AUTOMOBILE ANSWER BOOK

Bill & Hunter Harris

Reston Publishing Company, Inc.
A Prentice-Hall Company
Reston, Virginia

Library of Congress Cataloging in Publication Data

Harris, Bill.
  Automobile answer book.

  Includes index.
  1. Automobiles—Miscellaneous. I. Harris, Hunter.
II. Title.
TL154.H368   629.2′222   81-12027
ISBN 0-8359-0271-4   AACR2

Every effort has been made to ensure that the information contained herein is accurate. However, specific problems and/or questions should be referred to a professional.

©1982 by T H Marketing
3400 Sausalito Drive
Corona del Mar, California 92625

Printed in the United States of America.

FOREWORD

Congratulations on your acquisition of the *Automobile Answer Book*. It will go a long way in helping you to solve the mysteries of motor car ownership. This is not a repair manual. On the contrary, the *Automobile Answer Book* deals with the art and psychology of car ownership and tells how you can avoid costly ineffective repairs.

Based on thirty years of experience its logic is timeless. Hidden approaches to profits are revealed showing you how to make money, not lose it!

Cars fulfill fantasies and provide the answer to some of our most important needs. They represent success, freedom and self-expression. The mobility of an automobile is a prerequisite to success in America. But automobiles also represent the number one consumer complaint in America.

Yes, unfortunately, you need protection when dealing with the automotive establishment! There is no better way to protect yourself than by using the information you'll find in this book. Written in a clear simple style, the *Automobile Answer Book* arms you with the correct data to make intelligent automotive decisions. Bureaucratic jargon has been eliminated.

A unique and entertaining theme has been used throughout. The central character is a master detective from the turn of the century when the motor car first rolled onto the American scene. He skillfully unravels the mysteries surrounding automobiles in four extraordinary chapters: (1) How to avoid being taken, (2) How to stretch the buying power of your automobile dollars, (3) How to cope with red tape, traffic tickets and travel, and (4) How to relax and have fun with automobiles.

You'll find everything from gamesmanship techniques used in buying and selling to the art of protecting yourself from hidden surprises found in some car leases. Step-by-step outlines throughout the book simplify material and give you a confident first glance understanding. There are thousands of useful, easy-to-find, plainly labeled facts.

Obviously, not all car ownership poses a problem. Chapter Four, "Adventures With A Disappearing Breed," captures the magic charisma of the many relaxing, enjoyable and pleasurable aspects of the motoring life. Investment automobiles are discussed at length as well as building a kit car, racing, rallying and membership in car clubs. Full color illustrations of some of the world's finest classics provide "dream fodder" for the enthusiast.

Few writers can be considered as well qualified to write about automobiles as Bill and Hunter Harris. They've done it all: owners of car dealerships, restoration and repair shops, advertising and insurance, car builders, professional automobile racers, writers and book publishers. The combined experience of these two men includes an intimate working knowledge of the motor car from classic antique to the most sophisticated formula racing machine.

They use the theme of the book to give a light touch to a serious subject. You'll find enjoyment in simply turning the pages, looking at the illustrations and reading the comments of the super sleuth.

"Worth its weight in gold—a gem designed to give you the pure facts!" says the private eye. This book plants in your mind the right attitude—the correct way of thinking which enables you to pick cherries from lemons. It provides *Automobile Answers!*

S.P. Dibble - Editor
Tim Burgard - Illustrator

Table Of Contents

Chapter I

The Gamesmanship Caper
How To Avoid Being Taken

Chapter II

The Case Of The Shrinking Greenbacks
Stretch The Buying Power Of Your Automobile Dollar

Chapter III

The Riddle Of The Three T's
Red Tape, Traffic Tickets And Travel

Chapter IV

Adventures With A Disappearing Breed
Relax And Have Fun With Automobiles

The Gamesmanship Caper

How To Avoid Being Taken

The Easy Way
To Sell Your Car

Proceed. You can forget trying to impress the prospect with technical terms.

Even When She's A Burnin' Oil

Why can some people sell refrigerators to Eskimos while others couldn't sell bananas to starving gorillas? The answer is salesmanship! Becoming a dynamite salesperson is not difficult. But you must possess a desire to succeed and have belief in the value of your product (even when she's a burnin' oil).

Initial Impressions Are Important

Your appearance can make or break any sale. Dress neatly (not flashy or revealing) with hair combed and shoes polished. Keep cigarettes and cigars extinguished while greeting prospects even if they are smoking. Initial impressions can put potential buyers in a good frame of mind.

Let The Prospective Buyer Do The Talking

Never indulge in conversation off the subject. The subject is selling your car. Keep religious beliefs or world politics out of it. Become a good listener. Let the buyer do the talking and avoid any interruptions. This means you'll have to guard against outside distractions such as children playing, telephone calls and dogs in the garage. Don't expect a prospect to edge past your loveable pooch to purchase a car from you.

Successful Salespeople Sell Ideas

You want to make each prospect feel relaxed, welcome and glad they came. Offering a cup of tea, coffee or soda pop will help. Never mention alcoholic beverages. When wheeling and dealing use your best language and grammar. Forget trying to impress the prospect with technical terms! Remember, lay off the profanity. Remain calm, cool and courteous.

The Secret Qualities Of Professional Selling

There are simple basic methods of good salesmanship. The qualities of professionals. Aristotle Onassis used them. He could sell coffee to coffee growers. So can you! The secret? Sell ideas not objects! Even to an Eskimo, one of God's frozen children? Yes, if you want to sell a refrigerator to an Eskimo, you must first convince him he needs one. If you do, he'll buy. Automobiles are sold the same way. This chapter is filled with dynamite convincers! Use them. They'll make selling easier.

Your efforts will produce results!

Methods Used To Prepare
Your Car For A Quick Sale

Hum! Any appearance can be improved with resolution and energy.

It Really Does Make A Difference

Do you want to know the best way to go about selling your car? Everyone does. Questions. . .questions and more questions. Why should I recondition it? What difference will it really make? Should I just place a local ad and get rid of the beast? How do I word the ad? What ads sell? What should I tell the prospective buyer? Do I let them take my car for a test drive? Should I go with them? Will I need a deposit to hold the car? Should it be refundable? Well let's get down to the truth of the matter. And the truth of the matter is this!

The Key To Reconditioning—Keep It Original

Reconditioning your automobile will help you sell it faster for more money. Every dollar spent on reconditioning brings back two dollars in selling price. Don't expect this return when trading with dealers because this is true only when you sell it yourself.

Returning your automobile to original condition is the key to reconditioning success. Remove window stickers, dingle balls and fuzz dice from the rearview mirror. Replace broken knobs, handles and electrical switches. Any vehicle with missing pieces, ripped upholstery or a dash with holes in it becomes more difficult to sell. The goal to strive for is to make your vehicle look as original as possible. Most buyers will purchase an automobile having a pleasing appearance before buying one functioning perfectly!

Clean From The Inside Out

Prepare your car for sale by cleaning it from the inside out. First do the engine compartment, then the interior. Finish by cleaning the exterior. If time is scarce, I suggest you take the car to a professional auto detailer. You may not recognize the old buggy when it comes back looking like new. The usual charge is $50—$100. Remember. Quality reconditioning creates a car in top condition in the eyes of a buyer. This means quicker sales with less hassle . . . money well spent.

THE ENGINE COMPARTMENT

A clean engine compartment is as important as a clean interior. Pick up two cans of engine degreaser and proceed to your local self-service car wash. The car's motor should be fully warmed up so water sprayed on it will dry quickly. Steam clean both inner fender wells as well as the underside of the hood. Remove battery acid with baking soda rinsed with warm water. Spray WD-40 or Armor All on everything under the hood. Then wipe this area down. I advise against painting. Your engine compartment will have a new car shine. Correct as many rattles and noises as you can. Keep in mind that everything under the hood should look as original as possible!

Only Certain Repairs Can Be Justified

Many times what appears to you to be in need of repair will be overlooked by prospective customers. The truth is most buyers can't tell a good engine from a bad one by its sound. As a general rule if the car runs fairly well, don't monkey around with the mechanics. Keep enough gas in her for the test drive and avoid heavy engine work.

> He: "We're running out of gas."
> She: "No fooling?"
> He: "That's up to you."

When repairs are absolutely necessary, this is the order of importance for taking care of them:

1. Exterior—body and chrome work, paint, wheels, etc.
2. Interior—carpets, headliner and trunk areas.

3. Electrical—switches, gauges and lights.
4. Mechanical—engine, transmission, rear end, brakes and suspension.

If your car is idling rough, hard to start or losing power, consider an inexpensive tune-up. Many large national retail department stores offer these services in their automotive shops.

CHECK THE FOLLOWING:

1. Adjust or replace noisy or worn fan belts.
2. Install new freon in the air conditioning system if it does not blow cold.
3. Clutch and transmission problems are best taken to an independent shop, one having no factory affiliation. Their charges are generally lower than factory outlets. Although a shorter guarantee will be given, the work is usually comparable if not better!
4. If your engine oil is dirty, spend the money to change it and install a new oil filter.
5. Brake pedals that can be pushed to the floorboard when applied do not make a good impression. Have brakes adjusted or replaced if necessary.
6. While you're at it, make sure the emergency brake is in good order.

To Bring Top Dollar

Carefully weigh the automobile's retail value against all mechanical repair costs. You can't justify spending $500 for repairs on a $2,000 car. By the same token spending $500 on needed repairs for a $15,000 automobile is a must. This is a good general rule to keep in mind. The higher a vehicle's value the more perfect it must be!

THE INTERIOR

Clean both front and rear seats with a solution of hot water and dishwashing liquid using a soft scrub brush. Check for tears or rips in your upholstery. If found, have an upholstery shop repair each torn area by inserting matching fabric. Repairing in this manner is not only cheaper than reupholstering the entire seat but is virtually undetectable by anyone but you! Apply liberal amounts of Armor All to vinyl seats or a good preserver, like Lexol, to leather upholstery.

Many times rubber pads found on the clutch, brake or gas pedals are worn. Replace them. The driver's kickpad along with the surrounding carpeting can sometimes wear out. Simply have an upholstery shop insert a larger kickpad to cover both the existing one along with all surrounding carpeting!

Replace missing or unoriginal knobs, switches, gearshift levers and steering wheel assemblies. Have both the center console and armrests redone if torn. Be sure and leave the original owner's manual along with all miscellaneous sales literature in the glove box. Vacuum the entire trunk area including both spare tire and jack compartments. Remove all items, except your spare tire, jack and lug wrench.

AM-FM stereos, CB radios or special seats not intended to be sold should also be removed. Cover up all indications of their presence by tying up any loose wiring around the dash, door and seating areas. Oil squeaky doors at the same time you remove old service stickers and repair receipts from your car!

THE EXTERIOR

The first impression a car makes on a potential buyer usually makes or breaks the sale. Since this initial view is of the exterior, it's very important to devote time and care here. The sales impact of the appearance of your car can't be overemphasized! It must look in top quality condition.

Rust

Make a thorough examination for rust holes. The greatest single factor in losing a car sale is the presence of rust. If you are unable to do quality repair of this yourself, have it done professionally.

Paint

Don't consider a repaint of the entire car unless the following exist in abundance: rust, dents, scratches or heavily oxidized paint. Repainting or applying touch-up paint just to hide a few love taps (parking lot dings) or scratches is a mistake! Love taps are expected by buyers and usually will be forgiven.

First try applying a good rubbing compound to an oxidized finish. Only after repeated attempts with negative results should you consider a repaint. A word to the uninitiated. It's almost impossible to duplicate a factory paint job!

If a paint job is unavoidable, I would not recommend changing the color. However, you may feel this is necessary. Automobiles repainted in light colors hide imperfections and seem to sell better. Because of lower prices and better quality control, most used car lots sublet their body and paint work to outside shops. Ask a few lot managers where they have this type of work done, or select one of the many low-dollar auto painting outlets. Often paint overspray forms on the under carriage during repainting. Carefully apply black spray paint to those areas for a neater appearance.

Tires

Your tires may be in good shape but they probably need to be rotated. Front tires naturally wear faster on the outside edge. Potential buyers can't wait to point out your front end might be shot. You can replace a worn-out or mismatched set of tires for less money than you think. Call your local junkyard. Make sure to select tires from a similar vehicle.

You will seldom be compensated for mag type wheels in a sale. Put the originals back on before advertising the car for sale whenever possible. Use hot water combined with detergent to scrub each tire, including the spare. Then rub on Armor All to give those beauties the new look.

A Checklist

The following items should be replaced or put in working order: broken glass, windshield wipers, all lights, cracked tail lights and turn signal lenses, missing chrome trim items, bent or missing side moldings. Remove expensive trailer hitches, making sure to hide any loose wires or brackets a potential buyer might spot. Pick up two plain chrome license plate frames and install them. Finally, remove any bumper, body or window stickers.

Convertible and vinyl tops can look heavily weathered. First try a good vinyl top dressing. Apply one of the many vinyl coloring products as a last resort.

The Final Touches

Start cleaning the exterior of your car by using an extremely fine grade 0000 or 600 of steel wool on all chrome pieces. To be safe, first test a small inconspicious area. For your best car washing solution, mix a small amount of kerosene in water. Use Armor All on window and door moldings. Vinegar mixed in water cleans windows well. Finally, apply a good coat of high grade car wax.

If by now you haven't decided to keep the bloomin' thing, you're halfway towards a quick sale!

Composing Ads That Sell

Remarkable! You composed that ad?

The Secret Method Of Master Ad Writers

Some ads sell cars. Some don't! What makes the next door neighbor's jalopy sell quickly while your cream puff simply collects dust? You not only need ads that will sell refrigerators to Eskimos, but ones good enough to get them to want an icemaker as well. Yes, composing ads that sell is an art.

Only a few individuals possess this rare abitliy but the methods they use disclose some interesting secrets. I'm going to reveal these methods to you and take the mystery out of writing a good automobile ad. Your reward for success will be a quick sale!

The Mark Of A Professional

A good ad will be short, humble sounding and never insult the reader. It manufactures desire! There's no value in something not wanted. Potential buyers should feel as though they've just discovered something unique or special. When someone else blows your horn, it has the tone of a Cadillac. If you have to toot the thing yourself, it often resembles the sound of a Volkswagen.

Each ad should read as though a novice had written it! The mark of a true professional. Ads of this nature make the potential buyer less inhibited and more likely to call. Remember. The ad must create curiosity in the mind of the buyer. The number of calls you receive are directly related to its wording.

The Do's And Don'ts Of Ad Writing

THE BEST ADS ARE SIMPLE ONES

- When parts have been replaced such as a transmission, engine or front-end, don't indicate this in your ad. Readers ask, "I wonder what needs to be replaced next?"

- Don't mention "heavy-duty clutch," "mag wheels" or use "never raced" etc. These hint of abuse!

- Buyers look through used car classifieds in hope of obtaining a good automobile at a fair price. When you use the words "classic," "sacrifice," "blue book" or "wholesale" in your ad, most readers think you're too smart for them to receive a good buy!

- Too many abbreviations will make your ad jumbled and hard to read. Readers simply become frustrated and skip on to the next ad.

- Telling the car's color will cut your response in half. To most readers the word "repaint" signifies the car has been in an accident.

- It is unnecessary to say the car has a heater. The same is true of a radio unless it also has stereo or tape deck.

- Don't indicate if you have replaced one to three of the tires. This brings to mind too many questions about the condition of the car's suspension system.

- Words such as "cash only" and "firm" only aggravate the potential buyer. By using them, you're implying the reader can't afford this automobile. Never insult buyers by trying to qualify their credit or ability to purchase the car. They know it has to be paid for!

- Unless it is extremely low (for a quick sale), don't put price in a car ad. Make the reader call you to find out what it is. When you get them to call, you're already halfway home on a sale. The word "reasonable" infers overpriced.

- If you feel you must put in a price, the last two digits of the price should end in either 50 or 75. Round-figure prices and those ending in 99 tend to make readers feel you're too smart for them. Unless the car is unusual, keep your price somewhere between average prices being asked by private party sellers and those asked by dealers.

- "Best offer" forces readers to do something they don't want to in the beginning. They plan to make an offer later anyway. Leave "best offer" out of the ad.

- Insert one phone number. Pick one where you can be reached the greatest amount of time. Avoid wasting money on ads. Be available to answer calls.

- Avoid listing your address when advertising in local newpapers. Put your address in and leave the phone number out of an ad placed in a national publication. You'll appreciate the difference when you get your phone bill!

- Economy is important to most people. If your car comes equipped with a small V-8 (under 350 cubic inches) or a four or six cylinder engine mention this fact.

- When placing ads, choose the local newspaper with the largest circulation. Place the ad in two different papers to speed the sale and save your time (you need to be available anyway). Start ads on Wednesday or Thursday and let them run through the weekend. To save money cancel the ad immediately after the car is sold.

- Automobiles eight years or older sell well in smaller local newpapers or shopper guides.

- An inexpensive way to advertise is on local bulletin boards. Print your message neatly on white 3 X 5 inch file cards. Distribute these to markets, automotive supply stores, offices, spas, etc.

- Before placing any ad, check the paper for other cars for sale like yours. If there are a lot of them, hold off. Too many might indicate the market is soft (weak)! The advantage would then belong to the potential buyer. Remember. You want to make somebody out there feel as though they just found a one-of-a-kind jewel!

- Unusual or contemporary classic automobiles are most successfully advertised in the local newspapers of a resort area close to you. A Rolls Royce Corniche or a V-12 E-Type Jaguar tend to sell better in these locations.

● When placing a "For Sale" sign in the window of your car, never put a price on the sign. Just use your phone number. Make the letters at least three inches tall so the sign can be read from a distance of 25 feet.

 Indeed. Advertisements quickly reach far beyond your expectations.

Remember To Keep The Ad Simple

Every ad should include (a) year, (b) make, (c) model and (d) your phone number. One-liners or very short ads work best for private party sales. They not only lead to sales but cost a lot less to run. Use words such as these in your ads: (a) clean, (b) neat, (c) good condition, (d) original owner, (e) well-kept, (f) original, and (g) pretty.

EXAMPLES OF GOOD ADS

Ford Mustang, 1965, original, ph 900-1000

Chev Corvette, 1975, ph 831-5001

Cadillac Coupe de Ville, 1973, clean, original owner, ph 750-2500

Note: In some states you must list the license number. Insert it right after the date.

Simple ads cost less—sell more!

Common Automotive Abbreviations

Referral Brings Instant Understanding

Within this section you will find the abbreviations and their meanings relating to automobiles. These abbreviations are accepted for use in shortening automotive ads.

Abbreviations

AC	Air conditioning	Cpe	Coupe
A.C.	Air conditioning	cpe	Coupe
A/C	Air conditioning	crm puf	Cream puff
acc	Accessories	CST	Central Standard Time
all disks	4-wheel disk brakes	C/S	Convertible sedan
AM/FM	AM/FM radio	cu. in.	Cubic inch
Ant	Antique	CV	Convertible
/P	All power	Cvt	Convertible
Assys	Assemblies	CY	Cylinder
AT	Automatic transmission	Cyl	Cylinder
A/T	Automatic transmission	DC	Dual cowl
auto	Automatic transmission	DCP	Dual cowl phaeton
BG	Buggy	def	Defogger
bhp	Brake horsepower	DH	Drop head
blk	Black interior	Discs	Disc brakes front
blk/blk	Black interior & exterior	DL	Delivery
BR	Brougham	Dlr	Dealer
BRG	Bearing	DLX	Deluxe
Brg	British racing green	Dlx	Deluxe
brks	Brakes	dr	Door
BT	Boattail	DS	Dual sidemount tires
b/w	Black and white	EDT	Eastern Daylight Time
CB	Cabriolet	EL	Electric
cass	Cassette tape	EST	Eastern Standard Time
c.tape	Cassette tape	exc	Excellent
CB	Citizens Band Radio	fac	Factory installed
CC	Cycle car	F/BK	Fastback
CDT	Central Daylight Time	f/equip	Fully equipped
cid	Cubic inch displacement	FH	Fixed head
cln	Clean	FI	Fuel injected
cltch	Clutch	F.I.	Fuel injected
c/o	Care of	F/I	Fuel injected
CONT	Continental	FOB	You pay freight
conv	Convertible	FoMoCo	Ford Motor Company
CP	Coupe	f/pwr	Full power

gar	Garaged	PB	Power brakes
gd	Good	P.B.	Power brakes
GP	Grand Prix	pb	Power brakes
GT	Gran Turismo	p disc	Power disc brakes
GTS	Gran Turismo Sport	PDT	Pacific Daylight Time
h	Heater	PH	Phaeton
hdtp	Hardtop	PHA	Phaeton
HT	Hardtop	p/locks	Power door locks
hp	Horsepower	PO	Post office
hwy	Highway	P.O.	Post office
int	Interior	P/P	Private party
K	Thousand	p/p	Private party
K mi	Thousand miles	pp	Private party
Kph	Kilometers per hour	ppd	Postpaid
LD	Landau	Ps	Passenger
Lens	Singular	Pss	Passenger
Lenses	Plural	PS	European horsepower rating
Lf	Left front	P.S.	Power steering
Lhd	Left hand drive	p seats	Power seats
LHD	Left hand drive	PST	Pacific Standard Time
Lh	Left hand	PU	Pickup truck
Limo	Limousine	PW	Power windows
LM	Limousine	pw	Power windows
Lo	Low	Pwr	Power
LR	Lorrie	r	Radio
LTD	Laundalet	radials	Radial tires
Lthr	Leather	rblt	Rebuilt
Lr	Left rear	RC	Racing car
M	Thousand	Rdstr	Roadster
MAG	Magnesium	RDT	Roadster
mags	Custom wheels	rf	Right front
man	Manual transmission	rh	right hand
MDT	Mountain Daylight Time	rhd	right hand drive
mi	Miles	rr	right rear
Mil	Milestone Car	RHD	Right hand drive
mldg	Molding	RN	Runabout
M mi	Thousand miles	RP	Replica
MoPar	Chrysler Corporation	rpm	Revolutions per minute
mpg	Miles per gallon	RS	Rumble seat
mph	Miles per hour	RSC	Rumble-seat coupe
MST	Mountain Standard Time	S	Seats
NORS	New Old Replacement Stock	SASE	(Self addressed stamped envelope)
NOS	New Old Stock	SC	Supercharged
od	Overdrive	S.C.	Supercharged
OHC	Overhead camshaft	S/C	Supercharged
ohc	Overhead cam	SD	Sedan
OHV	Overhead valve	sed	Sedan
orig	Original	S.I.	Special interest car
p	Power	SL	Saloon sedan
pnt	Paint	SM	Sidemount
		snows	Snow tires

spd	Speed	uph	Upholstery
speedo	Speedometer	UTL	Utility
SPEC	Special	VERT	Verticle
Spl	Special	vg	Very good
SP	Sport	v/rf	Vinyl roof
SP DLX	Special deluxe	VT	Voiturette
Sp Dlx	Special deluxe	V top	Vinyl top
SPD	Speedster	w/	With
SS	Super sport	warr	Warranty
ss	Stick shift	WB	Wheelbase
std	Standard	wgn	Wagon
SV	Side valve	w/o	Without
SW	Station wagon	WS	Windshield
S/W/C	Split-window coupe	ww	White wall tires
Tape	Tape deck	www	Wide white wall
TC	Town car	Xlnt	Excellent
TK	Truck	2 Dr	Two door
TN	Tonneau	2S	Two door sedan
TR	Touring car	4 Dr	Four door
tr	Transmission	4S	Four-door sedan
trans	Transmission	4-wd	Four-wheel drive
trs	Tires	4-whd	Four-wheel drive
T/whl	Tilt wheel	8-tr	8-Track tape

Quick answers really help!

The Art Of Good Salesmanship

Ah, ha! Experience is what you get when you didn't get what you wanted.

Here's How You Get The Job Done

Do you think your talent for selling is limited? Have friends said to you, "I'd starve if I had to earn a living by selling anything?"

> *"It's starvation that's staring me in the face."*
> *"It can't be very pleasant for either of you!"*

Maybe you feel the same way about selling. But the time has come. The car must be sold. You already know you'll make a lot more money by selling it yourself. So, how do you get the job done? What's the answer?

To Sell, Eliminate The Barriers

When anyone tells me they can't sell, I answer by saying, "Hogwash!" Everyone of us was born to sell. And there are just as many people out there who want to buy (isn't owning an automobile a God-given right for everyone). Everytime the barriers between the two are eliminated a sale will take place. It's not necessary to possess indepth knowledge about your car to be able to sell it. Stay human; don't become a computer readout. Sales come easy when you keep the basic wants and needs of the other person in mind. Never sell your automobile to someone—help them buy it!

Talk Less—Listen More

Good salespeople all have these basic qualities: they talk in a cordial manner, radiate warmth and act humble. By nature they act calm, cool and collected. Fast talking sales pitches inhibit potential buyers by making them feel their chance of getting a bargain is remote. Do as little talking as possible. Be a good listener.

Turn Phone Callers Into Buyers

There are a couple of tricks to answering phone calls about the car. Talk in a normal tone. Speak slowly and hold the phone a couple of inches away from your mouth. A friendly, cheerful voice makes the caller feel at ease, comfortable and trusting. Apprehensions are eliminated. You have a much better chance of turning callers into lookers. Lookers become buyers!

Give Your Attack Dog The Day Off!

Use a little fundamental psychology. Set the stage first. Have your residence in tiptop condition! Clean the windows, vacuum a few carpets, mow your lawn and straighten up the garage. Give your attack dog the day off! This way customers will be thinking positive thoughts even before they meet you or see the car! First impressions play a large role in any decision to buy.

Increase The Desire To Buy By Reducing Fear

Before prospects arrive make your vehicle test track ready. Warm it up. Remove any "For Sale" signs in the windows. Later, when talking with potential buyers, never volunteer information or show receipts for major body or mechanical repairs. Even if you happen to be an expert mechanic, keep this fact to yourself. Buyer fear will develop when the buyer is confronted with a rebuilt engine, new paint or front end. Your job is to increase desire by reducing fear. Avoid such discussions. Answer questions honestly but be as brief as possible. Treat the buyer as you would like to be treated yourself. Be cordial and humble. There is no greater sales pressure than the pressure of silence at the right time. Win the argument—lose the sale!

Expect Offers For The Car

Adding a $100 to $200 margin to your selling price can be a good idea. You can always come down but never go up. In most cases be firm. Hold onto the price and don't be too quick to accept offers. Expect the prospect to bid on the car. If you can't accept the bid, be sure to get a name and phone number to call if the car doesn't sell in a few weeks. You may wind up settling on the original offer, but you have sold your car.

Typical Questions And Answers

Question: *How much are you asking?*
Answer: When talking over the phone never quote a price. Say something like this, *"The price is highly negotiable and I've got to sell my car."*

Question: *Will you consider anything less?*
Answer: Under no circumstances discuss this over the phone. When you are face-to-face you can talk price.

Question: *Can I drive the car?*
Answer: *Certainly, but we can't be gone for very long. I'm expecting another party to arrive shortly.*

Question: *May my mechanic look over the car?*
Answer: *Yes, though we'll have to schedule it in a few days. I've already committed myself to show the car today and tomorrow.*

Question: *What condition is it in mechanically?*
Answer: *Very dependable!*

Question: *You must have already cleaned up the engine compartment? I would like to have seen it before!*
Answer: *My engine compartment always stays clean so I can be aware of any problems developing.*

Question: *What condition is the paint in?*
Answer: *It looks very good.* Never mention you've had it repainted or the paint is new.

Question: *What shape is the body in?*
Answer: Simply say *"good condition"*. People expect small parking lot dings. If the car has a large dent, at least secure an estimate. Relay these repair figures to potential buyers. This eliminates guesswork (buyer fear).

It's not difficult to sell your own car. Just tell yourself the same thing every other car salesperson has said for years, "There's always an a__ for every seat!"

Sure enough, you'll find it's true.

A Test Drive That
Turns Prospects Into Buyers

Sell Only The Best Features—Avoid The Rest

The demonstration drive should clinch every car sale. It becomes the blue ribbon frosting on a sometimes plain cake. With good advance planning your test drive will turn prospects into buyers. It's elementary. Just avoid all the potential sources of buyer resistance. Sell nothing but the best points of your car, leave out the rest. Prospects will melt in your hands. Sound too good to be true? Not so. Here's how to get the job done!

Emphasize Your Car's Best Qualities

Successful test drives lead to sales. The seller should plan the route to follow in advance. This route will show the particular automobile for sale at its very best. Example: plan tight and twisty routes without long straight stretches of road for small sports cars with good suspension. Boring uncomfortable drives down straight highways only tend to emphasize the hard riding qualities of this car. The reverse in planning is true in demonstrating the best qualities of an easy riding luxury automobile.

In general select roads smooth and rut free. Routes having the fewest stop signs or traffic lights are best. Keep the potential buyer's driving time to a minimum. Defects in the engine, automatic transmission, clutch assembly or brakes are less apt to appear.

Don't Vary From Your Plan

Never allow a prospect to test drive your automobile without you! Though it may seem unnecessary, it pays to find out if the prospect has a current driver's license. Check with your insurance agent to make sure your coverage includes others driving your car. In case of accident you could be held liable.

There are also other reasons for this. When I had my sports car dealership, a very confident well-dressed man in his mid thirties drove up in a beautiful Lamborghini Espada. He was looking over one of our Porsches, a 911-S. Busy with another customer, I broke the rule and let him drive it alone. A little while later he returned, parked the Porsche on the lot, telling me he would bring his wife to see it the next day. When I tried to start the Porsche the following day, it would hardly run. Investigation disclosed my (unmarried) prospect had over-revved the engine, bending a valve! It was a very expensive lesson. Needless to say, the prospect never returned with his wife.

Never make stops during your test drive. About this time some prospects will want to have a mechanic look over the vehicle. Simply say, "In a couple of days you're more than welcome to but I have other people coming today and tomorrow and there isn't enough time. Let's arrange it later." Before each demonstration make sure your car has been warmed up and operating at peak performance. Check the amount of gasoline in the tank. Not many cars are sold after a hike back to the ranch. Don't bore the prospect with a filling station stop.

Summary

Remember. Propsects who stay around and pick the car apart usually are interested! Let them do the talking. Keep each test drive short but plan to follow a route that will show your car off to advantage. Discuss only the best features of the automobile. It's like giving a kid a taste of your apple pie—he can't wait to have the whole thing.

You're A Winner Every Time!

Accepting Deposits To Hold Cars

Qualify The Prospect

Accepting a small deposit (less than $50) from a buyer to hold your car is a mistake. Why? The prospective buyer can spend a day or two looking for a better car knowing yours can be purchased if another can't be found while you're prevented from a quick sale. Your advertisements are almost worthless during the waiting period. You are a serious seller. It pays to qualify the prospect as a serious buyer.

The Deposit Should Be Meaningful

Deposits should be at least $50 cash or cashier's check even on inexpensive cars. All deposits should be non-refundable in nature (if the buyer does not complete the transaction, the deposit is forfeited to you). Whenever you accept a deposit, always write out an agreement. This agreement should include the make, model, license number, serial number, depositor's name and address along with yours. Date it and be sure to include a statement as to how long the deposit to be good (2 to 4 days is sufficient). Both the buyer and the seller should sign it.

Adjust Deposits To Existing Facts

On certain cars you will receive lots of calls and action. The car is then said to be "hard" on the market! You can expect a quick easy sale. Adjust the conditions of the deposit to reflect these facts. Secure a deposit of at least 10 percent of your selling price before agreeing to hold this car. At the same time make the deposit good for 7 to 10 days. This method will save you from wasting time and effort. It will weed the tire kickers from actual buyers in a hurry.

You'll make the perfect choice!

Step By Step Directions
For Completing Private Party Car Sales

You Can Do It

Good news! Sell your car privately and you'll make more money every time. Myth? No. Absolute fact! In spite of this fact, we have long been conditioned to trade cars with dealers—losing money every time! It takes a powerful force to separate the public from their money. In this case some call it fear. I'd rather call it uncertainty. Better yet, I'm going to explain how to eliminate it!

Uncertainties: Is their check good? When should the money change hands? Am I still liable for the car? How can I protect myself legally? What's a Power Of Attorney? Am I safe in using one? What's a Federal Odometer Disclosure Statement? What do I have to do to meet Department of Motor Vehicle's requirements?

You need answers to make the transaction go smoothly. Let's take it step-by-step.

Is The Sale A "Cash" Or "Financed" Transaction?

Private party sales can be separated into two basic categories: cash transactions and financed transactions. There is one common link present in each. This is the agreement between the buyer and seller on the price. After agreement is reached, follow this procedure:

A CASH TRANSACTION

In this transaction we have a private party who is both the registered and the legal owner. There is no lien (loan) against the car. The ideal way to proceed with this transaction is as follows:

1. The Seller makes up a Bill of Sale. But it is not signed at this time by either seller or buyer.
2. Both parties set a convenient time to complete the sale.
3. The financial institution where the buyer does business is an excellent place to meet.
4. The seller brings pink slip or certificate of ownership to this location.
5. The buyer will have arranged a cashier's check made out to the seller for the amount of the sale.

6. The money is exchanged for the properly endorsed (signed off) pink slip or certificate of ownership.

7. Both parties sign and exchange a copy of the Bill of Sale. Have an officer of the financial institution serve as a witness.

8. The buyer and the seller proceed together to the closest Department of Motor Vehicle office and complete the transfer of ownership.

A FINANCED TRANSACTION

Both buyer and seller should discuss the procedure for payment. the present lien holder (lender) will have to be paid off or satisfied before the title can be transferred. Set aside at least a half day (avoid weekends) to consummate the transaction. The sale should proceed as follows:

1. Seller contacts the present lien holder to determine the amount owed (payoff).

2. Buyer makes out two cashier's checks. The first is in favor of the lien holder for the amount owed by the seller. The second is in favor of the seller for any difference between the lien (loan) payoff and the selling price agreed upon (use a cashier's check, not cash).

3. Seller makes out two copies of a Bill of Sale but leaves them unsigned.

4. Both parties proceed to the lien holder's place of business. Take the Bill of Sale along.

5. With the first cashier's check the buyer will pay off the lien holder.

6. At the same time the lien holder signs off the certificate of title or pink slip as legal owner of the car.

7. At this point any difference between the selling price and the amount owed to the lien holder is paid to the seller with the second cashier's check.

8. The registered owner (seller) will now sign off the pink slip (title). Titles registered in more than one name must be properly endorsed by each person. Some states require signatures to be notorized. Call your nearest Department of Motor Vehicle's office to check on this.

9. Both parties now sign and exchange copies of the Bill of Sale. Ask the person representing the lien holder (lending official) to witness the signatures.

10. Both the buyer and the seller should then proceed to the nearest Department of Motor Vehicles office to complete the transfer of ownership.

How To Protect Yourself When Selling

- Never sign off any title until you've received the money for your car.
- Don't treat a personal check as cash!
- If you feel you must accept a personal check, never complete the transaction over the weekend.
- Release the certificate of title only after the check clears. If necessary, present the check for payment at the buyer's bank first.
- Treat anyone who attempts to use a bank draft with extreme caution! Con artists love to use bank drafts.
- Never give a buyer a written affidavit or say anything concerning the car that could later prove to be false. You might be sued!
- Keep a copy of the purchaser's name and address handy for future reference.

(Note: The answers to other questions regarding the responsibilities of buyers and sellers, Department of Motor Vehicle procedures and forms such as a Bill of Sale are found in "How To Ease Your Way Through The Department Of Motor Vehicles" in Chapter Three, p. 186.)

Now It's Time To Relax

Pour yourself a glass of your favorite beverage. Soak in a hot tub.

Relax. You've earned a rest!

Consigning Your Automobile

A Beneficial Way To Reach The Buyer's Market!

Tired of those low offers for old Betsy when it's trade-in time? You say you don't have the time or want the hassles it takes to sell your car privately? There is an alternative. Consign her with a local car dealer.

A number of dealers fancy consignment vehicles for two good reasons. First, these cars add to the dealer's inventory, and second, there's no large cash outlay and flooring cost involved. Now you can't expect dealerships to come begging for your automobile. They won't. And you may have to do some looking around to find the right one.

You'll benefit in four important ways by consigning your automobile to a dealer. First, it gets exposed to more people. Second, you save money on advertising. Third, it releases you from dealing with the public, and most important, it puts your car on display in front of the impulsive buyer's market! Does all this sound too good to be true? Well, hold on. Let's take a look.

How Consignments Work

Consignments are made in one of two different ways—either on a percentage basis or an agreed upon net figure.

With a percentage consignment, dealers simply take a percentage out of the actual selling price. Percentage basis consignments are the best way for you to go. Almost all dealers work within the 10 to 12 percent range. For example: on an automobile actually selling for $8,500 the net amount payable to the car owner is $7,650. The dealer makes $850 (10 percent).

Now on net-figure consignments, both dealer and owner must agree upon a price the owner will receive. Using this method of consignment, dealers have the option of asking whatever price the market will bear. For example: the owner agrees to accept $1,800 for the car. The dealer sells the car for $2,700. This dealer has earned a $900 (33 percent) sales commission.

Regardless of the method of consignment you agree upon, limit it to a specific amount of time. I recommend two weeks as the minimum and four weeks as the maximum. Remember. Get everything in writing!

 Not all tires are perfect. Some have air in them.

Your Best Bet

A successful consignment starts with a dealer handling the same make of automobile you own (Fiat dealers are not looking for Fords). When selecting a dealer consider that dealer's present inventory of automobiles. A lot holding 30 cars with only 18 on it will be more receptive to your consignment. If the lot is full, the dealership wants to sell its cars, not yours! Make sure your buggy is clean, mechanically sound and has a good overall appearance. By trying to consign a dirty, poorly tuned, dented automobile, probably all you'll hear are the words, "Don't let the front door hit you in the a__ on your way out!" As I've said before, most dealers have a good reputation. They work hard to keep it that way.

Specialize only in success!

Selling Your Car To A Dealer

Find One Handling Cars Like Yours

Selling to a dealer closely parallels selling the family jewels to a jeweler. If, for instance, you inherit grandmother's diamond watch and want to sell it, you might go to a diamond broker. A gold chain could be sold to a gold merchant. An Indian shop might be interested in your turquoise. The same holds true for your car. To sell it to a dealer find one handling the same make as your automobile. The one exception to this rule would be in selling your exotic or classic. Any dealer might have an interest in this automobile.

To Save Time

Look for a dealer with a low inventory of used cars. If the lot is full, they want to sell their chariots not buy yours. Talking to salespeople is a waste of your time and theirs. Ask to see the used car manager of franchised dealerships and the owner or general manager at independent lots.

Leave Major Repair Receipts At Home

Many owners have inflated opinions of the value of their automobile. Don't expect to receive retail price when selling to a dealer. The price quoted will be wholesale, minus dealer cost for reconditioning. Service records should be taken with you but leave major repair receipts at home! Learn the true value of your car before you approach any dealer. If your car is seven years of age or older, don't waste time trying to sell it to a dealer (sell it privately).

Five Factors Determine The Price Dealers Will Pay

1. *Kelly Blue Book* or N.A.D.A. wholesale values. *(Note: See "Estimating The Value Of Any Used Car" in Chapter One, p. 45.)*

2. Wholesale dealer auction prices for similar vehicles. Dealers will compare the book value figures against recent auction sales in their area.

3. The condition of your automobile. Used car appraisers place more emphasis on appearance than the mechanical condition of your car. *(Note: See "Methods Used To Prepare Your Car For A Quick Sale" in Chapter One, p. 14.)*

4. Mileage. Many franchised dealers won't buy a car with over 50,000 miles on it. Independents will!

5. The dealer's current selection of cars for sale. If the dealer has ten others just like yours already, a sale is not likely.

The Keys To
Successful Used Car Purchases

Any simple idea will be worded in the most complicated way.

Replace Emotion With Logic

Next to buying a house, cars, even used, are usually the most expensive items most of us ever buy. With a home, we inspect it thoroughly to determine whether the house meets our needs or contains faults to be corrected before we buy. Now, by strange contrast, car buyers often treat the purchase of an automobile far too casually. Emotion replaces logic. They buy cars with problems. The automobile turns out to be so bad you'd think it must have been manufactured secondhand!

Money may not go as far as it used to but it sure can go faster. Is it time to save some money instead of spending it? You be the judge. Would you rather purchase an asset than a liability? Want to make your money talk instead of stutter? Take a few minutes. Put a hold on your emotions. Let your fingers wander through this chapter. You'll like what you find.

The Advantages Of Buying Used Cars

If there is any question as to why buy a used car, it can be answered in one word—money! It doesn't take very many months for most automobiles to lose half their value. The Hertz car rental company estimates vehicles two years old have already depreciated by 50 percent of original cost. We're looking at figures of over 50 cents per mile or $10 dollars per day just to own and operate a standard size automobile! Why pay these exorbitant costs? There is an excellent alternative—a good used car.

Money can be saved on lower insurance costs, less excise or sales tax and cheaper registration fees. Previously owned vehicles depreciate more slowly. Today, many actually appreciate in value! New car owners often justify their purchases by saying, "It will cost less to maintain." Not so! Surveys of owners have repeatedly shown it takes between 20,000-30,000 miles just to get the bugs worked out of new cars—thousands of miles beyond any warranty.

New car prices have risen rapidly due to many factors: higher material and labor costs, tighter emission control systems and safety standards, engine changes and modifications in body designs. Because of this escalation, certain used automobiles are actually increasing in value—something unheard of a few years ago. When the price of gas went sky high and inflation simply ran rampant, certain used automobiles began selling well above their original purchase price! Even so, they were bargains. To those lucky or farsighted, this meant the net cost of owning such a car was zero.

You Will Need Patience

Approximately half of all used car sales occur between two private parties. We're talking about millions of transactions each year. In this category California happens to lead the nation. In this state over 80 percent of all used cars sold are sales between two individuals with no dealer involved. It's big business, one where it pays to know what you are doing. You're going to be hurt financially if you rely on secondhand information. Don't expect private parties to be more honest than anyone else!

> *"I make two hundred dollars a day."*
> *"Honest?"*
> *"What's the difference?"*

The wise car salesman always said, "Even a priest, rabbi or minister can avoid the truth."

By 1985, because of increased prices, most Americans will decide to purchase desirable late model used cars. Therefore, good used automobiles will become increasingly scarce! It has been estimated over 80 percent of all automobiles advertised aren't worth buying. You have to make careful choices. Keep in mind how much you're willing to spend, what you want and why you want it.

Generally, properly maintained cars meeting certain standards will hold their value. Some may even appreciate. These standards are: (a) fuel efficiency, (b) high quality and (c) advance design. All successful used car purchases call for patience, common sense and comprehensive knowledge. *Automobile Success* supplies the facts and answers. You'll develop the sixth sense—patience.

If you can buy used cars wisely, why buy new?

The Ideal Time To Purchase An Automobile

A Potential For Substantial Savings

There are particular times of day, month and year offering greater opportunities for savings and selection when it comes to buying your next car. The potential for substantial savings is worthwhile. Experience clearly shows us there really is an ideal time to purchase automobiles.

- Under no circumstances purchase at night, in the rain or under poor weather conditions. Flaws, such as wavy body panels (poor body work) are hidden.

- When purchasing from a dealer, do so towards the end of each month. Many times salespeople and managers are working on quotas, a bonus, or just worried about paying their monthly living expenses. They could be more receptive to making a deal!

- Purchase during winter months. Government price indexes show used car prices rise 9-11 percent between March and June and fall 5-6 percent between December and February.

- Because of new car trade-ins, the months October through February offer the best price and selection on used cars.

- Both private party and dealer sales fall dramatically during late December! Most people are buying Christmas presents, not cars. Your chances of a better deal are much greater.

- If you live in a city or state where taxes are placed on all inventory, buy just before tax time. Dealers want to make money—not pay taxes.

- Historically, interest rates go down during a major election year. Money can be saved on finance charges. Be alert! Modern politicians do not always believe or follow the lessons of the past.

- Purchasing a contemporary classic or sports car during the spring months is a mistake. These automobiles tend to become hard (cost more) on the market. During spring a surprising number of people think about cleaning, love and sporty automobiles! Not necessarily in that order.

What To Buy
How To Pick A Winner

Sir, I'll loan you my crystal ball.

To Be Ferrari Or To Be Volkswagon. That Is The Question

If you frequently change cars, select one having a slow deprecia-tion rate during its second and third years. Look for automobiles with a history of few or no body changes. Purchase the car when it's a year old and sell it the next.

When long-term ownership is desired, purchase automobiles two or three-years-old. Remember. Automobiles at least two-years-old have already taken their biggest drop in value (depreciation), while traveling only one-fourth their life span!

If transportation is your sole purpose, select a three-year-old vehi-cle and sell it in three or four years.

Buy Loaded Models

Whether you're debating the purchase of a Toyota, Datsun, Hon-da or Ford, choose top of the line, loaded models. Such vehicles hold their resale value better and are more enjoyable to own.

Example: If you've decided on a 1979 Cougar, select a Brougham or XR-7 version.

Look for motorcars having a sun roof, turbo-charged engine, power seats and windows, AM-FM cassette stereo, computer package or special wheels, etc. There's an old saying, "Buy a stripped car, sell at a cheap price!"

People Still Want Fancy Gadgets

Purchase of a smaller, special-order car with unique options can give you a good chance for inflation to overcome depreciation. Why? More and more drivers (both young and old) are downsizing from large luxury bombs to more fuel efficient buggies. Nevertheless, they still desire both fancy gadgets and plush interiors. Anyone owning such a beast will have a distinct advantage when it comes time to sell!

Check Market Value Carefully

Individuals sometimes sell their leased automobiles. Usually a high residual (payoff) remains, making it almost impossible to purchase any of these at the right price! I don't recommend purchasing a private party leased vehicle. If you decide to do so, be sure to check market value carefully before you attempt a purchase. *(Note: See "Estimating Used Car Values" in Chapter One, p. 45.)*

They Devour Gas . . . But

High fuel costs have made large luxury cars soft on the market. True, they devour gas. On the other hand these cars are comparatively cheap, dollar for dollar, to buy if compared to small automobiles. There's a lot to be said in favor of safety, comfort and dependability. A vehicle's mechanical condition should be the deciding factor, not the name on the grill. If you drive under 8,000 miles per year, large automobiles can be excellent buys!

Diesel Equipped Automobiles

The demand for cars equipped with diesel engines is growing. This is a good indication their resale value will remain high. Why? Diesel engines have no points, sparkplugs, rotors, or distributors to go afoul. Consequently tune ups of this nature are not required! If frequent oil changes are made (every 2,000 to 3,000 miles), diesel motors can last over 200,000 miles. Since our huge trucking industry uses diesel fuel, it will probably never be in short supply.

Lower maintenance costs lead to less expensive transportation. It is very important to take into account an automobile's total lifetime cost before purchase. Don't leave out repair and upkeep. A car bought at a good price but having a high maintenance factor (Jaguar) can be devastating on your bank account. Think it over!

Car Selecting Ideas

- Purchasing a rare vehicle as your only automobile is a mistake. On second or third car purchases it can be a good hedge against inflation. Scarcity will increase its value.

- Stay clear of vehicles no longer in production when purchasing a first car for basic transportation.

- Spare parts are scarce or hard to obtain on older cars. By law manufacturers must make spare parts for each model year for seven years.

- Police, taxicabs and delivery vehicles make poor buys. This includes cars driven by salespeople.

- Convertibles, hardtops and station wagons develop leaks, squeaks and rattles first.

- For a list of good used buggies check the annual April issue of *Consumer Reports*.

- The older the automobile the more variable mileage and wear can be.

- Beware of foreign or out-of-state motorcars!

- Consider where the vehicle can be serviced! If the car can't be maintained within 25 miles of your home, it can quickly become useless.

- Late model cars with high mileage make me suspicious of low maintenance. Beware!

Uniqueness is lasting!

Estimating The Value Of Any Used Car

AIR CONDITIONING
PLUS RADIO =
$700.00

$7,000 + $400 FOR POWER
STEERING AND BRAKES
$200 + $100 + $45
etc.

One accurate guide is worth a thousand expert opinions.

It's Easy When You Know How

Estimating automobile values can be compared to hunting for oil in Texas. The secret is knowing where to dig! To achieve a highly accurate idea of worth, look in all the following areas: current value guides, local newspapers and dealership lots. Compare prices for like automobiles in all three areas.

You'll Find Official Used Car Pricing Guides In Libraries

First, obtain current issues of either the *Kelly Blue Book Auto Market Report* (a bi-monthly western publication) or *National Automobile Dealers Association Official Used Car Guide* (N.A.D.A., a monthly eastern publication) covering the wholesale and retail market value of automobiles up to seven years of age (older vehicles are covered separately elsewhere). These publications are official guides for automobile dealers on used car prices.

How do you obtain one of these manuals? And how do you read one of them after you've found it? Although the *Kelly Blue Book* is generally regarded as a western publication it does have a national circulation. The N.A.D.A. guide is more widely used in the eastern half of the United States. They're very similar in style with each one listing the current values of all late model used cars popular in the United States. You may gain access to these publications through public libraries, insurance companies, banks or loan companies. Ask for either one or better yet, both.

When It's Older—But Not Old Enough

What about older vehicles? These are the cars still too young to be classified either antique or classic. Still they are over seven years old. There are two excellent publications dealing with these cars, the *Gold Book* and the *Kelly Blue Book No. 2*. The *Gold Book Official Used Car Value Guide*, as it is officially called, is published twice a year. It can be found in most bookstores or you may purchase a copy by writing: *Gold Book*, 910 Tony Lama Street, El Paso, TX 79915. Unfortunately, the *Kelly Blue Book No. 2* can't be obtained by a private party. Contact your local library, insurance company or bank to look at a copy.

How To Read The Kelly Blue Book

Now that you've found a current copy, how do you find anything in it? To the uninitiated user finding the eighth wonder of the world would be easier than finding the true value of a particular automobile in the value guide. It's easy if you know how! Yet often even the humanoids of insurance companies, loan institutions and

 *So it was said. Intelligent people seek advice.*

banks can't tell the front cover from the back pages! Consequently, true wholesale or retail values are seldom reached. Remember. This is the guide most loans and insurance payoffs are based on. By correctly reading this "Bible," the amount of a loan can be much higher. In other instances the amount of an insurance payoff can be adjusted upwards. There is no substitute for knowing how to do something yourself. This is no exception. You'll save money.

READING THE KELLY BLUE BOOK

- The wholesale and retail prices of all automobiles are recorded for the seven most recent model years.
  a. For example the 1981 book will only list prices for 1974-81 vehicles.
  b. It's published every two months. You'll find values can change considerably in this amount of time.
- The major manufacturers are listed in alphabetical order starting with American Motors.
  a. Imported cars are at the rear of the guide with the pages marked "Imports" also listed in alphabetical order.
  b. Trucks and vans are listed in the last portion of the guide in the section entitled "Trucks".
- Follow these easy steps and you will arrive at accurate wholesale and retail values for any automobile listed.

EXAMPLE:

A 1979 Buick Regal 2-door coupe with 26,000 miles equipped with moon roof, tilt wheel and AM-FM stereo with 8 track player.

Note: The method of using the guide remains the same regardless of the car you select. Of course the figures will change to reflect current values.

1. Look at the top of the pages for the heading marked "Buick". Under this heading find the year and model in question.
2. There are two columns of figures on the righthand side of each page. The column to the far left is wholesale and the column to the right of it is retail.
3. By drawing an imaginary line from the name "Regal" to the column of figures, you find a wholesale base of $4,675 and a retail base of $6,010 (these figures would vary of course depending on the date of Kelly Blue Book used). At this point most people stop! They don't take into consideration mileage and optional

equipment. Unless you continue on, you haven't found the true wholesale or retail value!

4. At the end of each model heading a statement of this kind will appear, "For equipment and mileage adjustment use schedule A, B, C or D." These schedules are usually found on pages 4-11. We are instructed to use schedule B for this 1979 Regal.

5. Turning to schedule B, the lefthand pages are always mileage figures. Any figure found in the shaded area can be added to both wholesale and retail figures. Figures found in the white areas are a deduction from wholesale and retail values. You must deduct $50 from both the wholesale and retail base figures because the car has 26,000 miles on it. We now have a wholesale cost of $4,625 and a retail cost of $5,960.

6. On the right hand side of the page you'll find a column heading entitled "Wholesale Equipment Schedule B". These figures are to be added to the wholesale base only! For the moon roof add $400, tilt wheel add $100 and the AM-FM stereo with 8 track is a $150 add-on. With all these options added to the base, we how have a wholesale value of $5,275.

7. To find full retail value turn to page three. A heading marked "Retail Markup Charts For Equipment" is found here. You'll note, while the total wholesale equipment markup is $650, this translates to a retail figure of $870. The true full retail value of the automobile is $6,830—a far cry from the $6,010 figure found at first glance in step three above!

Comparing Used Car Prices In Local Newspapers

Now comes phase two. Look in the classified section of local newspapers for the automobile in which you are interested. Compare the ads as to price, mileage, options, equipment and condition. Call on a few ads. I suggesst you study the private party ad prices more than prices asked by dealers. Many dealerships advertise vehicles at ridiculously low prices in the hope (often successful) of attracting prospective car buyers. These dealer practices are known as "come ons" or "bait and switch" tactics. *(Note: See "Auto Jargon Used By Salespeople" in Chapter One, p. 62.)* I would not patronize a dealership using these methods.

Shop Dealerships To Determine Used Car Prices

As the last phase of estimating automobile values, visit at least two car dealerships. Make sure you are comparing similar automobiles for an accurate evaluation. Compare condition, mileage and optional equipment as well as price. When judging mileage, allow 12,000 miles per year. To estimate value you can deduct $40 for each 1,000 miles traveled above this figure (deduct

$120 for a car two years old with 27,000 miles on the odometer). In estimating the value of full-sized American automobiles, as a general rule, you may deduct $100 if there are no power brakes, $200 for no power steering, $200 if it has no air conditioning and $50 if the automobile is not equipped with power windows.

Discovering True Market Value

Here's the "coup de grace". You can arrive at the true market value! Take the prices found in newspapers and dealerships and compare them with the retail figures of the value guides. You'll find instances where automobiles are selling for less than the stated values found in either of these guides. This is not unusual. These cars are termed to be "soft" on the market. It can also go the other way. When the only way an automobile can be purchased is for more money than they are listed for in the guides, they are said to be "hard" on the market.

Another way to determine the "soft" or "hard" position of an automobile is to look in your local newpaper. Count the number of ads for each make and type of car. As a general rule makes and models with few listed for sale are "hard" on the market. Knowing if an automobile is "hard" or "soft" is extremely important.

This is exactly how you gain the edge at the bargaining table!

What To Look For When Selecting A Used Car

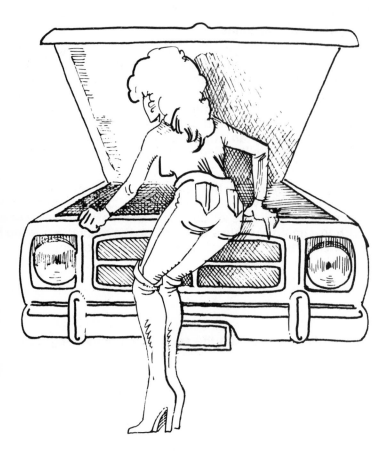

To judge like a fox, it helps to know the answers.

Build Judgement Confidence Through Awareness

Condition is the primary consideration when selecting any used vehicle! Approach each automobile with keen eyes and a rational frame of mind. Quickly look at the exterior and interior. If it doesn't look right, trust your own judgement and walk away. Don't let your desire to own any one particular car (because of color, styling, etc.) obstruct common sense! Take a friend along to better prove or disprove your line of reasoning.

Items needing repair are for you to find. Nobody will tell you everything wrong with a car! Seek information concerning where each vehicle came from (rent-a-car, lease turn-back, private party, etc.) to better understand its condition.

Before You Go A-Hunting

Before you start used car shopping, here are three glance-through lists. You won't use all of these in evaluating each car. They are meant to alert you to some telltale signs indicating the condition of an automobile. Obviously they can be put to use when you suspect a problem. To make it easier, I've separated the information into three categories: (a) mechanical, (b) interior and (c) exterior.

MECHANICAL

Top mechanics suggest 50,000 miles on the odometer as the maximum you should consider when purchasing a used car. Never assume low mileage is a true indication of less engine wear. Pay the relatively small fee to have an independent mechanic analyze the mechanical condition of the car before you buy! If the transmission, engine or rear end have to be torn down for repairs, skip the sled. Here's a general mechanical checklist:

- Look under the car for fluid on the ground or floor.
    a. Oil is heavy and dark.
    b. Transmission and power steering fluid is usually red.
    c. Brake fluid is clear in color.
- Don't worry if the engine compartment has been steam cleaned. Leaks can be spotted quickly and easily with a clean engine.
- Check all radiator, heater, air conditioner and power steering hoses for leaks. Beware of black spray paint used to make them look new.
- Have all fluid levels checked: brake fluid, coolant, power steering, oil and transmission. Units low on fluid may signify a leak.
- All fan belts (water pump, air conditioner, power steering, air pump, generator, etc.) should be tight. Check each belt for cracks or fraying. Low mileage cars usually don't have worn belts. Beware!
- Each belt is driven by a pulley. Shake each pulley from

side to side, making sure there isn't a large amount of play. Pulleys with play indicate worn-out bearings.

- Rust stains around the radiator, freeze plugs (located on each side of the engine block), water pump and adjoining fittings indicate a leak.

- Pull the oil dipstick out and check the oil's color.
  a. Black oil doesn't indicate a bad engine but a black, sludgy substance can.
  b. A milky grey color shows water is present meaning a cracked head, block or blown head gasket.

- Start the car. Then remove the radiator cap. Check for signs of bubbles or floating oil. If found, a blown head gasket is usually the culprit.

- Check the oil pan for dents. A deformed pan may indicate engine oil pick-up problems, a major accident or oil leaks.

- With the center wire removed from the ignition coil, crank the engine ten to twenty seconds. Uneven cranking usually indicates low compression in one or more cylinders.

- Have a compression check performed on any prospective purchase. Each cylinder should be within 10 to 20 pounds of one another. If not, beach this whale!

- Remove the air filter. How clean is the inside of the carburetor? Large deposits of a black, sludgy substance may indicate an overhaul.

- Engines rocking from side to side (when idling) probably have bad motor mounts.

- Brake pedals that feel firm but stop on the floor indicate a need for adjustment or replacement.
  a. A "spongy" pedal can indicate air in the system or a leak.
  b. Cars equipped with disc brakes on all four wheels can not be adjusted.
  c. Automobiles with low mileage and worn brake pads means someone speaketh with forked tongue!

- A bulging battery, loose or broken terminal posts are indications of a dying battery.
  a. White powder deposits along with corrosion may mean it's being overcharged.
  b. Most batteries have a date stamped on them. The older the battery the sooner it will need replacement.

- Taping or sectioning of electrical wiring in the engine compartment may be the signs of a major accident.

- Are the ignition wires, distributor cap or spark plugs cracked, melted or brittle? Replacement is necessary.

- Test for bad shock absorbers. Place your hands on each fender and push down hard. Good shocks will go down, bounce up and stop. Bad shocks allow a car to rebound several times.

- Check the integrity of the exhaust system. Do this by shaking the tailpipe.

   a. Examine the system for patches and repair tape.
   b. If suspect, use pliers to tenderly squeeze the exhaust pipe intermittently along the entire system. If it gives easily, replacement will be necessary.
   c. Examine the inside of the tailpipe. Any trace of oil or water indicates a major engine problem.

- If a trailer hitch is present, have the universal joints checked. Towing destroys these items.

- Check all five tire tread depths. Tires with less than 1/16″ of tread remaining are shot!

   a. Use a penny. Insert it between the tread with Lincoln's head toward the tire.
   b. The tire needs replacing if Lincoln's entire head is showing.

- All tires of a low mileage automobile (15,000 to 20,000 miles) should be the same brand and model. If there is a mixture, tread lightly.

- Tires having uneven wear, bald spots, bulges and missing pieces indicate suspension troubles.

   a. Make sure to check the spare on cars having four new tires.
   b. A spare tire in poor condition will show the car's true suspension condition.

- Grasp each front tire (on top) and shake vigorously. Excessive play or a clunking sound indicates worn out wheel bearings, ball joints or bushings.

- Look at the front of the car from a distance of about 20 feet. Front wheels leaning inward at the top need alignment.

- Inspect all wheels on their inner side for a black greasy build-up. If present, either a wheel cylinder or grease seal is leaking.

Take time to relax. Have a coke. It's not quite that serious.

INTERIOR

Ever watch youngsters at an auto show? They get in each seat of every car. Then proceed to pull, twist and press every button, switch and knob in sight! What fun. My advise is for you to do exactly the same thing. It's time well spent. Surprisingly, first impressions lie! The interior should look about the same age as the exterior. This quick initial three-point inspection can be backed up by a more in-depth examination when warranted.

1. Is the carpeting and upholstery clean?
2. Are the sunvisors, headrests and armrests worn or missing?
3. What is the condition of the seats, headliner, door panels and carpeting?

If the automobile passes your initial three-point exam, here are some other areas you may want to look over.

- Check each door latch (both inside and out), making sure they're in working order. All door locks should work by using the same key! Be suspicious if they don't.

- Both front and rear seats should be checked to see if they adjust properly. Look for broken or sagging springs.

- Worn out carpeting is a sign of high mileage.
  a. Look under each floor mat for rust or wavy floorpans.
  b. Welding in these locations can indicate the car may have been in a major accident.
  c. Silt and sand under carpets may indicate the car is a flood victim!

- Be leary of seat covers. Look under them.

- If the brake, clutch and gas pedals are heavily worn and the car has low mileage, I would question it. Equally suspicious are pedals with new rubber. The amount of rubber on each pedal should reflect a vehicle's mileage.

- Remove both jack and lug wrench from the trunk. Check

the jack's ability to raise the vehicle. Make sure the lug wrench fits all lug nuts.

- Check for missing knobs on dash controls. Beware of newly painted dashes. This one might have been used as part of a state, fire department, police or taxi fleet.

- A glove compartment having a missing interior box is useless. They're not very valuable if they won't open or close either.

- While you're playing with things, try out the operation of these electrical items: horn, radio (AM and FM), windshield wipers (all speeds), clock, dashboard lights, electric seat adjustments, cigarette lighter, electric windows, cruise control, interior lights and windshield washer.

- Roll all windows up and down. Windows not operating in a smooth manner might indicate previous body damage.

- Check for etched windows. This is a good indication the car has long been exposed to salt air.

  a. Terminal body rust may also be present. Tread with caution.

  b. Windshields with damage obstructing the driver's view will fail state inspection.

- Try the headlights (low and high beam), brake lights, turn signals, emergency flashers and back-up lights to make sure they're working.

- With the headlights on, rev the motor. A substantial difference in brightness while varying engine speeds indicates a faulty voltage regulator.

- Raise and lower the top on convertibles. Make sure it operates smoothly and there are no tears, broken or foggy rear windows. Tonneau covers come with every convertible! Is it there?

- Look up under the dashboard. Factory wiring is tied together in nice neat bunches. Hanging wires along with taped leads indicate electrical problems. Be prepared.

- Turn on both heater and air conditioner systems. Heaters refusing to blow hot usually have a faulty heater core. Air conditioners blowing warm either need recharging or are leaking. They can be expensive to repair.

- A steering wheel with two inches or more of play before activating the front tires is hazardous!

- Turn the ignition key to the "on" position. Both oil and generator lights should light up.
- Start the engine. Count the number of seconds it takes for both oil and generator lights to go out. Five seconds is allowable. Any more indicates worn out engine bearings or a faulty regulator and generator.
- Watch the oil pressure gauge closely. Oil pressure dropping while the car is in operation is an indication of worn rings or bearings.
- While you're at it, take a look at all gauges (fuel, oil, amp-meter, speedometer, tachometer, water) to make sure they're working.

EXTERIOR

 Let's go look. I've been fooled before!

Looks Go A Long Way

Ah, those beautiful lines! They can be a lovely sight or the devil in disguise. A magnificent outer surface may really be mud (body filler) underneath. If you think taking the time to investigate is expensive try ignorance. We all talk a lot about buying a car just to get from point A to point B but the truth remains. A buggy's looks (color and style) go a long way in determining the length of time you will keep her! For a long and happy relationship look over these items before you buy:

- Gaze down each body panel for wavy sheet metal. Ripply sections indicate a rebuilt area. Open all doors and check for sag. One or two precisely repaired panels are nothing to worry about.

- Check the distance between body panels (trunk lid to fender or hood to fender etc.). Body sections with unequal spacing indicate a major accident.

- Avoid one to three-year-old carriages with new paint.
  a. Look for overspray deposits on the muffler system, outer trim, door jambs, inside wheel wells, gas tank area and along the weather stripping.
  b. Rubber moldings along both front and rear windows can be pried up carefully. Look for differences in paint color underneath. Steer clear of cars whose original color has been changed!

- Make sure there is a flush fit between all adjoining sheet metal.

- When you are unsure of the extent of body damage or the method used to repair it, run a magnet over any questionable area. Magnets won't cling to fiberglass, body filler (bondo), or lead!

- Avoid cars infected with rust. The cost of the cure is usually prohibitive.
  a. Rust will often show up as tiny bubbles under the paint. Check for rust on lower portions of each fender, rocker panels (metal beneath each door), trunk lid and the metal strip surrounding the windshield.
  b. Be extra careful of automobiles with recent paint jobs! New paint is often used as a cover-up for hiding rust, especially in older cars.

- A car's frame or subframe should be checked for weld marks, odd bends or ripples.

- Does the car set level on all four tires? No, it isn't always the uneven surface of the parking lot.

- Take a gander at the basic suspension system. Do any of the pieces look newer or cleaner than others?

If the car you've found can pass 90% of the items on these lists, buy it.

You've found a cream puff!

Use Gamesmanship
Don't Pay Too Much For Your Next Car

Quite right! There are gamesmanship secrets.

Gamesmanship And Success Go Together

You don't have to make someone wealthy when you purchase a car but a lot of us do. Don't pay too much! Never underestimate the money you can save by the proper use of gamesmanship (at least $500-$1000 per deal). To become a winner, you're going to need a plan. Otherwise you enter the battle of wits—gamesmanship— half-armed. "Off the top of the head" ideas often turn out like dandruff—small and flaky. They just don't work! God still seems to be helping those who first help themselves.

As a buyer, if you follow your plan of gamesmanship, remaining honest, flexible and mixing in a great deal of patience, you'll come out a winner.

Negotiation Is The Secret Of Gamesmanship

Your plan has to include negotiation. It's the secret of gamesmanship. We're all negotiators at heart. To be successful in negotiating a car purchase you must make the seller feel they have gained something. Never initiate any negotiation you expect to win in a highly competitive manner. The spirit is one of cooperation. An automobile is only purchased at a bargain price when both parties are satisfied with the deal. To buy any car at its lowest possible price follow this plan. It's basically designed to make the seller doubt the validity of the asking price. This results in compromise.

Every intelligent compromise saves you money!

GAMESMANSHIP

- You just can't put yourself in the position of having to buy a certain car by a given date. Necessity never made a good bargain.

- Stay away from the squeeze. Even though you may feel pressured to buy, never show or reveal these thoughts to a seller.

- Once you have selected the buggy you want, have it mechanically checked.
    a. Use faults to carefully batter down the asking price.
    b. Deduct all repair cost estimates from the asking price. If repair costs aren't acknowledged by the seller move on. You need patience to be a winner.

- When you can't come to agreement on your terms or price, leave the deal. Come back to it in a day or two. You'll find many people are more receptive then.

- The price often becomes more flexible when a seller believes you might buy from someone else.

- You're always in a better position to negotiate a bargain when you don't have a car to trade.
    a. Sell your car yourself. You'll get just as much money, maybe a lot more than trading in and you'll be able to deal on the next car at rock bottom price.
    b. If you feel you must trade your car in, on the initial visit park your car away from the dealership. Don't discuss this car at all.
    c. Once you feel you've negotiated the bottom price, you can say, "After looking over my financial situation, I find I can't afford to keep two cars. How can we

trade?" Now you're in a position to find out just what the salesperson is willing to give for your car!

- There's no substitute for bargaining with cash. The leverage moves immediately to the buyer. Substantially lower offers can be made using this method!
  a. Buyer drops a hint. "I can draw the cash out of the bank today!" or "I'll give you ____ dollars right now."
  b. Getting yourself ready to offer cash really means securing your financing before you start looking. Don't wait. It'll cost you money every time!

- How you appear to a seller could reflect the deal you will finally negotiate. If you walk up flying diamonds, gold and designer clothes, most sellers will try to extract the highest price possible. Be neat, clean and dress in an unfadish manner. It's your best gamesmanship outfit.

- A salesperson or seller possesses the same feelings, desires and ambitions as anyone else. When you are less than honest with them, they're going to fight back. Sellers have often used the words, "bury 'em" to describe what they do in these situations. Remember. You're trying to get this person to fight for you, not against you. When you're honest with others, they'll be honest with you!

- A private party selling a car usually has just purchased a new automobile or is about to. If they didn't trade-in their old car or don't plan to, these people make excellent choices to deal with.
  a. By this time the dealer has offered less. The seller now has a clearer picture of the true value of the car. This is to your advantage.
  b. Soon these people will need money to accomplish their goal. To get it, they're apt to accept less.

- Weed the jalopies from the jewels by qualifying the seller. Try this one. Place a "Car Wanted" ad in your local newpaper. State the model and year you are interested in. When phone calls are received, ask each seller to bring their car to you! A little different twist. Sure. Why not. After all you have the money! You'll find out quickly how much they want to sell.

  a. Your chances of finding a cream puff are better and you have enhanced your bargaining position.

  b. This method is especially useful in buying an antique or contemporary classic. *(Note: See "Adventures With A Disappearing Breed" in Chapter Four, p. 270.)*

Know When To Stop Talking

You probably won't get an answer to all your questions. Don't let this discourage you. Try to discover why the automobile is for sale and how soon it must be sold. Your offer should be influenced by both. If the seller is leaning toward accepting your offer, stop talking! This convinces a seller they've heard your final and best offer. Take along a friend, husband or wife. A second party who talks against the purchase provides a good cover for you to make a low bid. Pay no attention to reports of other offers. Remember. If you don't buy this particular automobile, there's another one just like it somewhere else. Once you start making counter offers, the buyer knows you're bluffing. Be courteous but firm!

Everyone Can Play

There's just no substitute for patience when it comes to looking for a used car to buy. Gamesmanship. Sure it takes time to play.

The rewards make it worthwhile.

Auto Jargon Used By Salespeople

A Unique Vocabulary

Have you ever felt a little uneasy while talking with someone selling automobiles? Does their language seem like it's from outer space or just spaced out? I mean, really, why would anyone attempting to sell you a car talk about bird dogs at a dog show? The answer is simple. Automobile salespeople have a vocabulary of their own and it's quite unique. Some of their most common words and phrases are defined below.

Average
A car showing signs of wear but still in good shape.

Bait-and-switch
Attracting the customer to the dealership by advertising a deal on a car the dealer never intends to make available. There are many variations of this.

Bird dogs
Individuals who recommend a specific dealer and receive a kickback if this person eventually buys.

Bushing
The trade-in allowance is established and then lowered, or a deposit is made and the price of the vehicle is increased.

Buy at once
A selling trick. Many variations. Used by sellers to discourage comparison shopping. There is never any real need to hurry when buying a car.

Car-of-the-year
Every car built could be considered ''car-of-the-year'' by someone and usually is if you read enough different magazines.

Clean
An automobile in excellent condition both inside and out.

Cream puff
Cars in excellent condition regardless of age.

Dog show
A used car auction.

Doping
Various methods used to disguise a car's faults. A supposedly reconditioned vehicle. Usually ends up a lemon.

Easy credit
Probably never true. Large monthly payments usually mean lower interest rates. Low monthly payments spread out over many extra months go hand-in-hand with a higher interest rate.

Hard and soft
Cars currently selling well are called "hard" on the market. Those you can hardly give away are considered "soft" on the market. Also known as "hot" and "cold".

Highballing
The car salesman quotes a high trade-in price; then, after you've come to at least a preliminary agreement, the salesperson suddenly discovers there has been a big mistake. A variation of this method is used when the salesperson comes back after discussing your deal with the manager and it is changed. Another variation would be a change in the terms of your sales agreement before final approval by the credit department. In all instances the dealer wants to get you thinking you own the car.

House cars
Automobiles bought new, serviced, and then traded-in on a new model, all at the same dealership.

Late model
Automobiles one to three years of age.

Lemon
A car continually breaking down and in need of repair.

Low balling
A salesperson quotes one figure but puts another on the contract. When and if you question this, they usually claim you just misunderstood.

Mouse house
Independent dealers who specialize in older automobiles (not classics). They cater to people with low incomes and usually sell these cars at high prices. These dealers are also known as "iron peddlers."

No cash deal
Dealers where there is more than one profit: the profit from the sale of the car, the financing profit and the insurance profit. This allows waiver of down payment.

Red line
The bare minimum price a dealer will accept for an automobile. This has been established long before the customer arrives.

Rough
A serviceable but below average automobile.

*Working tight
Some used car dealers spread the cost of doing business over their entire inventory of used cars. In this way a certain car might be sold for less money than the dealer has in it. This is called "working tight." By lumping the costs of repair for this car along with those of other cars (with larger profit margins) the dealer can still show a profit on the car for the lot.

Where To Buy Your Next Used Car

What? You can make a choice by looking down the road?

Choose The Source Meeting Your Needs

Where should I buy my car? This question is frequently asked of me. Although not an easy one to answer, you do have quite a few choices. First ask yourself four determining factors:

1. How much money can I afford to spend?
2. What type of vehicle do I want?
3. How much time do I have to look?
4. How much inconvenience can I take?

To make a good choice, keep your answers to these four questions in mind as you read through...

THE SIX SOURCES OF AUTOMOBILE PURCHASE

Franchised dealership
Independent dealership
Pirvate party
Auto auction
Rental car agency
Bank or credit union repossession

The pros and cons of each of these six sources are discussed in the following pages. Since dealerships and private party sales account for the largest percentage of automobile sales, most of the information relates to these sources.

Buying A Used Car From A New Car Dealer

America's first automobile dealership was founded in 1898 by Mr. H.O. Koller. He had the exclusive rights to sell Winton Motor Cars in Reading, Pennsylvania. Although the Winton Motor Carriage Company went out of business in 1906, the concept remained to play a large role in today's automotive world! Dealerships can be divided into two categories: **franchised** or **independent.**

- **Franchised dealerships** can best be described as those given the right by an automobile manufacturer to distribute and sell their products.
  a. Each dealer is usually given a predetermined area called a territory where they have exclusive rights to sell the manufacturer's vehicles and spare parts.
  b. On their premises, dealers usually have a new car least seven years), a used car division, leasing division, repair facilities and a body shop. New car dealers acquire used vehicles from new car trade-ins, auto auctions, wholesalers and trading with other franchised dealers.

ADVANTAGES

1. You have a greater chance of finding a vehicle in better condition than on an independent lot.
2. New car dealers usually keep the best car trade-ins and wholesale the rest.
3. They're more likely to deal on a straightforward basis.
4. All DMV paperwork will be taken care of by the dealer.
5. Repair facilities are on the premises.
6. Convenient financing and insurance can be arranged.
7. A guarantee will come with the car. If not, forget this car and forget this dealership!

DISADVANTAGES

1. Usually you will pay top dollar.
2. You will have less time to check over the vehicle.
3. Reluctance might be encountered on a trade-in.

Buying A Used Car From An Independent Dealer

William E. Metzer organized the first independent dealership in 1898. There were so few motor cars then that most thought he was foolish. Time proved his foresightedness to be correct.

- **Independent dealers** have no affiliation with any manu-facturer. Usually they're strictly in the business of selling used cars.
  a. Today, independent dealers work one of two ways. Some will farm out all mechanical and body repairs their cars need to outside repair shops. Others have in-house repair facilities at the back of the lot or dealership.
  b. Independent used car dealers acquire cars from dealer auto auctions, wholesalers, new car dealer trade-ins, private parties and trade-ins on the vehicles they sell.

ADVANTAGES

1. The vehicle will probably cost less than one purchased from a francised dealer.
2. A guarantee should come with the car.
3. All DMV paperwork will be done by the dealer.

DISADVANTAGES

1. Chances of the car being a "lemon" are greater.
2. Often you will have to arrange your own financing.
3. If the dealership has no repair facility, your guarantee may not be worth much.

Selecting The Right Dealership

Who should you purchase from? It all depends on the automobile you're looking for! If you want a late model Oldsmobile (not more than two years old), I would begin looking at a franchised Oldsmobile dealership. Why? If this is the car of your choice, they will have a far greater selection. For customers who don't want to pay the price of a new car, dealers stock clean late model vehicles of the same make they are franchised to sell. Look for a car bought new at the same dealership a year or two ago now being traded on a current model. This holds true for foreign as well as domestic car models.

Often used car buyers overlook dealerships in high-priced neighborhoods who specialize in used luxury cars. This can be a mistake. As a rule, the previous owner had the money to service the car on a routine schedule (a most important point). Compare prices with other dealerships. You might be surprised!

When you're looking for a three to eight-year-old automobile, I would recommend finding a good independent dealership. Vehicles of this age are generally cheaper than comparable autos found at franchised dealers. Independents come in many shapes and sizes—from corner gas station lots to big glitter dealerships. How do you choose one?

1. Pick one having repair facilities.
2. Locate one in business for at least five years.
3. Find one where you can still negotiate with the owner.
4. Clean dealerships reflect pride. This increases your chances of finding a good used car.

Unless you are buying a special interest or contemporary classic, purchasing a car over eight years old from a dealer can be a waste of money. Why? In a car of this age you're looking for basic transportation at a low cost. A dealer can't buy this type of car any cheaper than you! Take the extra $300 to $500 you would pay the dealer and upgrade by purchasing the car yourself from a private party!

Additional Tips On Choosing A Dealership

- Pick a dealer who has been in business a long time. No one stays in this business very long selling defective merchandise or failing to answer the needs of customers.

- Call your local Better Business Bureau and check for recent complaints.

- Have an outside mechanic check the car before you buy.

- Avoid dealers who use "come-ons" in their advertising like black cats under ladders. "Come-ons" get prospects in the door. They're never quite what you imagine.

- Consider doing business with a young car salesperson. You just might get a better deal. Use to your advantage the ego, drive and desire to impress the boss this young person often has.

- If you finance, check first with your credit union, then your bank, next your dealer and finally a finance company.

- Check insurance costs with companies not affiliated with the dealer. It will probably be less expensive.

- There are two basic reasons for buying from a dealer: (a) convenience and (b) guarantee. If either ingredient is lacking, you can do better elsewhere!

- Dealers often figure they must make as much money as possible when selling a car to a personal friend. Why? If this friendship is valued, everytime parts fail or trouble develops the dealer will have to fix them free of charge.

- I advise staying away from any dealer advertising "No money down, only a few dollars per week."

- Every dealer must be licensed by the state to do business. In contrast to purchasing through a private party, any complaint you have doing business with a dealer can be taken to the appropriate authorities.

- Dealers operate on either the "turnover" or "straight" system of selling cars. Look for dealers operating under the "straight" system. Prices in "turnover" dealerships are generally higher in order to pay for the extra staff.

  a. Dealers working on the "straight" system have one salesperson take you through the entire transaction.

  b. "Turnover" houses have salespeople welcome you and give you a test drive. Then you're turned over to a "closer." This person attempts to close the deal on the car with you.

You're on the track of the correct choice.

Buying From A Dealer

Indeed! There are no real mysteries.

You Have Options—Use Them!

There are common situations with which car buyers are confronted. By becoming aware of them, you can avoid or use them to your advantage.

A SALESPERSON MIGHT SAY:

- "I have four parties interested in this automobile and expect a call this afternoon. I'll need your answer in a few hours!" Remember. Where there's one there's always another. Don't be in a hurry.

- "The price will go up in a couple of days. My manager is on vacation and when he sees the price, etc., etc." If the prices does go up, head for the next dealership.

- "I've got the perfect car for you if you can afford $__ per month." This is no way to be trapped into buying a car you can't afford.

- "I can see you feel the price is a little high. We can take a small amount down, stretch out the payments and keep your monthly payment low." (The smaller your monthly payments the more interest you're paying!)

Keep Your Options In Mind

- When you're paying cash, don't fill out a credit application.

- It is against the law for any dealer to sell a car containing "hidden defects." A sales contract can be cancelled if an independent repair shop will state the car is unsafe.

- Dealers can be sued for using misleading advertising or verbally misrepresenting a car.

- All conditions of sale and promises made by sales personnel should be written into the purchase contract.

- Sometimes dealers will increase your trade-in allowance above wholesale. When this happens, they usually reduce any discount from the list price you might have otherwise received. You will be financially ahead by selling your automobile privately.

- Never purchase a car from a dealer who refuses either a test drive or the opportunity to have the car checked by a mechanic of your choice.

- Beware of a salesperson's first estimate as to the value of your trade-in. It's almost always high. In this way you're already thinking positive thoughts about buying.

- Good salespeople never use the entire amount of their appraisal of your trade-in unless this becomes necessary in order to close the deal.

- Never sign an incomplete contract. Make sure all blanks are either filled in or crossed out. Remember to take your copy with you.

Everything will go your way.

Buying From A Private Party

This Can Be Your Best Bet!

No doubt about it. Purchasing a used car directly from the owner (private party) can be your best bet! You have more time to make a thorough examination of the car. Use it wisely! Have a mechanic check the car. If the owner doesn't want the car checked, go on to the next one. Believe me, the right automobile is waiting for you somewhere. High pressure sales tactics are seldom used by private parties when selling their cars. If you do find this, simply move on.

Exactly What You Should Look For

Individuals are easier to bargin with. They don't need to keep a reserve to pay for guarantees. There's no commission to be paid or set profit to be made. In some instances the sale of one car may be holding up the purchase of another. Most private parties can't afford or don't want to hold on to their car for the time it takes to get full price. This situation is exactly what you should look for.

When You Can't Save, Don't Buy

The biggest reason for buying any automobile from a private party is lower price. Dealers are able to sell the same cars for $300 to $800 more than an individual can! If you can't save this much, I wouldn't consider buying from a private party. And there are some good reasons for this.

1. Individuals can't be expected to give a guarantee. Once bought it's yours. You have no legal way to obtain your money back or get the car repaired at the previous owner's expense.
2. All transfer of ownership paperwork with the Department of Motor Vehicles will be handled by yourself (there are lenders who do help with the DMV paperwork).
3. Private owners usually don't offer financing or insurance for the car (this can be an inconvenience).

Look For A Private Party Who Fits This Description

Ideally, you should find a one-owner automobile. Never purchase from a friend. This can put a great strain on the relationship. Even the best friendship can turn sour! Look for a person over 30 years of age living in a house, condominium or townhouse. Preferably one they own. Generally these people have enough income to properly

71

maintain their cars. And they have respect for possessions.

If the car is in good condition, start by offering a wholesale or current low market value figure. Once you have made an offer between wholesale and retail and it is not accepted, move on to the next car. You're paying too much! *(Note: See "Estimating Used Car Values" in Chapter One, p. 45, and "Step By Step Directions For Completing A Private Car Sale" in Chapter One, p. 32.)*

TIPS ON PRIVATE PARTY PURCHASES

- Make sure you're dealing with an individual. Salespeople often attempt to sell a dealer-owned automobile privately. They are also sometimes involved in selling private party automobiles for the owner. In both instances you'll pay more for the car.

- Be sure all serial numbers (engine and identification) match those on the registration and pink slip. Car thieves sell cars too. If you purchase a stolen vehicle later recovered, your money and the car are both lost!

- Beware of the unlicensed car! It could be a car once totaled then rebuilt. Have your local DMV run a history check on the automobile. *(Note: See "How To Find A Car's History And True Mileage" in Chapter One, p. 85.)*

- In states where smog certificates are required for registration, the seller is responsible for all repairs needed to meet the standards.

- Hand over money only when you possess a valid legal clear title, bill of sale, odometer statement and have a power of attorney to make registration easier.

- Check the cost of insuring the car before you buy.

The right automobile is always waiting for you.

The Truth About Auto Auctions

Well now. You've discovered the truth. Does the temptation still linger?

On Buying Your Used Car At An Auction

It's impossible for me to think of an automobile auction without visualizing the typical auction patron: semiheavy male with Gucci briefcase and open collar. Lots of gold rings, dangling things. Oozing with confidence and sometimes polite. Aching feet, blood-shot eyes. Only carnivals produce such sights.

Auctions. There you buy automobiles at rock bottom prices . . . or do you? Not necessarily! Auctions are created to generate excitement. This excitement can transform the most casual onlooker into an impulsive buyer. Auctions offer greater car exposure before a group of impulsive buyers in a carnival atmosphere, a sure-fire winner. Sales are sure to follow.

But Where Do They Get Those Cars?

Auction vehicles come from private parties, dealers, bank repossessions, auto wreckers (totaled vehicles rebuilt), leasing companies and government pools. All state government agencies auction cars from their motor pools. These cars are subject to hard use, have excessive mileage and are stripped of frills (radio, electric windows, sun roofs, etc.). Contact your closest general administration's business service center for the nearest auction. Prices usually reflect exactly what you get. Dealers who possess too many cars of the same model or have a cash flow problem will consign their excess and problem cars to auctions. All of these sources treat automobile auctions as avenues of disposal.

And The Truth About Auctions

ADVANTAGES

1. You get a feel for the market. An accurate appraisal of current market values can be made by watching this circus.
2. Occasionally there are good buys.
3. It is a way for you to develop contacts in the car market field. Knowledge and experience can be gained by association with auction patrons.
4. A good automobile auction can beat most movies for sheer entertainment value. All you have to do is look around you. The action is hectic.

DISADVANTAGES

1. Your time is limited for presale inspection of the automobiles. Pretty much what you see is what you get.
2. Test drives or learning about the history of the cars on the block are generally not possible.
3. You will be subject to shill bids. These are bids made by the car owner, the car owner's friends or auction house employees for the sole purpose of upping the ante on the purchase price of the car.
4. Shill bids are a constant problem. To spot them you must look for these bidders carefully!
5. There usually are many dealers in attendance. Dealers have well-defined goals as to the price they will take and conditions of sale they will accept. At an auction, it's difficult to strike a bargain with a dealer's car.

6. To avoid impulsive buying you must have extremely strong convictions as to the exact car you want and know its worth. The aura of a good auction has been carefully planned to make buyers out of innocent bystanders.

Auction Tips

- Get to the auction early. This gives you a better opportunity to look the merchandise over carefully.

- Often the best buys occur when there are few bidders (lunchtime, early evening or late at night).

- Even at an auction a car owned by a private party is usually your best bet. You can find out by asking.

- When the cream puff comes up you want, start bidding early. Know your limit!

- If the car of your choice has gone through the auction and didn't sell, approach the owner with an offer. At this time, owners are often discouraged and might accept an offer (probably your best bet to make a good auction buy)!

- Go to the auction prepared to immediately remove your new acquisition. Shipping and storing are hassles.

Are You Accustomed To Pressure?

Unless you're an experienced horse trader (car buyer in this case) approach auctions with caution. Pressure is applied on a buyer to act in a hurry. True, there are some good buys, but they are the exception rather than the rule. *(Note: See "Auto Auctions Are Fun" in Chapter Four, p. 304.)*

You've stumbled onto the truth!

Special Advice On Buying A Rental Car

They May Look Alike But They're Not

Can you imagine going to a candy store selling all the same candy only in different colored wrappers? At first glance, this is similar to viewing a selection of used cars from a car rental agency. When you first look, it seems to be a lot full of just two and four door domestic sedans. The only difference is color! If you look more closely, you'll find most of these lots actually do carry a wide selection of cars.

Their Problem Can Become Your Advantage

One of the biggest problems rental companies have is the disposal of their used vehicles. Generally, they use a formula of mileage, age or a combination of both to determine at what point their cars will be put up for sale. By selecting a car two years old, you take advantage of the big depreciation any car has in the first two years. For you, this adds up to owning a car at one of the least expensive cost per mile possible!

World's Largest Seller Of Used Cars

Rental agencies sell their used cars to large wholesalers who, in turn, sell them to used car dealers. Some rental agencies retail the automobiles themselves. Avis, Hertz and National have so many vehicles they can stock their own retail lots. In fact, Hertz is Detroit's largest buyer of autombiles. This makes them the world's largest seller of used cars! Other companies such as Budget will designate specific independent dealers to sell their cars.

Some Interesting Advantages And . . . Disadvantages

Although some automobile rental companies do carry financing and a few will take a trade-in, most will not. Cash and carry is the financial situation in which you will find yourself. Liquidation of the used car fleet is their prime objective.

There are some other interesting advantages and disadvantages to purchasing a used car from a rental fleet.

ADVANTAGES

1. The biggest advantage you have is saving money. You can buy a late model automobile below current retail value!
2. Our survey showed Avis (the condition of their cars was better) averaging just under $400 savings per car and Hertz an

astonishing $840. Vehicles were priced at or near wholesale levels found in the *Kelly Blue Book Auto Market Report*.

3. Rental vehicles have been serviced on a regular basis. Records for all service work and repairs performed can be obtained before you buy. Hertz displays service records in every automobile while you shop.

4. Avis, Hertz and National carry "after-market" warranties on all their cars.

5. The warranties of Avis and Hertz cover internal parts of the engine, transmission, differential and drive train for a period of 12 months or 12,000 miles.

6. National's warranty is a little more extensive covering not only the drive train components but electrical, air conditioning and front end parts.

7. A warranty is good to have. However, don't base your purchase decision on this alone.

8. Because of the chance of previous abuse, I would lean toward buying six or eight-cylinder models. They tend to hold up better under adverse conditions.

9. Financing can be arranged through Avis, Hertz and National.

DISADVANTAGES

1. The unknown treatment these automobiles received from past drivers is the biggest strike against a rental car. On the average more than 80 different people drive each car over 14,000 miles a year!

2. A great many drivers abuse rental vehicles. Even with good maintenance there is premature wear on suspension and drive train components. This is the reason why rental companies don't keep them long.

3. Most rental cars have high mileage on their odometer. Compared to an average of 12,000 to 15,000 miles on most privately owned cars, 20,000 miles per year is high.

4. If the company or used car lot sells only rental vehicles, they won't take your car in trade. Independent car lots handling both rental cars and their own used cars will take trades.

5. Thrifty, for example, turns a great number of their cars over to independent lots.

6. Your best procedure is to sell your present vehicle first.

7. The selection of cars is limited. Almost no foreign makes are found with the exception of a few Datsuns or Toyotas. Finding one with a manual transmission would be like searching for the Titanic in outer space!

8. Don't expect to find any unusual accessories.

And You Can Call Toll Free

There is a large selection of rental companies to choose from. Any one of these will sell you a car. To easily find the location of a company with a sales office near you, use the list of toll free phone numbers. *(Note: See "Automobile Rental Companies" in Chapter Three, p. 221.)* Ask the operator for the used car sales department. They'll be glad to help you.

Good hunting!

If You're Thinking Of
Buying A Repossessed Automobile

Some Are Potentially Good Buys

Does the word repossession conjure up visions of luxury car ownership at mini-car prices? Unfortunately today, receiving something for nothing is practically impossible! So it is with repossessed automobiles.

Lenders take back motor cars for one reason—lack of payment. I have found non-payment to be closely related to non-maintenance. Beware! If there is one possibility of making a good buy here, it is because default usually occurs within the first year. This makes some almost new repossessed cars potentially good buys!

The Selection Is Limited

Most of these cars are purchased by auto wholesalers or retailers. Although individuals may buy repossessions, selection is extremely limited. Because of their age along with probable poor maintenance, you should stay away from car over three-years-old. Most repossessed cars advertised in the paper are usually poor buys. Why? Wholesalers and retailers have already refused them for good reasons.

Make Your Interest Known

When searching for the best buy, time is your best ally. There are ways to sound the market. Contact a number of lending institutions. Describe the type of vehicle you desire. Leave your name and phone number. Follow up by sending a brief summary of this same information to those lenders whose response to your call is favorable. This will make your interest a matter of record. It generally takes time but they will call you.

Might as well relax while waiting.

State Abbreviations

Approved by the United States Post Office

Matching The Letters With The States

Searching through the classified section of your favorite automotive magazine, you finally run across your dream machine! It's hard to believe, but there it is. Wait. Oddly, there's no phone number, only an address. This brings up your first question, "How far away is this beast?" This list will provide a quick answer. Simply look to the left of the zip code. Then match the two capital letters (abbreviations for states) to the corresponding state on this list.

AL	ALABAMA	MT	MONTANA
AK	ALASKA	NE	NEBRASKA
AZ	ARIZONA	NV	NEVADA
AR	ARKANSAS	NH	NEW HAMPSHIRE
CA	CALIFORNIA	NJ	NEW JERSEY
CZ	CANAL ZONE	NM	NEW MEXICO
CO	COLORADO	NY	NEW YORK
CT	CONNECTICUT	NC	NORTH CAROLINA
DE	DELAWARE	ND	NORTH DAKOTA
DC	DIST. OF COLUMBIA	OH	OHIO
FL	FLORIDA	OK	OKLAHOMA
GA	GEORGIA	OR	OREGON
GU	GUAM	PA	PENNSYLVANIA
HI	HAWAII	PR	PUERTO RICO
ID	IDAHO	RI	RHODE ISLAND
IL	ILLINOIS	SC	SOUTH CAROLINA
IN	INDIANA	SD	SOUTH DAKOTA
IA	IOWA	TN	TENNESSEE
KS	KANSAS	TX	TEXAS
KY	KENTUCKY	UT	UTAH
LA	LOUISIANA	VT	VERMONT
ME	MAINE	VA	VIRGINIA
MD	MARYLAND	VI	VIRGIN ISLANDS
MA	MASSACHUSETTS	WA	WASHINGTON
MI	MICHIGAN	WV	WEST VIRGINIA
MN	MINNESOTA	WI	WISCONSIN
MS	MISSISSIPPI	WY	WYOMING
MO	MISSOURI		

What Test Drive Clues Can Reveal

It's easier to find a problem than to repair it later!

How To Make A Test Drive Have Meaning

With hands twitching and heart throbbing you ease the throttle down. Your mind races with images and fantasies of ownership. Subconsciously you think, "At last! I'm really driving the car of my dreams." Totally oblivious of anything, you drive the treasure back to its home and prepare to pay the seller. Sad but true. Many buyers test drive as though they're being propelled forward by some kind of automatic pilot. Take command! Put real meaning into the words "test drive." Mentally picture these events.

Sounds Reveal The Causes Of Problems

Each test drive should incorporate: rough roads, stop-and-go traffic, freeway driving, twisting country roads and hilly terrain (if possible). The motor car being tested should be fully warmed up and driven (by you) a minimum of ten miles. Listen carefully. Serious problems in automobiles make sounds revealing their cause.

Testing The Brakes

First, test the brake system. Pump the brake pedal several times. Good brakes will stop in exactly the same position with each pump. Put the emergency brake on and try to accelerate. It should be almost impossible to move! Approaching a stop sign take your hands off the wheel and apply normal pedal pressure. As the car comes to a stop, it should not swerve to either side. If your foot receives a rhythmic pulsation under heavy braking, one or more brake drums or rotors are out of round.

A Simple Way To Determine The Carburetor's Condition

With the car in neutral check for a smooth low idle. Place your hand behind the tailpipe. The exhaust should blow out evenly, no popping. A fast idle will hide any malfuntioning carburetor or valve train. Automobiles should idle at no more than 1,000 rpm. Cars equipped with automatic transmissions should not inch forward while idling. Before purchase have the idle turned down and rechecked. A car shaking violently when idling should be avoided.

Smoke . . . Smoke . . . Smoke—Then What?

Watch from your rearview mirror for smoke coming out of the tailpipe. These are the meanings of tailpipe smoke:

- **Blue smoke** coming from the tailpipe when the car is **under acceleration** means the automobile is **burning oil**. Worn out piston rings are usually the culprit.

- **Bluish smoke** when **decelerating** indicates **bad valve guides**. I would leave a gem with either of these problems for some other buyer!

- **Black smoke** may look to be the worst but indicates only a **simple carburetor adjustment is needed**.

🐾 *Yes, examine! There's no substitute for the personal touch.*

Is Everything Headed In The Same Direction?

Look down the line of the car's wheels. Are the front and rear wheels in line with one another? Does the car's body seem to sit at a different angle to the direction of travel? If so, it may be a battle victim of the highway wars. Throughout the road test, check for steering wheel shimmy or vibration. A wheel shimmy occurring between 40 and 50 mph then disappearing around 55 to 60 mph, indicates unbalanced tires. Low speed vibrations are usually due to a bad front end. Vehicles shaking at all speeds usually have suspension problems.

As you make each turn and maneuver, ask yourself:

1. Is there an enormous amount of play before the wheels turn?
2. Does the steering seem tight or bind in turns?
3. Do I hear grinding or squealing from the steering mechanism?
4. At freeway or highway speeds, how well does the car hold a straight line?
5. You can test for a possible bent frame by making a right and then left turn with the steering wheel held at full lock. Any significant difference between the radius of each turn could spell trouble.

The Suspicious Clutch

On cars equipped with a manual gearbox check both clutch and transmission. Upshift and downshift into every gear! Some vehicles tend to pop out of gear, whine while running or grind going into gear. Stay away from these. A clutch pedal should travel 1 1/2 to 2 inches before disengaging. Pedals traveling to the floor before releasing indicate hydraulic, cable or adjustment problems. A clutch releasing immediately is a good candidate for replacement.

Investigate any suspicions of a slipping clutch. Proceed along in 3rd gear at 30 mph and press the accelerator pedal down. As the engine increases in rpm's so should the vehicle's speed. If this doesn't happen, the clutch assembly is over the hill. Remember. The clutch should never grab or chatter, causing the car to buck or jerk.

The Jerky Transmission

Automatic transmissions will shift automatically and smoothly to the next higher gear. Any gearbox not reacting in this manner is going to be a problem to you. Check automatic transmissions for signs of slippage, whine or whistling sounds. Another problem indicator would be its lack of ability to hold the car in a park position on hills.

How To Unveil Drive Train Weakness

The condition of the car's u-joints and drive train is easily determined. Back the car up about 10 feet. Stop. Then drive forward approximately 10 feet. If you hear a clank or clunk as you start your forward motion, bad u-joints are usually the cause. To unveil weakness in the drive train, at 40 mph back off the accelerator, then accelerate. You'll have the answer.

If These Sounds Persist

Clicking, tapping and clattering. A new dance step? No. They're just other telltale sounds the car makes when something's wrong. If these sounds persist during idle or full throttle, the car's valves are improperly adjusted or it has bad hydraulic valve lifters. On some automobiles these can be very expensive to repair!

Rounding Out The Test Drive With Some Finishing Touches

- Roll up all windows and turn off the air conditioner, heater and radio. Listen for a howl coming from the rear end of the car. This sound can mean a worn ring and pinion gear.

- Listen for a pinging noise emitted from the engine when accelerating. Motors knocking for long periods of time may have damaged pistons, valves or both.

- Perk up your ears for grinding sounds seeming to come from the front wheels especially when you are turning. The car could have poor wheel bearings or brakes.

- Years of experience tell me there is only one action to take with an overheating car—don't buy it!

- Observe the automobile in motion. As it moves slowly look for bent wheels (rims).

- After the test drive let the car stand idle for awhile. Look for leaks underneath it.

- Put the icing on the cake. Drive the car through a car wash before you decide to buy. If real leaks (not drips) are spotted this indicates previous major structural damage!

You Can't Buy From 'Em All

I suggest you discuss problems found in the test drive with the seller. If you still want the automobile, the seller should either repair the problem or agree to deduct the estimated cost of repair from the price of the car. There are sellers who will not do this. Don't buy from them.

You spent your time wisely!

How To Find A Car's History And True Mileage

Find the meaning of it all . . . analyze the obvious.

The Records Are Available

Whether you are a dealer or a private car owner, it is against the law to turn back the odometer on your car. Every time there is a change of ownership a signed statement indicating the true mileage must be given to the buyer upon request. Falsifying either the mileage or turning back the odometer is a federal offense subject to prosecution. You can be sued for $1,500 or three times the amount of damages for tampering with an odometer. In one instance a buyer received a court settlement of over $50,000 after it was proved the vehicle purchased had more miles than stated. Keep in mind, dealers can sue a private owner for falsifying mileage the same as a buyer can sue a dealer!

A Car's Past Is As Close As The Nearest Phone

True. Mileage figures alone will not tell you how hard the automobile has been used. There are some clues that will. Before buying ask to see previous service records. When no records can be found, look in the glove box for receipts or on the door jams for stickers indicating service or repair shops. Call these places and ask for the car's mileage on the date work was performed. Now you're getting accuracy plus the true history.

If you purchase from a dealer, ask to see the odometer statement from the previous owner. Write down this owner's name and address. Call the owner and discuss the car before you buy. Generally previous owners won't mind this call. It can be very informative.

Avoid Surprises

You can get answers to your questions when buying from a private owner by asking. How long have you owned the car? Where do you have it serviced? When was it last serviced? Do you drive it to work? Does anyone else use it besides you? Do you have service records or work receipts? May I see them?

Simple But Important Questions

If you think these are simple questions, you're right. When investigating the unknown, you never know what you'll turn up. You may not be pleasantly surprised with your purchase if you fail to ask questions before you buy!

My Auto Nose Tells Me Some Deals Are Best Forgotten

As a last resort, contact the Department of Motor Vehicles. Ask for the histories' department. For information on any automobile be prepared to send them the year, make, serial number, license number and a small search fee (usually under $5). You receive a computer print-out indicating traffic accidents, out-of-state ownership and a list of different owners. In cases where no records or information can be obtained, my auto nose tells me this forgetable deal smells a little fishy.

A Globe-Trotter's Past

Cars can have interesting pasts also. A DMV check I ran on one disclosed this gem was a girl with a figure like a deck of cards. Well-stacked but she'd been shuffled around quite a bit. The car was being offered for sale by a dealer in Sacramento, California. He bought it from a used car dealer in Portland, Oregon, who, in turn, bought it from a New Jersey dealer. The New Jersey dealer had taken it in trade from a local man! The car was young in age—it had just served too many masters. She may have been an innocent heiress but she had an heirloom's past. The words "Don't Buy" were written all over this globetrotter!

SAMPLE FORM FOR REQUEST OF INFORMATION

**INFORMATION REQUEST FROM
REGISTRATION RECORDS**

Notice to Requester: As a condition to disclosure of information from records which it maintains, the Department of Motor Vehicles will provide the subject of the request with the name and address and telephone number of the requester, and the reason for requesting the information.

DATE OF REQUEST

REQUESTER: (PRINT CAREFULLY)

YOUR NAME

TELEPHONE (IF NONE, SHOW "NONE")

YOUR ADDRESS   CITY   STATE   ZIP

DESCRIPTION OF VEHICLE ON WHICH INFORMATION IS REQUESTED.

VEHICLE LIC. NO.   IDENTIFICATION NO.   MAKE   YEAR

LAST NAME   FIRST NAME   M.I.

LOCATION (LAST KNOWN ADDRESS, CITY OR REGION)

INFORMATION REQUESTED

Owner(s) as of (date) _____ ☐ Other (explain)

REASON FOR REQUESTING INFORMATION AND THE INTENDED USE (BE SPECIFIC)

I certify under penalty of perjury that the foregoing is true and correct and that the reason(s) I have given is factual for requesting vehicle registration information on the above vehicle and that the information received will not be used for any unlawful purpose and I understand that I may be subject to prosecution under Penal Code Section 118 for making a false statement.

Executed at _____ on _____
     CITY   COUNTY   STATE   DATE

FOR DMV USE

OWNER'S NAME

ADDRESS

CITY   STATE   ZIP

X _____
     SIGNATURE OF REQUESTER

Requester's Driver's License or Identification Card No.

FIELD OFFICE IDENTIFICATION

Complete only if making request by mail. Please submit the required fee and include a pre-addressed stamped envelope.

DEPARTMENT OF MOTOR VEHICLES
DIVISION OF REGISTRATION
VEHICLE INFORMATION—HISTORIES UNIT

Send information to (Print carefully):

Name _____

Address _____

_____

_____

You've found it!

The Facts About Automobile Warranties

Ah ha. At the moment I'm speechless.

What They Conceal

They don't make cars like they auto. To many of us this may be true, but don't depend on warranties to solve this problem. To better understand why, we'll have to look over a few statistics. You know what statistics are. Like a bikini, what they reveal is suggestive, but what they conceal is vital. Let's start by arming ourselves with basic facts about warranties. Then the word warranty will no longer conceal reality.

Designed To Sell Automobiles

The first thing you should remember about warranties is they are **designed to sell automobiles**—not fix them! It is not difficult to justify this statement when you learn the dollar amount companies expect each warranty to cost: Oldsmobile, $27.50; General Motors, $30.00; Toyota, $47.50. This current warranty coverage is good for only 12 months or 12,000 miles, whichever comes first. This is a far cry from the older five years or 50,000 mile warranty auto manufacturers began cutting back on in 1972. These warranties were costing too much.

What To Base Your Decision On

Take this interesting fact into account if you are contemplating whether to buy new or used. Buying a new car gains you a warranty, but it also pledges you to a schedule of maintenance, at your expense, to keep the warranty alive. If you are basing your decision on the fact a new automobile comes with a warranty, don't give it a second thought!

Stated Clearly In Writing

The second largest category of complaints to reach the Office of Consumer Affairs in Washington, concern warranties. This fact led to a new law called the Magnuson-Moss Warranty Act (nicknamed the "Lemon Law") on January 1, 1977. Among other provisions, this law states that warranties on products costing more than $15 must be made available to the customer before sale. Every term of the warranty must now be clearly stated, not just in fine print. There are to be no fine print clauses at the bottom of the page stating, "If transmission fails between the hours of 2:00 a.m. and 6:00 p.m., this warranty is void!" Additional assurances by salespersons at the time of sales **do not count!** In simple language all terms of the warranty must be clearly and easily understood by all customers, not just by lawyers. There can be **no** fine print.

Make Sure Covered Items Are In The Contract

Regardless of these protective features you should read the contract. Have all the items to be covered by the warranty/guarantee stated clearly in writing before you sign the contract. It is still difficult and time consuming to bring action against a dealer or manufacturer over a warranty.

You should not expect a warranty/guarantee from a private party selling an automobile. By the same token, when you sell your own car, never attempt to give one.

Get Your Money Back

Warranties are classified under either **full, limited** or **implied**. It is important to know the difference between the three.

A **full warranty** is the best protection. It provides that a defective product will be fixed or replaced free, including removal and installation, if necessary. This means, after repeated attempts to repair by the dealer over a fair amount of time, the buyer can either get his money back or a replacement vehicle, if the automobile does not perform satisfactorily. This type of coverage is good for anyone who owns the product during the warranty period. Unfortunately, 98 percent of the car manufacturers do not offer this form of warranty on their new cars. Within our current laws, customers can't sue in federal courts to make a car manufacturer repurchase a car needing frequent repairs unless the vehicle is covered by a full warranty.

A **limited warranty** means you will not receive your money back or find a replacement car parked in your driveway if you have trouble with your purchase. Limited warranties only cover specific items on an automobile. Examples would be internal engine parts, transmission, drive line, axle housings—all covered only for a specific amount of time. Many limited warranties cover replacement parts only, no labor costs. However, no warranty can force you to use a particular product. This form of warranty makes it difficult to sue in federal courts to make a car manufacturer repurchase an automobile. If you've purchased a lemon, you own it!

An **implied warranty** is an unwritten but legally binding promise the seller gives you simply by selling you a product. It guarantees the product being sold is what the seller says it is and will perform the function ordinarily expected of it or the function you and the seller have agreed it will perform. This law not only applies to automobiles but also in the sale of parts, accessories and the repair of automobiles.

Dealer Prep Checklist

Dealers, like other businessmen, have been known to have a clear conscience with a foggy memory. To fight truth decay make sure you receive a copy of the dealer preparation checklist **at the time you buy a new car.** This list itemizes the things a dealer is supposed to do to make your car ready for use after it is shipped to him. These are called "dealer prep charges." Be sure the dealer has signed the list! This will make it much easier for you to get an item repaired later at no cost to you. Figures show even when repairs are absolutely free, only about two-thirds of the car owners take advantage of this service.

Good heavens! Does everything that begins bad have to end worse?

Get Agreements In Writing

A guarantee is the written agreement a dealer gives you at the time of sale. It describes the extent he will stand behind a used car. The agreement will be in effect for a certain length of time or so many miles. Be sure to get this in writing because the word "guaranteed" means nothing used by itself. You'll then know exactly what is guaranteed and for how long.

State All Facts In The Sales Contract

The guarantee should cover specific components of the automobile such as the motor, transmission and drive line. Do not expect it to cover upholstery, etc., or abuse of car in any way. Here is a very important tip! Carefully consider where and from whom you purchase your used car. Does the dealer, for example, have the garage facilities to honor the guarantee?

The best guarantee by far is the original factory-backed one. If the used car is less than a year old, it may still be covered. When any car is represented as having this type of coverage, be sure to have this fact added to the sales contract before it is signed.

Things Not Looked For Are Seldom Found

On any repair including guarantee or warranty work visually check your car to determine for yourself if the service work was performed. Look over the problem area before the work starts. There will later be clues in the form of alterations to help you determine what repairs were made. Remember. Those things not looked for are seldom found! Leave enough time in the normal working day when picking your car up to look things over without being rushed. Except for warranty work on a new car, you have a right to the old parts.

Don't Trust To Luck. Send A Registered Letter

It's possible you may have a car problem just before the guarantee is due to expire. Do not let the dealer stall you. If the car can't be repaired before the expiration date, send the dealer a registered letter proving you asked for the repair within the time limits of your guarantee. Once again, don't just "trust to luck." If you do, you won't have any!

Dealer Pays All Parts And Labor

Never accept a 50-50 guarantee. Here the dealer promises to pay half the repair bills for a specified time. You are to pay the other half. Make no mistake, you are at a big disadvantage in this one! Who knows more about the actual cost of parts and labor, the dealer or you?

The Only Worthwhile Guarantee

The only guarantee worth a grain of salt is one with the dealer paying all costs for parts and labor on covered items for a period of at least thirty days. This will give you enough time with the car to determine if any major problem exists. Before you settle for anything less, here's a good statistic to keep in mind. The auto industry's average repair guarantee covers parts and labor for 100% of cost for 90 days.

Promises Are Not Enough

If a dealer will not give you a guarantee on a used car, don't buy it—unless you enjoy working by day and playing mechanic by night! Goes hand in hand with not eating at restaurants named Mom's, playing poker with anyone named Doc, or buying used cars from a dealer named Frenchy. All reliable dealers strive to maintain a good reputation. It's a fact. Generally cars with good guarantees reflect the condition the dealership thinks the car is in.

At the time of purchase of a used car, the dealer promises to repair certain items. Make sure a notation as to the items to be repaired is added to the contract and initialed by the dealer. If the car is represented as reconditioned, add details about this to the guarantee. A few dealers feel they can fool some of the customers all of the time and all of the customers some of the time—and that's sufficient! Be sure to take the signed or initialed dealer checklists with you when you leave. These written statements will prove valuable if referral proof is needed later.

Automobiles Sold "As Is"

Buyers should realize that "as is" in a contract means the buyer has no guarantee what he purchases will work. The dealer does have an obligation even on an "as is" vehicle to recondition it to the extent it is safe to be driven. Once the dealer has conditioned the automobile in this manner, what you see is what you get!

TYPICAL "AS IS" CLAUSE

THIS AUTOMOBILE IS BEING SOLD ON AN

AS-IS

OR "WITH ALL ALL FAULTS" BASIS.

THE ENTIRE RISK AS TO THE QUALITY AND PERFORMANCE OF THIS AUTOMOBILE IS WITH THE BUYER. SHOULD THE AUTOMOBILE PROVE DEFECTIVE FOLLOWING ITS PURCHASE, THE BUYER AND NOT THE MANUFACTURER, DISTRIBUTOR, OR RETAILER ASSUMES THE ENTIRE COST OF ALL NECESSARY SERVICING OR REPAIR.
BUYER ACKNOWLEDGES COPY OF ABOVE IS ATTACHED TO VEHICLE.

BUYER_____

Dealer Safety Requirements

At the time of sale a dealer is required to have each of these items in working order, even if the automobile is sold "As-Is".

BRAKES

> Brakes must be in good working order. Fluid can't be leaking from wheel cylinders and there must be a reasonable amount of brake lining left.

SEATBELTS

> No dealer shall sell or offer for sale any used passenger vehicle manufactured on or after January 1, 1962, unless it is equipped with at least two seatbelts installed for the use of persons in the front seat.
>
> No dealer shall sell or offer for sale any used passenger vehicle manufactured on or after January 1, 1968, unless it is equipped with seatbelts for each seating position.

TIRES

> No dealer shall expose for sale a tire so worn that less than 1/16" tread depth remains in two adjacent grooves at any location on the tire.

WINDSHIELD WIPERS

> Every automobile must have its windshield wipers in good working order.

SMOG

> States vary. California says it's the seller's responsibility to bring the car into compliance with the code. This applies to individuals as well as dealers.

HORNS

> Every motor vehicle operating on a highway shall be equipped with a horn in good working order.

LIGHTS

> All lights (headlights, turn signal lights, running lights, etc., must be in good working order.

WINDSHIELDS

> Windshields must be free of defects so as not to obstruct the driver's view. There can be small rock chips but not a large crack in front of the driver.

When To Use The Small Claims Court

You may not discover life is more than a bowl of cherries 'till after you've eaten them. It can be the same with some car transactions. After repeated unsuccessful attempts to get satisfaction from the dealer on guarantee/warranty matters, your best chance for resolving the problem can be found in small claims court. This holds true also for an automobile sold "As Is" if there is a safety-related defect!

Be Sure Of Your Facts!

Before you enter the courtroom, arm yourself with as many facts as possible. First determine if your problem is covered by the guarantee. Make sure that before your warranty expires repeated attempts have been made to have the dealer solve the problem.

Take Copies Of Everything To Court

Before expiration of the warranty/guarantee send the dealer a registered letter explaining your complaint in clear, precise terms. Secure two written estimates regarding your problem from other repair shops. Keep copies of everything and take these to court. You'll find no substitute for a genuine lack of preparation. Them that has also gits!

Your Small Claim Trial Costs Are Minimal

The amount of money you can sue for in small claims court varies in different states from $100 to $3,500. Your costs in bringing this action to trial are minimal. Records show around 35 percent of the cases don't ever go to trial. Filing shows the dealer you mean business. Most dealers would rather settle out of court. Small claims courts allow consumers the right to subpoena important company records. Most manufacturers and dealers would prefer to keep these secret!

Secret Warranties

Everyone has secrets. Usually when it comes to a secret the more you are told the less the teller really wants you to know. This was never truer than the relationship between automobile manufacturers and the millions of car buyers. **Each company has warranty extensions to compensate consumers for defective parts that either fail prematurely or never fuction properly from the start.** These warranty extensions often offer free parts and labor up to five years or 50,000 miles, regardless of the number of prior owners.

Secret Warranty Funds

Here's a well-kept secret. The auto industry has built up secret warranty funds. These pay for warranty work carried out after the normal warranty period has expired. This work is carried out as quietly as possible. Most manufacturers still deny extended warranties even exist. The policy has been to notify only dealers of these factory defects. To find out if your problem is covered by such a warranty, take the car to an authorized dealer and ask. If you're still in doubt or receive no satisfactory answer, write to:

FEDERAL TRADE COMMISSION
Washington, DC 20580

How To Contest A Repair Bill

This is an excellent method to follow when you wish to contest a repair bill that you feel may be covered by a warranty extension.

First, write a registered letter to your dealer and also to the car manufacturer. *(Note: See "How To Settle Disputes Fast" in Chapter Two, p. 169.)* Ask that the necessary repairs be covered by the extended warranty. If this request is refused, pay for the repairs and then file claim for reimbursement through small claims court in the county you made the purchase.

Send a subpoena to the manufacturer ordering the deposit of all internal documents relating to the warranty extension for your model car. Take all records to court. Prepare a simple statement telling the judge what has happened and why you should be reimbursed. Back this up with evidence. This method works!

Extended Service Plans

Make no mistake about it. Extended service plans (contracts or warranty plans) are a way for dealers to make more profits when they sell either new or used automobiles. Need proof? To start with, only one of four buyers purchasing such a plan will ever file a claim! Consider this ad, one of many similar, quoted word for word from a company offering extended service contracts to automobile dealers, "(Name of the service contract company) is an expert at unlocking profits in automotive dealerships." There are many variations but all tell the dealer a way to make extra profit.

The basic service contract extends the 12 month or 12,000 mile warranty on new autos to 36 months or 36,000 miles— with certain limitations.

MOST SERVICE CONTRACTS . . .

1. Do not cover the cost of routine maintenance services.

2. Have a provision whereby the customer pays the first $25 of any repair bill.
3. Are not transferrable to subsequent owners of the car.
4. Are written on vehicles driven only for personal use.
5. Are not written to cover a used vehicle with over 60,000 miles.
6. Do not cover most vehicles if they are over three years old.

WHAT IS COVERED BY SERVICE CONTRACTS

1. All internal engine parts—block, cylinder heads, intake and exhaust manifolds, etc.
2. Steering assembly, some suspension components, axles, drive shaft assembly and most electrical components.
3. If your car has to be serviced overnight, you will be reimbursed up to $15 per day (five day limit) with a maximum allowance of $75 on a rental car.
4. Some service plans will help on towing expenses by paying up to $25 of each towing bill.

Your Money

Think this out. Any new vehicle given proper routine maintenance (oil changes, tune-ups, etc.) will probably never need such a plan. Even on a good used car, repairs usually do not occur until the 75,000 to 100,000 mile mark. By this time your extended service contract is void anyway. In some cases it is easy to unknowingly purchase an extended warranty contract. The used car dealer has simply added it to the selling price. Check this out before you buy. If you find this provision, ask the dealer to deduct the cost of this warranty and replace it with no less than a 30-day full parts and labor guarantee of his own. If he won't do this, you either have the wrong car or dealer—maybe both. Buy in haste. Repair at leisure!

Warranty Contracts Play The Odds

Today, extended warranty contracts are written not only by the big automobile manufacturers, but also by many smaller independent companies. In essence, what these companies do is play the odds. Just as they are for any other professional gambler, these odds are heavily stacked in their favor.

Listening to some of the sales pitches for extended service contracts are from the land of make-believe. It's like driving with all your windows closed in hot weather to make-believe the car is air conditioned. What you have to make-believe you've got—you ain't!

Your Money More Wisely Spent

Rather than purchasing an extended service contract, this same money can be more wisely spent having an option of your choice installed on a new car or upgrading your choice of cars when buying a used one. Better still, keep the money in your pocket!

Complaints Against A Dealer

In spite of all the precautions you may take, there may come a time when you feel you have been gypped by a dealer. If you can't come to a satisfactory settlement, all is not lost. Complaints against dealers may be filed with the Department of Motor Vehicles.

The various types of complaints include past ownership misrepresentation, turning back the odometer and a dealer who will not honor the warranty. The DMV will send a representative to investigate your complaint. If negligence is found, action will be taken against the dealer. Here is a sample of a form used for this purpose. Each state uses a slightly different form.

Division of Compliance – Consumer Complaint

You now know how to take action!

What To Do About A Defective Automobile

Your Assurance Recall Items Are Repaired

Many used cars still have safety defects even though the manufacturer may have issued notice of recall. Statistics show over 30% of all recalled automobiles go unrepaired. The manufacturer is obligated to repair each vehicle involved in a recall campaign regardless of mileage, number of owners, or age of the car. When purchasing a used car from a dealer selling new cars of the same make, you have the absolute right to assurance all recall items have been repaired.

Collection Is Often Difficult

If independent testimony can show a part was designed or produced in an unsound manner, the manufacturer involved can be held liable. In these cases an automaker is responsible for repair or replacement of defective parts. Any damages caused by the part's failure, bodily injury, loss of wages and personal inconvenience can be collected from the manufacturer although it may be difficult.

To Find Out About Recalls

Call the manufacturer's district service manager to find whether a certain automobile has been recalled. You'll find this phone number in the owner's manual. If this is missing, be ready with the make, model and indentification number of the car. Then call:

**NATIONAL HIGHWAY
TRAFFIC SAFETY ADMINISTRATION**
Office Of Consumer Services
PH: 202 426-0670 or 426-0671
Toll free—800 424-9393

Or write:

NHTSA
Department Of Transportation
Washington, DC

Buying A New Car

Does This Sound Familiar?

At 3:00 a.m. you awake in a cold sweat. Both palms are like melting cheese. The sheets are ringing wet from perspiration. You're thinking, "Gee, I really can afford a brand new Wonder Buggy Sport Coupe!" Secretly, you've already picked it out, convinced yourself, made up your mind. Yesterday an office buddy fed your desire by flapping about how he stole a brand new Sport Coupe from Bobby Bozo's Lincoln Mercury.

While lying in the dark you formulate a plan. "Let's see, I'll call in sick tomorrow, scarf down a little breakfast, proceed to Bozo's dealership, buy that red beauty and celebrate by taking Nancy out to dinner." Sound typical? It should. People do it every year.

You're Convinced It's A Bargain?

I'm not advocating that there's anything wrong with this method. On the contrary, buying a new motor car should be fun and exciting! I don't want to apply scare tactics, but neither do I want to disillusion anyone.

Have you ever noticed purchasers of new cars rave about what bargains they received? Well, if everybody received a bargain, why are there so many wealthy dealers?

The art of selling automobiles is a direct carry-over from selling horses. Hence, the slang term for an automobile salesperson is "horse trader." These people don't feel they're cheating—their tactics are simply rules of the game. Therefore, you must make it a point to understand this game!

A Difference That Means A Lot

Let's face it, everybody must eat and sleep. This includes all personnel in the automotive industry. But, there's a big difference between making a good living and being rich! You needn't make a dealer wealthy. On the contrary, you should keep as many of those hard-earned greenbacks as possible. That's the name of the game!

Before The Attack!

Before you're attacked by someone wearing white shoes, pink tie and plaid jacket, ask yourself this question, "What vehicle really fits my needs?" I've sold many motor cars to individuals who had no business owning them! Although I recommended against the purchase, I once sold a family man a two-seat Porsche as his first car. Don't ignore reality by assuming the car satisfying your desires in style, gas mileage and roominess will also satisfy your specific driving requirements. Imagine you have several tall children who will sit in the back seat. Take into consideration that amount of head and leg room in this area!

Resale Value—The Most Important Factor

Once you've selected those automobiles realistically matching your needs, examine the market. Study each vehicle's resale value. Ultimately, this new purchase will be sold again (by you). You'll want to retain as many precious greenbacks as possible. There are important ways to accomplish this.

Obtain a copy of either the *Kelly Blue Book* or N.A.D.A. value guide. *(Note: See "Estimating The Value Of Any Used Car" in Chapter One, p. 45.)* With each automobile, look up the value for a three-year-old model. If all vehicles are similarly priced, your final choice should be obvious! Choose the motor car with the highest resale factor.

The Value Of Magazine Road Test Summaries

Now, look up past road tests for the automobile you're contemplating buying. Most public libraries carry magazines such as *Road & Track* or *Car & Driver*. *(Note: See "Outstanding Publications" in Chapter Three, p. 237.)* Avoid the creatures with poor reliability. This factor will come back to haunt you!

When "Extras" Become A Must

Prior to leaving the old homestead you must know what you want and how much you're willing to spend. Determine the specific amount of money you can afford. Stick to this limit. Unless you're paying cash, don't purchase a motor car when the payment exceeds 20-25 percent of your monthly income.

It's An Option

Carefully consider all the optional equipment you want. Those "extras" directly influence the length of time you'll own this vehicle and the amount of pleasure you will derive from it. Having them is very important!

Optional equipment is not new to American car buyers. However, most of us are continually amazed at how long some options have been around. Packard offered optional air conditioning on their 1939 models. Oldsmobile in 1940 appeared with the first trustworthy automatic transmission. Today, it's not uncommon for optional equipment to equal or exceed the base price paid for an automobile. The "stripped" model just doesn't exist anymore. An American-built vehicle without an option would have to be ordered.

Some Things Are Just Better With Than Without

Optional equipment will effect the car's resale value and dramatically increase ownership enjoyment. But, more options mean higher maintenance and operating costs. In spite of this, don't skimp on options. The more the better!

Good salespeople try to fast-talk you into every option. This is to be expected. But don't let yourself be talked out of options just because the car is not in stock. The right car can usually be found. The delay is worthwhile.

A Right Time And Wrong Time To Order

Options installed by the dealer (add-on equipment) can cost you two or three times as much as factory-equipped options (OEM)! Certain options must be obtained from the manufacturer. These include automatic transmission, power steering and power brakes. Items such as stereo radios, air conditioners and vinyl tops are a dealer's bread and butter. The dealer installs these or contracts the job with an independent firm. You'll be charged accordingly.

Some Of The Basic Options

There are hundreds of options available to the new car buyer. Obviously, I can't list every one. All options and prices are listed in either the *Consumer Car Guide* (current year) or *Edmund's New Car Prices*. Here are a few basic ideas.

1. Every car manufactured in the U.S. (compact size or larger) should come with at least air conditioning, automatic transmission, power steering and power brakes. Without these items, resale could be greatly impaired.

2. Options you pick should reflect the amount of time you plan on keeping this motor car. Example: For a short period of time (1-2 years) fancy frill items like AM-FM stereo, electric sunroof, custom wheels or special interiors should be added first. These will make the automobile easier to sell when the time comes. For cars to be kept longer (4-5 years), add options that will reduce maintenance costs—a special rear axle for better fuel economy, heavy-duty suspension, larger radiator and heavy-duty battery.

3. Some items can save you money. Light-colored roofs reflect heat and reduce air conditioning costs.

4. Radial tires are well worth the extra money. They increase gas mileage, give you better handling and average 25,000 more miles of wear than regular tires.

5. Purchase your own stereo radio and have it installed by an independent firm. You can save between 10-30 percent.

6. If you plan to keep your car over three years, it would pay to have it rustproofed.

7. If you pay for an option, make absolutely sure you receive it! Believe it or not, people do pay for many options they never receive (especially undercoating and rustproofing).

8. Options you can't have installed yourself should be ordered from the factory.

9. Select options providing durability. Avoid adding to the complexity. It all boils down to how much you can afford and how long you plan to keep the car.

Wheeling And Dealing

Holding Four Aces

Would you stay in the poker hand holding a pair of queens if you knew the next player had three kings? You've got to know when to fold 'em. Bill Jones, a famous card player from Canada, was often quoted as saying, "It's morally wrong to allow suckers to keep their money." Imagine the poker player as a car dealer, the sucker a new car buyer. You better hold all four aces—then deal for that new Wonder Buggy Sport Coupe.

You Select The Time To Play The Game

Probably the best time to buy is in midwinter—February to be exact. Because of weather and the after-Christmas lag, few buyers are out. Both the dealer and salespeople are hungry. However, don't make the mistake of buying at night or in the rain! Tuesday is the most advantageous day to shop. Why? Tuesday is removed from the weekend rush when sales activity is heaviest. And plan a midmorning arrival at the dealership. Before you go, here's how to deal yourself a better hand.

Determine How Long To Hold The Cards

"Interim pricing" is the latest in automotive pricing policies. In essence, it means spaced price increases throughout the model year. There is a smaller than usual hike at introduction time. If you plan to keep your new purchase three years of less, purchase it as soon as possible! Maybe you like to hold 'em. Keep your new motor car for four or five years? If so, purchase in September or just before the new models are introduced. Factories give dealers rebates as incentive to clear out their current inventory.

Deal Yourself An Ace!

Put the ace of hearts in your hand. Use this formula to discover how much the dealer pays for each vehicle!

1. Add up a vehicle's sticker price. Be sure to include the transportation costs.
2. Subtract the transportation charge.
3. Use this figure. Take (a) 80 percent of the balance on full-sized motor cars, or (b) 81 percent of the balance on intermediate-sized or (c) 85 percent of the balance on compact cars.
4. Now add back the transportation cost.
5. This new figure will be close to the dealer's actual cost.

For retail and actual dealer costs on foreign automobiles write:

EDMUNDS
Subscription Department USC-778
515 Hempstead
New York, NY 11552

Go With A Winner

Dealers selling more than two makes of cars can spell trouble to you. Operating expenses usually are sky-high and the manufacturer could cancel the franchise in favor of an exclusive franchise elsewhere. Dealerships handling three or more different makes undoubtedly will have an inadequate supply of replacement parts. The rule of thumb is to purchase from a dealer who specializes in one or two makes.

Now you know when, what, where and from whom to buy. You've selected all the optional equipment and have a ballpark figure on dealer cost. You're ready for the lions. Let the games begin!

The Only Foolproof Method

That Tuesday finally arrives. You decide, with lump in throat, to visit a few dealerships. You are mentally prepared to negotiate the price. You know every dealer is different. Some will make deals that others won't. The essential agreement needed is what you want to pay versus the price at which the dealer wants to sell. Only one method is foolproof—a visit to at least two dealerships, preferably four. You must compare dealers and prices!

Smile Through It All

As you walk into the showroom, prepare for an invasion of salespeople. Be straightforward about discussing your needs in general terms. It does help to treat each salesperson with the same respect you would treat any business associate. At the appropriate time ask, "If I wanted to buy this car today without a trade-in, what kind of deal would you make?" Your salesperson will then respond with "their best deal." Get this figure in writing! Compare this to your estimated cost figure. Gad zooks! There's a vast difference!

Proceed to the next dealer and ask them to better the "deal." No need to be shy about this. Salespeople are quite used to beating other deals. Keep your honest and humble attitude. Repeat this procedure as many times as possible.

Success! You've Established Competitive Bargaining

While it may seem tedious, patience is your greatest virtue. Only by comparison shopping can you buy at the lowest price! With this method you'll find yourself at the base of a bidding triangle. Competitive bargaining between dealers is your greatest advantage. In the end, you should be able to come relatively close to dealer cost (within $200). If not, try a new tactic—the automobile broker!

Auto Brokers

This Can Be The Answer

Ordering autos and trucks from brokers could be considered a little like automobile mail order. Simply fill in your name and address, and drop in any mailbox and presto, chango, you're billed ten bucks. Three to four months later that shiny new creation is delivered to your nearest dealer! Sounds easy, right? Surprisingly, this can be one of the cheapest ways to buy a new car.

You Can't Be In A Hurry

Most of the big auto brokers (Montgomery Ward Auto Club, Nationwide Auto Brokers and United Auto Brokers) advertise cars for sale at $125 over dealer's cost. You may purchase any American and some foreign automobiles. The Montgomery Ward Auto Club will require you to become a member before making use of this service. Sound too good to be true? It's not.

Because of their large business volume, these companies have great purchasing power. They buy automobiles at a very low price! The price range does vary. Some makes and models can be purchased for cost plus $50. A few foreign makes may be slightly over cost plus $125. Brokers can also arrange financing, licensing and titling. Remember. You can't be pressed for time. Delivery may take three to four months. But, you can save a great deal of money!

Send For The Information—You'll Learn A Lot!

Contact any of these brokers. Tell them the make and model you want. A computer print-out will be sent back giving wholesale and retail price together with a list of all possible options and their cost. Prices fluctuate throughout different parts of the country. This is reflected on the card you receive. Even if you choose not to purchase through a broker, the price knowledge you'll acquire can become invaluable in future transactions!

These two companies sell nothing but information:

Car/Puter
Department A78
1603 Bushwick Avenue
Brooklyn, NY 11207

COMPUTERIZED CAR COSTS CO
P.O. Box 2090
Eleven Mile, Lasher Station
Southfield, MI 48037

These companies broker automobiles:

COMPUTERIZED CAR COST SYSTEM, INC
14411 W 8 Mile Road
Detroit, MI 48235

MASTERSON FLEET AUTO, INC
1957 Chestnut Street
San Francisco, CA 94123

MONTGOMERY WARD AUTO CLUB
1400 Greenleaf Avenue
Chicago, IL 60626

NATIONWIDE AUTO BROKERS, INC
17517 W Ten Mile Road
Southfield, MI 48075

UNITED AUTO BROKERS
Car/Puter
1603 Bushwick Avenue
Brooklyn, NY 11207

UNITED BUYING SERVICE
1855 Broadway
New York, NY 10023

Collecting The Pot

When To Consider Buying New

The purchase of a new car today requires a large capital outlay. Before deciding to buy, carefully weigh your alternatives. Quite often I'm asked, "When is the best time to sell my present car?" The answer is simple—only when maintenance and repair costs are about to outrun depreciation costs.

Before you sign any contract, look through the ideas listed below. You may find one enabling you to prevent a future problem.

- Automobile companies exist on volume and expect dealers to achieve this volume. The discount you receive depends strictly on how close a dealer is to meeting sales quotas and how well the cars are selling.

- When you first start negotiations, never mention a trade-in. Only after hearing a salesperson's bottom cash price should you introduce this fact. Then determine the bottom line—how much will I have to pay to complete this deal after deducting the trade-in.

- Customers who guard against paying too much for a new car quite often are the same ones who sell their trade-in for too little. Beware!

- Occasionally salespeople may (after a chat with their sales manager) return saying the list price is actually $500 more than the window sticker. This is called "packing." Packing is not illegal so long as the government sticker is on the car. Remain firm. By this time you should already have a written sales agreement.

- Never sign a sales agreement until you're positive it's written exactly as you want the car. Make sure all services, equipment and accessories itemized on the window sticker are actually included! Remember. Until the window sticker, bill-of-sale and car all match, don't sign any contract.

- Talk with the service manager before you buy. Ask questions about "loaner car" arrangements, etc. If the manager doesn't have a few minutes to spare before you buy, he probably won't listen to your problems once you've purchased the car!

- Before you sign the final acceptance papers, make sure all dealer preparation adjustments have been made to your satisfaction. Any vehicle equipment changes should be written on the window sticker and dealer initialed.

- On the bill-of-sale all dealer preparation charges must be marked, "Paid in Full." If you're not charged for these, the Bill of Sale should indicate, "Dealer preparation completed—no charge."

- Most new cars have some miles on the odometer. Before purchase, make sure you receive an odometer disclosure statement. Compare this to the car's actual mileage.

- The location and convenience of the dealership are factors that should override small price differences.

- If you move, notify your car manufacturer. Send a letter to the customer relations office at the manufacturer's headquarters. *(Note: See addresses in "Protect Yourself When Repairs Are Needed" in Chapter Two, p. 163.)* Include information such as the make, model, year and vehicle identification number. Your car may be involved in a recall campaign. You could end up driving an automobile with safety defects!

Lingo Used By New Car Salespeople

Have you ever felt lost in the fog when salespeople start to talk about "oversteer" or "understeer?" Maybe this person mumbled something about "OEM?" Once you return home are you confused by all this gibberish? These terms unravel many mysteries surrounding new car sales terminology. Glance over them before you go car shopping.

Add-on
A dealer adds an item to a car that the car was not originally equipped with by the manufacturer.

After-market
Customer takes delivery of a new car and later adds an option.

Automatic transmission
A transmission that shifts its own gears according to the prevailing speed, load and road conditions.

Compact car
Car having a wheelbase 100 to 111 inches.

Coupe
Car with a smaller interior than a sedan.

Cubic inches
The total number of cubic inches found in all cylinders (size of the engine).

Economy car
Car with a wheelbase under 100 inches (subcompact and minicar). Generally has an engine displacement of less than 2.5 liters.

Fastback
A car design having an unbroken curved style line from the top of the roof to the rear bumper.

Four-wheel drive
Power is transmitted to all four wheels instead of just the rear two. An advantage in rough terrain and muddy areas.

Fuel injection
A precise system which injects metered amounts of fuel into an engine.

Intermediate size car
An automobile with a wheelbase 112 to 118 inches.

Hardtop
Automobiles having no metal post (only rubber molding) between the front and rear side windows.

Hatchback
A car of the fastback design. The rear window opens to the rear of the car for storage space.

Limousine
A closed, chauffeur-driven automobile.

Luxury car
A well-equipped, appointed, designed and constructed automobile. Usually has a wheelbase of 119 inches or over.

Notch-back
A car body shape with a roof line that has an abrupt vertical drop at the rear window. The line returns to near horizontal at the trunk.

OEM
Stands for original equipment from the manufacturer.

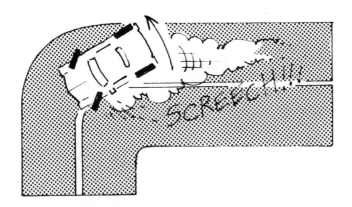

Oversteer
The reaction of a car to a turn. If the tendency is for the rear of the car to slide out while the front wheels hold stable, the car is said to oversteer.

Production
A car made in large quantities for street use.

Rack-and-pinion steering
A steering system having a pinion gear at the lower end of the steering column. A more precise way to turn the front two wheels.

Revolutions (revs)
The number of times the crank shaft rotates in one minute. Also expressed as RPM's (revolutions per minute).

S.A.E.
Society of Automotive Engineers. A group recognized for publishing research papers and defining standards of measurement.

Sedan
Automobile having either two or four doors. It's a closed car capable of carrying four or more passengers. These vehicles have a metal post between the front and rear side windows.

Sports car

An agile vehicle that is easily maneuverable, accelerates briskly, brakes positively, handles well, steers precisely and gives a taut performance. The car is tightly sprung and does not have the wallow and heave of a conventional passenger car. For this reason it is usually not as comfortable.

Sporty car

This automobile has only some of the true sports car characteristics.

Standard size car

An automobile with a wheelbase of 119 inches or over.

Subcompact car

An automobile with a wheelbase of 101 inches or less.

Tachometer

An instrument indicating the number of revolutions per minute of the engine's crankshaft.

Turning circle

The diameter of a circle made by an automobile when the steering wheel is fully turned or locked in one direction.

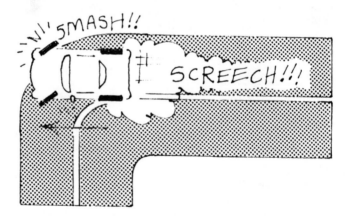

Understeer

The reaction of a car to a turn. If the tendency is for the front of the car to proceed relatively straight ahead instead of following the direction the wheels are turned, the car is said to be understeering (pushing).

Wheelbase

The distance between the centers of the front and rear wheels.

Auto + Thief + 30 Seconds = Stolen!

Really? You thought it couldn't happen to you?

Are You Alert Or Asleep?

Dishonesty is not accidental. Good men, like good women, never see temptation when they meet it. When it comes to the automobile or items within it, the temptation to steal is too much for some. We are bombarded with reasons for protecting the sanctity of our home from theft. Yet, in reality our financial losses due to thefts of automobiles (including accessories and personal possessions left in them) stagger the imagination by comparison. Think it can't happen to you? Do nothing and wait! Your turn will come. Don't be surprised when it does!

Protection At No Cost To You

Your first line of defense against car theft is simple. It costs you nothing. Keep the car in a locked garage if you have one. Lock the car anytime you're not in it. Never leave items in plain view inside the car. Put them in a storage compartment or inside the trunk. Make sure all windows are tightly closed when the car is unoccupied. Remember. A car cover never prevents burglary. The thief simply takes the cover. These are basics. They won't prevent thefts but they will deter them.

It Pays To Out Think The Burglar!

Stronger measures? Yes, you can do a lot better! Install or have installed an ignition cut-out switch in the dash area of your car. This is an inexpensive but hidden toggle switch. Wire the switch into the input side of your ignition coil. Always turn the switch off when leaving your car. This prevents electricity from entering the coil or distributor. The result—your engine turns over but the car will not start (even when the ignition has been jerked out and the wires bridged). Very discouraging to anyone in a hurry!

The Art Of Disguise

A quality stereo radio is a prime target for theft. It makes little difference whether it is factory-installed or otherwise. Here are some suggestions. Remove, hide or disguise the identification or nameplate panels on the radio. Construct a false face plate that snaps into place and covers up the real thing. Another suggestion— install it in the glove box where it will be concealed. A word of caution. If the reach is a long one, keep eyes on the road while operating the radio in this location!

Exotic Wheels And How To Keep Them

Put lug nut locks on the wheels. However, use two different sets of locks. Place one of each opposite one another on the lug nut pattern of each wheel. Then, have the tires rebalanced.

If you have the car burglar alarm system I will describe next, there will be little need to add locking lug nuts.

The Ultimate Protection!

A customized car burglar alarm system has to be professionally installed. **This is the only effective solution.** It provides you with the ultimate protection from theft. Your peace of mind will be directly related to the quality of the installation. Do-it-yourself kits slow a thief about as long as it took you to read this sentence! Don't waste your time or money.

Faster Than A Speeding Bullet

Car thieves are experienced, quick and highly skilled. First, the car is quickly tested to detect the presence of an alarm system. If no alarm sounds, a window or door is attacked by force. Almost any object in the car can be taken within **10 seconds**. The entire car can be driven away within **30 seconds**. If protection is what you want, you'll need the help of an expert!

A word of caution. Never make the mistake of confronting the would-be thief face-to-face. That's a job for police!

Let Me Describe A Good Alarm System

- It will be made up of a series of different alarm devices designed and installed to back each other up in case one fails to do the job. These descriptions will include most of the possibilities.

- It will be an instantaneous alarm as opposed to a time delay one.

- Triggers if the automobile is jacked up or attempt is made to tow away. System is not effected by gusts of wind or side-to-side movements of the car.

- The motion detector must have a sensitivity adjustment.

- The locking device for that phase of the system should be armor-plated and tamper-resistant with built-in tamper alert switches. The best ones are designed to blend with the car's side marker.

- Plunger switches are installed on each door, the hood and trunk. These are set by the locking device. None are connected to the car's entry or dome light system!

- The entire system should have a timer limiting the length of time it will remain on after being activated. The alarm is automatically reset.

- It should be equipped with a mechanical siren. This is preferred over the plastic type for durability plus the ability to resist sound deadening efforts.

- When the siren sounds, all parking lights also flash.

- A panic switch allows operator to activate siren and flashing lights from inside the vehicle. This is an extra safety feature, especially for women.

- The system is coupled with ignition cut-off—car can't be started when alarm is set.

- For an additional cost, a handheld transmitter (no lock on car's exterior) can set the system. A pocket beeper can also warn you of an attempted theft. Range is about one mile. This electronic radio receiver is coupled with a transmitter in the car.

- Glass breakage sensors are available. This is an electronic microphone inside the automobile.

- A finished wiring job by a professional is almost indistinguishable from the car's original wiring.

If You Need It, Here's Where To Get It

By now the picture is clear. You need back up devices to make the system effective. Everything should be installed by an expert!

Call or write Chuck Luttenbacher. If you do not reside in his area, he can refer you to an expert anywhere in the United States.

VIKING AUTO ALARMS
Chuck Luttenbacher, President
1601 West MacArthur, Suite 28R
Santa Ana, CA 92704
PH: 714 641-1711

You'll make the right choice!

CHAPTER II

The Case Of The Shrinking Greenbacks

**Stretch
The Buying Power
Of Your Automobile Dollars**

Stretch Your Gas Dollars

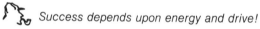
Success depends upon energy and drive!

Americans Became Fuel Conscious

When the price of fuel reached a dollar per gallon, we finally became aware of a fact Europeans have known for years. Gasoline is expensive! With over 125 million of the more than 300 million cars in use in the world, the United States really became dependent on gasoline supplies. If you think gasoline is expensive, try comparing the price of a gallon of gas with a gallon of plain soda water. The fuel is the bargain. Our problem is we use so much of it!

Driving Habits

Regardless of politics, statistics or comparisons, your real concern is, "What can I do to keep my own gas bill as low as possible?" A mystery? It really is no mystery—**our driving habits either in-**

crease or decrease our fuel consumption. To follow the tips listed below, you may have to change your driving habits somewhat. You hold the cards. How they are played will determine the results. As the song says, "You gotta know when to hold 'em and know when to fold 'em . . ."

Heavy City Traffic Vs Less-Crowded Areas

To gain perspective it is necessary to see the difference between driving in heavy city traffic and driving in less crowded areas. There is a big difference! Pressure is put on you by other motorists in heavy city traffic. This means you will have to double your efforts to change your driving habits before you can save gas. You can do it! Worthwhile? Is saving money important?

Stretch Those Precious Gas Dollars

Use the following tips. They will actually put money in your pocket regardless of the size car you drive.

> **Eliminate fast getaways**
> **Accelerate smoothly**
> **Anticipate traffic lights**
> **Limit accessories**
> **Minimize lower gears**
> **Drive at steady speeds**
> **Don't idle the engine**
> **Keep the speed down**
> **Avoid downshifts to increase speed**

- Fast getaways, racing the engine, jumpy starts or pumping the accelerator when the car isn't moving can burn 50 percent more gasoline.

- Accelerate smoothly and gently.

- Minimize traffic lights. When approaching intersections, take your foot off the gas and let the vehicle coast up to the traffic signal. Save fuel by using the brake rather than the accelerator to hold your car in place on a hill.

- Limit the use of energy-consuming accessories such as air conditioners, stereo systems and lighting fixtures. The alternator is required to work harder placing a greater strain on the engine.

- Get into high gear by not pausing long as you shift through each of the lower gears (manual shift automobiles). With an automatic take your foot off the accelerator to make it shift earlier.

● Drive at steady speeds. Even varying your speed as little as 5 mph can cut gasoline mileage.

● Don't idle the engine for more than a minute when stopping your car. It uses less gasoline to restart the car than it does to idle it.

● Automobiles get about 21 percent better fuel economy driven at 55 mph than at 70 mph. Most cars get their best mileage around 35 mph.

● When downshifting avoid blipping the throttle. Downshifts made in order to increase vehicle speed are fuel burners.

Do You Want Your Car To Run Economically?

Sure you do! All people expect in life is a fair advantage. You gain this advantage with your automobile by knowledge about its performance. Performance is directly related to care the car is given. Everyone wants good gas mileage. If your car was designed to produce 20 miles per gallon, tuning it properly will not give you 40 miles per gallon. But it may give you an honest 20 instead of 13! In addition to better gas mileage, the car will be more enjoyable and dependable. If you don't want to spend the money to have your car tuned, you can count on spending it on the price of gas.

When Your Car Works Harder Than It Should

Anything making the engine of your car work harder than it should will reduce gasoline mileage. Some of these causes of poor gas mileage are simple to correct and can be taken care of easily at home or any service station. Others require help on a more professional level. Well-tuned automobiles can be expected to get about 25 percent better gas mileage than those in poor shape.

Common Factors Determining Gasoline Mileage

This is a good list. I'm not going to attach a meaningless percentage of improvement to each item. Like the shoe, if it fits wear it. By the way did you notice—the shoes you hate last the longest.

These Items Increase Fuel Consumption

Dirty air cleaner
Worn out piston rings
Idle adjustment

Incorrect thermostats
Partially blocked exhaust system
Dirty oil

Gasoline leaks	**Hills**
Too much gasoline	**Traffic congestion**
Worn out tires	**Rolling the windows down**
Weather and wind	**Air dams**

- A dirty air cleaner will reduce air intake and increase the fuel mixture.

- Worn out piston rings and bad valve seals reduce engine power making the engine work harder.

- Having the idle adjustment set too high wastes fuel.

- An incorrect thermostat or one which is malfunctioning will open too soon allowing the engine to warm-up more slowly than normal. This results in the choke operating longer and wasting fuel.

- Plugged exhaust systems, even those partially blocked, will waste fuel.

- At the same time you have your car tuned-up have the oil changed. Use a multigrade oil such as 10 W-40 W or one of the new synthetic oils instead of a straight 30 or 40 weight oil. These types will flow more freely and cut drag while the engine is warming up.

- Gasoline leaks are expensive. If you smell gas vapors, have your car checked by a repair shop. This is more than just a fire hazard. A fuel tank losing one drop per second loses 3.9 gallons a day at a cost of over $150 per month.

- When filling your tank don't top it off. Fuel, when warm, can expand and spill out the gas cap.

- When buying new tires, steelbelted radials produce the best gas mileage.

- Weather and wind are factors effecting fuel consumption. Summer temperatures are better for fuel economy than winter. Rain or snow will cause a loss in fuel economy. A headwind can cause a loss; while a tailwind produces a gain in fuel economy. Consider buying a car more aerodynamically sound than the one you presently own. Wind resistance becomes a big factor, especially as your speed increases.

- Fuel saved going down a hill will not equal the fuel used to go up it.

- Stay away from areas of heavy traffic congestion to save

fuel. Poorly regulated traffic signals are one of America's biggest wasters (20%) of fuel.

- Using your air conditioner will save fuel compared to rolling the windows down during highway driving.

- Aftermarket air dams, unless tested and proven, will more likely increase air drag resulting in greater fuel consumption.

These Items Decrease Fuel Consumption

Wheel bearing packing
Front end alignment
Brake adjustments
Automatic cruise control
Pointless distributor
Larger tires

Exhaust headers
Higher axle ratio
Manual transmission
Proper Brake Usage
Early morning driving

- Cars roll easier when the front and rear wheel bearings are greased on a regular maintenance schedule.

- At the time of your tire replacement, have a front end alignment. This will decrease the rolling resistance of your car increasing gasoline mileage.

- Keep drum brakes adjusted properly if your car is equipped with them. Drum brake shoes can rub against the brake drums causing an increase in rolling resistance. Disc brakes are self-adjusting.

- Automatic cruise control is fantastic for maintaining steady long distance driving speeds.

- On older vehicles equipped with point-type distributors you could replace these with aftermarket pointless units.

- By using larger tires you can reduce the number of revolutions per mile.

- Aftermarket exhaust headers and some intake manifolds can improve exhaust back pressure.

- Install a higher axle ratio to reduce engine rpm's.

- Manual transmissions, used properly, are more fuel efficient than automatics

- Carefully plan where and when to use your brakes. Rushing up to a stop signal only to sit and wait uses additional fuel.

- Start driving your car in the mornings as soon as the engine will stay running. Be sure to keep the rpm's down and use part throttle (go slowly) for the first couple of miles. This will not appreciably increase wear on the motor.

Note: If all else fails, sell that bomb. Buy a horse and buggy and a ten-year supply of hay!

Only through past experience can you see clearly.

He Wasted His Time

Living in California with its smog laws, I'm always hearing about someone who has disconnected the smog devices on their car to **save gas. They not only wasted time,** but more than likely increased fuel consumption. Experts agree emission control systems hurt fuel consumption. However, these systems are so well-integrated into overall engine designs, disposing of them is almost impossible—and illegal. Here you have a choice between two evils. Do nothing. Leave the system alone!

If Your Engine Knocks Or Pings

Let's exclude those cars that use only unleaded gas for a moment. Even today over 50 percent of all gasoline sold is premium, yet only 10 percent of the automobiles on the road need it. **You will not get more power from highter octane.** Here is a simple test to see which gasoline you should use.

Step One

Have your car tuned by a competent mechanic. Make sure its in good mechanical condition.

Step Two

Wait until the gas tank is low; then fill up with the brand you usually buy, specifying the grade premium or regular as recommended by your owner's manual.

Drive a few miles until the engine is warmed up—come to a complete stop—then accelerate hard. If the engine knocks or pings on the gasoline with the recommended rating, use up the tank and refill with the next higher grade.

Step Three

Repeat the acceleration test. If the engine does not knock, this is the octane your car needs. Should it still knock on this higher octane, you have mechanical trouble.

Step Four

Naturally, you can reverse the test going from a higher to lower octane rating. If the engine does not knock, you can probably use this lower grade.

Diesel Power Vs Gasoline Power

Let's dispel one myth. Today, diesel fuel costs almost the same per gallon as gasoline. True, automobiles with diesel engines cost less to maintain. This is offset by the higher purchase price of the diesel car itself. You can justify this extra cost only if you plan to keep the car over three years. If you are a person who changes vehicles frequently, a diesel won't save you money!

For A List Of Diesel Stations Write

Diesel fuel is not as hard to find as many think. For a list of diesel stations across the country write:

UNION OIL COMPANY OF CALIFORNIA
1650 East Golf Road
Schaumburg, IL 60196
(No charge)

MERCEDES BENZ OF NORTH AMERICA
1 Mercedes Drive
Montvale, NJ 07645
(Send $2)

Manufacturers Using Lightweight Materials

Automobile manufacturers are responding to the need for cars capable of better gas mileage by changing the two major factors within their control:

1. **Reducing the size of the engine.** The size of the engine is probably the largest single factor concerning gas mileage.

2. **Decreasing the weight of the standard automobile.** Within limits, of course, fuel consumption will increase or decrease by 1-2 percent per 100 pounds of vehicle weight. More and more manufacturers will use lightweight materials such as aluminum, fiberglass and plastics in order to reduce weight and thereby increase gas mileage.

How To Check Gas Mileage

Fill the gas tank until exactly full. At the same time record the mileage reading on your odometer. Drive until the gas tank is almost empty. Refill tank. Write down the gas pump reading in gallons and your new odometer reading in miles. Subtract the original odometer reading from the new one to obtain the miles traveled between gasoline fill-ups. Divide the miles traveled by gallons required to refill gas tank. The answer is miles traveled on each gallon of gas—the gasoline mileage.

Note: To change liters on the gasoline pump into gallons divide the number of liters by 3.7854 (in round figures by 4).

The Easiest Way To Make Money

Now you have a plan to stretch your gas dollars. It's surprising just how much you can do. Most of these methods are similar to preparing a Soap Box Derby entry—you definitely must keep the rolling resistance of the car to a minimum. In addition, keep your car in good mechanical condition. **By far, the most important factors in stretching gas center around your own driving habits.**

Save Money On Gasoline

There are those who drive and never look back. Something might be gaining on them. There are also drivers who rush to the next stop light only to wait minutes for it to change. A minute wait can be a long one. It depends on which side of the bathroom door you're on. Use these tips. They'll save money on your automobile expenses.

Note: If you feel a service station has made an unjustified fuel-related price increase, this can be reported by phoning the toll free hotline number: 1 800 424-9246

Sometimes the easiest way to make money is to stop losing it!

Negotiate With Lenders
For The Best Auto Loan

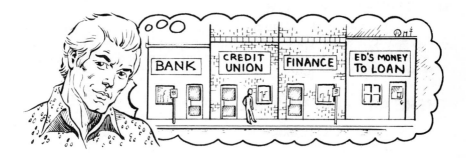

Options, my dear friend, are your keys to success.

You Do Have Choices

Money is what loans are all about. Loaning money has always been surrounded by mystery. If you are satisfied with the first loan offered, don't care about the interest rate, or don't believe there is a better loan available, join 75 percent of the borrowers today. Lenders are aware of this. Fortunately you do have choices. The first good one is to put yourself into the 25 percent group of borrowers who do care.

The Metz Plan

In history almost everything from tobacco and salt to the mulberry paper of Kubla Khan has been used for money. The United States established the dollar as our money unit in 1785 and soon minted the first coins (from George Washington's silverware). An interesting variation of the automobile loan was the Metz Plan of the early 1900's. C.H. Metz sold his 12hp, 2-cylinder roadster in fourteen separate packages. You bought these packages as you could pay for them, took the packages home and assembled the car.

A Game Plan To Bag The Best Loan

Automobile loans are big business. It takes a debtor and a creditor to make a loan. Simply put, debtors owe money. Creditors think they are going to get it! These two truths provide clues for securing the finest loan available.

It's impossible to find the best until you look for it! Investigate. Shop around. Sounds easy. Sure, but what do I look for? What should I do after I've found it?

This outline answers those questions and more. It tells how you discover (from among the many) that one lender who is currently making the best auto loans. After you find this lender, I'll explain how to negotiate the loan!

THERE ARE FIVE MAJOR LENDERS

Commercial banks
Credit Unions
Automobile dealers
Finance companies
Savings and loans (no auto loans)

A. COMMERCIAL BANKS (MAKE AUTO LOANS)

1. Lend money to make profits.
   a. They are chartered either nationally or by the state itself.
   b. Provide all forms of banking services.
2. Specialize in consumer loans (autos).
   a. Make over 60% of all auto loans.
   b. Compete for business with convenient locations (14,000 banks with another 28,000 branches).
3. How banks are organized.

> DIRECTORS
> (Chairman of the board)
> OFFICERS
> (Pres., v. pres., treasurers, cashiers)
> PERSONNEL
> (Tellers, processors, routine)

4. Banks often buy the loans auto dealers make.
5. Many banks have a *preferred interest rate* available to retain customers who could finance with a credit union.

B. CREDIT UNIONS (MAKE AUTO LOANS)

1. Do not loan to make a profit.

    a. There are over 22,000 credit unions in the United States.

    b. Credit union members can receive dividends.

    c. Credit unions want to offer more services to customers.

2. Usually make only consumer loans (autos).

3. Generally have some of the best loan rates.

4. To be a borrower you usually have to become a depositor.

5. Credit unions compete for loans on a more personal basis.

    a. Individual relationships promoted.

    b. Members are able to obtain loans more easily and at good terms.

    c. Consider saving your loan availability for ready cash on your signature—even though some other auto loan rate is higher.

C. AUTOMOBILE DEALERS   (MAKE AUTO LOANS)

1. Dealers often sell their auto loans to banks.

    a. Interest rates charged borrowers may be higher.

    b. For some borrowers it is easier to get an auto loan through a dealer than a bank.

2. Most auto dealers have several different loans available.

    a. Each loan has terms and rates to fit certain buyers.

    b. Some large automobile manufacturers have nationwide companies that make consumer loans on their cars (called captive companies).

    c. These loans are available to customers through participating dealers.

3. Dealers also act as a go-between car buyer (borrower) and the bank (lender).

4. There are two very different forms of dealer auto loans.

    a. The United States is divided into two regions.

    b. These loans are made in a different way within each of these regions.

East And Midwest

(No recourse loans)

- Bank makes loan to the car buyer. The dealer acts as a middleman.

- While the loan is secured by the car, this is only used as a reason to make the loan.

- The dealer is not responsible for the credit worthiness of the customer (car buyer).

- Withholding payment to resolve a problem with the dealer will not work in this case.
- Bank may repossess car in case of loan default.

West And South
(Recourse loans)

- Bank lets the dealer make the loan, then buys this loan from the dealer.
- In case of default, banks reserve the right to ask a dealer to take back the car and repay the money.
- This loan is secured by the car. But as far as the bank is concerned, a dealer must stand behind the loan.
- In default a car may be repossessed by the dealer.

Note: These regions overlap a great deal. When financing an auto through a dealer, ask which method (non recourse or recourse) is being used. It could be important to you.

D. FINANCE COMPANIES   (MAKE AUTO LOANS)
1. Charge maximum interest the law allows.
2. Finance companies often borrow funds from banks.
3. Compete by making the customer feel at ease.
   a. The questions on the loan form are easier to answer.
   b. It's easier to qualify for the loan.
   c. Tangible items such as furniture can be used as collateral.
   d. However, in the case of automobile loans, finance companies are prohibited from securing the sales contract balance with any property other than the car in most states. For many reasons, violations of this can be very unfair to the consumer.
   e. Provides a source of loan money to those without established credit histories.
4. Usually do not make new car loans.

E. SAVINGS AND LOANS   (DO NOT MAKE AUTO LOANS)
1. Includes thrift institutions, savings and loan associations and mutual savings banks.
2. We have over 6,000 of them in the United States.
3. Their range of services is expanding rapidly. Generally they deal in mortgage loans.

A 30-Year Education In Auto Loans in 5 Minutes

Can you afford it
Join a credit union
Shop for your loan
Talk with bank officers
Advertising methods
Prepayment penalties
The right of offset
Property pledged as security
Lenders don't want cars back
Hold car price to 60% of annual income
Lenders want to make car loans
Quoted loan rates
Long repayment schedules
Understand the APR
Credit Life Insurance
Look For Your Own Loan
Discrimination
Used car loans
Book value
Shop for your own car insurance
Go slow on refinancing
Loans from relatives
When you can't solve a problem

(Random order)

- It may not seem necessary to say this, but I'm going to anyway. Don't take the loan, even if offered, unless you can afford it!

  The only sure way to reduce bills is to pay them or put them on microfilm.

- Become a member of a credit union if possible.

  Losers let money manage them. Winners manage money.

- Lenders count on borrowers not shopping to save money.

- Always direct your questions to an officer of the bank or lending institution.

- The advertising of some savings institutions infers more frequent compounding leads to more interest for you. This may be misleading. It really depends on how long you leave your money in the bank and that bank's crediting rules.

Unless you put your money to work for you—you work for your money.

- Ask exactly what the prepayment penalties are on the loan. Penalties can triple the apparent interest rate. Sometimes the prepayment penalty can be eliminated if you ask.

- Ask the officer if funds can be withdrawn from any other accounts you may have to cover a payment.

- Property pledged as security can be repossessed without notice. An auto taken back by a lender or dealer does not always completely wipe out your debt.

- If you find you can't make your loan payments, contact the lender right away. Most lenders will work with you to solve the problem.

  If you think nobody cares if you're alive, try missing a couple of car payments.

- As a general rule keep the total price of any car you buy to less than 60 percent of your annual income.

  Anything left over today will be needed tomorrow to pay an unexpected bill.

- Most dealers and lenders have more than one loan package they can offer you.

- In spite of your feelings as you read over the loan application, lenders do want to make loans.

  Never get angry. Never threathen. Reason with people.

- Loan rate and terms quoted from two different officers within the same bank can vary.

- Loan rates and terms quoted from two different branches of the same bank can vary.

- Go slow on taking a longer loan repayment period.

  The slight reduction in monthly payments isn't worth the higher interest rate and the extra months or years you have to make those payments.

- Make sure all fees are included in the calculation of the Annual Percentage Rate (APR).

- Avoid the purchase of Credit Life Insurance if possible. Covering your life with enough insurance is important, but Credit Life Insurance isn't any bargain for a young borrower in good health. They help subsidize everyone else.

- You can count on a clause in the loan agreement where you agree to cover the automobile with a collision and comprehensive auto insurance policy.

- Negotiate with lenders for your best loan.

  When you let someone else take care of anything for you, you'll pay extra for that service.

- If you are sure you are being discriminated against, tell the loan officer. If not resolved, send a letter to the lender and a copy to your state consumer department.

- Don't expect to receive the same interest rate and terms for a used car as the lender may offer on a new one.

  Your largest savings with a used car comes in the purchase price (it can and should be substantial) not in the financing costs.

- Loan amounts and sometimes even terms are very dependent on the make, model and year of car purchased.

  Ask the loan officer to show you the book comparing past history. They use these price comparisons in figuring all used car loans.

- Lenders have the right to require you to insure the car (at least to their minimum requirements), but you may purchase this insurance anywhere.

- Be very cautious with any finance company before you agree to extend a loan period or take on a new loan to replace an old one. These changes can really put debt pressure on you.

  If you're already in a hole, there's no use to keep digging.

- If a relative or friend is going to finance a car, the person who lends should be sure their name appears on the certificate of title as the legal owner of the car. Legal owners must make sure the car is insured at all times! They can be held liable.

- In case you have a lending problem you can't resolve, contact your local or state consumer affairs office, the state attorney general's office or the state banking department.

- If you are trying to establish your personal credit rating, using the established credit of someone else (co-signing, etc.) will not help you much.

Establishing credit is essential to a young person. By using a co-signer, even though you make all the payments, a future lender will not recognize that loan as having established a personal credit worthiness. It may benefit you in the long run to pay more for a loan in your name only. Then when the loan is successfully paid, you have a good credit history to refer to in the future.

You Too Can Have Loan Appeal

You say you don't really need it? The door is open.

Fly With The Eagles

Were you born liberated? Ever say to yourself, "If I have to, I can do anything?" You know you can and here's a good place to start. There's no substitute for taking the time to compare (shop) one lender with another. It's like minting your own money. When looking for the best loan, if you want to fly with eagles, don't mix with parakeets. Nobody else can do it quite like you, no one can do it better and nobody can do it for you. If is impossible to win by a nose if you never stick your neck out.

Atlas! A Successful Plan

When working toward the solution to any problem, it always helps to know the answer. Now the answer to finding the best auto loan is simple. **Go shopping for your loan with an honest, organized plan!** I want to stress honesty. Honesty really is the best policy—there's less competition.

Biggest Fish Are Caught By Baiting The Hook

Loan shopping without a plan and fishing without bait are about the same thing. Give yourself a chance. You catch some, you lose some, but you gotta bait up for 'em all. By now are you saying to yourself, even with a nightcap on, the wolf looked nothing like Grandmother. You say you've never tried anything like this. So what! There's only one good thing about living in the past—it was cheaper. Let's get going. Here's how to do it!

A. ORGANIZE BEFORE YOU START TO SHOP

1. Use this outline as your guide. Compose the best possible presentation of yourself.

   a. Visualize how you want to appear as an applicant.

   b. Take a copy of this summary with you.

   Include:
   - All your addresses and phone numbers within the last three years.
   - Age and birthdate.
   - Social security number.
   - Marital status. If you are married, include the same information found in this outline for spouse. Lenders in most states ask few questions about marital status today.
   - Recent job history. How long you have been employed and name, address and phone of employer.
   - Previous and most recent job history.
   - Monthly earnings and monthly expenses.
   - Whether you own or rent.
   - Monthly mortgage or rent payment. If there is a mortgage, the name of the lender.
   - The name and age of each of your dependents.
   - The total amount of any other loan you may have other than a mortgage loan. Be prepared to show loan balances.

135

- The name and address of your bank and the types of accounts you have.

- The name and address of your nearest relative.

- Three to five names, addresses and phone numbers of places where you have credit or references.

- The amount of life insurance you carry and the name of the company.

B. LEARN WHAT LENDERS ARE LOOKING FOR

1. Automobile loans are among the easier ones any lender can possibly make.
   a. The car itself becomes additional security for the lender.
   b. Lender has fewer decisions to make on a new car. The full retail price can be used as a basis for the loan. Your downpayment will also be based on this figure. New car loans are easier to make than used car loans.
   c. To make a loan on a used car the lender has to evaluate more items (age, make, model, past history of value at the end of the loan, present conditon of auto, mileage on the car now and the miles you expect to drive).
   d. All of these factors will effect the interest rate and terms of your loan.
   e. In general, as in all loans, the lender is evaluating the degree of difficulty in getting the loan money back if there is a problem in the future.

2. Most banks and all credit unions are more interested in making loans to borrowers who are also depositors.
   a. Establishing your relationship before the time you need a loan can help.
   b. Agree to become a customer if you're not one already.
   c. A savings account is established when you join any credit union.
   d. Loan officers don't select good risks, they just eliminate the poor ones. If they don't find anything negative, you're probably going to be approved.

3. The best credit risks are usually over 30 years of age.
   a. You can't change age but you can always play up your strong points.
   b. Regardless of your age, show confidence in yourself and your financial position. Dress neatly. Appearances do make a difference.

4. Being married indicates a willingness to assume respon
   sibility. Don't volunteer extra information about your per
   sonal life.
5. One full year with your present employer helps.
   a. Numbers (5) and (6) indicate strong reasons for staying
      put and becoming established. However, there are many
      valid reasons for moving or changing to better yourself.
   b. If you have changed jobs and the reason was a good one,
      say so!
6. Stability at your place of residence shows you are established in the community.
7. Your credit record, especially the past two or three years, is
   very important.
   a. Be ready to answer questions accurately. Take your
      outline and answers with you. This will show you have
      already carefully considered the loan—a good sign in
      any business transaction.
   b. Never be on the defensive.
8. Loan officers are trained to ask themselves certain
   key questions.
   a. The most important one is, "Could I meet the payments
      of this loan if I made the same salary and had the
      monthly expenses the applicant does?"
   b. If your monthly debt payment (exclusive of house
      payments) exceeds more than 20% of your monthly in-
      come, you may have a problem.
9. Expect questions asking whether there is a secondary
   source of repayment if your monthly income is interrupted.
   a. A borrower can be required to purchase insurance
      guaranteeing repayment of the loan in case of death or
      medical disability.
   b. However, lenders can't dictate where such insurance is
      finally purchased.
   c. The insurance you presently have may cover this.

Throughout a lender's evaluation of your application, it's easy to
see a direct relationship between their questions, your answers and
getting the loan you want!

Summary

In searching for the best loan available, you really are your own
master. Now you have the facts and a plan enabling you to find and
qualify for it. Take your notes and answers with you. To a loan officer, what you appear to be, you are. There's no substitute for effi-

ciency! Maybe you're weak in some qualifying areas. Set goals to correct these before you buy.

What You Appear To Be, You Are!

When it comes to credit, most of us are far stronger than we realize. Get out and talk with lenders. They want to make loans. Your need for an automobile loan is something they'll easily understand. Organize and prepare yourself in advance with honest answers. Be willing to shop around. Present the facts clearly. The result for you will be the best loan available.

Now that's just what we set out to accomplish isn't it!

Terms Associated With Loans

Acceleration clause
Clause in a loan agreement stating all payments may become due at once if payments are not made on time.

Adhesion limitation
Clause in a loan agreement by which you agree to limit how far you drive. Courts have usually ignored these restrictions.

Annual Percentage Rate (APR)
The interest paid divided by the average amount of money the borrower has for use during a year.

Collateral
Any property pledged as security for a loan.

Community property states
Certain states where the earnings and property belong to both the husband and wife, not just to the spouse who produced those earnings. Hence the word ''community'' is used.

Co-sign
A second person signing on a loan as additional security for repayment. Don't be surprised if the lender asks for this in the case of a very young borrower.

Credit bureau
An agency collecting consumer credit information and then distributes this information to lenders. You have the right to know all the information in your file. Look under ''Credit Reporting Agencies'' in the Yellow Pages.

Creditor
A lender or one who permits extended payments.

Effective interest rate
The annual percentage rate with all fees and costs added in.

Equal Credit Opportunity Act
It shall be unlawful for any creditor to discriminate against any applicant on the basis of sex or marital status. An inquiry of marital status shall not constitute discrimination for the purpose of ascertaining the creditor's rights.

Fair Debt Collection Practices Act
Prohibits abusive, deceptive and unfair debt collection practices by debt collectors.

Loan fee (points)
Not usually asked for by lenders making automobile loans. An additional fee paid to the lender in advance for the lender agreeing to make a loan. One point equals one percent of the amount borrowed and increases the lender's true yield one-eighth percent in total.

Loan tie-ins
A lender who requires borrowers to open checking or savings accounts before agreeing to make a loan.

Magnuson-Moss Warranty Act
Provides minimum disclosure standards for written consumer product warranties. Improves consumer protection.

Mickey
A loan used to make the downpayment on an automobile. Not considered to be a sound business policy.

Paper down
A dealer faking the downpayment.

Preferred interest rate
Rate available to certain customers. Usually those who otherwise could go elsewhere for the loan.

Prepayment penalty
A charge by a lender for paying the loan in full ahead of final due date.

Recourse
In auto loans the right of the lender to collect for the loan.

Right of offset
Lender who can withdraw from a borrower's checking or savings account any amount due on a loan without recourse.

Truth In Lending Act
Protects consumers against inadequate and misleading leasing (loan) information. Assures meaningful disclosure of terms and limits liability.

Wage assignment
A loan agreement used by credit unions whereby the lender is able to directly secure the loan payment from the borrower's wages in case of late payment or non payment. Sometimes used when loan is not secured by deposits.

Modern Car
Parts, Products And Services

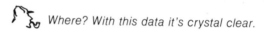

Where? With this data it's crystal clear.

You Know Where To Find It When You Need It!

Way back in 1899, the first auto parts supply house was opened in St. Louis, Missouri, by A.L. Dyke. Considering the number of cars on the road then, it's hard to imagine to whom he sold any parts. Persistence is important. If you keep your socks clean and run around with the right people—things fall into place. And so they did in the case of auto parts stores.

Looking For The Unusual

Today there are parts suppliers in almost every town in the United States. However, you may have a question about a certain part, service or book. Maybe you're just looking for an unusual one. Then it becomes important to know where to write or who to call for the information.

Accessories, International
Vilem B. Haan, Inc
11401 W Pico Blvd
Los Angeles, CA 90064
PH: 213 272-4455

Accessories
Pep Boys
1122-24 W Washington Blvd
Los Angeles, CA 90015
PH: 213 748-5571

Additives
Bardahl MFG Corporation
1400 N W 52nd Street
Seattle, WA 98107
PH: 206 783-4851

Additives
Pyroil Company
Albion, IL 62806
PH: 618 445-2395

Additives
Marvel Oil Company Inc
331 No Main
Port Chester, NY 10573
PH: 914 937-4000

Additives
Wynn's Friction Proofing Inc
2600 E Nutwood Av
Fullerton, CA 92631
PH: 714 992-2000

Additives
STP Corporation
1400 W Commercial Blvd
Fort Lauderdale, FL 33310
PH: 305 771-1010

Additives
Ethyl Corporation
330 So Folurth Street
Richmond, VA 23219
PH: 804 644-6081

Air Conditioner Parts
Murray Corporation
Schilling Circle
Cockeysville, MD 21030
PH: 301 666-0380

Alternators, Starters, Generators
American Gen. & Armature Co
6100 W Grand
Chicago, IL 60639
PH: 312 622-9292

Armor & Safety Devices
Global Coach & Armor Mfg
3527 Forsythe Rd
Orlando, FL 35808
PH: 305 671-0384

Batteries
Prestolite Battery Division

511 Hamilton Street
Toledo, OH 43694
PH: 419 244-2811

Batteries
Globe-Union Inc
5757 N Green Bay Av
Milwaukee, WI 53201
PH: 414 228-1200

Belts (V)
Dayco Corporation
333 W 1st Street
Dayton, OH 45402
PH: 513 226-7000

Bearings
Federal-Mogul Corp
26555 Northwestern Hwy
Southfield, MI 48076
PH: 313 354-7700

Bolt-On Accessories
A & E Systems
1101 S Linwood
Santa Ana, CA 92705
PH: 714 558-0811

Books (Racing Preparation)
Steve Smith Autosports
P.O. Box 11631
Santa Ana, CA 92711
PH: 714 639-7681

Books (Tune-Up)
Clymer Publications
222 North Virgil Avenue
Los Angeles, CA 90004

Books (Everything Automotive)
Classic Motorbooks
P.O. Box 1
Oscelola, WI 54020
PH: 715 294-3345
Orders PH: 1 800 826-6600

Books (Hobbyist)
Hemmings Bookshelf
Box 76
Bennington, VT 05201

Books (Special Interest)
Bookman Dan
P.O. Box 13492
Baltimore, MD 21203

Brake Linings
Raybestos
100 Oakview Drive
Trumbull, CO 06611
PH: 203 371-0101

Brake Parts
Gibson Products
4953 E 154th
Cleveland, OH 44128
PH: 216 581-0633

Burglar Alarms
A.R.A. Mfg Company
P.O. Box 870
Grand Prairie, TX 75050
PH: 214 647-4111

Carburetors & Parts
Holley Carburetor Division
11955 E Nine Mile Rd
Warren, MI 48090
PH: 313 536-1900

Carburetors, Rochester
Rochester Products Division
P.O. Box 1790
Rochester, NY 14603
PH: 716 254-5050

Carpets & Seat Covers
Newark Auto Products
177 Main Street
West Orange, NJ 07052
PH: 201 731-7200

Clocks, Digital
Airguide Instrument Company
2210 Wabansia Avenue
Chicago, IL 60647
PH: 312 486-3000

Corvette, Fiberglass Parts
Eckler's Corvette Parts
Box 5637
Titusville, FL 32780
PH: 305 269-9680

Electrical Products
Bosch, Robert, Corporation
2800 S 25th Avenue
Broadview, IL 60153
PH: 312 865-5200

Engine Components
Eaton Corporation
436 No 29th Street
Battle Creek, MI 49016
PH: 616 962-7571

Engines, Remanufactured
National Engines
Box 14169
St. Louis, MO 63178
PH: 314 533-8484

Fuel Injection Equipment
AMBAC Industries Inc
3664 Main
Springfield, MA 01107
PH: 413 781-2200

Gasoline & Kerosene
Sun Company Inc
100 Matsonford Rd
Radnor, PA 19087
PH: 215 293-6000

Gasoline & Oil
Ashland Oil, Inc
P.O. Box 391
Ashland, KY 41101
PH: 606 329-3333

Gasoline & Oil
Atlantic Richfield Co
515 So Flower Street
Los Angeles, CA 90071
PH: 213 486-3511

Gasoline & Oil
Chevron U.S.A. Inc
Perth Amboy, NJ 08861
PH: 201 738-2000

Gasoline & Oil
Cities Service Company
P.O. Box 300
Tulsa, OK 74102
PH: 918 586-2211

Gasoline & Oil
Continental Oil Co
High Ridge Park
Stamford, CT 069904
PH: 203 359-3500

Gasoline & Oil
Exxon Corporation
1251 Av of the Americas

New York, NY 10020
PH: 212 974-3000

Gasoline & Oil
Gulf Oil Corporation
Gulf Bldg
Pittsbury, PA 15230
PH: 412 391-2400

Gasoline & Oil
Mobil Oil Corporation
150 E 42nd Street
New York, NY 10017
PH: 212 883-4242

Gas & Oil
Pennzoil Company
Pennzoil Place
700 Milam
Houston, TX 77002
PH: 713 236-7878

Gasoline & Oil
Phillips Petroleum Co
Bartlesville, OK 74003
PH: 918 661-6600

Gasoline & Oil
Shell Oil Company
P.O. Box 2463
Houston, TX 77001
PH: 713 220-6161

Gasoline & Oil
Standard Oil Of Indiana
200 E Randolph Drive
Chicago, IL 60601
PH: 312 856-6111

Gasoline & Oil
Texaco Inc
135 E 42nd
New York, NY 10017
PH: 212 953-6000

Gasoline & Oil
Union 76
200 E Golf Rd
Palatine, IL 60067
PH: 312 529-7676

Glass, Safety
Libbey-Owens-Ford
811 Madison Avenue
Toledo, OH 43695
PH: 419 247-3731

Ignition Systems
Mallory Electric
18801 Oregon Street
Carson City, NV 89701
PH: 702 882-6600

Instruments
Stewart-Warner Corporation
1826 Diversey
Chicago, IL 60614
PH: 312 883-6000

Lacquer, Acrylic
Ditzler Automotive Finishes
Box 5090
Southfield, MI 48037

Lamps & Lighting Controls
Guide Division
2915 Pendleton Avenue
Anderson, IN 46011
PH: 317 646-4244

Lighting Devices
ESB Incorporated
5 Penn Center Plaza
Philadelphia, PA 19103
PH: 215 564-4030

Leather (Special)
Eagle Ottawa Leather Company
200 N Beechtree Street
Grand Haven, MI 49417
PH: 616 842-4000

Lubricants
Valvoline Oil Co
P.O. Box 391
Ashland, KY 41101
PH: 606 329-3333

Mufflers
Walker Mfg Co
1201 Michigan Blvd
Racine, WI 53402
PH: 414 632-8871

Nitrous Oxide Systems
Marvin Miller Systems
15611 Product Lane
Huntington Beach, CA 92649
PH: 714 898-9645

Oils
Quaker State Oil Corporation

143

Box 989
Oil city, PA 16301
PH: 814 676-0661

Oil Filters
Fram Corporation
105 Pawtucket Avenue
Providence, RI 02916
PH: 401 434-7000

Paints
Beck Chemicals, Inc
3350 W 137th Street
Cleveland, OH 44111
PH: 216 941-8355

Parts & Service
General Motors Corporation
General Motors Bldg
Detroit, MI 48202
PH: 313 556-5000

Performance Parts
TRW Inc
8001 E Pleasant Valley Rd
Cleveland, OH 44131
PH: 216 383-2121

Piston Rings
Muskegon Piston Ring Co
Muskegon, MI 49443
PH: 616 726-5226

Radios
Delco Electronics
700 E Firmin Street
Kokomo, IN 46901
PH: 317 459-2453

Regulators, Voltage
Windshield Wiper Motors
American Bosch
Electrical Division
McCreary Rd
Columbus, MS 39701
PH: 601 328-4150

Roof Racks
AMCO Mfg. Corporation
7425 Fulton Avenue
North Hollywood, CA 91605
PH: 213 875-2470

Rubber Bonding Products
Yale Rubber Mfg Co

180 N Dawson
Sandusky, MI 48471
PH: 313 648-2100

Rubber Products Custom Molded
Acushnet Co., Rubber Division
744 Belleville Avenue
Bedford, MA 02719
PH: 617 997-2811

Rustproofing Products
Ziebart International Corporation
1290 E Maple
Troy, MI 48099
PH: 313 588-4100

Sealed Beam Lights
Wagner Electric Corporation
100 Misty Lane
Parsippany, NJ 07054
PH: 201 386-9300

Service Contracts
American Warranty Corporation
9841 Airport Blvd
Los Angeles, CA 90045
PH: 213 776-4100

Shifters
Hurst Performance, Inc
50 W Street
Warminster, PA 18974
PH: 215 672-5000

Shock Absorbers
Monroe Auto Equipment Co
International Drive
Monroe, MI 48161
PH: 313 241-8000

Silicone & Sealants
Dow Corning Corporation
2200 Salzburg
Midland, MI 48640
PH: 517 496-4000

Sound Equipment
J.I.L. Corp of America
737 W Artesia
Compton, CA 90220
PH: 213 537-7310

Spark Plugs
NGK Spark Plugs U.S.A.
1652 W 240th Street

Harbor City, CA 90710
PH: 213 539-4842

Spark Plugs
Champion Spark Plug Co
P.O. Box 910
Toledo, OH 43661
PH: 419 535-2567

Speed Controls
Zero-Max
2845 Harriet Av
So Minneapolis, MN 55408
PH: 612 827-6261

Steering Wheels, Air Horns
A.I.A. Auto Import Associates
7815 N W 72nd Avenue
Medley, FL 33166
PH: 305 885-6635

Switches, Controls, Batteries
Delco-Remy
2401 Columbus
Anderson, IN 46011

T-Roofs (Corvette)
Cars And Concepts
2500 E Grand River
Brighton, MI 48116
PH: 313 227-1400

Telephone Systems
Executone, Inc
29-10 Thomson Avenue
Long Island City, NY 11101
PH: 212 392-4800

Tires
The Gates Rubber Co
999 So Broadway
Denver, CO 80217
PH: 303 744-1911

Tires
The Armstrong Rubber Co
500 Sargent Drive
New haven, CO 06507
PH: 203 562-1161

Tires
The Cooper Tire Co
Lima & Western Av
Findlay, OH 45840
PH: 419 423-1321

Tires
Dunlop Tire & Rubber
P.O. Box 1109
Buffalo, NY 14240
PH: 716 877-2200

Tires
Atlas Supply company
11 Diamond Rd
Springfield, NJ 07081
PH: 201 379-6550

Tires
Goodyear Tire & Rubber Co
Akron, OH 44316
PH: 216 794-2121

Tires
The Gates Rubber Co
999 So Broadway
Denver, CO 80217
PH: 303 744-1911

Tires
Firestone Tire & Rubber Co
1200 Firestone Pkwy
Akron, OH 44317
PH: 216 379-7000

Tires
Michelin Tire Corporation
2500 Marcus Avenue
Lake Success, NY 11040
PH: 516 488-3500

Tires
Pirelli Tire Corporation
600 Third Avenue
New York, NY 10016
PH: 212 490-1300

Tires
Uniroyal
1230 Ave. of the Americas
New York, NY 10020
PH: 212 756-5840

Tires
The Seiberling Tire & Rubber Co
Barberton, OH 44203
PH: 216 745-1111

Tires, Racing & Other
McCreary Tire & Rubber Co
1600 Washington Street
Indiana, PA 15701
PH: 412 357-6600

Tools
Snap-On Tools Corporation
Kenosha, WI 53140
PH: 414 654-8681

Transmissions, Remanufactured
B & M Automotive Products
9152 Independence Avenue
Chatsworth, CA 91311
PH: 213 882-6422

Trim, Interior & Seats
Allen Industries, Inc
143 Indusco court
Troy, MI 48084
PH: 313 588-2010

Turbochargers
Schwitzer
Engineered Components
1125 Brookside Avenue
Indianapolis, IN 46206
PH: 317 269-3100

Universal Joints
Zeller Corporation
P.O. Box 278
Ft. Wayne Rd.
Defiance, OH 43512
PH: 419 784-2244

Valve Springs, Engine Parts
Associated Spring
18 Main Street
Bristol, CT 06010
PH: 203 583-1331

Wheels, Custom
American Speed Equipment
300 Beth Page Rd
Mellville, NY 11747
PH: 516 420-9595

Wheels, Pipes & Accessories
Rocket Industries, Inc
9935 Beverly Blvd
Pico Rivera, CA 90660
PH: 213 699-0311

Winches
Superwinch, Inc
Conn. Rte. 52
Putman, CT 06260
PH: 203 928-7787

Windshield Wiper Blades
Anderson Company
1075 Grant Street
Gary, IN 46440
PH:219 885-4361

Terms Relating
To Operating Your Car

Descriptive And Basic

Automobile Success is not intended to be mechanical in the sense of an automobile repair manual. However, each driver sooner or later needs to know the meaning of words used to describe the basic operation of a car.

Engine Talk

Carden joint, cylinder block, displacement, methanol—these words and others relating to specific car and engine parts are used by service managers, mechanics and referred to in automotive articles. It's a very good list to have when you want to know exactly what someone's talking about.

Aerodynamics
The behavior of air flow as it passes around a moving car and the forces air exerts on an automobile.

Aftermarket
Products developed for sale to automobile buyers after the intial purchase of the car is made.

Air-cooled engine
An engine cooled by the direct flow of air moving over it.

Air intake
An opening at the front or side of the car designed to let in air.

Axle
A shaft on which a wheel revolves. This rod can also revolve with the wheel.

Ball joint
Part of suspension/steering system. It reduces the bearing load making steering easier.

Battery
A device for storing electrical energy. Used to start the engine.

Bearing
A support and/or guide for car parts that rotate, slide or pivot.

Belt drive
A system driven by belts placed on pulleys.

bhp. (brake horsepower)
A measure of an engine's power without auxilliaries (like a water pump) attached. The actual power an engine can deliver to the drive wheels is less than the bhp.

Blipping the throttle
Used in driving when slowing down vigorously. Pushing in the clutch at the same

time applying a short quick pressure on the accelerator, then quickly shifting into the next lowest gear, releasing the clutch. Done to match the rpm's of the engine with the speed of the gear box. Places less strain on the engine.

Body

The portion of a car enclosing the passengers.

Bonnet

Term for hood of a car.

Boot

The trunk of a car.

Brake

Term for engine power-testing equipment.

Brakes

Parts fitted to the wheels for stopping a car.

Brake fade

When brakes lose effectiveness after constant use. Usual cause is heat build-up.

Bucket seat

Seat shaped to provide better body support.

Cardan joint

A universal joint.

C-post or c-pillar

Structural pillars supporting the rear roof section of cars.

Caliper

A device holding two brake pads. It forces both pads onto the rotor when brake pedal pressure is applied.

Cam (camshaft)

An enlargement or projection attached to a rotating shaft in an engine. When the shaft rotates these projections (on the camshaft) give motion to push rods. These in turn provide motion to the valves.

Camber

Inward or outward tilting of your car wheels.

Canted engine

An engine designed to lay flatter reducing the hood line of an automobile. Also called: lay down, slanted or tilted.

Carburetor

A part designed to mix air and fuel together. It usually sits on top of the motor.

Caster

The angle steering parts of your care are set.

Catalytic converter

Anti-pollution device in exhaust system of cars. Part of the emission control system. Replaces one form of air pollution with another—this one a fine mist of sulfuric acid. Exhaust vapors have a rotten-egg odor. Requires automobiles to use unleaded gasoline. Increases fuel consumption.

Chain drive

Shaft driven by a toothed wheel and chain.

Chassis
The basic frame of your automobile.

Choke
A control attached to carburetors. By reducing air and increasing the flow of fuel, it helps start your engine.

Clutch
A device connecting the engine to the transmission. Used in changing gears. It can either connect or disconnect the engine from the transmission.

Coil
A device increasing the electrical volts to jump the gap in the sparkplugs of your engine.

Combustion
The exploding of mixture of air and fuel in the combustion chamber of a cylinder. This explosion creates pressure forcing a piston located in the cylinder down. This produces power making your engine go.

Compression
In your car's engine this is the squeezing together of the air-fuel mixture in the cylinders. When the functioning parts of the cylinder (rings, valves, sparkplugs) are new, this squeezing is more effective and your engine more efficient.

Connecting rod
Engine part (arm) connecting piston to crankshaft. Changes the up and down movement of the piston into the needed rotary movement of the crankshaft.

Cowl
The part of a car's body containing heater and air-conditioning ducts. Located between the engine compartment and driver.

Crankcase
A metal pan-shaped housing covering the bottom of the engine. Encloses the crankshaft and connecting rods. Contains oil for the engine.

Crankshaft
The main shaft of an engine. Delivers a rotary motion. Driven by connecting rods.

Cylinder
The cavity in the cylinder block in which the pistons travel and combustion takes place.

Cylinder block
The basic body of the engine. All other engine parts are attached.

Cylinder head
Contains all the valves, valve train, sparkplugs and combustion chambers. This part is removable from the engine block.

Dashboard
Term used to denote the instrument panel.

Diesel engine
Fuel in this engine is ignited by the heat of compressed air inside the combustion chambers. No sparkplugs, ignition wires or distributor required.

Differential gears
Gears conveying engine power to the driving axles.

Disc brakes
Brakes in which pads of friction material clamp onto a disc turning with the wheel. Provide a stable braking effort. Self-adjusting.

Distributor
This part directs the electrical current from the coil to the sparkplugs in the proper firing order.

Displacement
An engine measurement describing the capacity of each cylinder usually in cubic centimeters (cc) or cubic inches (ci).

Drive shaft
A shaft transmitting power from the transmission to the differential gears (rear end of the car).

Drive train
All the gears, clutches, shafts, etc., transmitting engine power to the wheels.

Drum brake shoes
Brake lining that tightens against the inside of the brake drums attached to your wheels. Produces braking action to the car.

Ethanol
Fuel made from food and fiber wastes. This is the only alternative fuel commercially available now. Probably the one likely to be available in any sizeable amount in the near future.

Flywheel
A large disc attached to the crankshaft. This disc smooths the power impulses from the cylinders.

Front end alignment
Adjustments to the front wheel suspension parts of an automobile. Reduces rolling resistance of the wheels. Camber, castor and toe-in adjustments are included.

Gasohol
Term generally accepted for a blend of 90 percent gasoline and 10 percent ethyl alcohol or ethanol.

Gasoline
Fuel for automobiles. A hydrocarbon mixture made from petroleum, coal or natural gas. A highly volatile petroleum fuel.

Heat exchanger
The best example of one is an automobile radiator. It transfers the heat of the water circulating through the engine to the outside air.

Hydraulic valve lifter
Valve lifter in an engine using hydraulic oil pressure to operate.

Hydrocarbon
A compound composed entirely of hydrogen and carbon, such as petroleum products. When these products burn, they make up principal ingredient of smog.

Hydroplaning
Loss of traction due to tires riding on top of water.
Ignition
The firing of the fuel/air mixture in your engine.
Induction
The inlet side of your engine where fuel and air is taken in.
Jet
A calibrated nozzle in a carburetor. Fuel is drawn through it and mixed with air.
Lug nuts
The nuts used to hold the wheels to the car.
Magneto
A device that generates electricity. It steps up the voltage.
Main bearing
Special lubricated metal support in your engine in which the crankshaft revolves.

Manual transmission
A gearbox needing to be shifted manually by means of a shift lever. The driver operates this lever in conjunction with the clutch to change gears.

Methane gas
Can be made from a variety of growing things—also from waste products. The product is heated and this heat produces gas. This gas is then processed to remove carbon dioxide and hydrogen sulfide. It is then compressed and dispensed into pressurized tanks.

Methanol (methyl alcohol)
A distillate fuel. Engines run well on it. Not a petroleum product. It is a colorless, volatile, watersoluble, poisonous liquid. Pure alcohol fuel can be produced synthetically from carbon monoxide and hydrogen and made from coal. Germany used this source as its primary engine fuel during the Second World War. However, this alcohol fuel is highly corrosive.

Needle and seat
Small carburetor parts controling the flow of fuel into the carburetor.
Octane
A number designated to rate the anti-knock qualities of gasoline.
Oil cooler
A small heat exchanger similar to a radiator. Cools lubricating oil of the engine.

Oil pan
The removable bottom piece of the crankcase. It functions as the reservior for the engine's lubricating oil.
Oil pump
A pump driven by the engine. Sends oil to the engine's moving parts.
Oil shale
Found mostly in Colorado, Wyoming and Utah. Can be used as engine fuel after refining.

Pinion
A smaller gear designed to mesh with a gear of larger diameter.

Pneumatic tire
Tire filled with compressed air.

Pointless distributor
A distributor using a beam of light to perform the same function as a set of points. Advantage—never needs adjustment. (Electronic ignition)

Propane
A flammable gas occurring in petroleum and natural gas. Used as a fuel.

Pushrod
A rod connecting the valve lifter or camshaft with the valve rocker arm on overhead valve engines.

Radial ply
A tire in which the fabric cords run around the tubular shape of the tire. Makes for a stiffer tread area.

Resonator
A small noise muffling device. Usually aid the main muffler. Located behind the main muffler.

Rocker arm
Converts the upward action of the pushrods to a downward push on the valve stem.

Rotor
A small rotating device located in the distributor. It transfers an electrical impulse from the coil to each ignition wire in the proper sequence.

Rpm's
Revolutions per minute. The number of times in one minute the engine crankshaft is forced to turn over. This motion is activated by movement of the pistons.

Sealed beam
A lens and bulb sealed as a single unit.

Semi-elliptic springs
Term for leaf springs.

Shims
Strips of thin metal used as spacers between parts.

Shock absorbers
Parts that absorb the energy (bump force) wheels convey to the springs.

Shrink fit
This is an interesting term that describes the tight fit obtained when the part to be inserted into a cavity is slightly larger than the cavity itself. The cavity is heated and the part is chilled. After insertion, when both have returned to normal temperature, a very tight fit has been created.

Sparkplug
A small part inserted into the top of the combustion chamber of your engine. It pro-

vides the gap across which the high-tension voltage jumps. This jump creates a spark that ignites the compressed fuel-air mixture. The resulting explosions make the engine run.

Stroke
The up and down motion of the piston.

Suspension
The combined assembly of springs, shock absorbers, torsion bars, joints, arms, etc. Cushions the shock of bumps on the road and keeps the wheels in contact with the road.

Transmission
A unit filled with gears and shafts. An engine's rpm's can be reduced or amplified as this power is being transmitted to the driving wheels.

Valve
Allows the fuel-air mixture to enter a combustion chamber and provides a means for exhaust to exit the chamber.

Valve stem
Part of the valve that is activated by the camshaft or rocker arm.

Water jacket
Chambers surrounding the cylinders and combustion chambers of your engine filled with water.

Wheel bearings
Lubricated supports for the revolving shaft of the wheel. If these function properly, the wheels turn easier.

Buy Quality Auto Insurance
At The Lease Expensive Rates

I have the answer. Now what was your question?

Save Up To 40% On Car Insurance

Way back in 1897 Gillbert Loomis became the first motorist in the United States to purchase automobile insurance. After building his one-cylinder car, Gilbert insured it for $1,000 liability coverage at a staggering premium of $7.50.

Times have changed. Today with over 125 million drivers there are real **differences in the prices companies charge for exactly the same coverage.** Many individuals have saved up to 40 percent! So can you.

One word of caution. Experience has shown you are wise to stick with your present insurance company when you have been with them a number of years and have a satisfactory relationship. If not, let's see what your alternatives are.

Companies Are Forced To Compete With Each Other

First, you'll want a basic understanding of automobile insurance. From there it's a matter of shopping and comparing prices and services. Each time you shop and compare companies are forced to compete with one another. This is the free enterprise system. Everyone benefits.

This Plan Is Uncomplicated

Our plan is easy to follow but you must put it to use to reap the benefits. Help yourself! Read through the outline. Once you get an idea of the type of insurance and service you're looking for, ask several friends for the name of an insurance agent they recommend. Good ones are recommended!

Using these names and, if necessary, by looking in the yellow pages under automobile insurance, talk with agents from at least five different companies. You can start by simply making phone calls, but most agents want to talk with you in person before giving firm price quotes.

Select the best agent whose office is close to your home. When you need your insurance agent, you need one who is accessible.

Why We Don't List Rates

There is no reason to list rates. Rates change often. Almost every town or area in every state has a different set of rates. In *Automobile Success* we want to establish a general method you can follow to obtain the best auto insurance. This is important for once you have the method it can be used regardless of the town, city or state you live in to buy quality auto insurance at the least expensive rate.

The General Procedure

This outline details the method. Use it as a guide. After you've determined the coverage you need, you're ready to talk with different insurance company representatives on a knowledgeable basis. During your comparison search, don't let the salesperson (agent) change the coverage you've decided on. This way all companies will be compared alike. Take notes as you make each call. You'll be very surprised at the variations in cost. The rates are often astoundingly different.

While talking with different agents, you will establish a feeling for the one who will give you the best service. This is the one you should do business with.

METHOD FOR OBTAINING BEST INSURANCE RATES

A. THIS IS THE WAY STATES DIFFER ON AUTO INSURANCE

1. Thirty-five states use the liability system.
   a. This insurance provides a fund for paying damages based on the degree of proven fault.
   b. While you're traveling, the coverage of most companies automatically extends and conforms from liability states to the requirements of "no fault" states.
2. Fifteen states have forms of "no fault" insurance.
   a. This insurance provides a fund for paying claims based on damages suffered, not on fault (liability).
   b. Payments come from your own insurance company.
   c. "No-fault" extends to medical benefits, income loss, funeral expenses, survivor benefits and loss of services.
   d. Under no-fault there is no change in collision or comprehensive coverages.
   e. The standards of qualification for insurance in "no-fault" states are more strict.
3. Companies are testing experimental concepts.
   a. Plans with varying deductibles are being compared.
   b. There is an interesting plan providing discounts for drivers with accident-free driving.

B. THIS IS THE WAY AUTO INSURANCE COMPANIES DIFFER

1. Who sells automobile insurance.

   Independent agents can sell policies for several different companies.

   Brokers can negotiate with all agency companies to write insurance policies. If you are not a "preferred driver," you may get the best rate through a broker.

   Exclusive agents are employed by (direct writer) auto insurance companies. They sell only that company's policies. Exclusive agents (also called captive agents) can usually give a "preferred driver" the best rates.

2. What you'll want to compare when looking.
   a. How friendly and helpful does the agent seem to be?
   b. Is the agent willing to discuss insurance with you?
   c. The price charged (rate) is very important.
   d. How fast and fair are claims processed by the company?
   e. What conditions can lead to cancellation of your policy?
   f. For what reason does the company not renew a policy?
   g. The extent and under what conditions will your rate be raised following an accident or citation?

C. HOW AUTO INSURANCE COMPANIES SET RATES

1. Each company's rates reflect its recent profit experience.
   a. Companies keep about 33% of your premium dollars to pay expenses and as profit.
   b. Insurance companies can be effected by profits or losses from their investments.
2. Every company has a method for rating drivers.

   a. Each driver is placed in one of four catagories.

   PREFERRED
   STANDARD
   SUBSTANDARD
   ASSIGNED RISK

   b. Drivers in each catagory after "preferred" are charged a higher rate for their insurance policy:
3. Answers to application question are used to rate you.
4. Citations and chargeable (your fault) accidents raise rates.

   a. *Example:* One company will give a preferred rate to a driver with no more than one ticket in the last eighteen months or two within a three-year period. This same driver can have no more than one chargeable accident in a three-year period. If the accident is chargeable, it is up to the company to decide if the driver will be given the preferred driver rate.
   b. As with all insurance company evaluations, the poorest record of anyone who normally drives your car is used for rating purposes.
   c. Auto insurance companies have access to driving records through centralized reporting agencies and the state department of motor vehicles.
   d. **Everything is not on record!** When you apply for insurance, it is not necessary to tell about an accident for which no insurance company paid any money or claim was submitted.

D. HOW APPLICATION ANSWERS AFFECT YOUR RATE

1. The neighborhood you live in.
   a. More congested areas have more cars, more accidents and more lawsuits.
   b. Because their exposure is greater, the insurance company raises premiums. They are in business to make profits—not losses.
2. Your age.
   a. Beginning drivers don't qualify for preferred rates. The risk factor for drivers under the age of 25 is high.
   b. Young drivers can usually save money by insuring through their parents' company.
   c. Drivers with good grades who have taken driver's education in school are eligible for large premium discounts (up to 50%).
   d. The age a company considers you an adult (you pay less premium) varies with different companies. This is one good reason for comparison shopping.
3. Your sex.
   a. Women usually drive fewer miles than men so they pay less premium.
   b. This mileage difference is less each year due to greater freedom women now enjoy.
4. Your marital status.
   a. Married women pay more than single because husbands drive their car.
   b. There are discounts for a married couple who have their second (or more) cars insured with the same company. The company knows each car will be driven less.
5. Your driving record.
   a. Insurance companies have access to your records.
   b. If you had a poor driving record but it has now improved, bring this to the attention of your insurance agent just before each renewal period. You may qualify for a better rate in the future
6. Your reliability.
   a. People usually don't qualify for the best rate if they have driven without liability insurance. Insurance companies consider this person as one willing to take risks.
   b. Loaning your car to a friend who has an accident with it can raise your insurance rate.
7. The make, model and age of your car.

a. High performance cars can cost up to 40 percent more to insure.

b. Cars are classified into groups according to make and model. Each group is assigned a cost-to-insure factor. The amount of accessories added to the car does not effect this premium charge.

c. Companies take a close look at the age of the driver and the type of car when establishing rates.

d. After a car reaches ten years of age, some companies have a set maximum limit they will pay out for collision damage regardless of the car's value.

e. If you own a valuable car this old, check with your insurance company about a "stated value" policy!

f. It usually isn't prudent for a single male under the age of 30 driving an older car to cover this car for collision.

8. How you use the car.

a. Whether the car is used only for pleasure driving, business or some of both effects the rate charge.

b. The distance you drive each year effects the rate. Be accurate in your estimate.

c. The distance you drive to work is very important. Be accurate in this estimate also. A few miles can make a great difference in premium.

d. This is an area for real comparison shopping, since so many companies have a different set of standards.

9. Your job.

a. People in certain jobs have more accidents in their personal cars than others. However, this is another area where shoppers can save money.

b. There are several companies today who do not consider a person's job as effecting their personal automobile insurance rate.

E. THERE ARE THREE DIFFERENT BASIC COVERAGES

Liability coverage
Physical damage coverage
Medical payments coverage

1. Your liability insurance compensates the other person.

a. It does not cover damage done to your car.

b. In most states you have two choices of coverage:

Split limit sets limits covering bodily injury to one person—another covering bodily injury to two or more persons—a third covering property damages. This plan has the most flexibility.

Single limit liability insurance covers each of the above up to the one amount of coverage you choose.

   c. There is no deductible amount on liability coverage.

   d. Do not insure for the minimum. The additional cost is small. When you need it, there are many advantages to larger coverages.

2. Physical damage insurance pays for damage to your car.

   a. There is no need to prove who was at fault.

   b. This insurance comes in two coverages:

Collision insurance pays for damage done to your car by you or another car.

Comprehensive insurance pays for damages to your car such as fire, flood, vandalism, theft etc.

   c. Both can be purchased with a deductible.

   d. This is the amount you agree to pay out-of-pocket (self insure) before the insurance is used.

   e. Keep the deductible high. This can save lots of premium dollars over time.

   f. Yes, you can carry collision without comprehensive or visa versa.

   g. Comprehensive coverage is always recommended. With most older cars, consider carefully before adding collision coverage.

   h. Don't count on the theft clause of comprehensive insurance to cover objects stolen from inside your car. It covers theft of the entire car only. A homeowners, renter's or personal property policy is needed to protect the other.

3. Medical Payments Insurance covers bodily injury.

   a. It covers you and any passengers regardless of fault.

   b. You are also covered when driving or riding in other cars or walking.

   c. You need Medical Payments Insurance to cover other passengers in your car regardless of your personal health plan.

   d. I suggest carrying more than the minimum coverage.

Auto Insurance Ideas

- Uninsured motorist insurance coverage does not pay for damage to your car. It covers you and occupants of your car for personal injuries caused by an uninsured motorist or a hit-and-run driver.

- When you buy a new car, your present insurance policy covers it automatically for 30 days, but with the same coverages (only) as the old one. If you need different coverage, call your agent right away.

- Eighty percent of the one million cars stolen each year were left unlocked.

- **Under-insured motorist** insurance protects you if you are hit by a driver who carries inadequate insurance. Usually this coverage is available only in "no-fault" states.

- Young drivers approaching an age change should call their agent. Companies don't always automatically reduce your rate.

- To determine the amount of liability coverage you need, compare its cost to the value of your assets.

- Some cars can be repaired more easily than others. There are companies offering discounts on these cars.

- Don't let your present policy expire until you're accepted by another company.

- About 50% of the companies give substantial discounts to drivers age 65 and over.

- Non-smokers and drinkers also get insurance discounts with some companies.

- Large group auto insurance plans can save you money if you qualify.

- Farmers and ranchers using cars and trucks only on the ranch are often eligible for discounts.

- Don't submit claims just over your deductible amount. This can lead to the loss of your preferred driver rating.

- Comprehensive coverage plans of some companies allow you to limit the perils you want covered. This can reduce your premium.

- No company will normally pay a claim for more than the book value of a car. If you have a restored vehicle worth more than book value, it is important to verify this with your insurance company at the time you insure. This is called "stated value" coverage.

- A tax deduction is allowed for money paid by you to repair accident damages.

- Assigned Risk, Automobile Insurance Plan, and the Auto Insurance Fund are names of insurance plans for drivers turned down elsewhere.

- If an accident does occur:
    1. Notify the police immediately.
    2. Write down names, addresses, telephone and license numbers of persons involved along with any witnesses available.
    3. Notify your insurance agent. When someone is injured, phone the agent immediately.
    4. Never admit fault and don't discuss the accident with anyone except the police or your agent.

- Five keys to keeping the best auto insurance rate:

    > Operate your car safely
    > Don't drive after drinking
    > Don't drive when you are tired
    > Don't drive after taking certain medication
    > Always drive defensively.

Knowledge Produces Intelligent Choices

Never was this truer than in buying automobile insurance. I've organized the basics of insurance coverage. Many of the frill plans have been left out. They only tend to confuse buyers. Here you have just enough information to enable you to discuss automobile insurance easily with any agent. Before you comparison shop, use this outline as a guide to establish your needs. Review the method—then go after the policy you want.

A logical purchase will soon follow!

Protect Yourself
When Repairs Are Needed

He saw clearly what was about to happen!

On Occasion They Require Tender Loving Care

When it comes to automotive repair, does it seem like you're a victimized pawn in one giant chess game? It might. After all, automotive repair is this nation's number one consumer complaint! Experts refer to it as, "The Tool Chest Thieves."

In recent years, the cost of owning and operating your motor car has risen faster than the cost of living. Consequently, today, unlike the past, more automobile owners consider their car an investment rather than a disposable item. Unfortunately, every motor carriage on occasion requires a little tender loving care. Remember Hunter's Law: "Anything made by man can and will fail!"

The Five O'Clock Surprise

One of the biggest horrors of automobile repair is receiving a bill much larger than you thought it would be. According to a Department of Transportation study, more than 50 percent of our dollars spent on repairs are wasted! Twenty-five billion dollars each year!

This figure translates into $150 per person in overcharges. Your chances of having the problem fixed correctly at the right price are about 50-50. You can do better! Here are some good ways to improve those odds.

Common Schemes Used To Defraud Customers

1. You're billed for good parts needlessly replaced.
2. "The sunshine treatment"—charged for work not performed.
3. Parts that can be repaired are simply replaced.
4. A mechanic tears down your motor car and then you're warned about a serious safety defect. In reality this deficiency does not exist.
5. Estimates are not given or signed by the customer and the bill is then ballooned—referred to as, "The five o'clock surprise."

There Are Many Honest Repair Facilities

While the automotive repair industry is full of incompetence and overpricing, there are still many honest and qualified repair facilities. Obviously, a solution to this madness must be found, one giving both the consumer and mechanic a fair shake.

First, analyze the symptoms and determine what is wrong with your car. Then, carefully select a repair facility. Here are some guidelines to help in your choice.

- Check with your friends or fellow co-workers for personal recommendations and experiences.
  a. Follow up all leads by inquiring at your local Better Business Bureau for complaints against these repair facilities recommended.
  b. Your closest Better Business Bureau can be found in the telephone white pages.
- Now comes the foot work. Repair facilities passing the first two tests should be investigated further.
  a. Look for a clean and neat shop. This signifies pride in ownership indicating quality work!
  b. Do they appear to have the proper tools to do the job?
  c. Any good repair shop will offer a written estimate, return any replaced parts and guarantee repairs for 90 days or 3,000 miles.

For a list of quality garage and service centers write:

AUTOMOTIVE SERVICE COUNCILS, INC
4001 Warren Boulevard
Hillside, IL 60162

Shops on this list give you a written guarantee covering parts and labor. Faulty repairs may be corrected at any other participating shop if you can't return to the original one.

Continue To Patronize A Good Repair Shop

Once a good repair facility has been located, continue to patronize this establishment! There's an old saying, "If you don't know car repair, know a good mechanic."

- Avoid repair work on a Friday, Saturday or Monday if at all possible. These are usually their busiest days and a mechanic (even a good one) in a hurry might make a mistake in the repair!

- Before any wrench twisting, insist all repairs must be approved by you on a work or repair order form. While this advise may seem unnecessary, only about 10 percent of the customers sign a work order. Without a written estimate signed by you, any legal action you take becomes futile!

  a. Make sure this repair order says exactly what you want it to!

  b. Be specific about your motor car's ailments.

  c. Under no circumstances sign a blank work order or say, "Do whatever is necessary."

  d. On the whole, most mechanics have only those words to go by. Anything vague or misinterpreted could result in unwanted and unneeded repairs.

  e. An estimated cost must be included on the repair form. Draw an arrow from the amount estimated to your signature. Allow for a 10% difference in final cost. Never accept additional repair or cost without prior consent.

  f. Request all replaced parts be returned. This leads a repair shop to believe the quality and honesty of their work might be verified by someone else.

  g. If the repair people are convinced you have pinpointed or fully grasp the problem, chances are they won't attempt to hustle your okay for a valve job because your tire is flat.

Take Your Mechanic For A Test Drive

The principal cause of any auto repair problem stems from a mechanic's inability to precisely diagnose your car's ailment! In fairness to him, part of this inability often lies with the customer's

It's elementary my dear friend.

failure to fully explain what they want fixed. Along with the information you give, take your mechanic for a test drive. There's usually nothing better than direct experience with the problem!

When all repairs are complete, road test the car again before you drive home. Return it to the garage immediately if she's not performing well. Don't wait until tomorrow. Your claim for corrective service will be weakened! Remember. If you're rational with repairmen, they'll be more receptive to you. The alternative to this is usually the mushroom treatment—keep the customer in the dark and spread manure on him at frequent intervals. It's best not to let emotion aggravate the situation!

Directory Of Certified Mechanics

What makes a good mechanic? First, it's someone who won't jump to conclusions. The amateur is usually the one with all the answers. Good mechanics spend the time needed for a diagnosis.

Neatness and cleanliness go hand-in-hand with quality repairs. Certified and licensed repairmen have experience. Find one! You'll be a lot happier with the results. For a 200 page directory of certified mechanics write:

EMPLOYERS DIRECTORY
National Institute
For Automotive Service Excellence
1825 K Street, NW Suite 515
Washington, DC 20006
Include $1.75

Shop Each Item

There is a solution to every problem; the only difficulty is finding it. Get a second opinion on estimated repairs over $100 or when the problem seems less urgent than the mechanic implies. Double check with other garages to see if your motor car "doctor" has given a proper diagnosis. For a good unbiased view contact an independent diagnostic center, one not repairing automobiles.

Separate all repairs according to cost and need. Example: Your transmission is retiring, the upholstery is torn and she needs a new left front fender. Fix the gearbox first! Even if you can afford all the above repairs, never get them done at the same garage. Shop each item! Usually it's cheaper to have mechanical objects repaired versus replaced. Example: The muffler system has a few tiny holes. Have your mechanic weld them instead of replacing entire system.

Repairs Under Warranty

Recent federal emission regulations pertain to cars with less than 50,000 and less than five years of age. Should an original part malfunction, causing the car to fail emission standard tests, the manufacturer must repair it free of charge. This applies to both new and used cars. For repairs still under warranty, you should take the car to an an authorized dealer.

However, there's a way to relieve you from most of this madness! Any well-conceived maintenance plan along with careful driving will provide reliable transportation for years to come. *(Note: See "Pamper Your Antique" in Chapter Four, p. 310.)* Allow between $400-$500 per year on general upkeep. Your motor car and bank account will thank you!

How To Tell An Expert From A Mud Mixer

Unfortunately, all of us, at one time or another, could use a body and fender shop. Whether you left both front fenders on the Santa Monica Freeway, the Cross Bronx Expressway, Florida's Turnpike or just acquired a small love tap, good body shops are hard to come by. Selecting an expert fender pounder from the many mud mixers can be difficult. Here are some guidelines:

- Single out a garage that is a member of the Independent Garage Owners Association or Auto Body Association. Members abide by strict trade standards.

- Your insurance company's accident adjuster will know the bondo fillers from the craftsmen. From among the many suggested body shops, obtain three estimates— select the middle one.

- Yes, you can choose your own preferred body shop. As

long as estimates are within reason three written estimates aren't required!

● Insurance companies may refuse to pay for any new part and might authorize a repair instead. Both the insurance agent and company adjuster usually decide between repair or replacement. You can see why it's a good idea to know your automobile insurance agent!

● Never sign authorization forms offered by a friendly tow-truck operator if you're an accident victim. You may find once you return to claim your car the repair work has already begun!

● It is physically impossible to duplicate a factory paint job! Many new paints (especially metallics found on BMW, Mercedes Benz, etc.) when spot painted will never match the original. Use this as a consideration when selecting your next automobile.

How To Settle Disputes Fast

Occasionally, controversies will arise concerning repair. Don't panic. Attempt to resolve disputes with a calm and collected temper. Be polite. There's an old saying, "If you appear intelligent and rational, you will be treated in the same manner." But, at times neither party will budge on their position. Now's the time to bring in the heavy artillery!

At a dealership, talk to the owner about poor service or inadequate repairs. If he refuses to give you satisfaction, contact one of the pilot project Automotive Consumer Action Panels (AUTOCAP). These panels seek to resolve customer difficulties. To learn if an AUTOCAP has been established in your locality and if it can handle your particular problem inquire at a local dealership or write:

NATIONAL AUTOMOBILE DEALERS ASSOCIATION
1640 Westpark Drive
Mclean, Virginia 22101

My lady, it's really quite simple.

Where are they located?

At the same time complain to the manufacturer! Describe your motor car, problems encountered, the dealer involved and your attempts to correct the problem. Send the first letter to your manufacturer's "Zone" or "District" representative. Their address and toll free phone number can be found in your owner's manual. If necessary, send the next letter to the Customer Relations Office of the manufacturer by writing:

ALFA ROMEO
250 Sylvan Avenue
Englewood Cliffs, NJ 07632
PH: 201 871-1234

AMERICAN HONDA
American Honda Motor Co
100 W Alondra Blvd
Gardena, CA 90247
PH: 213 327-8280

AMERICAN MOTORS CORP
27777 Franklin Rd
Southfield, MI 48034
PH: 313 827-1000

ASTON MARTIN LAGONDA
14 Weyman Avenue
New Rochelle, NY 10805
PH: 914 576-3202

AVANTI MOTOR CORPORATION
765 S Lafayette Blvd
South Bend, IN 46637
PH: 209 287-1836

BMW OF NORTH AMERICA

Montvale, NJ 07645
PH: 201 573-2000

BRITISH CARS
British Motor Car Distributors
19100 Susana Road
Compton, CA 90221
PH: 213 636-9831

BUICK MOTOR DIVISION
General Motors Corporation
Flint MI 48550
PH: 313 766-5000

**CADILLAC MOTOR
CAR DIVISION**
General Motors Corporation
2860 Clark Avenue
Detroit, MI 48232
PH: 313 556-6000

CHEVROLET MOTOR DIVISION
General Motors Corporation
General Motors Bldg
Detroit, MI 48202
PH: 313 556-5000

CHRYSLER
Chrysler Corporation
P.O. Box 857
Detroit, MI 48288
PH: 313 956-5741

FERRARI
Chinetti-Garthwaite Imports
1100 W Swedesford Rd
Box 455
Paoli, PA 19301
PH: 215 647-6665

FIAT
Fiat Motors
Of North America
155 Chestnut Ridge Rd
Montvale, NJ 07645
PH: 201 573-3700

FORD
Ford Motor Company
P.O. Box 4331
300 Renaissance Center
Detroit, MI 48243

GENERAL MOTORS CORP
General Motors Bldg
Detroit, MI 48202

JAGUAR MG ROVER TRIUMPH
600 Willow Tree Rd
Leonia, NJ 07605
PH: 201 461-7300

JEEP
940 N Cove Blvd
Toledo, OH 43657
PH: 419 470-7182

LINCOLN MERCURY
Division Ford Motor Company
300 Renaissance Center
P.O. Box 4322
Detroit, MI 48243

MASERATI
Maserati Automobiles, Inc
Box 8786
Baltimore, MD 21240
PH: 301 796-8485

MAZDA
Mazda Motors of America, Inc
3040 E Ana Street
Compton, CA 90221
PH: 312 537-2332

MERCEDES
Mercedes-Benz Of
North America
One Mercedes Drive
Montvale, NJ 07645

NISSAN   (DATSUN)
Nissan Motor Corp., U.S.A.
18501 Figueroa street
Carson, CA 90248
PH: 213 532-3111

OLDSMOBILE
Oldsmobile Division
General Motors Corporation
920 Townsend Street
Lansing, MI 48921

PEUGEOT
Peugeot Motors
Of American, Inc
One Peugeot Plaza
Lyndhurst, NJ 07071
PH: 201 935-8400

PONTIAC
Pontiac Division
General Motors Corporation
1 Pontiac Plaza
Pontiac, MI 48053

RENAULT
Renault U.S.A. Inc
100 Sylvan Avenue
Englewood Cliffs, NJ 07632
PH: 201 461-6000

ROLLS ROYCE
Rolls Royce Motors, Inc
West 75 Century Road
Box 189
Paramus, NJ 07652
PH: 201 165-8300

SAAB
Saab-Scania of America, Inc
Saab Drive
Orange, CT 06477
PH: 203 795-5671

SUBARU
Subaru of America, Inc
7040 Central Hwy
Pennsauken, NJ 08109

TOYOTA
Toyota Motor Sales, U.S.A.
2055 W 190th Street
Torrance, CA 90503

VOLKSWAGEN PORSCHE AUDI
Volkswagen of America, Inc
27621 Parkview Blvd

Warren, MI 48092
PH: 313 574-3300

VOLVO
Volvo of America Corporation
Rockleigh, NJ 07647
PH: 201 768-7300

When You Have A Repair Problem With A Private Garage

With a private garage or service center, talk with the owner about a complaint. If the problem is not resolved, check to see if a municipal, county or state consumer agency can help you. Your consumer protection agency is listed in the phone book under local government. Appeal to your local office of the Better Business Bureau. Write:

U.S. OFFICE OF CONSUMER AFFAIRS
Washington DC 20201

There's an excellent example of an automotive consumer protection agency in California. The California Bureau of Automotive Repair will take complaints about repair services and attempt to settle disputes. California residents can request complaint form 771-3 by writing:

DEPARTMENT OF CONSUMER AFFAIRS
Bureau of Automotive Repair
28 Civic Center Plaza, Room 360
Santa Ana, CA 92701
PH: 800 952-5210 or (916) 445-4751

If all else has failed, send in the marines—Nader's Raiders! Write of your complaint to:

RALPH NADER
Center For Auto Safety
1223 Dupont Circle Bldg
Washington, DC 20036

You May Have To Take Your Case To Court

For perhaps your best shot at obtaining satisfaction, sue in small claims court! By doing this, you not only convey your seriousness, but express how far you're willing to go. Arm yourself with as many facts as possible before you enter the courtroom. *(Note: See "The Facts About Automobile Warranties" in Chapter One, p. 88.)* The amount of money you can sue for varies in different states from $100 to $3,500. Your costs for bringing this action to trial in this manner are minimal.

If you are talking larger sums of money, explore the problem with an attorney. Most state bar associations have a local referral service. They will refer you to a competent attorney, knowledgeable in laws pertaining to your automobile problem. If your attorney advises you to file suit under the Magnuson-Moss Warranty Act the Federal Trade Commission wants to be informed. *(Note: See "The Facts About Automobile Warranties" in Chapter One, p. 88.)* Write:

WARRANTIES PROJECT
Bureau Of Consumer Protection
Federal Trade Commission
Washington, DC 20580

For Safety Related Defects

On occasion you may feel your motor carriage has a safety related defect. For prompt action call or write:

OFFICE OF DEFECT INVESTIGATION
NES 30
400 7th Street, SW
Washington, DC 20590
PH: 800 424-9393
Washington DC residents call: 426-0123

All-Time Automobile Repair Ripoffs

You've heard of television's great all-time bloopers? You know, where they show portions of shows never before seen by the public. Most deal with the humorous side of life. Melt the butter—they're poppin' 'em tonight!

J. C.   *Hold it! Stop the show! I think I see Sophia Derek in the eighth row!*

E. M.   *Sophia Derek? Are your sure?*

J. C.   *Either that or it's two Yul Brynners!*

Well, I don't have any film clips to show you, but here're some of the all-time repair gimmicks, scams and cons of the automotive repair industry. These deal with a serious side of life—fradulent automobile repair! Read carefully. Be on the look out.

Imagine you're on vacation. You stop at a local gas station to have the tank topped off. Then the friendly attendant proceeds to . . .

1. Drop a seltzer tablet into your battery, causing it to boil over.
2. Check your motor oil but "forgets" to push the dipstick all the way down.
3. Slash a fan belt so it hangs by a thread.
4. Puncture a tire while checking its pressure.
5. Squirt oil on the shock absorbers to make them appear to have a broken seal.

Be alert! Under no circumstances leave your car unattended at interstate gas stations! Remember. With any suggested repairs, get a second opinion!

Clues. Only through careful examination could you tell.

Beware Of The "Tricks Of The Trade"

● Picture a mechanic or service station attendant spraying oil on your starter, generator or alternator. He then claims one of these parts needs replacement. These parts do not contain or require oil!

- You've just received a repair bill and it contains charges for shop supplies (probably rags, paper towels, etc.). Never pay these charges.

- "The sunshine treatment." A repair shop leaves a customer's car outdoors for the day (there is no repair) and then charges for repairs.

- Many times when old Betsy is getting tuned-up your "Doctor " will call requesting permission to install a rebuilt carburetor.
  - a. Question this request. Get a second opinion.
  - b. If, indeed, another carburetor is required, purchase a brand new unit versus a rebuilt one. Reconditioned carburetors are notoriously bad.
  - c. The same holds true for your power steering pump and power brake booster.

- A considerable number of car dealers sell new motor cars through their body shop.
  - a. Here's how it's done. They make it a practice to talk to anyone with a repair estimate over $200 suggesting a trade for a new car instead of repair.
  - b. If you encounter this, pack your bags and leave.

- Many automobiles (especially foreign) contain two muffler systems: (1) the muffler, and (2) the resonator. Muffler shops like to replace the entire system when often just one or the other has failed. Replace what is necessary.

- At a body shop you could be billed for new parts when, in fact, these components have been obtained from wrecked vehicles.

- When the air conditioner doesn't blow cold, add freon and check the system for leaks. No, your compressor doesn't need to be changed.

- One of the biggest money makers for a tire and brake store is brake rebuilding. Before having this work done, check for yourself.

  - a. Drum brake shoes don't need to be replaced unless they have worn past 1/16" in thickness or 1/32" above the rivets.
  - b. Disk brake pads with less than 1/16" of lining are past history!

Repair Your Car Correctly 100% Of The Time

I've given you the facts and answers to solve one of our most irritating and expensive problems—automobile repair. Use them! You'll improve the chances of having your auto repaired correctly at the right price by 100 percent! There are many honest, reputable repair shops. Choosing the right one is the secret! Each of us evaluates before making correct choices. Now you have the clues to make this evaluation.

Look forward to success!

Automobile Leasing

Without the proper analysis it could be a fox hunt!

The Plan With One Big Advantage

Motor car leasing is a monthly time-payment plan with one big advantage—you pay only for the time you use the automobile! Leasing should be looked upon as a long-term form of renting. This enables you to drive a new car every two or three years without administrative and disposal problems. You pay the leasing company for this convenience and service but the rewards found in leasing are certainly appealing.

It's Not An Investment!

A lease can be written for any time period seven months or longer. As a lessee (customer) it is very difficult to acquire equity in any car. Equity is the difference between the selling price and the amount you owe. With certain lease contracts you are responsible to make up the difference at the end of the lease period should the car not sell for a price equal to the remaining balance of the car's original cost. You can see why leasing is considered an expense rather than an investment!

Leasing Frees Your Capital for Use Elsewhere

There are certain advantages to leasing. It allows you to manipulate your savings in more ways than an outright purchase. Why? When you buy, you can't borrow 100 percent of a new car's value. With a lease you effectively borrow this 100 percent and pay back only 50-70 percent.

Often a down payment is not required beyond a security deposit.

This deposit consists of one monthly payment plus good faith money equal to approximately one month's payment. Most automobile leases call for the payment of all license fees along with the initial payment.

When you purchase a car, all sales tax (if applicable) must be paid up front. This requires an additional initial cash outlay on your part. In leasing the total sales tax is divided into equal payments and added to your monthly payment. It is another way to defer expenses. Beyond these, leasing frees capital normally required for a downpayment for use elsewhere.

Since there is no loan involved, leasing becomes a financial transaction rather than a sale. For this reason automobile leases are not shown on financial statements.

Important Reasons Why Leasing Is Popular

Automobile leasing is growing in popularity for three main reasons. First, new car prices are rising at an alarming rate making the expense of a purchase less justifiable. Second, provided you have picked the right car (one having a proper depreciation rate) and have a good credit rating, no down payment will be necessary. Third, for the self-employed there are advantageous tax considerations. Leasing will provide you with precise expense and accounting records for tax reporting. If the vehicle is leased and used strictly for business purposes, the entire cost of the lease payments is tax deductible, along with the expenses of upkeep, repair and gasoline. All of these factors have contributed to a tremendous growth in the leasing industry. Some inside sources predict over 50 percent of all new motor cars will soon be leased rather than purchased outright!

Myths And Mysteries Surrounding Leasing

By now you may have some questions. Does leasing fit my needs? Do I qualify to lease? Can I really lease my dream machine? Will leasing cut my monthly automobile expenses? Let's answer these questions along with unraveling other myths and mysteries surrounding leasing. Read on!

What Is Leasing?

Leasing is simply an agreement between two individuals—the lessor and lessee. A lessee agrees to pay a predetermined amount of money each month for the use of the lessor's automobile. Also agreed upon is a lease termination date (usually 36 months). The lessee's monthly payments are based upon:

1. The automobile's depreciation rate (the difference between

what the lessor pays for an automobile and the amount the car can be expected to sell for after the lease has expired). Remember. The lessee pays only for that part of the automobile actually used (another way of saying depreciation).

2. The car's residual value (its estimated net worth at the termination of the lease).
3. The lessee's estimated driving mileage per year.
4. The reliablility factor of the motor car chosen.
5. The cost of writing the lease (the interest, overhead and profit going to the company writing the lease).

The Two Basic Forms Of Automobile Leases

Basically there are two different forms of automobile leases—open or closed end. This is a summary of their differences.

OPEN-END LEASES

An open-end lease is also known as a finance or equity lease. This lease is actually a promissory note to pay the entire amount of the capitalized (initial total cost) of the motor car! A lessor will estimate what the value of the vehicle will be at the end of the lease (also called the "bring back" or "residual value"). The lessee then remains liable for paying the lessor this depreciated or residual value upon termination of the lease.

If, at the end of a lease, the automobile is not worth the residual value (as originally estimated), you make up the difference! On the other hand, if the motor car sells for more than the predetermined residual value, you can receive a rebate at the end of the lease.

Note: Federal laws in effect since March of 1977 limit your liability to a maximum amount equal to three monthly payments unless you turn the car in with abnormal wear or excessive mileage.

The open-end lease can be the cheapest form of leasing. It can also be the most expensive! The key to success rests in your selection of a car. It must have a strong record of good resale value and a history of easy maintenance.

With open-end leases you can sell the car at any time, providing the lessor is paid-off. This enables you to trade for a new car before the scheduled lease termination date.

CLOSED-END LEASING

Closed-end leasing is often referred to as a walk-away, straight or net-rental lease. Under a closed-end contract the lessee has no obligation in the disposal of the automobile. Assuming the car is in good condition when it is turned in, the lessor must swallow any loss or take any profit from its sale! Once the last lease payment is made, you simply turn the car in. You have no other responsibility.

All costs are structured to allow the lessee to walk away from the leased automobile without owing a nickel. As you may have guessed, this makes closed-end leasing very expensive and not too popular.

In a closed-end lease you do not have the option of selling your leased car privately. This makes the lease difficult to terminate before the contract has expired. However, a closed-end lease does protect you completely against abnormal depreciation. Unusual depreciation of a car not leased on a closed-end contract can lead to a balloon payment in the end. Don't kid yourself. It can happen!

Who To Lease From?

It is important to select a reputable leasing firm for two reasons. First, the timing on terminating your lease will effect the vehicle's residual value. Any good leasing company will staff qualified personnel who can administer your car lease much like a stock broker takes care of a client's investments. They watch the market and advise you what and when to lease. Second, if the lessor goes out of business, all customers with open-end contracts may have a difficult time recovering their security deposit! In certain instances the customer can also be held responsible for any shortage in the lessor's debt on the leased vehicle.

Investigate First

It does pay to investigate before deciding on a company to lease from. One question giving you a clue (usually not offending anyone) is to ask what lender finances the company's contracts. The length of time a company has been in business is also a good indication of its strength and dependability.

The Sources For Leasing Cars

There are three main business sources leasing cars: (1) banks, (2) car dealerships and (3) independent leasing companies.

1. **Banks:** For the most part banks are confined to open-end leases. Generally, they have no facilities to recondition an automobile. Therefore they must wholesale or auction off the car at the end of the lease. This increases your chance of a balloon payment. Banks tend to compute residual values

higher than either car dealerships or independent leasing companies. Yes, this does make the lease payments less. However, if the residual value was set unrealistically high at the start of the lease, this could spell trouble should the car not bring that price upon termination.

2. **Car Dealerships:** Normally dealerships only lease the make of motor car they carry. This limits your selection! However, your chances for satisfactory warranty and service work are better. Remember. A dealer can't lease a car any cheaper than an independent leasing firm or bank!

3. **Independent Leasing Companies:** These firms tend to lease those motor cars likely to have the best resale value. They may be able to tailor the lease more to your needs. Generally you'll get an unbiased opinion to help in your selection of the correct automobile to lease.

To Lease Or Not To Lease?

The one question I'm asked more than any other is, "Should I be leasing or buying my cars?" Here is my answer. I'll lay out the facts. You decide. Education is what you get from reading all the facts first. Experience is what you get when you don't. The most intelligent people I know ask advice. The successful ones follow it.

Who Should Lease Automobiles

These are classic examples of someone who should lease. You're a self-employed professional or commercial business owner earning a higher than average gross income each year. You drive over 14,000 per year and need or desire a new automobile every two to three years (if you drive 20,000 to 25,000 miles a year, hold the length of the lease to just two years). Or, you're in a semi-self-employed position where you can prove you receive no compensation for automobile expenses. You should consider leasing if you're buying your cars on a long-term contract (48 months or longer). Why? By the time this loan is paid off, you've very little equity to show for all those payments!

This Person Can Almost Justify Leasing

By contrast with the person above, this one earns about the average or maybe even a little less than the national average salary. The car is driven between 10,000 and 13,000 miles each year and it must double as a family car. If you fit in this category, ask yourself these questions:

1. Can I write off all or part of this car as a business expense?
2. Will my income stay constant?

3. Can my income support a leased vehicle?
4. Do I have a good to excellent credit rating?
5. Will I need investment capital in the future?
6. Do I maintain my automobile properly according to the owner's manual?

Leasing Is Not For Everyone

Are you a low-mileage driver (under 10,000 miles per year)? Do you desire a small inexpensive model car you'll drive at least three years? If you fit this description, you'd be better off buying your car! There's no sound way to justify leasing.

The Facts On Leasing

- You can drive any new automobile you desire. But, most companies won't lease a used car over two-years-old. The exception might be an exotic classic such as a Lamborghini. Keep in mind. The greater the vehicle's cost the more substantial your income and credit rating must be to qualify for a lease!

- Lease automobiles with a good resale history. The more equipment your buggy has the more value it will have at the end of the lease. Your leasing company will help you decide on the best accessories and options to add.

- Study the markets. Because of better design and workmanship, some rather exotic cars make excellent lease prospects. Some actually increase in value. Your best time to lease is from the time new models are introduced each year until about May 1. Avoid leasing after this date!

- Some leasing companies offer unbelievably low monthly payments. Be extremely cautious of these claims. Low monthly payments usually result in a high residual. A large balloon payment would be required at the end.

- Low monthly payments are also offered by companies who penalize you heavily (10 cents per mile) for any excess mileage you drive. The maximum miles allowed without penalty is usually between 15,000 and 20,000 per year. Beware!

- Shop for a car to lease the same as you would for one to buy. Basically you are trying to determine if the car will retain a high resale value at the end of the lease! Study used

car values to determine the ones holding their value best.
(Note: See "Estimating Used Car Values" in Chapter One, p. 45.)

- You are responsible for the insurance on a leased car. However, the lessor has a set of minimum standards your insurance coverage has to meet. These vary with lessors.
  (Note: Follow the guideline for insurance in this chapter, p. 154.)

- Every new leased automobile is entitled to warranty protection. If the leasing firm is not close to your home, ask if there are limitations where this work can be performed.

- Most leases carry a penalty clause for terminating the lease early. The cost varies depending on the leasing company. Simply returning the leased vehicle to the lessor ahead of contract expiration does not always avoid a repossession on your credit record!

- At the end of a lease the leasing company usually sells the car to the lessee, an auto wholesaler or at auction. From a financial point of view it is not wise to lease a car you believe you will buy at the end of the lease! This is a very expensive way to buy a car.

- It takes a superior credit rating to lease a car. Because you put less money into it, someone else has more money at risk! However, leasing companies can and do tailor contracts for individuals with strong credit ratings.

Leasing Vs Buying Dollar For Dollar

If you lease over a period of years, your automobile maintenance costs (not only money but your time) are reduced. Why? You're continually dealing with newer automobiles and the chance of major repairs are remote. Leasing is still not the answer for everyone. I wouldn't consider it unless I was able to write off at least 50 percent of the monthly payment! Don't spend your time attempting to lease until you have established a strong credit rating. Leasing is geared to the self-employed professional.

You've spent your time wisely!

CHAPTER III

The Riddle
Of The Three T's

Red Tape, Tickets And Travel

How To Ease Your Way Through
The Department Of Motor Vehicles

Well, I have learned the truth and it makes no sense.

The Proven Best Method

When in danger or in doubt, run in circles, scream and shout! Have you had those thoughts also? No part of any automobile transaction is more confusing than the red tape of the Department of Motor Vehicles. Each year millions of car deals are transacted strictly between private parties. No new or used car dealer is involved. This is absolutely the best method for sellers to get the most money for their car!

Don't Eliminate Your Opportunity For Profit!

In spite of this fact, millions of people don't take advantage of the profits to be made selling their automobile privately. The reason? A strong desire to avoid time consuming Department of Motor Vehicle paperwork. Sellers eliminate this concern by simply trading with a dealer. It's an expensive solution! Dealer trading eliminates your opportunity to personally profit from the sale of your automobile!

186

This Is The Way

Follow this guide. I have summarized the general requirements of the D.M.V. All states are not exactly alike but each uses the same general format of requirements These don't change much from the small D.M.V. office in a rural town to the largest D.M.V. offices in our biggest cities.

You Will Make More Money

When the time comes to trade your car, glance through this summary and simple explanations of the typical forms. It's guaranteed to help ease your way through any Department of Motor Vehicles. Now you can answer your questions about red tape and then make more money **(national average is $400-$800 more)** by selling your car by yourself!

D.M.V. Planning
For
Car Sales Between Individuals

(Private Party Sales)

Here's What To Do

By far the simplest way to avoid problems is for the buyer and seller to go to the Department of Motor Vehicles together. If there is any loan against the car, it will have to be paid before the seller's lender (lienholder or legal owner) will allow the car to be transferred to the buyer. You will also find it is easiest to take care of this payoff together. I strongly recommend this procedure.

Use A Bill Of Sale

Avoid completing a sale on the weekend. The business end of the transaction is more difficult then. An exception would be a seller holding a valid title and a buyer with cash or cashier's check. Then both parties to the transaction are protected. Always use a Bill of Sale in any automobile transaction. *(Note: See "Step By Step Directions For Completing Private Party Sales" in Chapter One, p. 32.)*

Department Of Motor Vehicles—The Paperwork

Here are the fees you should plan on paying, forms you will be asked to fill out and items you should take with you to handle the necessary paperwork for a private party sale with the Department of Motor Vehicles.

DEPARTMENT OF MOTOR VEHICLES

Excellent sir—a splendid way to do business.

Seller's Responsibilities In Private Party Car Sales

> **Certificate of title**
> **Current registration**
> **Smog certificate** (when required)
> **Notice of transfer**
> **Odometer statement**
> **Power of attorney**
> **Bill of sale**

The Seller Is Responsible For:
- Ownership certificate or Certificate of Title.
  - a. The seller should have this certificate if there is no lien on the car.

    b. If there is a lien, contact your lender for the payoff and arrange the manner they want this done (payoff funds usually come from the buyer).

    c. Take the ownership certificate with you to the D.M.V.

    d. Be sure to have proper signatures of each registered owner(s) and the lienholder (lender) of the car.

    e. These signatures must appear where it says "Release Interest In Vehicle" or similar wording.

● Bring evidence of current registration (the car's registration card). Pay penalties (if any) if car is not currently licensed.

● In any state requiring one (California), secure and pay for a valid Smog Certificate unless this is an inter-family sale or transaction.

● Immediately report the sale or transfer of ownership on a Notice of Transfer form to the D.M.V. Don't fail to do this in family transfers or in **divorce cases**.

● Supply an Odometer Statement (current mileage) for the car upon request.

● Give a buyer a Power of Attorney upon request relating to this transaction.

● Furnish the buyer a signed Bill of Sale.

Buyer's Responsibilities In Private Party Car Purchase

    Checking current license
    Checking the serial numbers
    Cooperating on lienholder payoff
    Indicate any new lienholder
    Pay transfer fee
    Pay current registration fee
    Pay current license fee
    Pay use tax (if any)
    Insurance requirements (if any)

The Buyer Is Responsible For:

● Determine if car is currently licensed.

● Check serial numbers of car to match with documents.

- Coordinating with the seller on payoff of any lienholder. *(Note: See "Step By Step Directions For Completing Private Party Sales" in Chapter One, p. 32.)* This will make it possible for the seller to present an ownership certificate to the D.M.V.

- If the car is to be financed, placing the name of the new lienholder or legal owner in the proper space on the certificate of ownership.

- Pay the transfer fee.

- Pay the current registration fee if due.

- Pay any current license fees if due. The current license fee many have been due prior to the date of sale. The seller and buyer will have to reach an agreement as to whom will pay.

- Pay the use tax (same as sales tax) in states having such tax. This does not apply in the case of some inter-family or certain other types of car transactions.

- Check on insurance requirements. Some states require a vehicle to have insurance before it can be registered. A call to your local D.M.V. office can verify this.

Sell it yourself. Keep the profit!

Four Important Forms Used By
The Department Of Motor Vehicles

The content of these forms will vary from state to state but the general infromation and questions asked remain about the same for all states. There are thousands of different forms. Frankly 99 percent of them are seldom used. Therefore I narrowed the field to just four. Each of these four, for one reason or another, is important to you when dealing with the Department of Motor Vehicles.

THE FOUR FORMS ARE:

    1. Bill Of Sale
    2. Notice Of Transfer
    3. Power Of Attorney
    4. Certificate Of Non-Operation

BILL OF SALE

LICENSE PLATE NUMBER

VEHICLE IDENTIFICATION NUMBER | MAKE | BODY TYPE | MODEL | YEAR

For the sum of _____Dollars

($ _____)and/or other valuable consideration, the receipt of which is hereby acknowledged, I/we did sell, transfer and deliver to

_____ (Buyer)

on the _____ day of _____19_____, my/our right, title and interest in and to the above described vehicle:

I/We certify under penalty of perjury I/We as lawful owner(s) of said vehicle, have the right to sell same, that I/We warrant and will defend the title to the vehicle against the claims and demands of all persons whomsoever except the lienholder noted below, and that said vehicle is free from all liens and incumbrances except lien * **in favor of**

_____
LIENHOLDER

* **If no lienholder shown in this space the Department of Motor Vehicles will assume title is clear.**

_____
ADDRESS   CITY   STATE

Signed this_____ day of _____19___.

Signature of Seller X _____

_____
ADDRESS   CITY   STATE

Bill of sale. Condensed version. This should be a part of every car transaction. It is not a requirement of the D.M.V. Don't let this stop you! Be smart. Get one and use it.

**NOTICE OF SALE OR TRANSFER
OF A VEHICLE**

_____
VEHICLE IDENTIFICATION No.

LICENSE PLATE NUMBER
_____

MAKE OF VEHICLE
_____

FOR CHANGE OF REGISTERED OWNER ONLY. NOT TO BE SUBMITTED FOR LEGAL OWNER TRANSFER.

Dept. of Motor Vehicles Upon transfer, or sale, seller must enter odometer reading here. →

						/
THOUSANDS		HUNDREDS			10ths	

This is to report that on_____, 19____

MONTH   DAY

I, as owner of the vehicle described above, sold or transferred my interest in and delivered possession of said vehicle to:

BUYER'S
NAME_____

ADDRESS_____

                                                        ZIP
CITY_____STATE_____CODE_____

SELLER'S
SIGNATURE_____

ADDRESS_____

                                                        ZIP
CITY_____STATE_____CODE_____

Most states use some variation of the **Notice of Transfer** to officially notify the Department of Motor Vehicles of a transfer of ownership. Usually this is necessary to relieve the previous owner of responsibility. A few states require you to mail it yourself. Do this immediately! Keep a copy for your records.

Some states call this a **Change of Ownership** and this must be reported to the probate court in the county where the car is registered or with the county tax-assessor collector. Still other states call this a **Statement of Transfer** to be completed on the registration renewal stub. This information is picked up by the DMV from the signing over of the title transfer form itself.

Act! You'll be glad you did.

POWER OF ATTORNEY

VEHICLE
LICENSE
NUMBER

VEHICLE IDENTIFICATION NO.

MAKE OF
VEHICLE

To the **Department of Motor Vehicles**   and to whom it may concern:

I (print full name) ——————————————————————
                       FIRST   MIDDLE   LAST

I (print full name) ——————————————————————
                       FIRST   MIDDLE   LAST
the undersigned do hereby duly appoint the following named person,

——————————————————————————————————————

to act as my attorney in fact, to sign papers and documents that may be necessary in order to secure   registration of or to transfer my interest in the above described vehicle.

I further agree to guarantee and save the State of   and the Director of Motor Vehicles from all responsibility which might   accrue from the issuance of   registration or transfer of such vehicle.

Note: An attorney in fact cannot make an affidavit or certificate of the truth of facts unknown to him.

SIGNED   ——————————————————————

SIGNED   ——————————————————————

This ——————— day of ——————— 19 ———
              DAY   MONTH   YEAR

Power of attorney. To many people this seems like giving away the farm. Not true! The use of this form was designed to allow another person to officially sign documents for you. It has important time-saving functions in automobile transactions.

The Power of Attorney is worded so it can only be used to secure registration for the car specified by serial number on the form. It is used by most dealers and can be a real help to individuals in a private party car transaction where one party can't go to the Department of Motor Vehicles.

This power is a time saver!

CERTIFICATE OF NON-OPERATION

VEHICLE
LICENSE
NUMBER

VEHICLE IDENTIFICATION NO.

MAKE OF
VEHICLE

The above described vehicle was not driven, moved, towed or left standing upon _____ public highways

from_____to_____inclusive.
     Month   Day   Year   Month   Day   Year

The vehicle has been located at_____
                               Street and Number

_____since last operated.
        City   State

The vehicle has been in my control since_____
                             Month   Day   Year

as a result of storage ( ) purchase ( ) repossession ( ) or other ( ) as explained on the reverse side.

I certify under penalty of perjury that the foregoing is true and correct.

Executed on_____at_____, _____
         Date   City   State

Signature_____

Certificate of non-operation or non-use affidavit.

In many states it is often possible to save lots of money legally by correct use of this form. Thousands of cars are sold each month on which the registration and license have expired. In some states these fees have to be brought current before a new registration and license will be issued.

This form certifies the car was not operated, moved or left standing on a highway causing registration fees to become due. Since the car was not operated, no fees were due. There's a **moneymaking tip**. Old hat to a dealer but not general knowledge. Check with your local DMV because not all states have this provision.

The buyer can't complete and sign a certificate of non-operation for the period of time the car was owned and in the possession of the seller. The seller must do this! In most states a motor vehicle must be registered within a limited amount of time (varies by state from 10 to 30 days) from first operation to avoid a late registration penalty.

Facts to save money by!

D.M.V. Requirements For
New Car Sales (Dealers)

When you buy a new car from a dealer, the responsibiltiy for securing license and title belongs to the dealer. The dealer will collect these fees from you:

A registration fee
The license fee
Sales tax (depends on state)

- You operate the car on temporary identification.
- The ownership certificate is mailed to the legal owner (lender, if any).
- The registration card is mailed to you.
- Plates are picked up by dealer or mailed to you.

D.M.V. Requirements For
Used Car Sales (Dealers)

In this case, just as in a new car sale, it is the dealer's responsibility to take care of the license, title and paperwork. The dealer will collect from you for:

Registration or transfer fee
License fee if due
Sales tax (depends on state)
Verification of pollution controls
(depends on state)

- The identification, ownership, registration permits and certificates are handled the same as for a new car.
- Plates are usually transferred with the car (unless they are out-of-state or personalized).

D.M.V. Requirements For "New" Cars
Purchased Out Of State
Or Imported From A Foreign Country

Imported Cars Must Clear Customs Before D.M.V.

In this case it is the responsibility of the purchaser, owner or lessee to apply for registration and title. To avoid penalties this usually must be done within 20 days once the car enters the state.

Exactly! You have it. This knowledge is your most valuable tool.

Secure these documents from your nearest D.M.V. office. You'll need the following:

Registration application
Certificate of origin
Statement regarding liens
D.M.V. inspection
Smog certification if required
Cost certification
Registration and license fees
Use tax

- An application for registration of a new or used vehicle. All cars are termed "new" the first time they are registered in a state.
- Manufacturer's Certificate of Origin endorsed to the dealer and then from that dealer to you. In some cases a Bill of Sate can be substituted.
- When you import a car from a foreign country, you'll have to state whether a title has even been issued and if there are any liens (debts).
- Car will be inspected by D.M.V. to match the title and the serial numbers.
- You'll need a Smog Device Certificate only if your state requires one (California). This certificate is issued at the inspection station or center not by the DMV.

- You will have to certify the cost. This includes accessories and optional equipment (no interest, insurance or sales tax).
- You pay a registration and license fee.
- In some states you'll pay a use tax. Credit is given for sales tax paid in another state.
- When you (the car owner) move from one state to another, any valid (passenger) vehicle registration (license plate) is good in the new state until the registration in the previous state expires.

Note: An excellent and inexpensive book summarizes the laws and regulations governing registration and operation of cars in each state and Canada. It is available from:

American Automobile Association
Order Department
8111 Gatehouse Road
Falls Church, VA 22042
PH: 703 222-6543

A quick review will ease you through.

Coping With Traffic Laws

 *Hand me my violin!*

Traffic Tickets

There are literally thousands of traffic laws. These vary from state to state, and naturally there can be a violation of any one of these laws. In dealing with violations, traffic officers issue traffic citations or tickets. Although the printed form for traffic tickets varies from one locale to another, they are basically all an evaluation of the traffic violation the officer says you committed.

Sign the Citation

A traffic citation or ticket is really a written promise on your part agreeing to appear. On the ticket is the standard information such as code infraction, date, time, place, etc. Since signing is necessary and does not ever mean that you admit guilt, go ahead and sign the citation when the officer requests.

No matter what the violation is issued for, all traffic tickets will fit under one of these four categories:

1. Moving
2. Pedestrian
3. Parking
4. Equipment

You may be lucky and just receive a warning. There are several types of warnings. Although these are not reported to the Department of Motor Vehicles, there is one called an equipment warning that does require you to have the faulty equipment corrected within a specific period of time.

How To Avoid A Traffic Ticket

Avoid Attention

Traffic officers usually do not carry the vehicle code book in the patrol car. Instead they are trained to watch for drivers with poor driving habits, especially the driver who is inconsiderate of other drivers. No driver can avoid violating some provision of his state's vehicle or traffic code book at some time or another. **Your best chance to avoid tickets is to avoid attention.** Rude and inconsiderate driving styles really attract attention, the kind no driver will be happy with. Perhaps the most careful driver is the one who just saw the driver ahead get a ticket!

> *No expert he on freeway speeds,*
> *Sober or with cider*
> *Finally now his headstone reads,*
> *"He crossed the Great Divider"*

In a few cases you may be able to talk yourself out of receiving a ticket, but this is not likely. The excuse has to be better than good. Usually the best procedure after you are stopped by the officer is to be very cooperative. Draw as little attention to yourself as possible.

After you receive a ticket, you may later want to know more about the violation you have been charged with. If so, most libraries have a copy of the State Motor Vehicle Code Book that can be helpful. Additional information can sometimes be secured by calling the **desk clerk** in the traffic officer's department.

How The Point System Works

The Point System

Many states have a point system used to rate drivers who have been convicted of driving offenses. This is one rating list you do not want to be on. Usually more serious violations count two points and less serious ones count one. The state has grounds for taking away your driver's license if you receive four or more points in one year, six in two years or eight in three years. Some drivers think the point system is unfair, but the records show the more traffic violation convictions a driver has the higher the odds he will have a traffic accident. As a general rule all but the most serious driving convictions remain on your record for a period of three years.

What To Do When
You Receive A Traffic Ticket

How To Plead

Hiring an attorney to represent you in court regarding a minor violation is not recommended. However, you should secure good legal help if you are charged with a serious one. Whether you try to avoid the ticket by going to court and trial will depend on your total evaluation of the circumstances. The only plea you can make enabling you to **contest** your ticket is one of "not guilty!"

Here are some factors to help you in making the decision on how to plead:

1. To be convicted you must be proven guilty **beyond** a reasonable doubt. A factor in your favor.
2. Ask yourself, "How did the officer catch me?" He will be at your trial.
3. Ask yourself, "Was I really in violation?"
4. Will the conviction affect your driver's license?
5. Will the conviction affect your insurance premiums?
6. Time is valuable. Ask yourself, "Will the time I spend appearing in court have a chance of being well spent?"

Most traffic convictions do effect insurance rates. However, unless you (a) have an accident, (b) submit a claim or (c) change insurance companies, your present insurance company will probably not know about the traffic conviction unless you tell them.

Call The Clerk Of The Court In Advance

If your final answer to the above questions is, "I'm going to contest this ticket," then you will be doing so in court. Take enough money when you appear there to cover the bond or cost of paying the ticket. I suggest you call the court clerk before the trial date to determine how much money you may need. Maybe you don't have enough money. In some cases, if you can show a reasonable way to pay as you go, this can be worked out with the court.

Don't Fail To Appear

Regardless of your decision regarding the ticket, do not make the mistake of failing to appear in court on the date and time the ticket specifies. This only makes your problem bigger. Sometimes it is possible to secure a different trial date. You must have a very good reason. When this becomes necessary, apply for the change with the court clerk well in advance of your original date. If the date is changed, my advice is to get this in writing. Failure to appear once you have received a traffic citation leads to a warrant for your arrest.

Computers Used To Track Drivers

Today, there is a federal clearing house containing the names of about 6.5 million drivers who have suspended or revoked driver's licenses. The purpose of this register is to stop dangerous drivers from jumping the state line in order to obtain a "valid" license. Because of a variety of reasons the system has been ineffective to date. There are strong indications, with the coming use of computers, this will change.

Understanding The Traffic Officer

The traffic officer really has but one job. His job is to issue traffic tickets! Once you understand this you have a much better chance of avoiding tickets. All of the officer's ticket "quotas" and "minimums" are placed on him by his department to force him to do this job—write tickets. Nothing improves your driving like a police car following you. Statistics are interesting. They show motorists who avoid tickets avoid accidents, a worthwhile achievement.

Heavily Patrolled

There are so many opportunities for officers to catch traffic violators. It is really more a process of elimination of the many rather than a search to find the few. Certain areas or stretches of road tend to be more heavily patrolled than others. Many drivers think of lurking patrol cars disguised to look like billboards or parked behind bushes. In reality, with the technical development of radar and communication systems, these methods aren't needed.

Random Stop

While findng a reason for stopping any driver is easy for a well-trained traffic officer, motorists can no longer be randomly stopped when not suspected of breaking a law. Now, police can't legally make a random stop of automobiles just to check driver's licenses and car registrations. This issue was recently decided by the United States Supreme Court.

The Facts About
Police Use Of Radar

The mystery! Hidden but not where people are looking.

A Controversial Device

Although challenged from time to time in different states, the use of radar by traffic police is here to stay. Learn something about radar. You'll be glad you did. What you learn may be surprising!

Echo

Radar has been used for many years, but only with recent technical advances has it become a major aid to traffic officers in their effort to monitor the flow of traffic. Basically a radar unit can determine the location and speed of an object, regardless of its size or shape. The radar unit sends out radio waves and then measures the time it takes for the *echo* of the waves to return from the object. This length of time is translated into the speed of the object.

Most courts of law accept the accuracy of radar, although every use of radar presents variables such as hills and angles used to measure by. What does this mean? Simply, errrors are made and radar findings can be questioned. However, you'll find it will take a lot of your own time, effort and money to do so. In the long run the chances of successfully defending yourself against a radar-backed traffic ticket are not too good! As in all traffic citations the best defense all motorists have is to drive in a manner that will avoid getting a ticket in the first place. **Do not draw attention to yourself.**

Inaccurate Clocking

In spite of careful driving you may find yourself receiving a traffic citation by an officer aided by the use of radar. If you question the accuracy of the speed written on that citation, the best question to ask the officer is, "When was the last time your radar unit was checked for accuracy?" Make careful note as to the officer's answer. One of the most common ways of **checking accuracy** of a radar unit is by use of a tuning fork. This is usually done by the officer himself. His answer to this question can later leave some doubt as to the accuracy of the speed he listed on your citation.

Radar is not "Big Brother" able to see you anywhere at any given time. The range of a good radar unit is about one mile for a large truck but becomes progressively less for a regular size car and even less for a compact. Don't forget your bicycle. Yep, even they can be and are clocked on radar. Radar devices do not work well in hilly sections of road nor do they have the ability to "see" around curves.

The accuracy of radar is effected by poor weather. Many vehicles traveling together also tend to read out on radar as nothing more than an average speed. All or any of the above can contribute to an inaccurate clocking by a traffic officer.

You may ask yourself, "Where and when should I be most aware of the possible use of radar by officers?" Watch for the following circumstances regarding the road and area you are traveling:

1. The road is flat, level and open.
2. I have just come over the crest of a hill.
3. The officer has clear view of my car.
4. The weather is clear—no fog, rain or high winds.
5. Traffic density is reasonable.
6. The street is wide.
7. There are few if any power or transmission lines in the area.
8. You are coming out of a sweeping curve.
9. There are posted speed signs
10. A residential road with any or all of the above conditions.

Being especially alert in the above situations can not only save you a traffic citation; it can also contribute to your peace of mind!

Radar Detector

There is one thing more . . . without a doubt the easiest legal method you can use to determine when radar is being used would be to install a radar detector in your automobile. Should you decide to purchase one, ask for the type that has the ability to scan across all of the frequencies. None are foolproof but they do work well in most cases. The units light up or buzz or do both when they pick up radar in use. Interestingly, the effective range of a good radar detecting unit is far greater than the working range of the police radar unit itself. A big advantage to the motorist.

Supplemental Equipment

You'll be happy to know you can be caught coming or going. With the advances made recently in radar and supplemental equipment, it really makes little difference if your car is approaching the well-equipped traffic officer or moving away from him. For that matter, he can even clock your car while *he* is moving. Today many patrol cars are being equipped with radar units plus VASCAR. This is a time-distance computer that uses two reference points as close together as one-tenth of a mile to determine your car's speed.

Summary

Radar is used in all fifty states and many foreign countries, including Mexico and Canada. While the California Highway Patrol does not use radar, many cities and towns in California do. Radar is also used in aircraft, but not in direct relation to traffic control. As a driver you should be aware it is perfectly legal to warn another driver radar is in use.

Radar—a small controversial device of which motorists should always be aware. It may not be "big brother," but **radar is watching all of us!**

Terms Associated With Traffic Laws

Here is a short list of terms you may refer to for a better understanding of the the technical language of police officers, the traffic laws and legal forms.

Accident citation
Traffic ticket given to a driver who, by violating a law, contributes to an accident.

Acquittal
A court verdict of not guilty.

Appeal
Asking a higher court to review a decision.

Arraignment
Going before the court to be advised of charges and entering a plea.

Bail
Security deposited with the court to assure a later appearance in court.

Bailiff
A person who is responsible for maintaining order in the court.

Bear
A slang term for police officer.

Burden of proof
A legal principal. It is the job of the complaining party to prove the validity of the charges.

Calendar
The order and dates of cases in court.

Calibrate
Verify the accuracy of a device.

Change of venue
Transferring of a court case to another court.

Citation
Official notice to appear in court in answer to a charge.

Citizens arrest
An arrest by a private citizen.

Clock
Recording the speed of another vehicle.

Continuance
Delaying the date of a trial to another date.

Contributory negligence
Carelessness helping to cause an accident.

Conviction
A guilty verdict.

Court
A place where trials are held.

Crosswalk
Area designated for pedestrian's use. May be marked, or an imaginary extension of the sidewalks.

Defendant
Any person charged with a crime.

Dismissal
A court decision to drop charges.

Disposition
The results of a trial.

Document citation
Ticket given for violation involving vehicle registration and driver's license.

Equipment violation
Ticket given for illegal or inoperative vehicle equipment.

Expunge
Any record of a violation removed from the records.

Fixit ticket
Term describing ticket given requiring equipment to be repaired.

Guilty
Offense committed as charged.

Hit-and-run
An act of leaving the scene of an accident without leaving information or notifying authorities.

Implied consent
Consent to submit to alcohol test inherent in accepting driver's license.

Infraction
Any violation of the law.

Jury trial
A trial decided by a body of citizens selected to hear the case in court.

Kiting
Indicating a speed on the ticket higher than the actual clocking.

Learner's permit
A temporary driver's license.

Marshal
An officer who has the power to carry out the orders of the court.

Median
The center of a highway.

Merging
The coming together of two separate flows of traffic vehicles to form one single flow.

Miranda decision
Court decision requiring an officer to inform suspect of constitutional rights.

Misdemeanor
Crime punishable by imprisonment in a county or municipal jail for less than a year.

Mistrial
Trial made void by a mistake in proceedings.

Municipal court
A court representing a local government.

Not guilty
A verdict by the court that the offense was not committed by the defendant.

Panning
Turning radar device so that it reads the background rather than the target. A way to get an inaccurate clocking.

Perjury
Willfully telling a lie when under oath to tell the truth.

Probable cause
Reasonable ground for suspicion that suspect committed a crime.

Prosecution
Legal proceedings against a defendent(s).

Radar
Electronic device used to determine the speed of vehicles.

Registered owner
Person recognized by the state as the licensed owner of a vehicle.

Speed trap
A location designated either by design or in the manner of enforcement to catch motorists violating vehicle laws.

Ticket
A citation issued for violation of traffic law.

Traffic school
Educational program conducted by some courts. Can sometimes be used as an alternative to a conviction.

Warrant
Authorization from a court for the arrest of an individual. Also a positive assurance.

Watch commander
Person in charge of an agency at a given time.

You can navigate within the system!

Basic First Aid

(The Essentials Only)

You have indeed been of the greatest help to me.

When You Need It
There may be a time when you will need to use some basic first aid. Knowing what to do for an injured person until a doctor or trained person gets to an accident scene can save a life. Here are some basic first aid measures.

Asphyxiation
Start mouth-to-mouth resuscitation immediately after getting patient to fresh air. Call physician.

Bleeding
Elevate the wound above the heart if possible. Press hard on wound with sterile compress until bleeding stops. Send for doctor if it is severe.

Burns
If mild, with skin unbroken and no blisters, plunge into ice water until pain subsides. Apply mild burn ointment or petroleum jelly if pain persists. Send for physician if burn is severe. Apply sterile compresses and keep patient quiet and comfortably warm until doctor's arrival. Do not try to clean burn, or to break blisters.

Chemicals In Eye
With patient lying down, pour cupfuls of water immediately into

corner of eye, letting it run to other side to remove chemicals thoroughly. Cover with sterile compress and call doctor.

Fainting
Seat patient and fan the face. Lower head to knees. Lay patient down with head turned to side if the patient becomes unconscious. Call doctor if faint lasts for more than a few minutes.

Falls
Send for physician if patient has continued pain. Cover wound with sterile dressing and stop any severe bleeding. Do not move patient unless absolutely necessary (as in case of fire) if broken bone is suspected. Keep patient warm and comfortable.

Shock (Injury Related)
Keep the victim lying down. If uncertain as to the injuries, keep the victim flat on the back. Maintain the victim's normal body temperature; if the weather is cold or damp, place blankets or extra clothing over and under the victim; if weather is hot, provide shade. Get medical care as soon as possible.

Unconsciousness
Send for doctor and place person on stomach with the head turned to side. Start resuscitation if the victim stops breathing. Never give foods or liquids to an unconscious person.

Asphyxiation
Losing consciousness because normal breathing has been impaired.
Foreign
Matter normally not present.
Ointment
A soft, creamy often medicated preparation for application to the skin.
Resuscitation
To revive or arouse from unconsciousness.
Sterile
Free from living germs.
Unconsciousness
Without awareness. Not awake.

MOUTH-TO-MOUTH RESUSCITATION

Your breath can save a life. The American Red Cross gives the following directions for mouth-to-mouth resuscitation. If the victim is not breathing. . .

1. Turn victim on back and begin artificial respiration at once.
2. Wipe out quickly any foreign matter visible in the mouth. Use your fingers or a cloth wrapped around your fingers.
3. Tilt the victim's head back.
4. Pull or push jaw into jutting-out position.
5. If victim is a small child, place your mouth tightly over the mouth and nose and blow gently into the victim's lungs about 20 times a minute. If victim is adult, cover the mouth with your mouth, pinch the victim's nostrils shut and blow vigorously about 12 times per minute.
6. If you are unable to get air into lungs of victim, and if head and jaw positions are correct, suspect foreign matter in the throat. To remove it, suspend a small child momentarily by the ankles or hold child with head down for a moment and slap sharply between the shoulder blades.
7. If the victim is an adult, turn on side and use same procedure.
8. Again, wipe mouth to remove foreign matter.
9. Repeat breathing, removing mouth each time to allow for escape of air. Continue until victim breathes for himself.

Information to live by!

How To Use Emergency Signals

On the contrary, it's always darkest just before the lights go out.

Who—Me?

Like the startled expert who, asked to quickly name two pronouns, responded with, "Who—me?" you may find yourself someday in real need of some basic knowledge of emergency distress signals. The best way you can gain the attention of someone else is by the use of more than one signal. Use as many as you can. By doing this your chances of being seen, heard or found are much better. Use common sense when setting up fire signals. In many regions of the United States rescue teams are on constant patrol in the back areas.

Signals And Ideas

- If you have a citizens band radio, use it.
- Gather firewood before dark if possible.
- Wave a light in a pattern of a cross, turning to face all directions as you wave. Then repeat with the light this time waving in a criss-cross pattern.
- Light three separate fires each about fifty feet from the other. This is an international distress signal.
- With care, a torch of fire could be waved in place of a light as above.

- Construct a sign visible from the air with rocks or what have you spelling out the word HELP.

- By day raise the hood on your vehicle. Find a way to put the work HELP on the hood if possible.

- Blowing the horn on your vehicle in an SOS manner from time to time could be helpful. This signal is three short, then three long, then three short honks (the international distress signal).

- Listen for sounds and watch for lights between your signalling efforts.

- Mark the direction you see any lights coming from at night so you can tell exactly where they were when daylight comes.

- If the wind is down, you can create black smoke to attract attention by lighting your dismounted spare tire. This can be done with wood placed in the middle or by use of a fuel soaking the tire. When you soak your tire with fuel, don't stand close to set it on fire. Toss the igniter from a safe distance. A thin layer of sand placed inside the tire will add to the time it will burn.

- Use one or more of the mirrors taken from your vehicle to act as a hand-held daylight signal. Stay in one spot when using a mirror.

- Remember! The international distress signal is flashed by a code of three short—three long—three shorts with **any device** at your disposal.

- If you must go away from your vehicle, leave a message as to your need for help. Be sure to tell where you are.

- In an emergency, extend motor fuel by diluting gasoline with up to 50 percent stove or lantern fuel.

- The international radio distress call is the repeating of the word **MAYDAY** over and over again.

You Are The Most Important Factor

Carefully think through your situation and your alternatives. Give yourself time to think. The mind will create solutions to most emergency problems.

The ability to help yourself is far greater than you imagine!

State Police

(Phone Numbers)

HIGHWAY PATROL

Yes, you may look them up in my index.

The Fast Way To Get Help

When you need to get in touch with the Highway Patrol in an emergency, these numbers will do the job for you. Give your present location to the dispatch officer. You'll receive a phone number for the nearest available patrol district. It's a fast way to get help when you need it!

AL	205 832-6448	IA	515 281-5261
AK	907 465-4300	KS	913 296-3801
AZ	602 262-8011	KY	502 564-4686
AR	501 371-2026	LA	504 389-7501
CA	916 445-2211	ME	207 289-2155
CO	303 757-9011	MD	301 667-1100
CT	203 566-4054	MA	617 566-4500
DE	302 734-5973	MI	517 332-2521
FL	904 488-6517	MN	612 296-6652
GA	406 656-6077	MS	601 982-1212
ID	208 384-3628	MO	314 751-3313
IN	219 633-5674	MT	406 449-3000

NE	. . . .	402	477-3951	RI	. . . . 401 647-3311
NV	. . . .	702	885-5300	SC	. . . . 803 758-2815
NH	. . . .	603	271-3636	SD	. . . . 605 224-3105
NJ	. . . .	609	882-2000	TN	. . . . 615 741-2101
NM	. . . .	505	827-5111	TX	. . . . 512 452-0331
NY	. . . .	518	457-6811	VT	. . . . 802 828-2104
NC	. . . .	919	733-7952	UT	. . . . 801 533-4900
ND	. . . .	701	224-2455	VA	. . . . 804 272-1431
OH	. . . .	614	466-2990	WA	. . . . 206 753-6540
OK	. . . .	405	424-4011	WV	. . . . 304 348-2351
OR	. . . .	503	378-3720	WI	. . . . 608 266-3212
PA	. . . .	717	783-5556	WY	. . . . 307 777-7301

Telephone Area Code Numbers

(Numerically)

We shall communicate again soon I presume.

How The Area Code System Was Set Up

When the telephone area code system was devised, it was set up so the more heavily populated areas received the code numbers with the shortest pulls on a dial type phone. Hence New York was given the code number 212, Los Angeles area 213—all short pulls.

No code numbers start with the number one as this was saved to be used as the first number in dialing out of your own area.

Note: Examples comparing the times of different areas with a Pacific time of 4:00 p.m. . . .

For Hawaii & Alaska Time subtract two hours (2:00 PM)
For Mountain Time add one hour (5:00 PM)
For Central Time add two hours (6:00 PM)
For Eastern Time add three hours (7:00 PM)
For Atlantic Time add four hours (8:00 PM).

201 . . . . . . NEW JERSEY	317 . . . . INDIANA	515 . . . . IOWA	715 . . . . WISCONSIN
202 . . . D. OF COLUMBIA	318 . . . . LOUISIANA	516 . . . . NEW YORK	716 . . . . NEW YORK
203 . . . . . CONNECTICUT	319 . . . . IOWA	517 . . . . MICHIGAN	717 . . . PENNSYLVANIA
204 . . . . MANITOBA		518 . . . . NEW YORK	801 . . . . UTAH
205 . . . . ALABAMA	401 . . . . RHODE IS.	519 . . . . ONTARIO	802 . . . . VERMONT
206 . . . . . WASHINGTON	402 . . . . NEBRASKA	601 . . . . . . MISSISSIPPI	803 . . . . . . S. CAROLINA
207 . . . . MAINE	403 . . . . ALBERTA	602 . . . . ARIZONA	804 . . . . VIRGINIA
208 . . . . IDAHO	N W TERRITORIES	603 . . . N. HAMPSHIRE	805 . . . . . . CALIFORNIA
209 . . . . . . CALIFORNIA	YUKON	604 . . . . . BR. COLUMBIA	806 . . . . TEXAS
212 . . . . NEW YORK	404 . . . . GEORGIA	605 . . . . S. DAKOTA	808 . . . . HAWAII
213 . . . . . CALIFORNIA	405 . . . . . . OKLAHOMA	606 . . . . . . KENTUCKY	809 . . . CARIBBEAN IS.
214 . . . . TEXAS	406 . . . . MONTANA	607 . . . . NEW YORK	812 . . . . INDIANA
215 . . . PENNSYLVANIA	408 . . . . . . CALIFORNIA	608 . . . . . . WISCONSIN	813 . . . . FLORIDA
216 . . . . OHIO	412 . . . PENNSYLVANIA	609 . . . . . NEW JERSEY	814 . . . PENNSYLVANIA
217 . . . . ILLINOIS	413 . MASSACHUSETTS	612 . . . . . . MINNESOTA	815 . . . . ILLINOIS
218 . . . . . . MINNESOTA	414 . . . . . . WISCONSIN	613 . . . . ONTARIO	816 . . . . MISSOURI
219 . . . . INDIANA	415 . . . . . CALIFORNIA	614 . . . . OHIO	817 . . . . TEXAS
301 . . . . MARYLAND	416 . . . . ONTARIO	615 . . . . . TENNESSEE	819 . . . . QUEBEC
302 . . . . DELAWARE	417 . . . . MISSOURI	616 . . . . MICHIGAN	901 . . . . . . TENNESSEE
303 . . . . . . COLORADO	418 . . . . QUEBEC	617 . MASSACHUSETTS	902 . . . . NOVA SCOTIA
304 . . . . . . W. VIRGINIA	419 . . . . OHIO	618 . . . . ILLINOIS	PRINCE EDWARD IS.
305 . . . . FLORIDA	502 . . . . KENTUCKY	701 . . . . N. DAKOTA	903 . . . . MEXICO
306 . . SASKATCHEWAN	503 . . . . OREGON	702 . . . . NEVADA	904 . . . . FLORIDA
307 . . . . WYOMING	504 . . . . . . LOUISIANA	703 . . . . VIRGINIA	907 . . . . ALASKA
308 . . . . . . NEBRASKA	505 . . . NEW MEXICO	704 . . . N. CAROLINA	912 . . . . GEORGIA
309 . . . . ILLINOIS	506 . . . N. BRUNSWICK	705 . . . . ONTARIO	913 . . . . KANSAS
312 . . . . ILLINOIS	507 . . . . . MINNESOTA	707 . . . . . CALIFORNIA	914 . . . . NEW YORK
313 . . . . . . MICHIGAN	509 . . . WASHINGTON	709 . NEWFOUNDLAND	915 . . . . TEXAS
314 . . . . MISSOURI	512 . . . . TEXAS	712 . . . . IOWA	916 . . . . . CALIFORNIA
315 . . . . . . NEW YORK	513 . . . . . . N. DAKOTA	713 . . . . TEXAS	918 . . . . . OKLAHOMA
316 . . . . KANSAS	514 . . . . QUEBEC	714 . . . . . CALIFORNIA	919 . . . . . N. CAROLINA

Telephone Area Code Numbers

(By States Alphabetically)

You may sometimes need a quick reference to match up the area code listed in an advertisement or article with the state it represents. Some states have more than one.

Time zones within each state are shown in parentheses:

Atlantic	**(A)**	**Mountain**	**(M)**
Central	**(C)**	**Pacific**	**(P)**
Eastern	**(E)**		

Note: To find a particular telephone number fast simply dial:
1 + (area code of city) + 555-1212.

Alabama (C) 205	Georgia (E) 404
Alaska (P - 2 hrs.). 907	912
Arizona (M) 602	Hawaii (P - 2 hrs.). 808
Arkansas (C) 501	Idaho (M & P) 208
California (P) 209	Illinois (C) 217
213	309
408	312
415	618
707	815
714	Indiana (C & E) 219
805	317
916	812
Colorado (M). 303	Iowa (C). 319
Connecticut (E) 203	515
Delaware (E) 302	712
Dis. of Columbia (E) 202	Kansas (C & M). 316
Florida (E & C) 305	913
813	Kentucky (C & E) 502
904	606

Louisiana (C) 318
504
Maine (E) 207
Maryland (E) 301
Massachusetts (E) 413
617
Michigan (E & C) 313
517
616
Minnesota (C) 218
507
612
Mississippi (C) 601
Missouri (C) 314
417
816
Montana (M) 406
Nebraska (C & M) 308
402
Nevada (P) 702
N. Hampshire (E) 603
New Jersey (E) 201
609
New Mexico (M) 505
New York (E) 212
315
516
518
607
716
914
North Carolina (E) 704
919
North Dakota (C & M) 701
Ohio (E) 216
419
513
614
Oklahoma (C & M) 405
918
Oregon (P & M) 503
Pennsylvania (E) 215
412
717
814

Rhode Island (E) 401
South Carolina (E) 803
South Dakota (C & M) 605
Tennessee (C & E) 615
901
Texas (C & M) 214
512
713
806
817
915
Utah (M) 801
Vermont (E) 802
Virginia (E) 703
804
Washington (P) 206
509
West Virginia (E) 304
Wisconsin (C) 414
608
715
Wyoming (M) 307
Alberta (M) 403
Brit. Columbia (P) 604
Manitoba (C) 204
N. Brunswick (A) 506
Newfoundland (A) 709
N. West Terr. (M & P) 403
Nova Scotia (A) 902
Ontario (E & C) 416
519
613
705
Pr. Edward Isl. (A) 902
Quebec (E) 418
514
819
Saskatchewan (C) 306
Yukon (P) 403
Caribbean Isl. (A) 809
Mexico (P & C) 903

Tips On Driving In Mexico

Professionally rather busy now.

"Si, Senor"

It is not absolutely necessary to speak Spanish when traveling in Mexico. I suggest taking a simple Spanish phrase book with you. For those who get lost remember "a" pronounced "ah" means "to." Point in the direction you want to go and say "ah" plus the name of the city or place. If you have pointed in the right direction, a friendly native will nod and say "Si, senor."

Auto Insurance While Traveling In Mexico

The Mexican government does not recognize American automobile insurance. Unless arrangements are made in advance, most American policies do not extend coverage beyond 50 miles from the border. There are several American insurance writers in the United States, also some with offices at the border, who represent Mexican companies. It's better to buy insurance coverage from a company licensed in Mexico. Be sure to carry comprehensive and collision as well as liability coverage. Don't declare a lower value than your car's worth! Estimate accurately!

On all trips take proof you own your car and an insurance policy. Also carry a valid driver's license and a Mexican tourist card. Don't go without them! Your insurance agent can help with most of these arrangements. Insurance is not compulsory; however, **it is a criminal offense in Mexico to have an accident**. Should this happen you will need all the help you can get.

Oil, Gas And Aid To Travelers

The entire oil industry in Mexico is controlled by the government. It is known as "Pemex." Check on the availability of unleaded fuel before you go. Speed limits and mileages on highway signs are shown in kilometers.

One mile is equal to 1.60 kilometers. If your speedometer indicates you are traveling **35 miles per hour,** this is equal to **56 kilometers per hour.** In another example when the speedometer reads 62.5 mph this is the same as 100 km/h. A town located 100 kilometers distance would be 62.5 miles away, etc.

Green-colored Tourist Aid trucks travel highways to assist tourists having car trouble. There is no charge except for parts.

Money And The Peso—A Duty Free Return

The peso is the basic unit of money used in Mexico. Don't expect to be able to cash personal checks. If you are going to need a large sum of money while you are in Mexico, plan for this in advance. Make out an international bank draft to a Mexican bank in the city of your choice. Take the draft with you and cash it at the bank when you arrive.

Residents of the United States returning from Mexico are permitted to bring back up to $300 worth of items duty free.

Travel In Canada

Carry Evidence Of Auto Insurance Coverage

Check with your insurance agent to make sure you are covered while traveling in Canada. Many American policies are not valid beyond a limit of 100 miles from the Canadian border. There is a card known as the "yellow card" you should have with you. It can be used to prove you carry adequate auto insurance coverage if the need arises. No lawsuits are allowed for bodily injuries caused by auto accidents in the province of Quebec. Most automobile policies have a clause automatically adapting your coverage to comply with the laws of the state (in the United States) or province (in Canada) in which you are traveling.

Automobile Travel In Europe

Credit Cards

Everywhere but in England gasoline is sold by the liter. In England the unit of measure is an "Imperial gallon" equal to 1.2 United States gallons. Although gasoline is sold by the same companies as in the United States, **don't count on using your American oil company credit card**. You can't.

Travel Long Distances At Nominal Cost

All of Europe is covered by a network we call auto-trains. These are used by people when they want the use of their car but don't want to drive long distances. The cars and their passengers are carried by special trains. You can cover long distances for a very low cost. Time, effort and gasoline are saved. This service is known as Motorail in Great Britain, Autoreisezuge in Germany and Treni per Auto Accompagnate in Italy.

You'll Need An International Driving Permit

Many European countries require an International Driving Permit for entry. This permit is written in nine different languages. It is available in the United States from any AAA office.

Automobile Rental Companies

Sir, does he know what game he is playing?

A Solution When It's Not Convenient To Phone

It's true. Most daily auto rental companies have offices in all large airports. Often you may need information as to availability and cost when it is not convenient to phone an airport. There is a solution to every problem—the only difficulty is finding it.

Phone The Company On Their Nickel

Here's a good one. When you need an automobile rental, this method is quick and efficient. Save money by simply phoning the rental company on their nickel over a toll free line. You'll get the same courteous service with less hassle.

Airways Rent-A-Car Systems, Inc.
800 648-5656
(Except Nevada)

Alfa Rent-A-Car
800 528-0535

American International Rent-A-Car
800 527-6346
(Except Texas)

Auto Europe
800 223-5740
NY & New England
800 223-5125

Avis Car Rental
800 331-1212
NY 800 632-1200
OK 800 482-4554

Brooks Rent-A-Car
800 634-6721
(Except Nevada)

Budget Rent-A-Car
800 228-9650
NE 800 642-9910

Dollar-A-Day Rent-A-Car
800 327-6362
(Eastern U.S. only)

Econo Car Rental
800 228-1000
FL 800 342-5628

Greyhound Rent-A-Car
800 327-2501
(Except Florida)

Hertz Car Rental
800 654-3131
OK 800 522-3711

National Car Rental
800 328-4567
(Except Minnesota)

Sears Rent-A-Car
6800 228-2800
(Except Nebraska)

Thrifty Rent-A-Car
800 331-4200
(Except Oklahoma)

Convenience! The name of the game.

National Weather Service

 *Good heavens! You didn't call?*

It Can Make Your Trip

All weather forecasters must start somewhere. One stayed up all night trying to figure out where the sun went down. Finally, it dawned on him. In spite of this, calling ahead for weather conditions can make your trip. Large cities often have a local weather information phone. However, in many towns weather service phones are not available. There is an answer to this. Here are the regional offices the National Weather Service. A call to the regional office of the area you'll be traveling in can make trip planning easier.

(Regional Offices)
States

Eastern
(CT, DE, ME, MD, MA, NH, NJ, NY, NC, OH, PA, RI, SC, VT, VA, WV)
PH: 516 222-2102

Southern
(AL, AR, FL, GA, LA, MS, NM, OK, TN, TX)
PH: 817 334-2660

Central

(CO, IL, IN, IA, KS, KY, MI, MN, MO, NE, ND, SD, WI, WY)

PH: 816 374-5464

Alaska

PH: 907 265-5701

Pacific

PH: 808 546-5680

Western

(AZ, CA, ID, MT, NV, OR, UT, WA)

PH: 801 524-5135

The Climate Month By Month
In 70 Selected Cities

How Travelers Anticipate Weather Conditions

Here are four pages of tables that can sure make your next trip more pleasant. Each table was taken directly from *The Statistical Abstract of the United States*. Don't be alarmed. They're not really difficult to read. I had fun with them and you will too. The four tables show the following facts for each month of the year:

A stroke of luck! Now we have a grip on the essential facts of this case.

Select a city and follow it through the four tables. You'll be able to estimate the weather for any month of the year in each of the 70 cities. With this knowledge you can plan a more pleasant trip!

Temperature Comparisons

Fahrenheit	Centigrade
0	-17.7
20	- 6.6
30	- 1.1
50	10.0
60	15.5
70	21.1
80	26.6
90	32.2
100	37.7

Looking for 80, but I'll accept 26.6!

The Four Tables Show:

1. Average percentage of sunshine each month
2. Normal monthly rainfall
3. Maximum daily temperature
4. Minimum daily temperature

Average Percentage Of Sunshine
Each Month

STATE AND STATION	Length of record (yr.)	Jan.	Feb.	Mar.	Apr.	May	June	July	Aug.	Sept.	Oct.	Nov.	Dec.	Annual
Ala._____ Montgomery [1]___	25	47	53	58	64	66	65	63	65	63	66	57	50	59
Alaska____ Juneau_____	32	32	32	37	38	39	33	31	32	26	20	23	20	31
Ariz._____ Phoenix_____	82	78	80	83	88	93	94	85	85	89	88	84	77	86
Ark._____ Little Rock_____	32	46	54	57	61	68	73	71	73	68	69	56	48	63
Calif._____ Los Angeles [1]_____	32	69	72	73	70	66	65	82	83	79	73	74	71	73
Sacramento_____	29	47	62	71	80	87	92	97	96	93	84	63	46	79
San Francisco [1]___	38	56	62	69	73	72	73	66	65	72	70	62	53	67
Colo_____ Denver_____	28	72	71	70	66	65	71	71	72	74	73	66	68	70
Conn._____ Hartford_____	23	58	57	57	57	58	58	62	63	59	58	46	48	57
Del._____ Wilmington [2]_____	25	50	54	57	57	59	64	63	61	60	60	54	51	53
D.C._____ Washington_____	29	49	52	56	58	59	64	63	63	62	59	52	47	58
Fla._____ Jacksonville_____	27	57	61	66	71	69	62	60	58	54	57	60	56	61
Key West [1]_____	17	72	76	81	84	80	71	75	76	69	68	72	74	75
Ga._____ Atlanta_____	42	48	54	57	66	68	67	62	65	63	67	59	50	61
Hawaii___ Honolulu_____	25	63	65	68	66	69	70	73	75	74	67	60	59	67
Idaho_____ Boise_____	36	41	52	63	68	72	75	88	85	82	67	45	40	67
Ill._____ Chicago [1]_____	33	44	47	51	53	61	67	70	68	63	62	41	38	57
Peoria_____	34	46	50	52	55	59	66	69	67	64	62	45	40	58
Ind._____ Indianapolis_____	34	42	51	52	56	62	67	70	71	66	64	43	40	58
Iowa_____ Des Moines_____	27	51	54	54	56	60	67	72	69	64	63	50	45	60
Kans._____ Wichita_____	24	60	61	61	62	65	70	74	74	65	66	60	58	65
Ky._____ Louisville_____	30	42	47	51	55	62	66	66	68	64	62	47	40	57
La._____ New Orleans_____	4	47	65	53	69	58	69	58	55	63	68	53	53	60
Maine_____ Portland_____	37	56	59	56	57	56	59	64	65	61	59	47	53	58
Md._____ Baltimore_____	27	52	55	55	56	57	62	65	62	60	59	51	48	57
Mass._____ Boston_____	42	54	56	57	57	59	63	66	67	63	61	51	52	60
Mich.____ Detroit_____	32	32	43	49	52	59	65	70	65	61	56	35	32	54
Sault Ste. Marie___	36	35	46	54	55	57	58	63	58	45	41	23	28	48
Minn._____ Duluth_____	27	49	54	55	54	56	58	67	62	52	48	34	39	54
Minneapolis-St. Paul_____	39	50	57	54	56	59	63	71	67	61	57	39	40	58
Miss._____ Jackson_____	13	49	57	59	62	62	69	62	62	58	64	53	47	59
Mo._____ Kansas City_____	5	62	61	65	72	74	76	82	68	57	64	53	59	67
St. Louis_____	18	54	53	56	57	62	68	72	65	63	63	49	43	59
Mont._____ Great Falls_____	35	48	57	67	62	64	65	80	77	68	61	46	45	63
Nebr._____ Omaha [1]_____	40	55	55	55	59	62	68	76	72	67	67	52	48	62
Nev._____ Reno_____	35	66	68	75	80	81	85	92	93	92	84	71	64	81
N.H._____ Concord_____	36	52	54	52	53	55	57	62	61	55	54	42	47	54
N.J._____ Atlantic City_____	17	50	51	53	55	55	58	60	63	58	56	49	43	55
N. Mex___ Albuquerque_____	38	73	73	74	76	80	83	76	76	80	79	78	72	77
N.Y._____ Albany_____	39	46	51	52	53	55	59	63	61	56	52	36	38	53
Buffalo_____	34	33	39	46	53	58	66	69	66	59	53	29	27	52
New York [3]_____	100	50	55	56	59	61	64	65	64	63	61	52	49	59
N.C._____ Charlotte_____	27	55	60	63	70	69	70	69	70	68	69	63	58	66
Raleigh_____	23	55	59	63	65	59	60	61	60	60	62	62	56	60
N. Dak.___ Bismarck_____	38	54	55	60	59	63	64	76	73	65	59	45	47	62
Ohio_____ Cincinnati [1]_____	60	41	45	51	55	61	67	68	67	66	59	44	38	57
Cleveland_____	34	32	37	44	53	59	65	68	64	60	55	31	26	52
Columbus_____	26	37	42	44	52	58	61	63	63	61	57	38	31	52
Okla._____ Oklahoma City___	23	59	61	63	63	65	73	75	77	69	68	60	59	67
Oreg._____ Portland_____	28	25	36	43	50	55	52	69	63	59	41	29	20	48
Pa._____ Philadelphia_____	35	51	54	56	57	57	62	63	63	59	59	52	49	58
Pittsburgh_____	25	35	39	46	49	53	58	60	59	59	54	39	30	50
R.I._____ Providence_____	24	57	56	55	56	57	57	60	59	58	59	49	51	56
S.C._____ Columbia_____	24	57	61	63	68	65	64	64	66	64	66	64	60	64
S. Dak.____ Rapid City [1]_____	33	54	59	61	59	57	60	71	73	67	65	56	54	62
Tenn._____ Memphis_____	27	49	55	57	64	70	74	73	76	69	71	58	50	65
Nashville_____	35	41	48	53	60	63	67	65	66	63	63	50	41	58
Tex._____ Amarillo [1]_____	34	69	68	71	73	73	77	77	78	74	75	73	67	73
El Paso_____	35	78	82	85	87	89	89	79	80	82	84	83	78	83
Houston_____	8	45	56	45	52	59	65	67	62	60	61	55	65	57
Utah_____ Salt Lake City____	40	48	56	64	67	73	79	84	83	84	73	54	45	70
Vt._____ Burlington_____	34	42	48	51	51	56	60	65	62	54	50	33	33	51
Va._____ Norfolk_____	19	57	58	63	66	67	68	65	65	64	60	60	57	63
Richmond_____	27	51	56	59	63	63	66	65	64	63	59	56	51	60
Wash.____ Seattle-Tacoma___	11	21	43	49	52	59	55	67	62	61	41	28	17	49
Spokane_____	29	26	40	53	60	63	65	80	77	70	51	29	20	57
W. Va.____ Parkersburg [1]_____	78	32	36	43	49	56	59	62	60	59	54	37	29	48
Wis._____ Milwaukee_____	37	45	47	51	54	59	64	71	67	60	60	41	38	56
Wyo._____ Cheyenne_____	42	61	65	65	60	58	64	68	67	69	68	60	59	64
P.R._____ San Juan_____	22	65	70	74	68	61	59	65	65	59	59	57	58	63

[1] For period of record through 1975
[2] Data not available; figures are for a nearby station.
[3] City office data.

Source: U.S. National Oceanic and Atmospheric Administration, *Comparative Climatic Data,* annual.

Normal Monthly Rainfall
70 Selected Cities

STATE AND STATION	Jan.	Feb.	Mar.	Apr.	May	June	July	Aug.	Sept.	Oct.	Nov.	Dec.	Annual
Ala.____ Mobile____	4.71	4.76	7.07	5.59	4.52	6.09	8.86	6.93	6.59	2.55	3.39	5.92	66.98
Alaska__ Juneau____	3.94	3.44	3.57	2.99	3.31	2.93	4.69	5.00	6.90	7.85	5.53	4.52	54.67
Ariz.___ Phoenix____	.71	.60	.76	.32	.14	.12	.75	1.22	.69	.46	.46	.82	7.05
Ark.____ Little Rock____	4.24	4.42	4.93	5.25	5.30	3.50	3.38	3.01	3.55	2.99	3.86	4.09	48.52
Calif.___ Los Angeles____	2.52	2.32	1.71	1.10	.08	.03	.01	.02	.07	.22	1.76	2.39	12.23
Sacramento____	3.73	2.68	2.17	1.54	.51	.10	.01	.05	.19	.99	2.13	3.12	17.22
San Francisco__	4.37	3.04	2.54	1.59	.41	.13	.01	.03	.16	.98	2.29	3.98	19.53
Colo.___ Denver____	.61	.67	1.21	1.93	2.64	1.93	1.78	1.29	1.13	1.13	.76	.43	15.51
Conn.___ Hartford____	3.28	3.17	3.82	3.75	3.50	3.53	3.41	3.94	3.55	3.03	4.33	4.06	43.37
Del.____ Wilmington____	2.85	2.75	3.74	3.20	3.35	3.24	4.31	3.98	3.42	2.60	3.49	3.32	40.25
D.C.____ Washington____	2.62	2.45	3.33	2.86	3.68	3.48	4.12	4.67	3.08	2.66	2.90	3.04	38.89
Fla.____ Jacksonville____	2.78	3.58	3.56	3.07	3.22	6.27	7.35	7.89	7.83	4.54	1.79	2.59	54.47
Miami____	2.15	1.95	2.07	3.60	6.12	9.00	6.91	6.72	8.74	8.18	2.72	1.64	59.80
Ga.____ Atlanta____	4.34	4.41	5.84	4.61	3.71	3.67	4.90	3.54	3.15	2.50	3.43	4.24	48.34
Hawaii _ Honolulu____	4.40	2.46	3.18	1.36	.96	.32	.60	.76	.67	1.51	2.99	3.69	22.90
Idaho__ Boise____	1.47	1.16	1.01	1.14	1.32	1.06	.15	.30	.41	.80	1.32	1.36	11.50
Ill.____ Chicago____	1.70	1.30	2.52	3.38	3.41	4.15	3.46	2.73	3.01	2.32	2.10	1.64	31.72
Peoria____	1.82	1.50	2.80	4.36	3.87	3.91	3.76	3.07	3.55	2.51	2.02	1.89	35.06
Ind.___ Indianapolis ___	2.86	2.36	3.75	3.87	4.08	4.16	3.67	2.80	2.87	2.51	3.10	2.71	38.74
Iowa__ Des Moines____	1.14	1.05	2.31	2.94	4.21	4.90	3.28	3.30	3.07	2.14	1.42	1.09	30.85
Kans.__ Wichita____	.85	.98	1.78	2.95	3.60	4.49	4.35	3.10	3.69	2.50	1.17	1.12	30.58
Ky.____ Louisville____	3.53	3.47	5.05	4.10	4.20	4.05	3.76	2.99	2.94	2.35	3.33	3.34	43.11
La.____ New Orleans___	4.53	4.82	5.49	4.15	4.20	4.74	6.72	5.27	5.58	2.26	3.88	5.13	56.77
Maine__ Portland____	3.38	3.52	3.60	3.34	3.33	3.10	2.61	2.60	3.09	3.31	4.86	4.06	40.80
Md.____ Baltimore____	2.91	2.81	3.69	3.07	3.61	3.77	4.07	4.21	3.12	2.81	3.13	3.26	40.46
Mass.__ Boston____	3.69	3.54	4.01	3.49	3.47	3.19	2.74	3.46	3.16	3.02	4.51	4.24	42.52
Mich.__ Detroit____	1.93	1.80	2.33	3.08	3.43	3.04	2.99	3.04	2.30	2.52	2.31	2.19	30.96
Sault Ste. Marie____	1.92	1.48	1.74	2.22	3.01	3.31	2.60	3.10	3.85	2.85	3.26	2.36	31.70
Minn.__ Duluth____	1.16	.85	1.76	2.55	3.41	4.44	3.73	3.79	3.06	2.30	1.73	1.40	30.18
Minneapolis-St. Paul____	.73	.84	1.68	2.04	3.37	3.94	3.69	3.05	2.73	1.78	1.20	.89	25.94
Miss.___ Jackson____	4.53	4.62	5.63	4.65	4.38	3.40	4.27	3.59	2.99	2.22	3.87	5.04	49.19
Mo.____ Kansas City____	1.25	1.25	2.55	3.50	4.28	5.55	4.37	3.81	4.21	3.24	1.47	1.52	37.00
St. Louis____	1.85	2.06	3.03	3.92	3.86	4.42	3.69	2.87	2.89	2.79	2.47	2.04	35.89
Mont.__ Great Falls____	.88	.75	.97	1.18	2.37	3.11	1.27	1.09	1.17	.68	.81	.71	14.99
Nebr.__ Omaha____	.76	.98	1.59	2.97	4.11	4.94	3.71	3.97	3.27	1.93	1.11	.84	30.18
Nev.___ Reno____	1.21	.86	.70	.47	.66	.40	.26	.22	.23	.42	.68	1.09	7.20
N.H.___ Concord____	2.67	2.45	2.77	2.92	3.02	3.35	3.14	2.89	3.06	2.68	3.96	3.26	36.17
N.J.____ Atlantic City__	3.56	3.37	4.31	3.37	3.54	3.38	4.36	4.90	2.99	3.46	4.21	4.01	45.46
N. Mex. Albuquerque___	.30	.39	.47	.48	.53	.50	1.39	1.34	.77	.79	.29	.52	7.77
N.Y.___ Albany____	2.20	2.11	2.58	2.70	3.26	3.00	3.12	2.87	3.12	2.63	2.84	2.93	33.36
Buffalo____	2.90	2.55	2.85	3.15	2.97	2.23	2.93	3.53	3.25	3.01	3.74	3.00	36.11
New York [1]____	2.71	2.92	3.73	3.30	·3.47	2.96	3.68	4.01	3.27	2.85	3.76	3.53	40.19
N.C.___ Charlotte____	3.51	3.83	4.52	3.40	2.90	3.70	4.57	3.96	3.46	2.69	2.74	3.44	42.72
Raleigh____	3.22	3.32	3.44	3.07	3.32	3.67	5.08	4.93	3.78	2.81	2.82	3.08	42.54
N. Dak. Bismarck____	.51	.44	.73	1.44	2.17	3.58	2.20	1.96	1.32	.80	.56	.45	16.16
Ohio___ Cincinnati____	3.34	3.04	4.09	3.64	3.74	3.81	4.12	2.62	2.55	2.15	3.08	2.86	39.04
Cleveland____	2.56	2.18	3.05	3.49	3.49	3.28	3.45	3.00	2.80	2.57	2.76	2.36	34.99
Columbus____	2.87	2.32	3.44	3.71	4.10	4.13	4.21	2.86	2.41	1.89	2.68	2.39	37.01
Okla.__ Oklahoma City_	1.11	1.32	2.05	3.47	5.20	4.22	2.66	2.56	3.55	2.57	1.40	1.26	31.37
Oreg.__ Portland____	5.88	4.06	3.64	2.22	2.09	1.59	.47	.82	1.60	3.59	5.61	6.04	37.61
Pa.____ Philadelphia__	2.81	2.62	3.69	3.29	3.35	3.70	4.09	4.11	3.03	2.53	3.39	3.32	39.93
Pittsburgh____	2.79	2.35	3.60	3.40	3.63	3.48	3.84	3.15	2.52	2.52	2.47	2.48	36.23
R.I.____ Providence____	3.52	3.45	3.99	3.72	3.49	2.65	2.85	3.90	3.26	3.27	4.52	4.13	42.75
S.C.___ Columbia____	3.44	3.67	4.67	3.51	3.35	3.82	5.65	5.63	4.32	2.58	2.34	3.38	46.36
S. Dak. Sioux Falls____	.57	1.04	1.40	2.30	3.37	4.32	2.94	2.84	2.85	1.50	.85	.74	24.72
Tenn.__ Memphis____	4.93	4.73	5.10	5.42	4.39	3.46	3.53	3.33	3.01	2.58	3.92	4.70	49.10
Nashville____	4.75	4.43	5.00	4.11	4.10	3.38	3.83	3.24	3.09	2.16	3.46	4.45	46.00
Tex.____ Dallas-Fort Worth____	1.80	2.36	2.54	4.30	4.47	3.05	1.84	2.26	3.15	2.68	2.03	1.82	32.30
El Paso____	.39	.42	.39	.24	.32	.60	1.53	1.12	1.16	.78	.32	.50	7.77
Houston____	3.57	3.54	2.68	3.54	5.10	4.52	4.12	4.35	4.65	4.05	4.03	4.04	48.19
Utah___ Salt Lake City_	1.27	1.19	1.63	2.12	1.49	1.30	.70	.93	.68	1.16	1.31	1.39	15.17
Vt.____ Burlington____	1.74	1.68	1.93	2.62	3.01	3.46	3.54	3.72	3.05	2.74	2.86	2.19	32.54
Va.____ Norfolk____	3.35	3.31	3.42	2.71	3.34	3.62	5.70	5.92	4.20	3.06	2.94	3.11	44.68
Richmond____	2.86	3.01	3.38	2.77	3.42	3.52	5.63	5.06	3.58	2.94	3.20	3.22	42.59
Wash.__ Seattle-Tacoma_	5.79	4.19	3.61	2.46	1.70	1.53	.71	1.08	1.99	3.91	5.88	5.94	38.79
Spokane____	2.47	1.68	1.53	1.12	1.46	1.36	.40	.58	.83	1.42	2.20	2.37	17.42
W. Va._ Charleston____	3.39	3.11	4.03	3.33	3.48	3.31	5.04	3.68	2.94	2.45	2.81	3.18	40.75
Wis.___ Milwaukee____	1.63	1.13	2.24	2.76	2.88	3.58	3.41	2.68	3.02	1.98	2.01	1.75	29.07
Wyo.__ Cheyenne____	.46	.46	1.05	1.57	2.52	2.41	1.82	1.45	1.03	.95	.58	.35	14.65
P.R.____ San Juan____	3.73	2.50	2.04	3.40	6.54	5.64	6.41	6.98	6.07	5.64	5.49	4.71	59.15

[1] City office data.

Source: U.S. National Oceanic and Atmospheric Administration, *Climatography of the United States*, No. 81.

Daily Maximum Temperature
70 Selected Cities

STATE AND STATION	Jan.	Feb.	Mar.	Apr.	May	June	July	Aug.	Sept.	Oct.	Nov.	Dec.	Annual avg.
Ala____ Mobile_____	61.1	64.1	69.5	78.0	85.0	89.8	90.5	90.6	86.5	79.7	69.5	63.0	77.3
Alaska__ Juneau_____	29.1	33.9	38.2	46.5	55.4	62.0	63.6	62.3	56.1	47.2	37.3	32.0	47.0
Ariz____ Phoenix_____	64.8	69.3	74.5	83.6	92.9	101.5	104.8	102.2	98.4	87.6	74.7	66.4	85.1
Ark_____ Little Rock_____	50.1	53.8	61.8	73.5	81.4	89.3	92.6	92.6	85.8	76.0	62.4	52.1	72.6
Calif___ Los Angeles_____	63.5	64.1	64.3	65.9	68.4	70.3	74.8	75.8	75.7	72.9	69.6	66.5	69.2
Sacramento_____	53.0	59.1	64.1	71.3	78.8	86.4	92.9	91.3	87.7	77.1	63.6	53.3	73.2
San Francisco___	55.3	58.6	61.0	63.5	66.6	70.2	70.9	71.6	73.6	70.3	63.3	56.5	65.1
Colo____ Denver_____	43.5	46.2	50.1	61.0	70.3	80.1	87.4	85.8	77.7	66.8	53.3	46.2	64.0
Conn____ Hartford_____	33.4	35.7	44.6	58.9	70.3	79.5	84.1	81.9	74.5	64.3	50.6	36.8	59.6
Del_____ Wilmington_____	40.2	42.2	51.1	63.0	73.1	81.6	85.5	83.9	78.2	67.8	55.2	43.0	63.7
D.C.____ Washington_____	43.5	46.0	55.0	67.1	76.6	84.6	88.2	86.6	80.2	69.8	57.2	45.2	66.7
Fla_____ Jacksonville_____	64.6	66.9	72.2	79.0	84.6	88.3	90.0	89.7	86.0	79.2	71.4	65.6	78.1
Miami_____	75.6	76.6	79.5	82.7	85.3	88.0	89.1	89.9	88.3	84.6	79.9	76.6	83.0
Ga_____ Atlanta_____	51.4	54.5	61.1	71.4	79.0	84.6	86.5	86.4	81.2	72.5	61.9	52.7	70.3
Hawaii__ Honolulu_____	79.3	79.2	79.7	81.4	83.6	85.6	86.8	87.4	87.4	85.8	83.2	80.3	83.3
Idaho___ Boise_____	36.5	43.8	51.6	61.4	70.6	78.3	90.5	87.6	77.6	64.7	48.9	39.1	62.6
Ill_____ Chicago_____	31.1	34.3	44.6	59.4	69.7	79.1	83.1	82.3	75.4	65.5	48.3	35.0	59.0
Peoria_____	31.9	36.0	46.5	61.7	72.3	81.7	85.5	84.0	76.4	65.9	48.7	35.7	60.5
Ind_____ Indianapolis_____	36.0	39.3	49.0	62.8	72.9	82.3	85.4	84.0	75.4	65.5	48.3	38.7	62.2
Iowa____ Des Moines_____	27.5	32.5	42.5	59.7	70.9	79.8	84.9	83.2	74.6	64.9	46.4	32.8	58.3
Kans____ Wichita_____	41.4	47.1	55.0	68.1	77.1	86.5	91.7	91.0	81.9	71.3	55.8	44.3	67.6
Ky_____ Louisville_____	42.0	45.0	54.0	66.9	75.6	83.7	87.3	86.8	80.5	70.3	54.9	44.1	65.9
La_____ New Orleans____	62.3	65.1	70.4	78.4	84.9	89.6	90.4	90.6	86.6	79.9	70.3	64.2	77.7
Maine__ Portland_____	31.2	33.3	40.8	52.8	63.6	73.2	79.1	77.6	69.9	60.2	47.5	34.9	55.3
Md_____ Baltimore_____	41.9	43.9	53.0	65.2	74.8	83.2	86.7	85.1	79.0	68.3	56.1	43.9	65.1
Mass___ Boston_____	35.9	37.5	44.6	56.3	67.1	76.6	81.4	79.3	72.2	63.2	51.7	39.3	58.7
Mich___ Detroit_____	31.7	33.7	43.1	57.6	68.5	79.1	83.1	81.6	74.2	63.4	47.7	35.4	58.3
Sault Ste. Marie_	22.0	23.7	32.5	47.2	59.4	70.0	75.1	73.4	64.5	54.8	39.0	26.8	49.0
Minn___ Duluth_____	17.6	22.1	32.6	47.8	60.0	69.7	76.4	74.4	64.0	54.3	35.3	22.5	48.1
Minneapolis-St. Paul_	21.2	25.9	36.9	55.5	67.9	77.1	82.4	80.8	70.7	60.7	40.6	26.6	53.8
Miss___ Jackson_____	58.4	61.7	68.7	78.2	85.0	91.0	92.7	92.6	88.0	80.1	68.5	60.5	77.1
Mo_____ Kansas City____	36.2	41.9	50.5	64.8	74.3	82.6	88.0	86.7	78.8	68.9	52.7	40.4	63.7
St. Louis_____	39.9	44.2	53.0	67.0	76.0	84.9	88.4	87.2	80.1	69.8	54.1	42.7	65.6
Mont___ Great Falls_____	29.3	35.9	40.4	54.5	65.0	72.1	83.7	81.8	70.0	59.4	43.4	34.7	55.9
Nebr___ Omaha_____	32.7	38.5	47.7	64.4	74.4	83.1	88.6	87.2	78.6	69.1	50.9	37.8	62.8
Nev_____ Reno_____	45.4	51.1	56.0	64.0	72.2	80.4	91.1	89.0	81.8	70.0	56.3	46.4	67.0
N.H.____ Concord_____	31.3	33.8	42.4	56.7	68.6	77.7	82.6	80.1	72.4	62.3	47.9	34.6	57.5
N.J.____ Atlantic City___	41.4	42.9	50.7	62.3	72.4	80.8	84.7	83.0	77.3	67.5	55.9	44.2	63.6
N. Mex. Albuquerque____	46.9	52.6	59.2	70.1	79.9	89.5	92.2	89.7	83.4	71.7	57.1	47.5	70.0
N.Y.____ Albany_____	30.4	32.7	42.6	58.0	69.7	79.4	83.9	81.4	73.7	62.8	48.1	34.1	58.1
Buffalo_____	29.8	31.0	39.0	53.3	64.3	75.1	79.5	77.6	70.8	60.2	46.1	33.6	55.0
New York [1]____	38.5	40.2	48.4	60.7	71.4	80.5	85.2	83.4	76.8	66.8	54.0	41.4	62.3
N.C.____ Charlotte_____	52.1	54.9	62.2	72.7	80.2	86.4	88.3	87.4	82.0	73.1	62.4	52.5	71.2
Raleigh_____	51.0	53.2	61.0	72.2	79.4	85.6	87.7	86.8	81.5	72.4	62.1	51.9	70.4
N. Dak. Bismarck_____	19.1	24.5	35.4	54.8	67.1	75.8	84.3	83.5	71.3	60.3	39.4	26.0	53.5
Ohio____ Cincinnati_____	39.7	42.7	51.8	65.0	74.4	83.2	86.5	85.8	79.7	68.5	53.2	42.0	64.4
Cleveland_____	33.4	35.0	44.1	58.0	68.4	78.2	81.6	80.4	74.2	63.6	48.8	36.4	58.5
Columbus_____	36.4	39.2	49.3	62.8	72.9	81.9	84.8	83.7	77.6	66.4	50.9	38.7	62.1
Okla____ Oklahoma City_	47.6	52.6	59.8	71.6	78.7	87.0	92.6	92.3	84.7	74.2	60.9	50.7	71.1
Oreg____ Portland_____	43.6	50.1	54.3	60.3	67.0	72.1	79.0	78.1	73.9	62.9	52.1	46.0	61.6
Pa_____ Philadelphia____	40.1	42.2	51.2	63.5	74.1	83.0	86.8	84.8	78.4	67.9	55.5	43.2	64.2
Pittsburgh_____	35.3	37.3	47.2	60.3	70.9	79.5	82.5	80.9	74.9	63.9	49.3	37.3	60.0
R.I.____ Providence_____	36.2	37.6	44.7	56.7	66.8	76.3	81.1	79.8	73.1	63.9	52.0	39.6	59.0
S.C.____ Columbia_____	56.9	59.7	66.5	76.9	84.5	90.3	92.0	91.0	85.4	77.1	66.9	57.9	75.4
S. Dak. Sioux Falls_____	24.6	29.7	39.7	57.8	69.7	78.9	85.1	83.8	73.0	62.7	43.5	29.6	56.5
Tenn___ Memphis_____	49.4	53.1	60.8	72.7	81.2	88.7	91.6	90.6	84.3	74.9	61.5	51.7	71.7
Nashville_____	47.6	50.9	59.2	72.1	79.8	87.5	90.2	89.2	83.5	73.2	59.0	49.6	70.1
Tex____ Dallas-Fort Worth_	55.7	59.8	66.6	76.3	82.8	90.8	95.5	96.1	88.5	79.2	67.5	58.7	76.5
El Paso_____	57.0	62.5	68.9	78.5	87.2	94.9	94.6	92.8	87.4	78.5	66.1	57.8	77.2
Houston_____	62.6	66.0	71.8	79.4	85.9	91.3	93.8	94.3	89.1	83.5	73.0	65.8	79.8
Utah___ Salt Lake City___	37.4	43.4	50.8	61.8	72.4	81.3	92.8	90.2	80.3	66.4	50.0	39.0	63.8
Vt_____ Burlington_____	25.9	28.2	38.0	53.3	66.1	76.5	81.0	78.3	70.0	58.7	44.3	30.3	54.2
Va_____ Norfolk_____	48.8	50.0	57.3	67.7	76.2	83.5	86.6	84.9	79.6	70.1	60.5	50.6	68.0
Richmond_____	47.4	49.9	58.2	70.3	78.4	85.4	88.2	86.6	80.9	71.2	60.6	49.1	68.8
Wash___ Seattle-Tacoma__	43.4	48.5	51.5	57.0	64.1	69.0	75.1	73.8	68.7	59.4	50.4	45.4	58.8
Spokane_____	31.1	39.0	46.2	57.0	66.5	73.6	84.3	81.9	72.5	58.1	41.8	33.9	57.2
W.Va.__ Charleston_____	43.6	46.2	55.2	67.9	76.6	83.4	85.6	84.4	79.0	69.1	55.8	45.2	66.0
Wis_____ Milwaukee_____	27.3	30.3	39.4	54.6	65.0	75.3	80.4	79.7	71.5	61.4	44.4	31.5	55.1
Wyo____ Cheyenne_____	38.2	40.7	43.5	55.4	65.1	74.4	83.7	81.9	72.8	61.8	47.5	40.3	58.8
P.R.____ San Juan_____	81.9	82.1	83.6	84.4	85.6	87.0	87.0	87.5	87.6	87.4	85.0	83.1	85.2

[1] City office data.

Source: U.S. National Oceanic and Atmospheric Administration, *Climatography of the United States*, No. 81.

Daily Minimum Temperature
70 Selected Cities

STATE AND STATION	Jan.	Feb.	Mar.	Apr.	May	June	July	Aug.	Sept.	Oct.	Nov.	Dec.	Annual avg.
Ala_____ Mobile _____	41.3	43.9	49.2	57.7	64.5	70.7	72.6	72.3	68.4	58.0	47.5	42.8	57.4
Alaska_ Juneau _____	17.8	22.1	25.6	31.3	38.2	44.4	47.7	46.2	42.3	36.4	27.6	22.5	33.5
Ariz____ Phoenix_____	37.6	40.8	44.8	51.8	59.6	67.7	77.5	76.0	69.1	56.8	44.8	38.5	55.4
Ark_____ Little Rock_____	28.9	31.9	38.7	49.9	58.1	66.8	70.1	68.6	60.8	48.7	38.1	31.1	49.3
Calif___ Los Angeles_____	45.4	47.0	48.6	51.7	55.3	58.6	62.1	63.2	61.6	57.5	51.3	47.3	54.1
Sacramento_____	37.1	40.4	41.9	45.3	49.8	54.6	57.5	56.9	55.3	49.5	42.4	38.3	47.4
San Francisco___	41.2	43.8	44.9	47.0	49.9	53.0	54.0	54.3	54.5	51.6	47.2	42.9	48.7
Colo___ Denver_____	16.2	19.4	23.8	33.9	43.6	51.9	58.6	57.4	47.8	37.2	25.4	18.9	36.2
Conn___ Hartford_____	16.1	17.9	26.6	36.5	46.2	56.0	61.2	58.9	51.0	40.8	31.9	19.6	38.6
Del____ Wilmington_____	23.8	24.9	32.0	41.5	51.6	61.1	66.1	64.3	57.6	46.5	36.2	26.3	44.3
D.C____ Washington_____	27.7	28.6	35.2	45.7	55.7	64.6	69.1	67.6	61.0	49.7	38.8	29.5	47.8
Fla_____ Jacksonville_____	44.5	45.7	50.1	57.1	63.9	70.0	72.0	72.3	70.4	61.7	51.0	45.1	58.7
Miami_____	58.7	59.0	63.0	67.3	70.7	73.9	75.5	75.8	75.0	71.0	64.5	60.0	67.9
Ga_____ Atlanta_____	33.4	35.5	41.1	50.7	59.2	66.6	69.4	68.6	63.4	52.3	40.8	34.3	51.3
Hawaii_ Honolulu_____	65.3	65.3	66.3	68.1	70.2	72.2	73.4	74.0	73.4	72.0	69.8	67.1	69.8
Idaho___ Boise_____	21.4	27.2	30.5	36.5	44.1	51.2	58.5	56.7	48.5	39.4	30.7	25.0	39.1
Ill_____ Chicago _____	14.7	17.8	26.7	38.2	47.0	57.0	60.7	59.9	52.0	42.0	30.1	19.2	38.8
Peoria_____	15.7	19.3	28.1	40.8	50.7	60.9	64.6	62.9	54.6	44.0	31.1	20.3	41.1
Ind_____ Indianapolis____	19.7	22.1	30.3	41.8	51.5	61.1	64.6	62.4	54.9	44.3	32.8	23.1	42.4
Iowa___ Des Moines_____	11.3	15.8	25.2	39.2	50.9	61.1	65.3	63.4	54.0	43.6	29.2	17.2	39.7
Kans___ Wichita_____	21.2	25.4	32.1	45.1	55.0	65.0	69.6	68.3	59.2	47.9	33.8	24.6	45.6
Ky_____ Louisville_____	24.5	26.5	34.0	44.8	53.9	62.9	66.4	64.9	57.7	45.9	35.1	27.1	45.3
La_____ New Orleans____	43.5	46.0	50.9	58.8	65.3	71.2	73.3	73.1	69.7	59.6	49.8	45.3	58.9
Maine__ Portland_____	11.7	12.5	22.8	32.5	41.7	51.1	56.9	55.2	47.4	38.0	29.7	16.4	34.7
Md_____ Baltimore_____	24.9	25.7	32.5	42.4	52.5	61.6	66.5	64.7	57.9	46.4	36.0	26.6	44.8
Mass___ Boston_____	22.5	23.3	31.5	40.8	50.1	59.3	65.1	63.3	56.7	47.5	38.7	26.6	43.8
Mich___ Detroit_____	19.2	20.1	27.6	38.6	48.3	59.1	63.4	62.1	54.8	45.2	34.4	23.8	41.4
Sault Ste. Marie_	6.4	6.7	15.5	29.2	38.5	47.3	52.5	52.9	46.1	37.6	26.5	13.3	31.0
Minn___ Duluth_____	-.6	2.0	14.4	29.3	38.8	48.3	54.7	53.7	44.8	36.2	21.4	6.3	29.1
Minneapolis- St. Paul_____	3.2	7.1	19.6	34.7	46.3	56.7	61.4	59.6	49.3	39.2	24.2	10.6	34.3
Miss____ Jackson_____	35.8	37.8	43.4	53.1	60.4	67.7	70.6	69.8	64.0	51.5	42.0	37.3	52.8
Mo_____ Kansas City____	19.3	24.2	31.8	45.1	55.7	65.2	69.6	68.1	58.8	48.3	34.5	24.1	45.3
St. Louis_____	22.6	26.0	33.5	46.0	55.5	64.8	68.8	67.1	59.1	48.4	35.9	26.5	46.2
Mont___ Great Falls_____	11.6	17.2	20.6	32.3	41.5	49.5	54.9	53.0	44.6	37.1	25.7	18.2	33.8
Nebr___ Omaha_____	12.4	17.4	26.4	40.1	51.5	61.3	65.8	64.0	54.0	42.6	29.1	18.1	40.2
Nev____ Reno_____	18.3	23.0	24.6	29.6	37.0	42.5	47.4	44.8	38.6	30.5	23.9	19.6	31.7
N.H____ Concord_____	9.9	11.3	22.1	31.7	41.5	51.6	56.7	54.2	46.5	36.3	28.1	14.9	33.7
N.J_____ Atlantic City___	24.0	24.9	31.5	41.0	50.7	59.7	65.4	63.8	56.8	45.9	36.1	26.0	43.8
N. Mex. Albuquerque____	23.5	27.4	32.3	41.4	50.7	59.7	65.2	63.4	56.7	44.7	31.8	24.9	43.5
N.Y____ Albany_____	12.5	14.3	24.2	35.7	45.7	55.6	60.1	57.8	50.1	40.0	31.1	17.7	37.1
Buffalo_____	17.6	17.7	25.2	36.4	45.9	56.3	60.7	59.1	52.3	43.7	33.5	22.2	39.1
New York [1]___	25.9	26.5	33.7	43.5	53.1	62.6	68.0	66.4	59.9	50.6	40.8	29.5	46.7
N.C____ Charlotte_____	32.1	33.1	39.0	48.9	57.4	65.3	68.7	67.9	61.9	50.3	39.6	32.4	49.7
Raleigh_____	30.0	31.1	37.4	46.7	55.4	63.1	67.2	66.2	59.7	48.0	37.8	30.5	47.8
N. Dak_ Bismarck_____	-2.8	2.4	14.7	31.1	41.7	51.8	57.3	54.9	43.7	33.2	18.3	5.2	29.3
Ohio____ Cincinnati_____	22.4	23.8	31.6	42.7	51.9	61.0	64.6	63.0	55.9	45.0	34.3	25.3	43.5
Cleveland_____	20.3	20.8	28.1	38.5	48.1	57.5	61.2	59.6	53.5	43.9	34.4	24.1	40.8
Columbus_____	20.4	21.4	29.1	39.5	49.3	58.9	62.4	60.1	52.7	42.0	32.4	22.7	40.9
Okla___ Oklahoma City__	26.0	30.0	36.5	49.1	57.9	66.6	70.4	69.6	61.3	50.6	37.4	29.2	48.7
Oreg___ Portland_____	32.5	35.5	37.0	40.8	46.3	51.8	55.2	55.0	50.5	44.7	38.5	35.3	43.6
Pa_____ Philadelphia____	24.4	25.5	32.5	42.3	52.3	61.6	66.7	64.7	57.8	46.9	36.9	27.2	44.9
Pittsburgh_____	20.8	21.3	29.0	39.4	48.7	57.7	61.3	59.4	52.7	42.4	33.3	23.6	40.8
R.I_____ Providence_____	20.6	21.2	29.0	37.8	46.9	56.5	63.0	61.0	53.6	43.4	34.6	23.4	40.9
S.C_____ Columbia_____	33.9	35.5	41.9	51.3	59.6	67.2	70.3	69.4	63.5	51.3	40.6	34.1	51.5
S. Dak_ Sioux Falls_____	3.7	9.0	20.2	34.4	45.7	56.3	61.5	59.8	48.7	37.6	22.7	10.4	34.2
Tenn___ Memphis_____	31.6	34.4	41.1	52.3	60.6	68.5	71.5	70.1	62.8	51.1	40.3	33.7	51.5
Nashville_____	29.0	31.0	38.1	48.8	57.3	65.7	69.0	67.7	60.5	48.6	37.7	31.1	48.7
Tex_____ Dallas-Fort Worth_____	33.9	37.6	43.3	54.1	62.1	70.3	74.0	73.7	66.8	56.0	44.1	37.0	54.4
El Paso_____	30.2	34.3	40.3	49.3	57.2	65.7	69.9	68.2	61.0	49.5	37.0	30.9	49.5
Houston_____	41.5	44.6	49.8	59.3	65.6	70.9	72.8	72.4	68.2	58.3	49.1	43.4	58.0
Utah___ Salt Lake City__	18.5	23.3	28.3	36.6	44.2	51.1	60.5	58.7	49.3	38.4	28.1	21.5	38.2
Vt_____ Burlington_____	7.6	8.9	20.1	32.6	43.5	53.9	58.5	56.4	48.6	38.8	29.7	14.8	34.5
Va_____ Norfolk_____	32.2	32.7	38.9	47.9	57.2	65.5	69.9	68.9	63.9	53.3	42.6	34.0	50.6
Richmond_____	27.6	28.8	35.5	45.2	54.5	62.9	67.5	65.9	59.0	47.4	37.3	28.8	46.7
Wash___ Seattle-Tacoma__	33.0	36.0	36.6	40.3	45.6	50.6	53.8	53.7	50.4	44.9	38.8	35.5	43.3
Spokane_____	19.6	25.3	28.8	35.2	42.8	49.4	55.1	54.0	46.7	37.5	29.2	24.0	37.3
W. Va__ Charleston_____	25.3	26.8	33.8	43.8	52.3	60.6	64.3	62.8	55.9	44.8	35.0	27.2	44.4
Wis_____ Milwaukee_____	11.4	14.6	23.4	34.7	43.3	53.6	59.3	58.7	50.7	40.6	28.5	16.8	36.3
Wyo____ Cheyenne_____	14.9	17.3	19.6	30.0	39.7	48.1	54.5	53.2	43.5	33.9	23.5	18.1	33.0
P.R_____ San Juan_____	68.8	68.4	68.9	70.6	72.8	74.0	74.8	75.1	74.6	73.7	72.3	70.5	72.0

[1] City office data.

Source: U.S. National Oceanic and Atmospheric Administration, *Climatography of the United States*, No. 81.

United States
Mileage Charts

 Be kind enough to tell me how far to Nottingham? Well how about Omaha?

	Atlanta, Ga.	Boston, Mass.	Cheyenne, Wyo.	Chicago, Ill.	Cincinnati, Ohio	Cleveland, Ohio	Dallas, Texas	Denver, Colo.	Des Moines, Iowa	Detroit, Mich.	Houston, Texas	Indianapolis, Ind.	Kansas City, Mo.	Los Angeles, Calif.	Louisville, Ky.	Memphis, Tenn.
Albuquerque, N Mex.	1381	2172	517	1281	1372	1560	638	417	977	1525	834	1266	782	807	1301	1010
Amarillo, Texas	1097	1897	511	1043	1096	1285	358	423	742	1269	596	991	547	1091	1019	726
Atlanta, Ga.		1037	1442	674	440	672	795	1398	870	699	789	493	798	2182	382	371
Austin, Texas	919	1911	994	1110	1083	1327	193	906	877	1315	164	1037	682	1374	982	615
Baltimore, Md.	645	392	1608	668	497	343	1356	1621	981	503	1412	563	1048	2636	598	904
Birmingham, Ala.	150	1165	1347	642	465	709	645	1286	787	724	639	475	697	2032	364	246
Bismarck, N. Dak.	1495	1794	572	831	1118	1166	1141	671	670	1097	1384	1012	777	1617	1123	1228
Boise Idaho	2174	2639	732	1683	1906	2011	1582	811	1359	1942	1778	1800	1382	849	1893	1832
Boston, Mass.	1037		1907	963	840	628	1748	1949	1280	695	1804	906	1391	2779	941	1296
Buffalo, N. Y.	859	446	1466	522	431	187	1346	1508	839	253	1460	481	966	2554	532	899
Charleston, S. Car.	289	929	1722	877	603	730	1072	1678	1150	842	1054	696	1078	2459	591	660
Cheyenne, Wyo.	1442	1907		954	1174	1279	869	100	627	1211	1107	1068	650	1137	1161	1101
Chicago, Ill.	674	963	954		287	335	917	996	327	266	1067	181	499	2054	292	530
Cincinnati, Ohio	440	840	1174	287		244	920	1164	571	259	1029	106	591	2179	101	468
Cleveland, Ohio	672	628	1279	335	244		1169	1321	652	170	1273	294	779	2367	345	712
Columbus, Ohio	533	735	1235	308	108	139	1028	1229	618	192	1137	171	656	2244	209	576
Dallas, Texas	795	1748	869	917	920	1159		781	684	1143	243	865	489	1387	819	452
Denver, Colo.	1398	1949	100	996	1164	1321	781		669	1253	1019	1058	600	1059	1120	1040
Des Moines, Iowa	870	1280	627	327	571	652	684	669		584	905	465	195	1727	566	599
Detroit, Mich.	699	695	1211	266	259	170	1143	1253	584		1265	278	743	2311	360	713
Duluth, Minn.	1139	1428	918	465	752	800	1086	994	402	707	1307	646	597	2016	757	943
El Paso, Texas	1415	2316	754	1430	1515	1704	620	654	1126	1674	748	1410	931	790	1438	1072
Flagstaff, Ariz.	1704	2495	757	1604	1695	1883	961	657	1300	1848	1157	1589	1105	484	1624	1333
Fort Wayne, Ind.	593	825	1093	156	153	197	983	1135	466	160	1105	118	586	2175	216	553
Fort Worth, Texas	826	1779	845	941	951	1183	31	757	708	1167	262	889	513	1356	850	483
Harrisburg, Pa.	700	373	1579	639	468	314	1383	1592	952	474	1439	534	1019	2607	569	931
Helena, Mont.	2030	2388	685	1425	1712	1760	1554	781	1161	1691	1792	1606	1251	1190	1717	1702
Houston, Texas	789	1804	1107	1067	1029	1273	243	1019	905	1265		987	710	1538	928	561
Indianapolis, Ind.	493	906	1068	181	106	294	865	1058	465	278	987		485	2073	111	435
Jackson, Miss.	391	1406	1257	742	655	899	404	1169	809	914	406	646	644	1791	554	212
Jacksonville, Fla.	306	1155	1748	980	746	915	990	1704	1176	1003	889	799	1104	2377	688	674
Kansas City, Mo.	798	1391	650	499	591	779	489	600	195	743	710	485		1589	520	451
Knoxville, Tenn.	193	911	1372	527	253	485	837	1328	800	512	893	346	728	2202	241	385
Las Vegas, Nev.	1964	2725	855	1772	1941	2097	1221	777	1445	2029	1417	1835	1365	282	1884	1593
Lexington, Ky.	362	896	1233	352	78	317	861	1192	636	337	970	171	592	2180	72	409
Little Rock, Ark.	509	1434	1035	640	606	850	314	947	561	838	427	560	389	1687	505	138
Los Angeles, Calif.	2182	2779	1137	2054	2179	2367	1387	1059	1727	2311	1538	2073	1589		2108	1817
Louisville, Ky.	382	941	1161	292	101	345	819	1120	566	360	928	111	520	2108		367
Mackinaw City, Mich.	935	916	1291	387	495	439	1281	1341	673	284	1427	460	864	2392	562	880
Madison, Wis.	812	1103	912	140	427	475	968	954	286	406	1137	321	483	2012	432	622
Memphis, Tenn.	371	1296	1101	530	468	712	452	1040	599	713	561	435	451	1817	367	
Miami, Fla.	655	1504	2097	1329	1095	1264	1300	2037	1525	1352	1190	1148	1448	2687	1037	997
Milwaukee, Wis.	761	1050	987	87	374	422	991	1029	361	353	1142	268	537	2087	379	612
Minneapolis, Minn.	1068	1368	788	405	692	740	936	841	252	671	1157	586	447	1889	697	826
Mobile, Ala.	335	1372	1443	851	706	950	590	1355	954	965	478	716	812	1977	605	363
Montreal, Que.	1181	318	1773	828	805	561	1705	1815	1146	562	1827	840	1305	2873	906	1273
Nashville, Tenn.	242	1088	1200	446	269	513	660	1156	628	528	769	279	556	2025	168	208
New Orleans, La.	479	1507	1361	912	786	1030	496	1273	978	1045	356	796	806	1883	685	390
New York, N. Y.	841	206	1746	802	647	473	1552	1771	1119	637	1608	713	1198	2786	748	1100
Norfolk, Va.	540	558	1764	831	604	508	1329	1758	1141	666	1328	700	1162	2694	642	877
Oklahoma City, Okla.	839	1641	697	787	840	1029	206	609	544	1013	449	735	349	1349	763	468
Omaha, Nebr.	986	1412	495	459	693	784	644	537	132	716	865	587	201	1595	687	652
Orlando, Fla.	435	1294	1876	1109	875	1054	1078	1815	1305	1134	968	928	1226	2465	817	775
Philadelphia, Pa.	741	296	1678	738	567	413	1452	1691	1051	573	1508	633	1118	2706	668	1000
Phoenix, Ariz.	1793	2604	892	1713	1804	1992	998	792	1409	1957	1149	1698	1214	389	1733	1442
Pierre, S. Dak.	1361	1726	434	763	1050	1098	943	518	492	1029	1186	964	522	1524	1055	1043
Pittsburgh, Pa.	687	561	1390	452	287	129	1204	1411	763	287	1313	353	838	2426	388	752
Portland, Me.	1139	106	1986	1042	942	707	1850	2028	1359	775	1906	1001	1486	3074	1043	1398
Portland, Ore.	2601	3046	1159	2083	2333	2418	2009	1238	1786	2349	2205	2227	1809	959	2320	2259
Raleigh, N. Car.	372	685	1695	784	534	561	1166	1661	1092	683	1160	631	1061	2545	541	728
Rapid City, S. Dak.	1487	1859	295	896	1177	1231	1050	394	618	1162	1288	1071	708	1363	1182	1159
Reno, Nev.	2374	2866	959	1913	2133	2238	1668	1011	1586	2170	1864	2027	1609	469	2120	2003
Richmond, Va.	510	535	1674	748	514	425	1266	1668	1058	583	1298	618	1072	2631	552	814
St. Louis, Mo.	541	1141	901	289	340	529	630	857	333	513	779	235	257	1845	263	285
Salt Lake City, Utah	1878	2343	436	1390	1610	1715	1242	504	1063	1647	1438	1504	1086	715	1597	1535
San Antonio, Texas	983	1988	1027	1187	1160	1404	270	939	954	1392	197	1114	759	1363	1059	692
San Diego, Calif.	2126	2955	1186	2064	2155	2343	1331	1108	1760	2308	1847	2049	1565	125	2084	1783
San Francisco, Calif.	2496	3095	1188	2142	2362	2467	1753	1235	1815	2399	1912	2256	1835	379	2349	2125
Seattle, Wash.	2618	2976	1228	2013	2300	2348	2078	1307	1749	2279	2274	2194	1839	1131	2305	2290
Spokane, Wash.	2340	2698	995	1735	2022	2070	1864	1089	1471	2001	2102	1916	1561	1205	2027	2012
Springfield, Ill.	592	1099	888	189	299	473	728	865	291	433	879	193	310	1899	275	370
Springfield, Mo.	652	1353	820	499	552	741	419	759	342	725	629	447	170	1636	475	281
Toledo, Ohio	640	739	1176	232	200	111	1084	1218	549	59	1206	219	687	2276	301	654
Topeka, Kans.	863	1456	595	562	656	844	480	535	549	806	701	550	65	1531	585	508
Tulsa, Okla.	772	1537	765	683	736	925	257	681	443	909	478	631	248	1452	659	401
Washington, D. C.	608	429	1611	671	481	346	1319	1616	984	506	1375	558	1043	2631	582	867
Wichita, Kans.	903	1587	583	696	787	975	365	509	392	945	608	681	197	1400	710	532

232

	Milwaukee, Wis	Minneapolis, Minn	New Orleans, La	New York, N Y	Omaha, Nebr	Philadelphia, Pa	Pittsburgh, Pa	Portland, Oreg	St. Louis, Mo	Salt Lake City, Utah	San Francisco, Calif	Seattle, Wash	Toledo, Ohio	Tulsa, Okla	Washington, D.C.	Wichita, Kans
Albuquerque, N Mex	1319	1190	1134	1979	856	1899	1619	1371	1038	604	1115	1440	1469	645	1824	593
Amarillo, Texas	1084	975	850	1704	643	1624	1344	1655	756	888	1399	1724	1210	361	1549	350
Atlanta, Ga	761	1068	479	841	986	741	687	2601	541	1878	2496	2618	640	772	608	903
Austin, Texas	1184	1129	517	1715	837	1615	1367	2069	823	1302	1748	2138	1256	450	1482	548
Baltimore, Md	755	1073	1115	196	1113	96	218	2751	798	2044	2796	2681	444	1194	37	1244
Birmingham, Ala	728	1006	342	969	898	869	741	2505	465	1781	2366	2535	665	647	736	778
Bismarck, N Dak	758	427	1583	1635	581	1569	1283	1265	979	916	1604	1195	1063	958	1502	776
Boise, Idaho	1692	1405	2078	2478	1227	2410	2122	432	1633	340	658	501	1908	1486	2343	1312
Boston, Mass	1050	1368	1507	206	1412	296	561	3046	1141	2343	3095	2976	739	1537	429	1587
Buffalo, N Y	609	927	1217	372	971	353	216	2605	716	1902	2654	2535	298	1112	356	1162
Charleston, S Car	964	1282	720	733	1266	633	666	2881	821	2158	2785	2890	783	1061	500	1192
Cheyenne, Wyo	987	788	1361	1746	495	1678	1390	1159	901	436	1188	1228	1176	765	1611	583
Chicago, Ill	87	405	912	802	459	738	452	2083	289	1390	2142	2013	232	683	671	696
Cincinnati, Ohio	374	692	786	647	693	567	287	2333	340	1610	2362	2300	200	736	481	787
Cleveland, Ohio	422	740	1030	473	784	413	129	2418	529	1715	2467	2348	111	925	346	975
Columbus, Ohio	395	713	894	542	750	462	182	2391	406	1671	2423	2321	133	802	387	852
Dallas, Texas	991	936	496	1552	644	1452	1204	2609	630	1242	1753	2078	1084	257	1319	365
Denver, Colo	1029	841	1273	1771	537	1691	1411	1238	857	504	1235	1307	1218	681	1616	509
Des Moines, Iowa	361	252	978	1119	132	1051	763	1786	333	1063	1815	1749	549	443	984	392
Detroit, Mich	353	671	1045	637	716	573	287	2349	513	1647	2399	2279	59	909	506	940
Duluth, Minn	392	153	1331	1267	510	1203	917	1705	662	1315	2044	1635	697	845	1136	794
El Paso, Texas	1468	1339	1098	2123	1007	2043	1763	1635	1175	868	1164	1704	1618	780	1939	742
Flagstaff, Ariz	1642	1481	1457	2302	1171	2222	1942	1241	1361	511	792	134	1792	968	2147	916
Fort Wayne, Ind	243	561	901	662	598	585	297	2239	353	1529	2281	2169	101	749	518	783
Fort Worth, Texas	1015	960	527	1583	655	1483	1235	1978	654	1211	1722	2047	1108	279	1350	359
Harrisburg, Pa	726	1044	1142	180	1084	102	189	2722	769	2015	2767	2652	415	1165	107	1215
Helena, Mont	1352	1020	2033	2227	1050	2163	1877	658	1493	477	1098	588	1657	1416	2096	1234
Houston, Texas	1142	1157	356	1608	865	1508	1313	2205	779	1438	1912	2274	1206	478	1375	608
Indianapolis, Ind	268	586	796	713	587	633	353	2227	235	1504	2256	2194	219	631	558	681
Jackson, Miss	824	1036	178	1210	845	1110	939	2401	495	1646	2157	2470	855	527	977	708
Jacksonville, Fla	1067	1374	555	959	1292	859	851	2907	847	2184	2743	2924	944	1075	726	1206
Kansas City, Mo	537	447	806	1198	201	1118	838	1809	257	1086	1835	1839	687	248	1043	197
Knoxville, Tenn	614	932	596	715	916	615	511	2531	471	1808	2510	2540	453	786	482	871
Las Vegas, Nev	1805	1607	1717	2548	1313	2468	2188	981	1621	433	564	1152	1994	1228	2393	1176
Lexington, Ky	439	757	727	703	758	623	343	2392	335	1669	2421	2365	278	731	514	782
Little Rock, Ark	715	813	418	1238	590	1138	890	2179	352	1438	1995	2228	779	271	1005	453
Los Angeles, Calif	2087	1889	1883	2786	1595	2706	2426	959	1845	715	379	1131	2276	1452	2631	1400
Louisville, Ky	379	697	685	748	687	668	388	2320	263	1597	2349	2305	301	659	582	710
Mackinaw City, Mich	368	508	1247	906	805	842	556	2128	651	1691	2443	2058	328	1047	775	1061
Madison, Wis	77	272	1006	942	418	878	592	1950	358	1348	2100	1880	372	727	811	676
Memphis, Tenn	612	826	390	1100	652	1000	752	2259	285	1535	2125	2290	654	401	867	532
Miami, Fla	1416	1723	856	1308	1641	1208	1200	3256	1196	2532	3053	3273	1293	1398	1075	1529
Milwaukee, Wis		332	994	889	493	825	539	2010	363	1423	2175	1940	319	757	758	734
Minneapolis, Minn	332		1214	1207	357	1143	857	1678	552	1186	1940	1608	637	695	1076	644
Mobile, Ala	933	1173	144	1176	1013	1076	982	2587	632	1832	2343	2651	906	713	943	893
Montreal, Que	915	1163	1591	378	1278	449	583	2755	1075	2209	2961	2685	621	1471	579	1502
Nashville, Tenn	532	826	517	892	744	792	553	2359	299	1636	2333	2376	469	609	659	699
New Orleans, La	994	1214		1311	1007	1211	1070	2505	673	1738	2249	2574	986	647	1078	816
New York, N Y	889	1207	1311		1251	100	368	2885	948	2182	2934	2815	578	1344	233	1394
Norfolk, Va	918	1236	1019	362	1273	263	384	2914	905	2200	2952	2844	607	1278	188	1352
Oklahoma City, Okla	861	796	668	1448	455	1368	1088	1841	500	1100	1657	1910	954	105	1293	159
Omaha, Nebr	493	357	1007	1251		1183	895	1654	449	931	1683	1638	681	387	1116	298
Orlando, Fla	1196	1503	634	1098	1421	998	990	3034	976	2310	2831	3053	1075	1176	865	1307
Philadelphia, Pa	825	1143	1211	100	1183		288	2821	868	2114	2866	2751	514	1264	133	1314
Phoenix, Ariz	1751	1616	1494	2411	1290	2331	2051	1266	1470	648	763	1437	1901	1077	2256	1025
Pierre, S Dak	690	394	1394	1565	391	1501	1215	1353	824	823	1575	1283	995	760	1434	578
Pittsburgh, Pa	539	857	1070	368	895	288		2535	588	1826	2578	2465	228	984	221	1034
Portland, Me	1129	1447	1609	308	1491	398	663	3125	1236	2422	3174	3055	818	1632	531	1682
Portland, Ore	2010	1678	2505	2885	1654	2821	2535		2060	767	636	172	2315	1913	2754	1739
Raleigh, N Car	871	1189	851	489	1214	389	445	2854	804	2131	2853	2797	624	635	256	1245
Rapid City, S Dak	840	565	1507	1698	507	1634	1348	1204	950	662	1414	1134	1128	873	1567	691
Reno, Nev	1946	1711	2164	2705	1454	2637	2349	538	1860	523	229	702	2135	1640	2570	1471
Richmond, Va	835	1153	989	339	1190	239	301	2831	815	2110	2862	2761	524	1211	106	1262
St. Louis, Mo	363	552	673	948	449	863	588	2060		1337	2089	2081	494	396	793	447
Salt Lake City, Utah	1423	1186	1738	2182	931	2114	1826	767	1337		752	836	1612	1172	2047	1003
San Antonio, Texas	1261	1206	550	1792	914	1692	1444	2086	900	1319	1737	2155	1333	527	1559	625
San Diego, Calif	2102	1938	1827	2762	1641	2682	2402	1084	1821	764	504	1256	2252	1428	2607	1376
San Francisco, Calif	2175	1940	2249	2934	1683	2866	2578	636	2089	752		808	2364	1760	2799	1695
Seattle, Wash	1940	1608	2574	2815	1638	2751	2465	172	2081	836	808		2245	1982	2684	1568
Spokane, Wash	1662	1330	2343	2537	1360	2473	2187	348	1803	712	882	278	1967	1726	2406	1544
Springfield, Ill	263	480	758	906	412	826	546	2047	100	1324	2076	2039	377	494	751	507
Springfield, Mo	573	594	636	1160	371	1080	800	1978	212	1254	1944	2009	666	185	1005	251
Toledo, Ohio	319	637	986	578	681	514	228	2315	454	1612	2364	2245		850	447	884
Topeka, Kans	598	508	863	1263	165	1183	903	1751	322	1028	1770	1802	750	223	1108	139
Tulsa, Okla	757	695	647	1344	387	1264	984	1913	396	1172	1760	1982	850		1189	182
Washington, D C	758	1076	1078	233	1116	133	221	2754	793	2047	2799	2684	447	1189		1239
Wichita, Kans	734	644	816	1394	298	1314	1034	1739	447	1003	1695	1808	884	182	1239	

Metrics Made Simple

Why Metrics?

The decision was made some time ago to standardize our methods of computing weights and measurements. Since the metric system of measuring was chosen, a comparison of our old system with the (new to us) metric one is important.

LIQUID MEASURE

1 fluid ounce	29.573 milliliters
1 quart	9.4635 deciliters
1 quart	0.94635 liter
1 gallon	3.7854 liters

Or

.033814 fluid ounce	1 milliliter
3.3814 fluid ounces	1 deciliter
33.814 fluid ounces	1 liter
1.0567 quarts	1 liter
0.26417 gallon	1 liter

LINEAR (LENGTH) MEASURE

1 inch	25.4 millimeters
1 inch	2.54 centimeters
1 foot	30.48 centimeters
1 foot	3.048 decimeters
1 foot	0.3048 meter
1 yard	0.9144 meter
1 mile	1609.3 meters
1 mile	1.6093 kilometers

Or

0.03937 inch	1 millimeter
0.3937 inch	1 centimeter
3.937 inches	1 decimeter
39.37 inches	1 meter
3.2808 feet	1 meter
1.0936 yards	1 meter
3280.8 feet	1 kilometer
1093.6 yards	1 kilometer
0.62137 mile	1 kilometer

WEIGHTS

1 ounce	28.350 grams
1 pound	0.45359 kilogram

Or

0.035274 ounce	1 gram
2.2046 pounds	1 kilogram

National Highway Traffic Safety Administration

(Transportation)

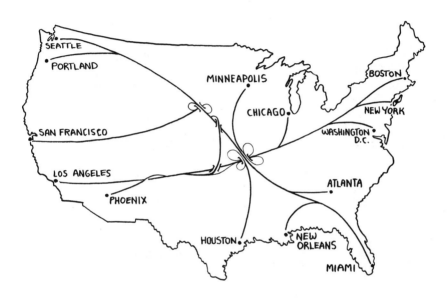

It shall be a secret no longer.

Government Agency Responsible For Car Recalls

I wonder what those men who poured the first rural mile of concrete pavement near Detroit in 1909 would feel if they could see the network of national highways today. The method of numbering national highways was started way back in 1920. North-south routes were assigned odd numbers—east-west received even numbers. The National Highway Traffic Safety Administration (NHTSA) is responsible for planning and building roads, recalls of cars and the importation of cars. One of the ten regional offices is located close to you.

Regional Offices

REGION I
Transportation Ctr
55 Broadway
Cambridge, MA 02142
PH: 617 494-2680

REGION II
222 Mamaroneck Ave
White Plains, NY 10601
PH: 914 761-4250

REGION III
Airport Plaza Bldg
6701 Elkridge Landing Rd
Linthicum, MD 21090
PH: 301 796-5117

REGION IV
Suite 501
1720 Peachtree Rd N W
Atlanta, GA 30309
PH: 404 881-4571

REGION V
Suite 214, Executive Plz
1010 Dixie Hwy
Chicago Heights, IL 60411
PH: 312 756-1950

REGION VI
819 Taylor Street
Fort Worth, TX 76102
PH: 817 334-3653

REGION VII
P.O. Box 19515
Kansas City, MO 64141
PH: 816 926-7887

REGION VIII
330 Garrison Street
Lakewood, CO 80226
PH: 303 234-3253

REGION IX
2 Embarcadero Ctr
Suite 610
San Francisco, CA 94111
PH: 415 556-6415

REGION X
3140 Federal Bldg
915 2nd Avenue
Seattle, WA 988174
PH: 206 442-5934

Setting safety standards to live by!

Outstanding Publications

(Automotive)

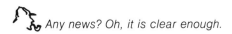 *Any news? Oh, it is clear enough.*

You can climb the ladder of success easier when you lay it flat. Likewise you will enjoy automobiles more by becoming a subscriber to one or more of these magazines. There are many to choose from. All are good, but each one treats the subject in a different manner. To make your choices easier I have made a capsule comment relating to the content of each publication. Many will be found on magazine stands, but just in case you need them, here are their addresses.

(Random Order)

**HEMMINGS
MOTOR NEWS**
Box 380
Bennington, VT 05201
For the investment
automobile enthusiast.

**SPECIAL
INTEREST AUTOS**
Box 7211
Stockton, CA 96207
Devoted to special interest
automobiles.

OLD CARS
Iola, WI 54945
Devoted to the location of
and stories about old cars.

CARS & PARTS
Box 299
Sesser, IL 62884
Details the locating of cars
and parts.

CAR MAGAZINE
England
FF Publishing Ltd
64 West Smithfield
London EC1
Tests and stories about new
car models.

SUPER STOCK CARS
Box RD 3
Flemington, NJ 08822

STOCK CAR RACING
602 Montgomery Street
Alexandria, VA 22314
Coverage of the sport of
stock car racing.

OFF-ROAD TRAVEL
12301 Wilshire Blvd
Los Angeles, CA 90025
Stories and tips on off-road
travel.

DEALS ON WHEELS
1499 Monrovia Avenue
Newport Beach, CA 92663
Blend of technical
information & entertainment.

KIT CARS
P.O. Box 9187
San Jose, CA 95157
For confirmed automotive
do-it-yourselfers

SPORT TRUCKING
12301 Wilshire Blvd
Los Angeles, CA 90025
Focuses on various phases of
the truck and van field.

**AUTOMOBILE QUARTERLY
MAGAZINE**
245 West Main Street
Kutztown, PA 19530
Outstanding pictures and
stories relating mostly to
older automobile history.
Quality hardcover.

**NATIONAL SPEED
SPORT NEWS**
The Kay Publishing Co
News Bldg
Box 608
Ridgewood, NJ 07451
Weekly coverage of racing news

COAST CAR COLLECTOR
P.O. Box 88427
Emeryville, CA 94662
Covers collector cars for
the western U.S.

CAR EXCHANGE
700 E State Street
Iola, WI 54945
For postwar car collectors

THE ROBB REPORT
P.O. Box 720317
Atlanta, GA 30328
Covers Rolls-Royce/Bentleys

ANTIQUE MOTOR NEWS
919 South Street
Long Beach, CA 90805
Features collectable antique
vintage, classic, and imported
automobiles

**VETERAN AND VINTAGE
England**
Bridge House

181 Queen Victoria Street
London, EC4 4DD
For collector car enthusiasts.

AUTOCAR
England
Dorset House
Stamford Street
London SE1 9LU
**Describes performance
testing along with general
interest articles.**

THOROUGHBRED AND CLASSIC CARS
England
IPC Business Press Ltd
Perrymount Road
Haywards Heath
Sussex
**For the collector car
enthusiast.**

VETTE VUES MAGAZINE
Drawer "A"
Sandy Springs, GA 30328
All about Covettes.

AUTO RACING DIGEST
1020 Church Street
Evanston, IL 60201
**Auto racing events
worldwide.**

AUTOWEEK
740 Rush Street
Chicago, IL 60611
**For car enthusiasts
and racers**

BOY'S LIFE
North Brunswick, NJ 08902
General automotive.

CAR COLLECTOR/ CAR CLASSICS
P.O. Box 28571
Atlanta, GA 30328
Articles on collector cars.

CAR CRAFT
8490 Sunset Blvd
Los Angeles, CA 90069
**Drag racing and high
performance.**

CAR AND DRIVER
One Park Avenue
New York, NY 10016
**Edited for automobile
enthusiasts**

SCHOLASTIC WHEELS
50 W 44th Street
New York, NY 10036
**For students enrolled in driver
education classes.**

SPORTS CAR
3629 W Warner
Santa Ana, CA 92704
**Devoted to the interests of the
members of the Sports Car Club
of America. Racing.**

STREET MACHINE
7950 Deering Avenue
Canoga Park, CA 91304
**For the late model hot rod
enthusiast.**

STREET RODDER
2145 W La Palma
Anaheim, CA 92801
**Concerns street related
automotive activites and
equipment.**

SUPER CHEVY
12301 Wilshire Blvd
Los Angeles, CA 90025
For the Chevrolet enthusiast.

TRAVELIN' VANS, MINI TRUCKS & PICKUPS
15825 Stagg Street
Van Nuys, CA 91423
**From the economy minded to
the exotic with how-to's
on customizing.**

TRUCKIN'
2145 W La Palma
Anaheim, CA 92801
**For the light truck, van and off
road enthusiast.**

VAN PICKUP AND OFF ROAD WORLD
16200 Venutra Blvd
Encino, CA 91436

Designed for the interests of
van enthusiasts.

VW & PORSCHE
12301 Wilshire Blvd
Los Angeles, CA 90025
For the Volkswagen and
Porsche enthusiast.

RACING PICTORIAL
P.O. Box 500B
Indianapolis, IN 46206
For auto racing fans.

1101 TRUCK & VAN IDEAS
12301 Wilshire Blvd
Los Angeles, CA 90025
''How to'' articles dealing
with customizing.

OWNER OPERATOR
Chilton Way
Radnor, PA 19089
For the independent trucker.

PICKUP, VAN & 4WD
1499 Monrovia Avenue
Newport Beach, CA 92663
For the enthusiast/owner.
Performance testing.
Buyers guides

POPULAR HOT RODDING
12301 Wilshire Blvd
Los Angeles, CA 90025
Emphasis on performance.

POPULAR OFF ROADING
7950 Deering Avneue
Canoga Park, CA 91304
Enthusiasts who prefer off-
pavement sport.

POPULAR SCIENCE
380 Madison Avenue
New York, NY 10017
Automobile developments
and new products mixed
with other new ideas.

RACECAR
11322 Idaho Avenue, Suite 102
Los Angeles, CA 90025
Racing enthusiast
and competitor.

MUSTANG MONTHLY
Box 5917
Lakeland, FL 33803
Mustang enthusiasts.

ROAD KING
233 E Erie Street
Chicago, IL 60611
For over-the-road truck drivers.

ROAD AND TRACK
1499 Monrovia Avenue
Newport Beach, CA 92663
For the knowledgeable
automobile enthusiast.

ROD ACTION
7950 Deering Avenue
Canoga Park, CA 91304
For the do-it-yourself street
rod enthusiast.

4X4's AND
OFF ROAD VEHICLES
15825 Stagg Street
Van Nuys, CA 91423
Off road enthusiast.

FOUR WHEELER
21216 Vanowen
Canoga Park, CA 91303
For four-wheel-drive enthusiasts.

4 WHEEL & OFF-ROAD
8490 Sunset Blvd
Los Angeles, CA 90069
For the outdoor enthusiast.

HOT ROD MAGAZINE
8490 Sunset Blvd
Los Angeles, CA 90069
Concerns modification to
automotive machinery.

MECHANIX ILLUSTRATED
1515 Broadway
New York, NY 10036
How-to-do magazine for
car repairs.

MINNESOTA AAA
MOTORIST
7 Travelers Trail
Burnsville, MN 55337
General interest auto
related articles.

**MONTGOMERY WARD
AUTO CLUB NEWS**
11400 Greenleaf
Chicago, IL 60626
Auto news for members.

MOTOR TREND
8490 Sunset Blvd
Los Angeles, CA 90069
General interest
automotive magazine.

NATIONAL DRAGSTER
10639 Riverside Drive
North Hollywood, CA 91602
Automotive enthusiasts,
especially those interested
in drag racing.

OFF-ROAD
12301 Wilshire Blvd
Los Angeles, CA 90025
Coverage of off-roading.

Now the choice is easy.

Miscellany Of Useful Addresses

Often too much of our valuable time is spent looking for hard to find addresses and phone numbers. Seems they can never be found when you need them. This list will save you lots of frustration. These businesses are related in some way to the automobile. You will find them, like a parachute, helpful to have when needed.

You are quite right. Interesting. Now let me have the details.

Peoples Trans-Share
258 S W Alder Street
P.O. Box 40303
Portland, OR 97240
PH: 800 547-0933
OR 503 227-2419
Membership service arranges cost-sharing cross-country transportation by car or plane

National Automobile Theft Bureau
17 John Street
New York, NY 10038
PH: 212 233-1400
Maintains a nationwide file on stolen vehicles

Federal Highway Administration
400 7th Street S W
Washington, DC 20590
PH: 202 426-0677

National Highway Traffic Safety Administration (NHTSA)
400 7th Street S W
Washington, DC 20590
PH: 202 426-4000

Consumer Product Safety Commission
Bureau Of Information
501 Westbard Avenue
Bethesda, MD 20207
PH: 301 496-7621

Insurance Information Institute
110 William Street
New York, NY 10038
PH: 212 233-7650

Motor Vehicle Manufacturers Assoc.
320 New Center Bldg
Detroit, MI 48202
PH: 313 872-4311

Nadar-Related
Center For Auto Safety
1346 Connecticut Av N W 1223
Washington, DC 20036
PH: 202 659-1126

**National Automobile
Dealers Association**
8400 Westpark Drive
McLean, VA 22101
PH: 703 821-7000

**Mailing Lists
(Add or substract your name)**
Write: Direct Marketing Asso.
6 East 43rd Street
New York, NY 10017

Consumer Publications (free)
Consumer Information Center
Pueblo, CO 81009

Radar Information
Federal Communications
Commission
2025 M Street, N W, Rm. 5308
Washington, DC 20554
PH:202 632-6475

Guard Service
Pinkerton's
100 Church Street
New York, NY 10007
PH: 212 285-4856

Car Auctioneers
Kruse Auctioneers, Inc
Kruse Building
Auburn, IN 46706
PH: 219 925-4004
**A collector car auction company
that hold auctions in various
cities across the United States
each year.**

**American Federation
Of Labor**
815 16th St N W
Washington, DC 20006
PH: 202 637-5000

**United Automobile
Workers Of America**
UAW Intern. Union
8000 E Jefferson
Detroit, MI 48214
PH: 313 926-5000

**United Steelworkers
Of America**
5 Gateway Center
Pittsburgh, PA 15222
PH: 412 562-2400

**International Brotherhood
Of Teamsters**
25 Louisiana Av N W
Washington, DC 20001
PH: 202 624-6800

**American
Petroleum Institute**
2101 L Street N W
Washington, DC 20037
PH: 202 457-7000

**Consumers Union Of
United States, Inc**
256 Washington Street
Mount Vernon, NY 10550
PH: 914 664-6400

**Council Of Better
Business Bureaus, Inc**
1150 17th St N W
Washington, DC 20036
PH: 202 467-5200

**Independent Petroleum
Association Of America**
1101 16th St N W
Washington, DC 20036
PH: 202 466-8240

You expected the answer. Now you have it!

Importing—The Right Approach

At last! This is the beginning of a beautiful friendship.

The Air Is Heavy With Castrol

You're screaming down a rolling, one-lane country road. Scarf flying, eyes watering, right foot buried deep in the firewall. As the tachometer continues to climb, lights begin to dance across a mile-long hood. The air is heavy with Castrol, making for short shallow breaths. Whether she's a Rolls, Jag, blood-red Ferrari or Porsche foreign motor cars are fun! But where can such a beast be found? Many times the answer comes back in one simple word—importing. Let's take a closer look.

The Good Ones Are Scarce

Although importing motor carriages can be a bed of wine and roses, I'm going to dispel some popular myths! If you're thinking of importing cars as a business, forget it! Several factors have changed, making this venture financially a poor investment. Unlike the late 60's and early 70's when motor cars were cheap and plentiful, today's European car market is inflated and scarce! Desirable automobiles in foreign countries have risen in price to comparable vehicles found right here in the United States. There's an old saying, "If a man fools me once—shame on him. If the same man fools me twice—shame on me." Vast quantities of these "desirable" cars have already been imported! This leaves good ones far and few in-between. To import cars large amounts of your capital will be tied up for long periods of time, producing months of negative cash flow! Not to mention it's time consuming and full of hassles.

Easy Sales To Starry-Eyed Buyers

A tiger and a lamb may lie down together, but the lamb won't get much sleep. Are car dealers or private parties in foreign countries really more honest than Americans? No! Some foreign dealers are expert in converting "junk sleds" into melting icicles! These "experts" apply a cosmetic treatment to cars including plastic patches, new paint, new chrome, steam cleaned and painted engine compartments, heavy asphalt undercoatings to hide serious rusting, etc. This results in easy sales to starry-eyed American buyers. A common stunt is to identify 1968 and later models with the selling point, "No U.S. Federal Motor Vehicle Safety Standards Apply." Beware! *(Note: See "What To Look For When Selecting A Used Car" in Chapter One, p. 50.)* It's easy to tell when you've got a bargain—it is too good to be true.

One Alternative Remains

Sure, I know, nothing would ever be attempted if all possible objections had to be overcome first. Why, then, would anybody import a European motorcar? The answers are quite simple. Say you take an extended tour of Europe, maybe two or three months. A Eurorail pass is considered but rejected because it hampers your flexible mobility. Renting a car is expensive with nothing to show for it after the vacation! Only one alternative remains. Purchase a European motor carriage. Drive it, bring her back home and use it as a second or third car.

Do All Modern Automobiles Look Like Clones Of One Another?

Maybe you're one of the growing number of people who look upon present day sleds as uninteresting or lifeless, having no aesthetic appeal? Do you crave English leather, real woodwork, a mile-long hood (bonnet), connected to beautiful curved fenders with large protruding headlights! Tired of buying American slugs that quickly depreciate into sawdust?

Yes, quite a few European automobiles can still be purchased, imported to the U.S., put in good running conditon then later sold for the total amount invested! You'll have the fun of owning it in the meantime. But be careful! First, determine what the precise value of the car will be in the United States by studying Chapters One and Four of *Automobile Success*.

Now you've got the right approach! Read on.

Environmental Protection Agency Requirements
(EPA)

Under the Clean Air Act of 1968 imported motor cars are subject to air pollution control standards. Beginning with the 1968 model year every car must meet U.S. standards applicable to the model year in which it was manufactured!

- **1968-70** All passenger cars, starting with the 1968 model year, must be certified to meet crankcase and exhaust emission standards (this is relatively easy).
  - a. Vehicles manufactured between 1968-70 in conformity with U.S. emission standards can be identified by a Department of Transportation door post label. This tag shows the vehicle as manufactured in compliance with federal safety standards.
  - b. Before purchase you should **double check** and verify conformity with the automobile's manufacturer!
- **1971-** With the 1971 model year, fuel evaporative emission standards must also be met (can get sticky)!
  - a. All complying 1971 and later models have a label in a readily visible position in the engine compartment. This label states the vehicle conforms to U.S. standards. It will read "Vehicle Emission Control Information" and include the full corporate name and trademark of the manufaturer.
  - b. Some 1970 model vehicles also have this label if the automobile was manufactured after March 9, 1970!
- **1976-** Beginning with the 1976 model year, motor cars are subject to EPA catalyst requirements.
  - a. Any 1976 or newer automobile manufactured in conformity can be identified by the statement

"Catalyst" appearing on or adjacent to the Department of Transportation door post label, or on the engine compartment emission control label.

b. Automobiles without this label are almost impossible to make comply with U.S. standards!

c. If the car is not labeled as described, it will not be released by U.S. Customs unless a bond is posted. This bond must be equal to the value of the car plus duty. *(Note: See "Importing A Nonconforming Motor Car" in this chapter, p. 258.)*

d. Motor cars not required to meet air pollution control standards are automobiles manufactured before the 1968 model year or vehicles with diesel engines manufactured before the 1975 model year!

For More Information Contact:

ENVIRONMENTAL PROTECTION AGENCY
Mobile Source Enforcement Division
401 M Street, N.W.
Washington, D.C. 20460
PH: 202 755-0944

There's Something Special About California

California emission regulations are the most strict of all the states. For California emission control requirements contact:

INFORMATION CENTER
California Air Resources Board
P.O. Box 2815
Sacramento, CA 95812
PH: 916 322-2990

The Form To File At Time Of Entry

No matter if she's a 1953 Royce Silver Dawn saloon or a 1977 twelve-cylinder Lamborghini Countach, all imported motor cars are declared to the United States Environmental Protection Agency. At the time of entry file E.P.A. form 3520-1. This form must be completed for every automobile (regardless of compliance)!

EPA FORM 3520-1

OMB NO. 158-R0150

U.S. ENVIRONMENTAL PROTECTION AGENCY	WARNING
IMPORTATION OF MOTOR VEHICLES AND MOTOR VEHICLE ENGINES SUBJECT TO FEDERAL AIR POLLUTION CONTROL REGULATIONS *(Read instructions on reverse side before completing form.)*	Any person who knowingly makes a false declaration shall be fined not more than $10,000 or imprisoned not more than 5 years, or both. 18 U.S.C. 1001.

PORT OF ENTRY		DATE OF ENTRY	ENTRY NO. *(if applicable)*

IMPORT VESSEL OR CARRIER	MAKE OF VEHICLE *(or engine, if not chassis mounted or if mounted in heavy-duty vehicle)*	MODEL OF VEHICLE *(or engine, if not chassis mounted or if mounted in heavy-duty vehicle)*

MODEL YEAR OF VEHICLE *(or engine, if not chassis mounted or if mounted in heavy-duty vehicle)*	VEHICLE IDENTIFICATION NUMBER	ENGINE SERIAL NUMBER *(if not chassis mounted or if mounted in heavy-duty vehicle)*

√ WITH REGARD TO THE IMPORTATION OF THE DESCRIBED MOTOR VEHICLE OR MOTOR VEHICLE ENGINE, I DECLARE THAT:

1. SUCH 1971 OR SUBSEQUENT MODEL YEAR MOTOR VEHICLE OR MOTOR VEHICLE ENGINE IS COVERED BY A CERTIFICATE OF CONFORMITY ISSUED BY THE DEPARTMENT OF HEALTH, EDUCATION, AND WELFARE OR BY THE U.S. ENVIRONMENTAL PROTECTION AGENCY, AND BEARS A CERTIFICATION LABEL OR TAG.

2. SUCH 1968, 1969 OR 1970 MODEL YEAR MOTOR VEHICLE OR MOTOR VEHICLE ENGINE IS COVERED BY A CERTIFICATE OF CONFORMITY ISSUED BY THE DEPARTMENT OF HEALTH, EDUCATION, AND WELFARE OR THE U.S. ENVIRONMENTAL PROTECTION AGENCY.

WITH REGARD TO THE IMPORTATION OF THE DESCRIBED MOTOR VEHICLE OR ENGINE, I DECLARE THAT SUCH VEHICLE OR ENGINE IS NOT COVERED BY A CERTIFICATE OF CONFORMITY ISSUED BY THE DEPARTMENT OF HEALTH, EDUCATION, AND WELFARE OR THE U.S. ENVIRONMENTAL PROTECTION AGENCY, BUT IS ELIGIBLE FOR ADMISSION INTO THE UNITED STATES BECAUSE

3. THE VEHICLE OR ENGINE IS BEING IMPORTED SOLELY FOR PURPOSES OF DISPLAY AND WILL NOT BE SOLD OR OPERATED ON THE PUBLIC HIGHWAYS.

4. THE IMPORTER OR CONSIGNEE IS A MEMBER OF THE ARMED FORCES OF A FOREIGN COUNTRY, OR MEMBER OF THE SECRETARIAT OF A PUBLIC INTERNATIONAL ORGANIZATION SO DESIGNATED PURSUANT TO 50 STAT. 669 (22 U.S.C. 288(h)) OR A MEMBER OF THE PERSONNEL OF A FOREIGN GOVERNMENT ON ASSIGNMENT IN THE UNITED STATES WHO COMES WITHIN THE CLASS OF PERSONS FOR WHOM FREE ENTRY OF VEHICLES HAS BEEN AUTHORIZED BY THE DEPARTMENT OF STATE AND THE VEHICLE OR ENGINE WILL NOT BE SOLD IN THE UNITED STATES.

5. THE IMPORTER OR CONSIGNEE IS A NON RESIDENT OF THE UNITED STATES IMPORTING SUCH VEHICLE OR ENGINE FOR PERSONAL USE FOR NOT MORE THAN ONE YEAR FROM THE DATE OF ENTRY, AND THE VEHICLE OR ENGINE WILL NOT BE SOLD IN THE UNITED STATES.

6. THE VEHICLE OR ENGINE IS BEING IMPORTED FOR THE PURPOSE OF TESTING AND WILL NOT BE SOLD OR OPERATED ON THE PUBLIC HIGHWAYS WITHOUT THE PRIOR WRITTEN CONSENT OF THE ADMINISTRATOR OF THE U.S. ENVIRONMENTAL PROTECTION AGENCY.

7. THE VEHICLE OR ENGINE IS INTENDED SOLELY FOR EXPORT.

8. THE VEHICLE OR ENGINE IS NOT SUBJECT TO THE REGULATIONS UNDER THE CLEAN AIR ACT BECAUSE IT IS A

   a. VEHICLE MANUFACTURED BEFORE THE 1968 MODEL YEAR.

   b. NON CHASSIS MOUNTED ENGINE TO BE USED IN A LIGHT DUTY VEHICLE. *(NOTE A light-duty vehicle is a vehicle designed primarily for transportation of property and rated at 6,000 pounds GVW or less or designed primarily for transportation of persons with a capacity of 12 persons or less.)*

   c. ENGINE MANUFACTURED BEFORE JANUARY 1, 1970 FOR USE IN A HEAVY DUTY VEHICLE. *(NOTE A heavy-duty vehicle is a vehicle designed primarily for transportation of property and rated at more than 6,000 pounds GVW or designed primarily for transportation of persons with a capacity of more than 12 persons.)*

   d. LIGHT DUTY NON GASOLINE FUELED VEHICLE. *(e.g. diesel-fueled light-duty vehicle)*

   e. MOTORCYCLE.

   f. RACING VEHICLE NOT TO BE OPERATED ON PUBLIC STREETS OR HIGHWAYS.

9. THE VEHICLE OR ENGINE IS ONE OF A CLASS OF VEHICLES OR ENGINES FOR WHICH AN APPLICATION FOR A CERTIFICATE OF CONFORMITY IS PENDING BEFORE THE ADMINISTRATOR OF THE U.S. ENVIRONMENTAL PROTECTION AGENCY, AND IS BEING IMPORTED UNDER BOND.

10. THE VEHICLE OR ENGINE IS NOT IN CONFORMITY WITH APPLICABLE EMISSION STANDARDS, BUT WILL BE BROUGHT INTO CONFORMITY WITH SUCH STANDARDS, AND IS BEING IMPORTED UNDER BOND.

11. NEITHER THE IMPORTER NOR THE ULTIMATE CONSIGNEE POSSESSES SUFFICIENT INFORMATION TO MAKE ANY OF THE PRECEDING DECLARATIONS, BUT THE IMPORTER OR ULTIMATE CONSIGNEE WILL SEEK TO DETERMINE SUCH INFORMATION, AND THE VEHICLE OR ENGINE IS BEING IMPORTED UNDER BOND.

WARNING: Entry under provisions 9, 10, and 11 requires posting of bond at the time of entry equal to the value of the merchandise plus duty for delivery of the vehicle or engine. In less than 90 days after entry to the District Director of Customs. Written notice that a vehicle or engine has been admitted under bond must be sent by the importer not later than 5 days after entry to the U.S. Environmental Protection Agency, Mobile Source Enforcement Division, 401 M Street, S.W., Washington, D.C. 20460. The information required in such notice is set forth in the instructions printed below on this form. A vehicle admitted under bond must be redelivered to port of entry unless certification is granted, or the Administrator makes a determination in writing that the vehicle has been modified to conform to applicable standards.

NAME OF IMPORTER *(Please print)*	NAME OF CONSIGNEE *(Please print)*

ADDRESS OF IMPORTER	ADDRESS OF CONSIGNEE

SIGNATURE OF IMPORTER OR CONSIGNEE	

National Highway Traffic Safety Administration Requirements
(NHTSA)

Imported motor carriages are subject to safety standards under the Motor Vehicle Safety Act of 1966. It was intended to "insure fast, safe, convenient and efficient transportation for the economic stabiltiy and general welfare of the country." All vehicles manufactured on or after January 1, 1968, must conform to these Federal Motor Vehicle safety standards.

- The regulations are quite extensive and cover items such as: occupant crash protection, brake hoses, side door strength, roof crush resistance, flammability of interior materials and bumper requirements.

    a. Not all individual safety regulations (there are over 45) will have to be changed. However, you'll have to demonstrate either they're legal or have been brought into conformity.

    b. On many cars the cost of compliance could be greater than the vehicle's actual cost!

- No automobile shall be refused entry by NHTSA if it bears a certification label affixed by the original manufacturer. This tag will be located on the driver's door post (next to the door latch) or driver's door (inside seam). In affect it will state, "This vehicle conforms to all applicable safety standards for 19__," or "This vehicle meets all bumper standards for 19__ motor vehicles."

    a. These certification statements in many cases are included on the vehicle's weight, load capacity, and body color tag located in the same area.

    b. If you doubt the validity of this tag (I would check in every case before buying), write the serial number down and contact the manufacturer. They will tell you when the car was officially manufactured.

- If the certification tag is missing, you will be required to file a Department Of Transportation (DOT) form HS-7. A statement from the original manufacturer must be attached to this declaration indicating the automobile was manufactured in conformity.

    a. Remember. Before purchasing any 1968 or later automobile lacking a tag, you should verify compliance with the manufacturer!

    b. The chassis serial number will identify any vehicle as to conformity. This is a very important point!

- Form HS-7 must also be filed when motor cars are brought into compliance after manufacture but prior to their importation.

    a. Include a statement from the person who brought the vehicle into conformity describing the work done.

    b. If either statement is not attached (to form HS-7), a bond equal to the automobile's value must be posted.

(Note: See "Importing A Nonconforming Motor Car" in this chapter, p. 258.)

● Anyone who attempts to import a nonconforming automobile and refuses to sign a declaration (form HS-7) will be refused entry! Study the declaration form closely.

FORM HS-7

Form HS-7 (R. 3-71)	IMPORTATION OF MOTOR VEHICLES AND MOTOR VEHICLE EQUIPMENT SUBJECT TO FEDERAL MOTOR VEHICLE SAFETY STANDARDS (P.L. 89-563 SECTS. 108 AND 114, 19 C.F.R. 12.80)		U.S. DEPARTMENT OF TRANSPORTATION NATIONAL HIGHWAY TRAFFIC SAFETY ADMINISTRATION
DISTRICT AND PORT		DATE OF DECLARATION	CUSTOMS ENTRY NUMBER AND DATE
MAKE OF MOTOR VEHICLE		YEAR	PORT CODE NUMBER
MODEL	ENGINE SERIAL NUMBER		BODY SERIAL OR OTHER IDENTIFICATION NUMBER
DESCRIPTION OF MOTOR VEHICLE EQUIPMENT			

I declare that the motor vehicle or motor vehicle equipment (merchandise hereafter) described above and offered for importation does not bear a certification label affixed by its original manufacturer as required by section 114 of PL 89-563 and regulations issued thereunder but that such merchandise is eligible for admission into the United States pursuant to 19 C.F.R. 12.80(b) because: (Check one)

☐ 1. The merchandise was manufactured on a date when there was no Federal Motor Vehicle Safety Standard in effect which was applicable to it.

☐ 2. The merchandise was not manufactured in conformity with applicable Federal Motor Vehicle Safety Standards, but has since been brought into conformity *in accordance with the attached statement of the manufacturer, contractor, or other person who has brought the merchandise into conformity and which describes the nature and extent of the work performed.*

NOTE: Where the statement is not attached, 19 C.F.R. 12.80 (c) requires entry to be made under bond.

☐ 3. The merchandise does not conform with applicable Federal Motor Vehicle Safety Standards, but I will bring it into conformity with such standards and will not sell or offer it for sale until the bond required by 19 C.F.R. 12.80 (c) has been released.

WARNING: Entry under this provision requires posting of bond, equal to value of the merchandise, for the delivery of a conformity statement no later than 90 days after entry to the District Director of Customs and the National Highway Traffic Safety Administration, 400 7th Street, S.W., Washington, D.C. 20590, Attn: 41-22 CUS. Vehicle *must be redelivered to port of entry* upon failure to provide satisfactory statement.

☐ 4. The merchandise consists of new vehicles being imported for purposes of resale, and such vehicles do not presently conform to all applicable Federal Motor Vehicle Safety Standards because readily attachable equipment items are not attached, but there is affixed to the windshield of each vehicle a label stating the standard with which and the manner in which the

vehicle does not conform and that the vehicle will be brought into conformity by attachment of such equipment items before it is offered for sale to the first purchaser for purposes other than resale.

☐ 5. I am a nonresident of the United States and I am importing the merchandise primarily for personal use, or to make repairs or alterations to it, for a period not to exceed one year from the date of entry and I will not resell it in the United States during that time.

☐ 6. I am a member of the armed forces of a foreign country, or member of the Secretariat of a public international organization and so designated pursuant to 59 stat. 669, or a member of the personnel of a foreign government on assignment in the United States who comes within the class of persons for whom free entry of vehicles has been authorized by the Department of State and I am importing the merchandise for purposes other than for sale.

☐ 7. I am importing the merchandise solely for purposes of show, test, experiment, competition, repairs, or alterations and the merchandise will not be sold or licensed for use on the public roads.

☐ 8. The merchandise was not manufactured primarily for use on the public roads and is not a "motor vehicle" as defined in section 102 of PL 89-563.

☐ 9. The merchandise was manufactured in conformity with applicable Federal Motor Vehicle Safety Standards, in accordance with the attached statement of the original manufacturer.

NOTE: If statement is not attached, 19 C.F.R. 12.80 (c) requires entry to be made under bond.

The information given above is true and correct to the best of my knowledge and belief.

PRINTED OR TYPED NAME OF IMPORTER	PRINTED OR TYPED NAME OF DECLARANT
	SIGNATURE
ADDRESS OF IMPORTER	CAPACITY OF DECLARANT
CITY AND STATE IN WHICH VEHICLE IS TO BE REGISTERED	ADDRESS OF DECLARANT

Motor Cars Constructed After September 1, 1972

True, importing a nonconforming car built between January 1, 1968, and August 31, 1972, can be relatively simple. But mountains of conversion work will be necessary on cars constructed after September 1, 1972. Especially those 1975 or newer. This is the date new bumper regulations for cars took effect. In 99.9 percent of the cases, the purchase of a brand new model produced in the United States would be less expensive than the conversion of a used foreign version. I highly recommend not importing such a beast!

Every automobile importer must file DOT form HS-189 (a statement of compliance) with United States Customs. This form contains information used by the Customs Service and NHTSA to monitor motor vehicles for compliance to federal safety standards. On the following pages, only pages 1 and 8 are shown.

FORM HS-189 PAGE ONE

DEPARTMENT OF TRANSPORTATION
NATIONAL HIGHWAY TRAFFIC SAFETY ADMINISTRATION
DIRECTOR, OFFICE OF STANDARDS ENFORCEMENT (N41–22) (CUS)
2100 2nd STREET, SW
WASHINGTON, D.C. 20590
(Complete this form and mail to above address)

Form Approved

O.M.B. No. 04R-5661

STATEMENT OF COMPLIANCE

"*This is to Certify* that the motor vehicle described below conforms to all applicable Federal Motor Vehicle Safety Standards (FMVSS) in effect on the date of manufacture, as indicated below."

Name of Importer as shown on Customs Entry *(Type or Print)*	Port of Entry	Customs Entry Number and Date

Make and Model of Vehicle	Year Manufactured

Complete Chassis Serial Number *(Include all Prefixes)*	Engine Serial Number	

Please Sign Here	Signature of Importer	PCI Number	Date

Please Note:

You must indicate on the line next to each requirement outlined below the status of compliance, i.e., indicate:

ORIGINAL _____ If the item was part of the original factory equipment;
MODIFIED O/S _____ If the modification was made overseas;
MODIFIED IN USA _____ If the modification was made in USA subsequent to importation.

You **must** attach to this Statement of Compliance all vouchers and receipted work orders identifying the modifier and describing the *exact* nature and extent of work performed.

The Applicability Key is as follows:

PC = Passenger Car   TRK = Truck
MPV = Multi-Purpose Passenger Vehicle   BUS = Bus

The numerals 1–68, etc., indicate that the requirement is applicable to vehicles manufactured on or after January 1, 1968, etc.

All subsequent pages and attached vouchers and documents must show the importer's name and vehicle chassis serial number.

The listing shown below is not intended to represent the complete or detailed requirements of the Federal Motor Vehicle Safety Standards, but only to indicate the areas of apparent noncompliance which may exist with respect to your vehicle.

Indicate if item is Original, Modified
O/S or Modified in USA

FMVSS 101   *CONTROL LOCATION, IDENTIFICATION, AND ILLUMINATION*

This part applies to: PC=1–68

The following controls, when mounted on the instrument panel, must be identified:

_____ Headlamps

_____ Choke (if manual)

_____ Windshield defrosting and defogging system

_____ Windshield wiping system

_____ Windshield washing system

This part applies to: PC=1–72   MPV=9–72   TRK=9–72   BUS=9–72

All manually-operated controls must be identified as follows:

Word or Abbreviation	Permissible Symbol
CHOKE	None
THROTTLE	None
LIGHTS	🔅
HAZARD	⚠
CLEARANCE LAMPS or CL LPS	⚞
IDENTIFICATION LAMPS or ID LPS	None
WIPER or WIPE	⊊
WASHER or WASH	⊛
DEFROST or DEF	None

Don't Become A Manufacturer

On page eight of form HS-189 is paragraph 15-USC-102-(5). It states, "Indicate whether the vehicle has been imported for resale within six months from the date of entry." Don't circle the word "Yes!" As an importer for resale, the law classifies you as a manufacturer. There are many additional regulations to comply with. Believe me. You don't want to become a manufacturer!

FORM HS-189 PAGE EIGHT

Indicate if item is Original, Modified
O/S or Modified in USA

FMVSS 216

ROOF CRUSH RESISTANCE

This part applies to: PC = 9–73 MPV = n/a TRK = n/a BUS = n/a

The vehicle's body must meet strength requirements equal to those incorporated in a model certified by the manufacturer to resist a force of 1½ times the unloaded vehicle weight of the vehicle or 5,000 pounds, whichever is less, applied to either side of the forward edge of the vehicle's roof.

FMVSS 217

BUS WINDOW RETENTION AND RELEASE

This part applies to: PC = n/a MPV = n/a TRK = n/a BUS = 9–73

The bus windows, other than windshield, must meet retention requirements specified in this standard.

Clearly identified emergency exits must be provided.

FMVSS 301

FUEL SYSTEM INTEGRITY

This part applies to: PC = 1–68 MPV = n/a TRK = n/a BUS = n/a

The fuel system must be equal in design to that installed in a model certified by the manufacturer, such system to prevent loss of fuel at a rate greater than one ounce *(by weight)* per minute upon termination of impact of barrier collision test at 30 mph. Fuel loss during impact shall not exceed one ounce *(by weight)*.

FMVSS 302

FLAMMABILITY OF INTERIOR MATERIALS

This part applies to: PC = 9–72 MPV = 9–72 TRK = 9–72 BUS = 9–72

Materials used in the occupant compartment, such as seat cushions, seat backs, seat belts, head-lining, convertible tops, arm rests, all trim panels including door, front, rear, and side panels, compartment shelves, head restraints, floor coverings, sun visors, curtains, shades, wheel housing covers, engine compartment covers, etc., must be essentially equal to those used by the manufacturer in his certified models, such is to have a burn rate across its surface at less than 4 inches per minute.

15 USC 102(5)

Indicate whether the vehicle has been imported for resale within six (6) months from the date of entry: Yes   No   If the answer is yes, attach to this compliance statement a sample of the certification label affixed to the vehicle.

A person importing motor vehicles for resale is a manufacturer under Section 102(5) of the National Traffic and Motor Vehicle Safety Act of 1966 (15 USC 102(5)) and must comply with the following regulations:

49 CFR 566—Manufacturer Identification
49 CFR 567—Certification
49 CFR 573—Defect Reports
49 CFR 574—Tire Identification and Recordkeeping
49 CFR 575—Consumer Information
49 CFR 577—Defect Notification
49 CFR 580—Odometer Disclosure Requirements

Copies of these regulations may be obtained by writing or telephoning this office (202–426–1693).

Printed name of importer	Complete chassis serial number

For more detailed information write or call

NATIONAL HIGHWAY TRAFFIC SAFETY ADMINISTRATION
Attention: N-41-22-CUS (Buzzard Point)
2100 2nd Street, S.W.
Washington, D.C. 20590
PH: 202 426-1693

U.S. DEPARTMENT OF TRANSPORTATION
National Highway Traffic Safety Administration
Two Embarcadero Center, Suite 610
San Francisco, CA 94111
PH: 415 556-6415

Procedures Before Shipment

Arrangements for shipping your car are made by you, the importer. Your responsibilities are:

a. A broker must be hired to arrange the exit papers and clear the car through customs in its original country.

b. The U.S. Department of Agriculture requires each chassis be free from foreign soil before entry into the United States. Have all under carriage components steam cleaned before embarking for the U.S.

c. All shipments must be cleared through Customs at the first port of arrival. Make sure the vehicle is being shipped directly to your nearest port! This enables you to personally clear it through Customs. Otherwise a bond will have to be posted and the car shipped in Customs' custody. If possible, avoid posting a bond.

d. Arrange to be notified in advance by the shipper of the date the car will arrive in the United States.

e. Expect a few small dings or dents during shipment. Photograph the car just before it is loaded. In order to collect on any insurance policy these photographs will be required.

f. Before shipment, contact your personal insurance agent and cover the motor car against damage. It's the only way to assure yourself you'll be able to collect!

Packing Personal Belongings In The Car

I feel you should not pack personal belongings in your car when it is shipped to the United States. Some of the reasons are:

- Personal possessions are very susceptible to pilferage and theft while the vehicle is at the dock awaiting shipment, in the open holds of the vessel bringing the car, and on the docks in the United States.

- Many shippers or carriers will not accept a vehicle for shipment if it is packed with personal belongings.

- The shipper or carrier is required to present to Customs a complete list of everything transported, including the contents of your car. When this is not done, the shipper or carrier is fined.

- Your car's complete contents must be declared at the time the car is presented to the U.S. Customs for entry into the United States. If this is not done, you are subject to fine and your car and its contents are subject to seizure.

Remove The Accessories

Before your new jewel is delivered to any port for shipment, have the following items removed: radio and speakers, tools, manuals, shift knob, hood ornament, outside mirrors, emblems, etc. If you can't take care of this yourself, have a shipping concern (agent) remove these accessories as per your instructions. They should be inventoried, packed and shipped separately by air express. Be sure to keep a copy of this inventory and its stated value.

Here's how to avoid paying a double-duty tax on these items! Give a Power of Attorney (form) to the Custom's representative working for your air freight company. U.S. Customs can now clear these articles and ship them directly to you without you personally being there. A 2.9 percent duty tax will be charged based on the appraised value. Pay it. When your car arrives at the pier, present your copy of the stated value of the accessories and the receipt for payment. Subtract this amount (the stated value of the accessories) from the appaised value of the car before you pay the tax on it!

Shipping Agents Offering Services

These shipping agents (concerns) offer services for international motor car shipment. Each will remove all accessories, steam clean the undercarriage and take photographs as per your instructions.

DANIAL HUSTINGS LTD
63 North Action Road
London NW 10 6PJ
PH: 01-961-1000
Telex 23563

ROLA SHIPPING LTD
4a Deodar Road
Putney, London SW 15
Ph: 01-789-7205

SWANSCOMBE AUTO EXPORTS
Swanscombe Garage
3 Swanscombe Road
Holland Park, London W11
PH: 01-602-3555

Shipping Options

Three shipping options are open to you: (a) air freight, (b) container and (c) open hold cargo. Air freight is fast and safe but expensive! Containerized cargo is moderately expensive, safe, but slow. Open hold cargo (frequently referred to as breakable cargo) is slow and dangerous but the least costly. Let's take a closer look at each—then you decide.

Air Cargo

Air cargo is based on price per pound or volume weight (amount of cubic feet it occupies) whichever is greater. On a Volkswagon weighing 2,100 pounds and a Rolls Royce weighing 5,000 pounds, these are current shipping costs.

Volkswagon

London to New York	*$2,000*
London to Los Angeles	*$3,000*

Rolls Royce

London to New York	*$4,700*
London to Los Angeles	*$6,800*

Before shipment, all petrol must be drained from the gas tank and the battery disconnected. Some freight lines even require the removal of the entire gas tank.

Containerized Cargo

Containerized cargo is one of the safest methods for motor car transport. Each container is packed and sealed, avoiding any chance of loose freight smashing into your beautiful buggy. The most widely used container for motor car shipment is the small 20 foot container (inside measurement 19' 3 1/2" long by 7' 7 1/2" wide by 7' 5" high). Two factors determine shipping cost:

(1) The number of cubic meters an item occupies inside (a small container has 33.6 meters), or

(2) The total weight. The cost will be whichever factor is greater.

Shipping lines carry a minimum charge per container, currently between $1,200—$1,500. It's very unlikely a motor car would fit these minimum charges! On containers shipped from England to Los Angeles, carriers are averaging $115 per cubic meter or $3,900 for the entire container. Large automobiles such as a Rolls Royce or Mercedes Benz will require the whole container. But, with smaller vehicles (MG or VW, etc.) it might be possible to place two automobiles in one shipment. Your shipping costs are cut in half.

Open Hold *(Breakable Cargo)*

Open hold or breakable cargo is definitely your cheapest shipping method, though not the safest! Automobiles are parked next to one another in the freighter's hold. Frequently, during the voyage, one or two vehicles will move about creating driverless accidents! These open hold charges are based on a car shipped from England.

Type of car	East Coast	West Coast	Gulf Ports
Mercedes Benz	$950	$1,000	$1,025
Volkswagon	$650	$ 700	$ 725

You can anticipate a minimum shipping time of 15 to 20 days to the East coast and 20 days to the West Coast.

Port Of Entry Procedures

Every Automobile Is Taxed

Once your car has landed stateside (whether new or used) it must be declared to United States Customs at the actual purchase price. A 2.9 percent tax will be assessed based on the Customs officer's appraised value. The selling price in the country of exportation will be taken into consideration but may not coincide necessarily with the Customs officer's estimated value! The Customs Service reserves the right to reaccess the car's value and may come around later demanding more money!

Keep in mind. All persons bringing an automobile into the United States for any purpose must pay tax. There is one exception. A car built in Canada by a Canadian manufacturer is admitted duty free. Imported vehicles from the Sino-Soviet block have a duty rate of 10 percent, although Poland, Rumania and Hungary are exempt from this high tariff!

Value Is Based On Actual Examination

On new cars duty tax will be based on a value (approximating the wholesale value) determined by the examining Custom's officer. Since used cars reflect different degrees of wear and tear, there are no established allowances for use or depreciation. The Custom's value of a used car depends solely upon actual examination. The value of a new car of identical year, make and model is used. This new car value is reduced as warranted by mileage, condition of body, engine, interior, wear of tires and the like.

Returning Resident's Customs Exemption

Returning U.S. residents may apply their custom's exemption (presently $300 per person) toward the taxable value of a foreign made car if:

a. The car accompanies you at the time of your return on the same carrier.

b. It was imported for your personal use or for use by members of your household.

c. The car was acquired abroad as a part of the trip from which you're returning.

Families May Make Joint Customs Exemptions

Any head of a family may make a joint declaraton for all members residing in the same household when returning to the United States. They may apply their custom's exemptions toward the value of the imported car.

Example: You're returning from Italy by cargo ship with your two children and wife. By using each family member's customs exemption, you may deduct $1,200 from the vehicle's appraised value!

Exemptions For Government Personnel

Government personnel (civilian or military) are exempt from any duty tax if:

a. You've been stationed in Europe, and
b. You have already purchased a vehicle for personal use before your government orders to leave are issued.

Obtain Needed Statements In Advance

Allow one whole day upon arrival at the port of entry for completing paperwork, going through customs and paying fees. Vehicles not conforming to EPA or DOT standards usually take longer! Remember. Any statements needed as to whether your vehicle conforms to federal safety and air pollution control standards must be obtained in advance of Customs!

What To Do When Notified Of Delivery

The shipping agent notifies you of delivery. Ask this agent how much you owe and in what currency they wish to be paid. Arrange this payment with your bank. With the original bill of lading from your carrier, the bill of sale, foreign registration and any other documents pertaining to the motor car proceed to U.S. Customs. Be prepared to:

- Pay an import duty tax of 2.9 percent of appraised value.

- File EPA Form 3520-1 regardless of compliance *(See "EPA Requirements" p. 246.)*

- File DOT Form HS-189 regardless of compliance *(See "NHTSA Requirements" p. 248.)*

- Post a bond on nonconforming vehicles and file DOT Form HS-7 *(See "NHTSA Requirements" p. 248)* and customs form 7551, 7553 or 7593 *(See "Importing A Nonconforming Motor Car" p. 258.)*

- Pay any Department Of Agricultural chassis cleaning fee (usually $50).

Note: A custom house broker can be employed to take an automobile through Customs. For a small fee (between $75 and $150) a broker will handle the above requirements. Brokers are listed in the yellow pages under "Custom." If you're importing a noncomforming car, I sure recommend using one!

Have Any Damage Acknowledged

Before driving off into the sunset, check for body damage! Compare the pictures taken before shipment to the car's present condition. Point out any new body wrinkles to the insurance company surveyor at the pier and have him acknowledge it on the spot! If there is damage, take close-up photographs to use later in filing your claim.

Importing A Nonconforming Motor Car

Under bond, any concomplying automobile may be admitted but must be brought into conformity within 90 days after importation! The posting of a custom's bond guarantees you will bring this car into compliance with U.S. regulations. This bond is obtainable from most custom's brokers (Yellow pages under "Custom"). There are some rather strict requirements for securing a bond to post.

a. A cash deposit will be held by the bond writer. The amount varies from 50 to 100 percent of the assessed value plus duty charges or . . .

b. A letter of credit will be issued from your bank in favor of the assurity (bond writer) plus duty charges.

Most bond writers charge a minimum of $20 or $1 per thousand dollars of assessed value (whichever is greater) for this service. The entry of your car will be accepted only if you post this bond on Customs Form 7551, or 7553, or 7593.

CUSTOMS FORM 7551

U.S. CUSTOMS SERVICE

No. ....

IMMEDIATE DELIVERY AND CONSUMPTION ENTRY BOND (Single Entry)

(To redeliver merchandise, to produce documents, to perform conditions of release, such as to label, hold for inspection, set-up etc. to be taken in all cases when release is requested prior to inspection, examination, or liquidation)

KNOW ALL MEN BY THESE PRESENTS That* ....

_____

of .... , as principal,

and* .... , of ....,

and .... , of ....

as sureties, are held and firmly bound unto the UNITED STATES OF AMERICA in the sum of_____

_____ dollars ($_____),
for the payment of which we bind ourselves, our heirs, executors, administrators, successors, and assigns, jointly
and severally, firmly by these presents.

WITNESS our hands and seals this _____ day of _____, 19___

WHEREAS, certain articles described in an application dated _____, 19___, for special

permit to land and deliver immediately are expected to arrive at the port of _____,

from _____, on _____, and the immediate delivery of such article is
necessary; and   (Vessel, vehicle, or aircraft)

WHEREAS, pursuant to regulations promulgated under the provisions of section 448 (b), Tariff Act of 1930,
the above-bounden principal desires the release of the articles described in the application prior to the making of
an entry therefor and the payment of duties thereon; or

WHEREAS, certain articles have been imported at the port of _____, and entered at

said port for consumption on entry No. _____, dated _____, 19___, and described
therein; and

WHEREAS, the above-bounden principal may request that the merchandise be examined elsewhere than at
the public store, wharf, or other place in charge of a customs officer; and

WHEREAS, the above-bounden principal desires release of the articles described in the permit or entry prior
to the ascertainment by customs officers of the quantity and value of such articles, and of the full amount of the
duties and charges due thereon, and prior to the decision by the proper officer as to the right of the articles to
admission into the United States;

NOW, THEREFORE, THE CONDITION OF THIS OBLIGATION IS SUCH THAT—

(1) The above-bounden principal, in consideration of the release of all or any part of the shipment covered
by the entry specified above before the full amount of duties and taxes imposed upon or by reason of importation
has been finally determined, and notwithstanding section 485 (d), Tariff Act of 1930, or any other provisions of
law, voluntarily undertakes and agrees to pay any and all such duties and taxes found to be due on the shipment

*If the principal or surety is a corporation, the name of the State in which incorporated also shall be shown.

CUSTOMS FORM 7551

Secure A Single-Trip Permit To Drive

Customs will not release your car until both freight and import duty taxes are paid. Once the automobile is released you're still not permitted to drive it away from the port of entry! A single-trip permit must be arranged with the Department of Motor Vehicles. Automobiles not driveable have to be transported to the location where the compliance work will be performed. At this time you can expect a minimum delay of 60 days before taking delivery.

Independent Garages Doing Conversion Work

For conversion work meeting federal requirements you'll get little cooperation from a factory-authorized dealer. An independent garage mechanic familiar with conversion work will have to be located. Information regarding modifications to bring a noncon-forming automobile into compliance can be obtained from the manufacturer or contact one of these qualified companies.

ACC
217 Smith Road
Spring Valley, NY 10977
PH: 914 425-3622

AMERISPEC
86 Mill Plaing Road
Danbury, CT 06810
or
P.O. Box 681
Ridgefield, CT 06877
PH: 203 744-0844

AUTOMOTIVE COMPLIANCE
25518 Frampton Avenue
Harbor City, CA 90710
PH:213 539-4880

CHINETTE INTERNATIONAL MOTORS
342 W Putnam Avenue
Greenwich, CT 06830
PH: 203 869-9210

Exhaust Emission Control Requirements Are Complex

Be sure to have all your compliance work documented including photographs, drawings and plans. These items will be required by both EPA and NHTSA agencies. The most difficult and complex por-tion of any conversion is in the area of exhaust emission controls. Your car must conform to the exhaust level for its particular year of manufacture! This can mean adding an air pump, thermal reactor or catalytic converter, etc.

The EPA now requires an exhaust emission test by an accredited emission laboratory. During these tests any slight malfunctioning of the carburetor, injector nozzle or fuel float can cause the car to fail these requirements. At $1,000 per test this can get expensive! For the emission test contact:

OLSON ENGINEERING
15512 Commerce Lane
Huntington Beach, CA 92649
PH: 714 891-4821

SATRA AUTOMOTIVE EMISSION LABORATORY
U.S. 1 and 9 South
Newark, NJ 07114
PH: 201 242-7665

What Happens If Car Doesn't Conform In 90 Days?

When NHTSA requirements and EPA emission tests are completed, all documentation (photographs, test results, etc.) are then sent to each respective federal agency. Upon their approval the Custom's bond can be released enabling you to legally register and drive your motor carriage—at last! But, keep in mind the car could be called back at any time for another inspection. You can later be required to prove your vehicle still complies with government regulations. This usually doesn't happen.

Once Started The Job Must Be Completed!

You can become subject to a penalty up to $10,000 if you fail to either bring your imported automobile into conformity or export it within 90 days. In addition, you will forfeit your Custom's bond. Remain alert!

Where To Find Detailed Information

If you think Customs is strict, you're correct! My advice is not to import any automobile unless you can determine (before purchase) the exact modifications required! For more detailed information write or call one of the nine regional custom's offices. Within these nine regions are 45 district offices and about 300 ports of entry.

REGION I CUSTOMS OFFICE
100 Summer Street
Boston, MA 02110

REGION II CUSTOMS OFFICE
6 World Trade Center
New York, NY 10048

REGION III CUSTOMS OFFICE
40 S Gay Street
Baltimore, MD 21202

REGION IV CUSTOMS OFFICE
99 SE, 5th Street
Miami, FL 33131

REGION V CUSTOMS OFFICE
1440 Canal Street
New Orleans, LA 70112

REGION VI CUSTOMS OFFICE
500 Dallas Avenue
Houston, TX 77002

REGION VII CUSTOMS OFFICE
300 N Los Angeles Street
Los Angeles, CA 90053

DISTRICT DIRECTOR OF CUSTOMS
Port Of Los Angeles-Long Beach
300 South Ferry Street
Terminal Island, CA 90731
PH: 213 548-2461

REGION VIII CUSTOMS OFFICE
211 Main Street
San Francisco, CA 94102

REGION IX CUSTOMS OFFICE
55 E. Monroe Street
Chicago, IL 60603

For further information contact:

U.S. CUSTOMS SERVICE
Department Of The Treasury
1301 Constitution Avenue NW
Washington, D.C. 20229
PH: 202 566-5286

Buying And Importing Sight Unseen

Yes, you can buy, import and own a Rolls, Jag, Mercedes or Ferrari without making the long journey yourself! Sound impossible? It isn't. I'll explain how.

An excellent selection of previously owned foreign, antique and late model automobiles is brought up to date each month in the ad section of some interesting magazines. There are ads from dealers all over the world. Single out your dream carriage from among the cars listed for sale. If not at the newsstand, write:

CAR MAGAZINE
64 West Smithfield
London, EC1

HEMMINGS MOTOR NEWS
Box 100
Bennington, VT 05201

THOROUGHBRED & CLASSIC CARS
IPC Transport Press Ltd
Dorset House
Stamford Street
London SE1 9LU

VETERAN AND VINTAGE
Independent Magazines Ltd
Bridge House
181 Queen Victoria Street
London EC4 4DD

Be Sure Photos Are Process Dated!

Once you have narrowed the field and located the machine of your choice, request photographs. Then, if the car still tickles your fancy, investigate further. Ask for a complete set of detailed current pictures of the automobile. Include the following photo angles: (a) front and rear, (b) left and right side, (c) inside the trunk compartment, (d) inside the engine bay and (e) complete interior. Don't expect anybody (dealer or private party) to take all these pictures for free! Include money to pay for this time and cost factor. Steer clear of anyone who does not agree to take these photographs!

In England, for a small fee, the Royal Auto Club will send a professional assessor to inspect the motor car and write an honest report. Pictures will be taken and process dated so you know they're current! Write:

ROYAL AUTO CLUB
80-91 Pall Mall
London SW1

The Importance Of A Phone Call

Carefully examine all photographs and reports. *(Note: See "What To Look For When Selecting A Used Car" in Chapter One, p. 50.)* With automobiles painted in dark colors, (burgundy, black, etc.) wavy body panels, dents and scratches tend to remain hidden in photographs. Don't be surprised if the European finish doesn't fit U.S. expectations!

Now, if you still like what you see, the time has come to place an all-important telephone call. In this phone conversation attempt to decipher the integrity and trustworthiness of the person you're talking to. With dealers, request the name, address and telephone number of private parties they have dealt with in the United States. Contact these people. Ask their opinion of the dealer's reputation.

Check back issues of the magazines I listed. Dealers who advertise year after year are more likely to be honest straight shooters. Why? Their business depends on the ads in these periodicals. Complaints sent to the editor usually produce negative publicity!

Procedures For Purchase

Before any automotive purchase, correspond with one of the many exporting agents. *(Note: Three are listed in section "Procedures Before Purchase" in this chapter, p. 254.)* With private party sales arrange for pickup and delivery by your shipping agent. Anticipate paying a little extra for this service. A dealer can be expected to deliver the automobile to the shipping concern.

1. Ask the dealer in what currency they wish to receive payment.
2. Arrange with your bank for the correct currency and amount to be wired overseas. A small fee will be charged.
3. Send only the exact purchase price! All shipping, custom brokerage and chassis cleaning fees will be paid by you at the port of entry.

4. Instruct the dealer to prepare a condition report (including pictures) before the vehicle is removed from their premises. These photographs serve as an excellent record of the car's condition before shipment.
5. Make sure the Bill of Sale is notarized and in U.S. dollars.
6. Both the Bill of Sale and report must be sent to you immediately. At the time of delivery, take all paperwork to Customs for a smooth entry.

Food For Thought

- Are replacement parts available and can this imported car be serviced?

- Compare prices between your selected foreign vehicle and a comparable U.S. one. Can you justify buying and importing this automobile?

- The 1967 and older vehicles are exempt from EPA and DOT requirements. These carriages are the prime candidates for importation.

- In many cases foreign automobiles contain "do-hickeys" defying American automotive explanation. Obtain an owner's manual!

- Collectors, recognized engineering facilities and racers may bring nonconforming cars into the country so long as they won't be driven on the street.

- Although a 1971 or newer nonconforming car may be admitted under bond, modifications may be impractical, impossible, or require extensive engineering.

- Late model vehicles manufactured abroad in conformity with U.S. standards are exported for sale in the U.S. Beware of claims by a dealer or other seller that a vehicle meets such standards.

- Even though Canadian automobiles are admitted without duty charges, they're not exempt from U.S. regulations!

- Be cautious with foreign dealers. A few unscrupulous ones place older EPA and DOT certification labels on late model automobiles. Substituted labels do not fool Custom's inspectors!

- Consider the time lag between cash outlay and possession of car.

- Before you act, ask yourself the one important question, "Do I really want the hassle of importing a 1968 or newer motor car?"

Is The Dream Of Importing Still There?

Probably! Nothing ever overcomes the lure of the unknown. Importing exotic automobiles fits this category to a tee. I know. I've been there. You're guaranteed to have the adventure of a lifetime. It can be lot's of fun—especially if you use the experiences of others to your advantage. Take heed! Stick with the older models (1967 and older). Then someday with pride you, too, may own a part of history, feel the wind in your hair, and smell the air heavy with Castrol.

**The tachometer continued to climb . . .
lights dance across the hood!**

Code For International License Plate Letters

Letter Combinations By Country

While examining that foreign "cream puff," you might run across an unusual combination of letters. Maybe they're stamped on the license plate or attached to a plaque? If you do see them, approach this motor car with caution! You have unveiled a clue as to this car's true history and condition.

Example: Say you're looking over a Rolls Royce with left-hand steering and the letters "GB" (Great Britain) appear on the trunk. In reality she could be a right-hand drive car converted to left-hand steering or worse yet have a terminal case of metal decay (rust)!

Albania	AL	Hungary	H
Algeria	DZ	Iceland	IS
Andorra	AND	India	IND
Argentina	RA	Indonesia	RI
Australia	AUS	Iran	IR
Austria	A	Ireland	IRL
Bahamas	BS	Isle of Man	GBM
Belgium	B	Israel	IL
Bolivia	BOL	Italy	I
Brazil	BR	Ivory Coast	CI
Bulgaria	BG	Japan	J
Canada	CDN	Jordan	HKJ
Chile	RGH	Kenya	EAK
China	RC	Kuwait	KWT
Colombia	CO	Laos	LOA
Costa Rica	CR	Lebanon	RL
Cuba	C	Libya	LT
Cyprus	CY	Liechtenstein	FL
Czechoslovakia	CS	Luxemburg	L
Denmark	DK	Malagasy Republic	RM
Dominican Republic	DOM	Malaya	MAL
Ecuador	EC	Malta	M
El Salvador	ES	Mexico	MEX
Egypt	ET	Monaco	MC
Ethiopia	ETH	Morocco	MA
Finland	SF	Netherlands	NL
France	F	New Zealand	NZ
Germany (E)	DDR	Norway	N
Germany (W)	D	Pakistan	PAK
Ghana	GH	Paraguay	PY
Gibraltar	GBZ	Peru	PE
Great Britain	GB	Phillippines	PI
Greece	GR	Poland	PL

Portugal . . . . P
Rhodesia . . . . RSR
Romania . . . . R
San Marino . . . . RSM
Senegal . . . . SN
South Africa . . . . ZA
South Korea . . . . ROK
South Vietnam . . . . VN
Spain . . . . E
Sri Lanka CL
Sweden . . . . S
Switzerland . . . . CH
Syria . . . . SYR

Thailand . . . . T
Trinidad . . . . TT
Tunisia . . . . TN
Turkey . . . . TR
United Arab Emirates . . . . TO
United States of America . . . USA
Uruguay . . . . U
USSR . . . . SU
Venezuela . . . . YU
Yugoslavia . . . . YU
Zaire . . . . ZAI
Zambia . . . . Z

CHAPTER IV

Adventures
With A
Disappearing Breed

Automobiles
Your Profitable Pastime

The World
Of
Classic Automobiles

The Secret Is

The world of classic, vintage, antique, collectable and investment automobiles (terms used interchangeably) encompasses hundreds of makes and models. Many one-of-a-kind vehicles are part of this historic past. These are every bit as original as a Picasso painting and have increased in value accordingly. Duesenbergs, for example, appreciated over 150 percent in a six-year time span.

For this reason, not to mention inflation, unpredictable economic and nostalgic reasons, owning these antiquated vehicles has become one of the fastest growing hobbies in the United States.

Vehicle age is not the most important consideration enabling you to make money with this enjoyable hobby. **The secret is to purchase the correct make and model.** Only then, will it provide a hedge against inflation.

Let Reason Hold The Reins

Automobiles are a fun and exciting hobby. The hobby can become a source of relaxation. It can also be a money-making pastime. However, approach it with caution. Study and investigate before you act. This is the reason we cover investment automobiles so thoroughly in *Automobile Success*. You must gain this knowledge to be successful!

Nothing is more frightening than ignorance in action. When it comes to collectable automobiles, passion may drive you, but let reason hold the reins. In the world of classic automobiles, one man's trash is not another man's treasure.

"Classic"—A Word Often Misused

When speaking of automobiles "classic" is the one word most often misused. Pick up any newspaper and look under antique autos in the classified section. You will find many "classics" for sale. Half aren't worth saving from the scrap yard. Two-thirds of those remaining are plain, old, doddering Detroit iron. They aren't classics—just junk! Sellers misusing words to entice buyers. If you have to tell people it's a classic—it isn't. I'll explain the difference. Collectable automobiles are probably one of the best investment choices in the world today—a disappearing breed. The challenge to you is there. The results can be spectacular.

Investing In Automobiles

Investing in automobiles can be compared to investing in diamonds. The sparkle may be beautiful, but if you don't know exactly what you are looking at, just enjoy the view. Time passes quickly. There are far fewer innovations than we are led to believe.

The Columbia Electric Truck offered power steering as an option in 1903. In the same year the Charter Mixed Vapor car operated on a fuel mix of 66 percent gasoline vapor and 33 percent atomized water. Across Europe, just one year before, an over supply of beets led to racing cars powered by alcohol fuel. By 1906 the United States produced a grand total of 33,200 cars—a record year. Then, in 1907 the Ford Company made over a million dollars in profit. The automobile age arrived! In those early days of the automobile, over 150 companies in the United States alone were manufacturing cars.

You Will Make Money

To a serious investor in collector automobiles, facts such as these show why you should arm yourself with the most up-to-date information available. Approach with care. If you want to make money with a hobby (and you can), then treat the hobby like you would a business. Follow price changes and market trends especially within the past two years. Then with good common sense, the information I'm going to give you in this book, a well-stocked bank account and some luck thrown in, you will make money. At times you can make a lot of money!

The First Cardinal Rule

● **Stick with automobiles well known by the general public!** Example: A 1911 McFarlan, 1928 Walter or 1927 Vulcan, though fine automobiles, would be difficult to liquidate other than to the true connoisseur of motor cars. The connoisseur is in love with a particular model. It is difficult to locate this person. When found, they, not you, are in the best position to bargain for your car!

   a. As a rule these types of automobiles present at least one problem to owners—their ownership can not be justified by a good return on invested money at the time of sale!

   b. Remember. Select automobiles everyone knows. Auburns, Cords, Duesenbergs, early Ford Thunderbirds, Pierce-Arrows, Lincoln Continental MK II's, MG-TC's, Packard's, all fall into this category. Choose top-of-the-line models along with those having unusual accessories and body styles. These automobiles will resale faster and your chances for higher profits will increase substantially.

Second Cardinal Rule

● **Never buy automobiles in need of extensive restoration or "basket cases".** Restoration work is very expensive! In general, you will spend more money completing a 95 point restoration than you can hope to sell it for in the immediate future. Both a large cash outlay and considerable time are involved. Forget working your fingernails to the bone! You will be time and money ahead buying a completely restored vehicle. This "Cardinal Rule" can't be over emphasized!

Third Cardinal Rule

● **Softop or convertible automobiles tend to rise in value faster than sedans or hardtops.** Naturally, these models sell easier, generally bringing more money. For example, 1961-64 Jaguar XKE's are contemporary classics. There is less demand for the coupe 2 + 2 version, but a true roadster, even one in poor condition, will sell faster for more money.

Fourth Cardinal Rule

● **Patience is a virtue.** Be prepared to wait for the right model at the right price. Then, when selling, prepare to wait for the right buyer. Make three correct guesses consecutively and you'll have established yourself as an expert. Everything will take longer than you expect. Don't plan to get rich quick! Time will be your ally.

    a. Example: As far as Ford Thunderbirds are concerned, only three models are considered true clasics—1955, '56 and '57. Now what vision do most of us have when discussing classic Thunderbirds? You can be sure it's porthole windows and a spare tire fitted onto the rear bumper assembly. And the year? Why 1955 of course. Wrong! This model came out in 1956, not 1955.

    b. All three models are collectable. All three are "Milestone Cars." Your best choice as an investor however, is the 1956 Thunderbird. This is the car the public visualizes whenever "Classic Thunderbird" is mentioned. To a future buyer there will be no need to qualify which Thunderbird you have. **You have the Thunderbird!**

It Takes Time To Play The Game

272

What Makes
One Model
Worth More Than Another

I WONDER WHAT THAT OLD CAR IS WORTH?

Ah, a mystery! The answer is elementary.

How Much Money Should I Sell My Car For

One of the most difficult problems in dealing with antique or collector automobiles is determining what makes one model worth more than another. Everyone has found themselves asking these questions: What should I pay for that car or what should I sell my own car for? The trouble with resisting temptation is it may never come again. As you get involved with automobiles you'll find great price differences between two cars of the same make, model and year. In some ways these two cars may be compared the way apple pie and kisses can. You know—apple pie without the cheese is like a kiss without the squeeze. Both lack something.

Prime Qualifications

Just what are the qualifications making one automobile worth more than another? Well, there are four. If the automobile you are thinking of buying or selling has one or more of these qualities, it definitely will be worth more than one not having any. If the car is to have value for investment or even just personal ownership, it must meet at least one of the four qualifications. These qualities are listed in the order of their importance.

Rarity

Condition

Quality Vehicle—Unique Styling

Previous Owners—History

- **Rarity:** This is of primary importance. The fewer produced or remaining always increases the value. Look for statements such as, "One of three known to exist." Request proof! A way to determine rarity is found in the book entitled *The Production Figure Book For U.S. Cars.* It lists over 50 marques, giving models, years produced and quantity of each. *(Note: Write Classic Motorbooks, P.O. Box 1, Osceola, WI 54020.)*

  a. There is a supply-restoration-demand cycle you should be aware of. Rarity is the main consideration in determining value in an antique automobile. As the car's price escalates, it becomes profitable to restore more of them. This increases the supply. Before long supply equals demand. Prices then stabilize.

  b. At this time the car may not be a money-making venture! Two good examples of this cycle are early Ford Thunderbirds and Mustangs.

  c. You must foresee trends to make money!

- **Condition:** Compare two automobiles, both the same make, model and year. Auto A is in fine running condition with good paint and tires. Auto B does not run and has been sitting in a field. Naturally A is going to be worth more than B. This is an easy comparison; however, I have developed a detailed checklist of condition. *(Note: See "The Easy Way To Initially Evaluate Condition" in Chapter Four, p. 285.)*

- **Quality vehicle—unique styling:** The race is not always to the swiftest, nor the battle to the strongest, but that's the way to bet. Compare a 1930 Model A Ford to a 1930 Pierce-Arrow. The Model A was a production car with no fancy frills, just a basic vehicle to transport you from one place to another. It did exactly what it was designed to do. On the other hand the Pierce-Arrow was a limited production auto with leather interior, side-mount tires, lots of chrome, powerful engine and some very unique styling.

  The Pierce-Arrow led the way for future car design. It

was ahead of its time. Obviously, the Pierce-Arrow has more value than the Model A Ford on this point alone. Today it would be like comparing a Ford Pinto to a Rolls Royce Corniche.

- **Previous Owners—History:** In any comparison of two identical automobiles, the one with a well-known previous owner or an unusual past history will have considerably more value than one without such a past. Usually the previous owner must be someone of national prominence.

    An automobile associated with a famous event in history draws attention and a corresponding increase in value. The ownership or association with an event must be documented. It isn't necessary to look at events of the distant past—history-making changes occur everyday.

Watch It Appreciate In Value

They say it's a great life if you weaken early enough to enjoy it. Owning automobiles as a hobby is rewarding. Hobbies should be work we don't have to do for a living. Like a good wine you can purchase the automobile of your choice—then watch it appreciate as it ages. What a satisfying way to make money.

Be selective. **Wait for the right car and the right moment to buy it.** The smart collector of cars thinks nothing of waiting years to find the right car at the right price. Make sure it meets at least one of the four qualifications making one car more valuable than another. Then, like the wine, hold on to it and watch it grow in value.

Now you have the advantage!

How To Successfully
Purchase Investment Automobiles

The faster the car, the narrower the seats.

Amateurs Hope. Professionals Work. Successes Play

And so it is in finding the investment automobile. To the sucesssful collector, what is called work by others has become play. The research, discussion, buying, restoration, and selling involved in the world of investment automobiles is play to them. Most successful people will tell you, because they enjoy their vocation so much, they have never worked a day in their lives.

The Ability To Foresee Trends

We all believe in luck. Luck is what people on the outside think those on the inside have. In successfully collecting investment automobiles, luck is the direct result of **an ability to foresee trends.** Sound simple? It is, each of us can acquire this ability. The first and most important step is to gain knowledge. Broaden and strengthen your background of the investment automobile through research. This knowledge is your key to success. Armed with it, you will be able to foresee the trend in investment automobiles. You will be able to recognize a mistake before you make it. By using knowledge as your sixth sense when negotiating, you will not need the other five.

Reading—The Quickest Way To Knowledge

One of the most enjoyable and enlightening things you can do is subscribe to and read regularly one or more outstanding automobile magazines. *(Note: See "Where To Buy, Sell Or Trade Collectable Automobiles" in Chapter Four, p. 292.)* These are the very largest and most complete of the car publications. Use your local newspaper for comparing prices in your own area. They may differ from those listed in the value guides. Clipping out the ads for these cars and dating them can later give you another indication of trends. You will be very surprised at what you can learn from this easy tip.

See For Yourself

There is not a substitute that can take the place of a first-hand look for yourself. Attend at least one antique car auction, a concours d'elegance and visit your closest automobile museum. As a guide to your scheduling, we have included lists of major events and museums. *(Note: See "Outstanding Automobile Events Around The World" in Chapter Four, p. 297 and "The Great Collector Car Museums" in Chapter Four, p. 318.)* Here you will be able to talk with car owners and **see for yourself** just what the cars actually are selling for. This will be your best appraisal of value because you will be able to compare price to your judgement of condition. It will give you an opportunity to talk with other car owners and get a feel for the antique and investment car market. Many lasting friends are found through discussions like these. These are your preliminary steps, but you'll need the more specific information I am going to discuss now to have success in the world of collectable investment automobiles!

You'll have the Midas touch!

Collectable Automobiles— Considerations Before Purchase

Good heavens, the name is familiar. Soon it'll be mine.

Nearly 5,000 different car marques have come and gone over the years. Quite a few unusual and collectable automobiles remain. "But what automobile should I buy?" This is a difficult question but here is the method that will lead you to the answer! I call it narrowing the gap.

First ask yourself: What type of automobile appeals to me the most? Does it come from the antique era (early 1900's through 1917) or do I want one from the classic era (around 1918 through 1941)? Can it be one of the great contemporary classics (1946 to around 1975)? Must it be a convertible, a sedan, have side-mount tires or a powerful engine, etc., etc?

What Kind Of Driving Will I Do With The Car

To answer this question ask yourself: What actual driving use will I make of the car? Do I wish to take extended trips? Would I rather transport the car or **enjoy driving it to events?** Is it large enough to carry a number of passengers or do I only want it to be a Sunday car just for myself?

Be Careful To Qualify

Once you have decided on the general type of vehicle you are looking for, research it. Go to the library, an auction, a concours. By doing this, you will find a make and model appealing to you. Take notes on what you see and hear. Keep notes on the prices of the automobiles in which you are interested. At auctions be careful to qualify whether sales are valid (many auctioneers are trained to give the impression every car is sold as it comes through the auction block—this does not happen). After attending a few auctions, you can usually recognize the difference between the valid car sales and the ones not really selling. Keep the investment potential of the automobile in mind at all times. *(Note: See "How To Successfully Purchase Investment Automobiles" in Chapter Four, p. 276.)*

Join A Car Club Before You Buy Any Car

Once you have selected the make of automobile, join a car club **to fit the marque.** *(Note: See "Car Clubs Essential and Enjoyable" in Chapter Four, p. 325.)* By joining one of these clubs you gain knowledge of this particular automobile and increase your chances of finding a desirable vehicle within your budget.

Each of your answers to all the above questions will depend on these four factors:

> **Your financial position**
> **Your mechanical ability**
> **Available storage**
> **The amount of time you can devote**

● **Unless you are experienced in restoring cars, never, under any circumstance, purchase one needing total restoration.** If you decide to tackle a restoration, carefully weigh the costs involved. Start by putting together your own estimate of the total restoration cost—most restoration estimates are far too low. Then, evaluate the worth of the automobile completely restored. Leave a margin for the months or years the job will take. Use value guides as a starting point. *(Note: See "Using Value Guides To Estimate Price" in Chapter Four, p. 289.)*

Now, multiply your estimate figure 2 1/2 times—finally, add in your original purchase price. This will be your true cost of restoration! Ninety-five percent of the time it is cheaper to buy a restored vehicle rather than one unrestored!

Never buy restoration projects someone has started and not completed. Don't buy "basket cases." If you can't afford to purchase your choice in restored condition, look for a car in good original condition—one showing it has been well-cared for. This usually will be a one-owner automobile.

Don't be too surprised if the car you want costs a little more than its actual present worth. Your plan must include holding the car for some time. This will give the car an opportunity to appreciate in value. From research of its past history, estimate the ability of the car to appreciate.

A word of caution. When you buy after your evaluation shows the car is not a worthwhile financial investment, you'd better be deeply in love with it! If you want something badly, that's how you get it. Many "get-rich-quick" schemes have made millionaries—out of multimillionaries.

Come sir, are you sure that's the one we're looking for?

● **At some time all collector automobiles will need repairs.** Unless you have unlimited capital, you will be doing some of this work yourself. Only you can assess your mechanical abilities. But the older the vehicle, the easier it is to work on. The sophisticated modern car, with all of its power options and electrical components, is more complicated to repair.

Imagine the Ford Model T—a very basic automobile. Compare the repair of the Model T with, say, a 1955 Mercedes Benz 300 SL. Your mechanical knowledge and tool inventory had better be far greater with the '55 Mercedes. Choosing a car you or a reasonably skilled mechanic can repair will increase your driving time (fun) and keep costs down.

● **Your available storage room should determine the type of automobile you purchase.** Like most babies, your investment or collector automobile needs a roof over its head. Most collectors first acquire the automobile then ask themselves the question, "Where will we keep it?" This is the wrong order of reasoning. You know, scarce as truth is, the supply is much greater than the demand. You can't fool "Mother Nature."

Think before you buy. It is foolish to purchase a vehicle in need of restoration unless you have at least a three-car garage or the equivalent in covered storage space. Room will be needed for parts, work benches, tools, etc. Without the necessary room the following sequence of events usually occurs:

> a. *You gradually begin losing parts.*
> b. *Garage looks like an A-bomb blast zone.*
> c. *You become discouraged.*
> d. *Helpers and friends become discouraged.*
> e. *Faithful dog leaves also.*
> f. *Eventually you sell car at a great loss.*

Plan for adequate storage and space for repairs before you buy. Consider these costs, if any, in your total restoration budget. Make sure you have the needed room to get the job done right! You will be rewarded on both emotional and financial levels. Without it you may end up losing your time, money and pride.

● **How much time should I plan to devote to my investment car?** Well for a starter you know the number of repairs you can make will correspond to the number of spare hours you have available. This is a good formula for estimating the amount of time needed to do a job. First, estimate the time you think will be needed—then multiply this figure by four.

If you know in advance only a few hours are available on weekends, stay with the purchase of automobiles either in very good original condition or fully restored. By not following this plan there simply will not be enough time to maintain your project and sell it for a profit. The rule must be—if you start it, finish it!

In Summary Consider The Four Factors

Yes, it's true. Of the four factors the financial consideration is the largest single factor determining the collectable automobile you decide to buy. Regardless of all else, you still must depend on your earning power, savings account, outside help or borrowed money to make your purchase. *(Note: See "Negotiate With Lenders For The Best Auto Loan" in Chapter Two, p. 127.)*

Ask yourself honestly how much money, mechanical ability, storage space and time you can devote to a collector car. These remain the deciding factors determining your choice. By using these answers as a guide, your choice will be a good one.

Shrewdly narrowing the gap!

Timeless Tips
On Buying And Selling
Investment Automobiles

Profit From Experience

The best way to improve your chances for success is to profit from the lessons *we* learned from years of experiences. Use these tips to *your* benefit. They are simple, but they'll make a dollar work hard for you!

Loaded	**Original condition**
Investment in mind	**Bodywork**
Long term	**Right-hand-drive**
Readvertising	**Exotics**
Rust	**Parts cars**
First/Last year of production	**Special styles**
Owner manuals	**Area effects price**
Previous ownership	**Recent articles**
Use of cash	**Current market trends**

- Try to find a car **loaded** with factory options. These will add to its mystique and give you great selling ammunition when that time comes.

- Purchase automobiles with **investment** in mind—not to satisfy dreams or personal preference of style.

- Think of your investment as a **long term** one. Don't invest until you can afford to tie up the capital for at least a year. Quick sales usually mean a loss of money. Turn this situation around. As an investor this is the type of seller you should be looking for.

- I don't recommend purchasing an automobile of the '50's priced in the $1,000 range, then **readvertising** it as a "classic" somewhere else for $2,500!

- Look carefully for signs of **rust**. A car badly rusted is almost impossible to work with! Dry climate vehicles such as those found in Arizona or California will generally bring more money at the time of resale.

- It is advantageous to buy the **first or last year of production** for a given model or make. For instance, purchasing one of the last big Lincoln Continentals and keeping it for at least five years will be a good investment. Incidentally, the last big Lincoln produced has the serial number 99Y5763622—a white with brown vinyl roof, two-door model. Can anybody find it?

- Automobiles found with original **owner manuals**, service manuals or parts books will have an edge over the same car without them. These are proven sales tools. Finding them in a car indicates pride of ownership. This in turn suggests a well-maintained automobile.

- Be suspicious of automobiles with a lot of **previous owners**. There is a reliable method to determine any automobile's past. *(Note: See "How To Find A Car's History And True Mileage" in Chapter One, p. 85.)* The chances are good there has been a great deal of speculation on this automobile.

- When you are ready to really bargain with the seller for the car, **use cash!** With cash you can sway a deal in your favor in a way that checks never can. There are ways to protect yourself when using cash. *(Note: See "Step By Step Directions For Completing Private Party Car Sales" in Chapter One, p. 32.)*

- Automobiles appreciating the fastest are ones in the most **original condition**.

- The condition of the **bodywork** plays a major factor in choosing a vintage car.

- Do not expect any **right-hand-drive vehicle** to be worth as much as a comparable left-hand model. They are not!

- **Exotic**, but well-known automobiles such as Ferrari and Porsche, etc., will be the first to go up in value. Exotic cars in excellent condition bring a very high price.

- Purchasing a **"parts car"** is unnecessary. Automobiles in excellent condition will disappear faster than parts will.

- Look for **special body styles** and makes. These will have the best appreciation.

- The general economic conditions in the **area where you live** effects collector car prices.

- **Recent articles**, books or publications relating to a particular automobile will effect its price. If the article is in favor of the car, the price will go up—or visa-versa.

- Become knowledgeable about **current market trends** and price changes. *(Note: See "Value Guides" in Chapter Four, p. 289.)*

Believe in your abilities—
> *Now, with all my lore*
> *I stand here*
> *Wiser than before*
> *There is no hobby near*
> *That to me could offer more*

The Easy Way
To Initially Evaluate Condition

CREEK!

SPROINK!!

Ah, ha! Reason for doubt is obvious.

Don't Depend On Beginner's Luck

Beginner's luck is a good description of those people born with a silver spoon in their mouth. Don't depend on luck. Well-informed personal effort comes first. Pursue my system. Luck will follow.

It is very important to first narrow the field to a few automobiles in which you are most interested. Select the make, model and year of collector car **before** you begin shopping. Then join an automobile club corresponding to that make. Here you can communicate with club members who have owned and worked on this particular automobile.

Take Experience With You

When looking for your car, take these people along. They will be able to pinpoint problem areas, availability of spare parts, prices—and, most important, help you accurately determine condition. Their good judgment comes from experience. Experience is the result of bad judgment. Take advantage of this hard-earned knowledge. You will find fellow club members willing and able to help. There also are evaluations to make yourself! I'm going to list the twelve most important evaluations you should use to determine condition. Using these, make a checklist. Take notes as you inspect each car. Following this checklist will improve your chances of accurately determining condition 100 percent.

Test drive	**Rust**
Time of day	**Accessory pieces**
The exhaust pipe	**Wood**
Acceleration/deceleration	**Convertibles**
Testing clutch	**Body**
Checking brakes	**Camera**

● **Always test drive.** Make this drive as long as possible. You will have a much better chance to discover the car's deficiencies before they become your problem.

● **Never look at a vehicle during twilight hours.** At this time of day body flaws become hidden (wavy body panels). Viewing the car in an area with overhead lighting (such as found in a garage) is not a good idea. Shadows are cast on areas which would be visible under normal lighting conditions. Shadows cover up lots of defects.

Automobile hunting is not advised on rainy days because so many problems are hidden. Regardless of the time or type of day you first look at the car, be sure your final inspection is done on a nice day in broad daylight!

● **Watch that exhaust pipe!** With clues learned from it you will be able to tell the general condition of the engine. When going for a test spin, you can make these diagnoses. If black smoke is coming out the exhaust, it simply means the carburetor is out of adjustment. An adjustment by a qualified mechanic will solve this problem. On the other hand, when blue smoke comes out the exhaust, it can mean major engine problems are present.

● **Observe the car closely under acceleration.** If blue smoke appears from the exhaust, it usually means bad rings in the engine. This will take a major engine tear down to repair. Should blue smoke appear under deceleration, this indicates bad valve guides. While this condition does not warrent a major engine tear down, it will require the removal of the cylinder head. New valve guides will have to be installed and the valves reground.

● **When the automobile you are testing has a manual shift, beware of the following:** The clutch pedal has to be pushed all the way to the floor (or visa versa). This action indicates the clutch will have to be replaced soon. This requires the removal of the transmission and, in some vehicles, the entire engine! Make sure some hills are included in your test run. On hills you will be able to determine whether the clutch is slipping. This is happening when the engine speed increases but your ground speed does not. If this situation occurs, correcting it will require a clutch replacement.

● **Checking out the brakes:** Make sure, under braking, the car does not pull strongly to one side or the other. Usually this pulling action indicates a bad wheel cylinder. You should not have to pump the brake pedal to get optimum braking results. This indicates a bad master cylinder.

● **In dealing with antique or older cars rust is always a possible factor.** Some of the most common rust areas are: the bottom portions of doors, rear trunk area, rear fender (especially around the rear door or inside the wheel arches), front fenders (also inside the wheel arch area), and finally the jacking points (places where jacks can be fitted). I would be very skeptical of a vehicle with lots of undercoating. Large amounts of undercoating may indicate major rust problems underneath.

● **Beware of owners' claims as to how easy or cheaply exterior or interior accessory pieces are to obtain.** Special badges, chrome strips, etc., can be some of the most expensive items to replace! Some can't be found at all and will have to be made. After all, why doesn't the present owner have them?

● **Many antique autos were constructed partially of wood,** especially older English vehicles such as Morgans and Rolls-Royces. Purchasing a car with rotted, broken or worn out wood can become expensive to repair.

Here are a few ways to evaluate condition. Open all the doors on the automobile. If they sag, once open, you can bet you have wood problems. Find several pieces of exposed wood. Dig your fingernail lightly into the wood (Don't try this test on a 100 point automobile). If you dig in with ease, you've got wood problems. Originally hard woods, such as English oak, were always used. Softness also can indicate replacement of the original wood.

● **Sedans will usually be in better condition than convertibles.** Don't let this steer you away from a convertible!

● **Recent repair to the body is more easily seen from a distance.** Look for different shades of paint or wavy lines to any area of the body.

● **Take a camera along.** Snap quite a number of pictures of the automobile from all angles (interior and dashboard also). Before you buy, compare these photographs to ones of a completely restored car of the same year, make and model. This comparison can yield important clues as to the originality and condition of your prospective purchase.

Quality Condition May Cost More

Now you have the simple clues to look for when evaluating condition. Quality condition may initially cost a little more to purchase, but it'll be worth it in the long run. Buying quality is like buying oats, it does cost more. If you are willing to settle for oats that have already been through the horse, that comes a little cheaper.

The best of good luck to you!

1929 Ford Model A Roadster
The Ford Motor Company
Dearborn, Michigan

The four-cylinder Model A first appeared in the autumn of 1927. Attesting to its roaring success, 3.5 million cars were sold in just four years.

1932 Chevrolet
General Motors
Detroit, Michigan

Starting in 1927, Chevrolet used beauty of line and decoration as sales' tools. The results—spectacular sales.

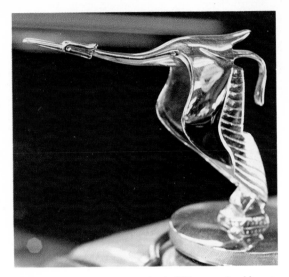

**1929 Dupont Model G
Convertible Sedan**
Dupont Motors Incorporated
Wilmington, Delaware

Dupont assembled a total of 537 cars in Moore, Pennsylvania. Grill concealed the radiator, a pioneering feature. Company combined with Indian Motorcycle Company in 1930.

1929 Isotta-Fraschini
Type A SS Carriolet Roadster
Fabbrica Automobili
Isotta-Fraschini
Milan, Italy

Founded in 1899, company developed four-wheel brakes and eight-cylinder engines. Company received early prestige from racing efforts.

1928 Diana Royal Roadster
The Light Straight "8"
Moon Motor Company
St. Louis, Missouri

1927 Stutz Custom Series
AA Blackhawk Speedster
Stutz Motor Car Company
of America
Indianapolis, Indiana

Last year of production. Company began as the Joseph W. Moon Buggey Company in 1905.

Known as the Ideal Motor Car Company until 1913. Car featured safety considerations.

1926 Franklin
Series 11-A Special Sedan
Syracuse, New York

Pioneered an air-cooled, six-cylinder 30 hp engine. These cars sold for $2,100 and were highly prized.

1910 Mercer Model 30 Speedster
The Mercer Automobile Company
Mercer County
Trenton, New Jersey

First year of production for this Finlay Porter design. Company owned by the same Roebling family who designed famed Brooklyn Bridge. Production never exceeded 500 units a year. Last Mercer built in 1925.

1913 Metz Model 22 Roadster
The Metz Company
Waltham, Massachusetts

One of the few light car manufacturers in United States at the time. Company developed interesting sales methods. Water-cooled engine produced 22 hp.

Using
Value Guides
To Estimate Price

Well, the answer is clear.

The Helpful Guides

Collector and special interest car prices vary from one extreme to the other for the same model. The following source materials will be helpful guides for determining values. I recommend using at least two or three of the "Value Guides" to form a rough idea of worth. Form an estimate only! Then, let your own reasoning and judgement direct your actions.

Build Your Own Composite Of Information

Again, I really advise a variety of different investigations of your subject. Build a composite of information about the automobile of your choice. Attend at least one car auction and a concours. *(Note: See "Auctions Are Fun" in Chapter Four, p. 304 and "Outstanding Automobile Events Around The World" in Chapter Four, p. 297.)* By talking with other car owners and seeing for yourself for what the cars are actually selling, you will gain insight to the collector car market. To appraise value subscribe to at least one of these automobile (story/advertisement) publications. *(Note: See "Where To Buy, Sell Or Trade Collectable Automobiles" in Chapter Four, p. 292.)* Prices for the same model also vary in different areas of the world. Use local newspapers for comparisons. Don't be surprised if they differ a little from those listed in the value guides.

This Is The Way You Make Money

I'm sure by now you have said to yourself, "All of these sections overlap." Yes, there is a direct relationship between each of them. By attacking our goal—knowledge of collector cars—from every angle, we get a grip on the real world of the classic automobile. With this knowledge you will be able to **substitute skill for luck in the art of negotiating.** When it comes to estimating value, nothing is more important to you. This is the way you make money!

VALUE GUIDES
(Most are updated regularly)

C.A.R. VALUES
P.O. Box 1399
Bloomington, IN 47401
Carries prices on cars going through auctions within past year. Contains actual sales figures. With "no sales" gives the reserve and highest bid made.

CLASSIC CAR GUIDE
Victortia & Co
Classic Car Guide
199 Buckingham
Palace Road
London, England S.W. 1
Good guide to English collector car values. Prices stated in pounds.

COLLECTOR CARS
300 South Union
Auburn, IN 46706
An automobile price guide starting with early 1900's to present.

INVESTMENT AUTO BUYERS GUIDE
M & W Publishing Ltd
8023 W Dodge Road
Omaha, NE
Contemporary classics from mid 1950's to present. Covers 63 vehicles.

KIPLING IMPORT MARKET REPORT
5 Holly Ridge
Ballwin, MO 63011
Monthly/Shows the wholesale values of imported and exotic automobiles

OLD CARS PRICE GUIDE
700 E State Street
Iola, WI 54945
Quarterly/Gives complete prices for most cars up to 1965.

OLD CAR
VALUE GUIDE
910 Tony Lama Street
E. Paso, TX 79915
Yearly/Covers automobiles from 1900-1967 with some photos. Gives good basic idea of worth.

THE GOLD BOOK
910 Tony Lama Street
El Paso, TX 79915
Covers automobiles/pickups, American and import 1946-72.

THE INVESTOR'S GUIDE TO AMERICAN CONVERTIBLE AND SPECIAL INTEREST AUTOMOBILES
Automobile Quarterly
245 West Main Street
Kutztown, PA 19530
Covers in detail postwar productions of American convertibles.

THE KRUSE GREEN
BOOK VALUE GUIDE

Kruse Building
Auburn, IN 46706
Contains results of Kruse auctions for the past year. Gives actual sales prices or highest bid. Does not give the reserve figure.

THE KRUSE REPORT
Kruse Building
Auburn, IN 46706
Bi-monthly/Shows market trends and the cars bringing the most money. If you plan to invest in collector cars this one is a must!

THE LEWIS GUIDE TO
1939-60 BRITISH
COLLECTOR CAR PRICES
Classic Motorbooks
P.O. Box 1
Osceola, WI 54020
Gives values for British cars in pounds. Over 1,500 listings. A great book if you plan to buy in England or Europe.

Substitute skill for luck!

Where To
Buy, Sell Or Trade
Collectable Automobiles

 *Quite so. I've found it.*

World's Best Collectable Automobile Magazines

All automobiles, collectable or otherwise, have devoted followers. Your first order of business is finding those people with the same interest as yourself. The publications listed here are hubs of information, bringing together writers, advertisers and readers from around the world for one purpose—automobiles.

Enthusiastic Readers

By mail and on news stands, magazines are purchased by automotive connoisseurs, hobbyists and enthusiasts everywhere. You can safely bet the first mail read when it arrives is the automobile magazine! These people are eager readers. They may be searching for a once-in-a-lifetime discovery or trying to sell or find a special auto or part. They may simply enjoy reading the stories and looking at the pictures. Regardless, all have one thing in common. They're bargain hunters—some call them headhunters!

Those Automobiles Still Exist But They Are Hidden

These factors make it difficult to find a true bargain in the classified section of a national publication. However, there is always that one find! I do advise selling through these publications. *(Note: See "Composing Ads That Sell" in Chapter One, p. 19.)* Try to purchase from a local source. Thousands of antique automobiles remain in existence hidden in out-of-the-way locations. Persistent travel, search and questions reveal them. Everyone will talk about old cars. Just get the conversation going. You'll soon find out where they are.

Collector Car Magazines

ANTIQUE MOTOR NEWS
Antique Motor News
919 South Street
Long Beach, CA 90805
Featuring collectable antique, vintage, classic and imported cars.

AUTOWEEK
Autoweek
13920 McCellan Blvd
Reno, NV 89506
Mainly a racer's magazine, but has a lot of classifieds on collector cars. A weekly publication.

CAR EXCHANGE
Car Exchange
700 E State Street
Iola, WI 54945
For postwar car collectors.

CARS AND PARTS
Cars And Parts
911 Vandemark Road
P.O. Box 482
Sidney, OH 45367
A serves the car hobbyist.

COAST CAR COLLECTOR
Coast Car Collector
P.O. Box 88427

Emeryville, CA 94662
Magazine covers western United States.

HEMMINGS MOTOR NEWS
Hemmings Motor News
P.O. Box 100
Bennington, VT 05201
World's largest collectable auto marketplace.

OLD CARS
Old Cars
700 E State Street
Iola, WI 54945
Very informative magazine.

ROAD AND TRACK
230 Mason Street
P.O. Box 8122
Greenwich, CT 06835
Has a good classified ad section for special interest automobiles. For knowledgeable enthusiasts.

THE ROBB REPORT
The Robb Report
P.O. Box 720317
Atlanta, GA 340328
Covers Rolls-Royce and Bentley only. Advertisements by present owners.

You may find some of the above at your local newsstand or automotive parts store. If you're looking to buy in England, the following magazines have great classified sections: *Classic Cars*, *Motor Sport*, *Mart*, *Veteran and Vintage Exchange* and *Thoroughbred*. You'll find their addresses in the complete list of automobile magazines. *(Note: See "Outstanding Automotive Publications" in Chapter Three, p. 237.)*

Concours d'Elegance

Yes, they may not pass this way again.

A Gathering Of Memory's Best

Elegance on wheels. That's what a Concours d'Elegance is all about. Automobiles may be planned obsolescence, but there will always be those never made quite the same again. Old, past, timeless things from long ago. Concours bring people together for the enjoyment, display and judging of automobiles. They are a relaxing, sporting happening.

Most concours or similar events are affiliated with car clubs or automotive organizations. In some cases, to be a participant, you need to be a club member. At most concours the public is welcomed as spectators. Basically, the cars are judged for originality as if they were brand new, showroom-fresh models. At some shows automobiles modified or customized are eligible to compete, but most concours function to preserve older vehicles in their original state. A Concours d'Elegance is organized in the following manner:

Judging
Classification
Points
Scoring

● **A chief judge is appointed,** usually by the sponsoring car club's officers. His or her job is to organize the car judges and act as decision maker in case of tie voting.

Car judges (usually between five and ten) are selected, either by the chief judge or the sponsoring car club. It's the job of these judges to personally inspect and evaluate each automobile in the show.

● **Similar cars are grouped in classes for judging.** A typical concours might have the following classifications: Vintage (cars built before 1912); Brass Era (1913-19); Classic (1925-48); Milestone (1945-67) and Contemporary (1968-).

● **Points are awarded by the judges for each area of the automobile.** Examples are: originality of paint and finish, upholstery, glass, chrome, stainless parts and mechanical condition.

The over-all winner in each classification is the vehicle totalling the most points. There may be a "best-of-show" award presented by the judges to one outstanding automobile or a "people's choice" award chosen by audience voting.

● **A score of 100 points would be a perfect score.** Ninety-eight point vehicles are not uncommon today, but a true 100-point car is rare. When you read an ad describing a "98 point car," it had better be just about perfect!

Memories Of Happy Times

Take your picnic basket with you. Concours and picnics go great together. A little cheese, salami, and a bottle of chablis are a definite must with many. Thinking of automobile events brings back memories of happy times, good times. Great places to take the girl friend, boyfriend, kids, meet new friends or talk with old acquaintances. Lasting friendships are made. They may not pass this way again. It's a darn good way to spend the weekend!

Fortune smiles on timeless things!

Outstanding Automobile
Events Around The World

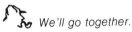 *We'll go together.*

How to use this section:

Pebble Beach
Concours d'Elegance
P.O. Box 597
Pebble Beach, CA 94953
*Monterey, CA

Actual location
Name of event
Address to write

*Indicates closest city

JANUARY
Middle East
Rothmans Rally
Challenge
Bahrain

FEBRUARY
Rotorua, New Zealand
Intern. Antique Rally
2220 Raymond Drive
Lansing, MI 48906

MARCH
Geneva, Switzerland
Geneva Auto Show

Middle East
Rothmans Rally
Challenge
Kuwait

Emporia, KS
Antique Car Show
1911 Briarcliff
Emporia, KS 66801
PH: 316 342-0215

Lake Worth, FL
Pioneer Day Car Meet
Bryant Park
799 Ivory Lane
West Palm Beach,
FL 33406
PH: 305 683-4406

APRIL
Costa Mesa, CA
Indoor Car Show
South Coast Plaza
PH:714 545-0062

New York, NY
Auto Expo/New York
New York Coliseum

**Coquitlam
British Columbia**
Vintage Car Meet
Civic Arena
2760 East 27th Avenue
Vancouver, BC, Canada
PH: 604 433-6738

St Louis, MO
Concours
Forest Park

7240 Henderson Road
St Louis, MO 63121
PH: 314 389-9795

Long Beach, CA
Grand Prix Concours
Queen Mary
PH: 213 436-0709

Pomona, CA
Antique Car Display
Los Angeles Co
Fairgrounds
PH: 714 547-1502

Yankton, SD
Annual Meet
4-H Grounds
507 Burleigh
Yankton, SD 57078

Pecatonica, IL
Collector Car Show
Winnebago Co Exh Ctr
Box 368
Forreston, IL 61030
PH: 815 938-2250

South Bend, IN
Antique Car Show
4-H Fairgrounds
922 E Jefferson
Mishawaka, IN 46455
PH: 219 255-1916

Winchester, VA
Apple Blossom Show
1744 Stanley Drive
Winchester, VA 22601

MAY
Los Angeles, CA
Auto Expo
Los Angeles
Los Angeles
Convention Center

Hillsborough, CA
Concours d'Elegance
William H. Crocker
School

Winter Haven, FL
Cypress Gardens
Meet
2402 Constitution Blvd
Sarasota, FL 33581

Tucson, AZ
Car Show
3501 E Broadway
Tucson, AZ 85713

West Hartford, CT
University Car Show
On Campus
23 Chestnut Hill Road
Glastonbury, CT 06033

Fort Wayne, IN
Antique Auto Show
Washington Blvd
10615 Steelhorn Road
New Haven, IN 46774
PH: 219 749-0317

Bozeman, MT
Big Sky Meet
PH: 406 586-2606

Dearborn, MI
Annual Meet
4391 Yorkshire
Detroit, MI 48224

Chillicothe, OH
Annual Car Show
Central Shopping Center
341 Plyleys Lane
Chillicothe, OH 45610
PH: 614 772-2538

London, England
London To Brighton Run
Beaulieu, Hants

Golden, CO
Old Car Meet
Heritage Square
Golden, CO
PH: 303 934-1507

JUNE

Reno, NV
Harrah's Annual Meet

Lexington, KY
Blue Grass Annual Meet
Kentucky State Horse Park
346 Bassett Avenue
Lexington, KY 40502

Newport Beach, CA
Concours d'Elegance
Newporter Inn

Morrilton, AR
Automobile Show
Museum Of Automobiles
Route 3
Morrilton, AR 72110

England
Bristol Run
National Motor Museum
Beaulieu To Ashton
Court Estate

York, PA
Concours d'Elegance
York Interstate
Fairgrounds

JULY

Quebec
Concours d'Elegance
Quebec City, Canada
PH: 514 733-8127

Traverse City, MI
Motorwheels
P.O. Box 425
Acme, MI 49610
PH: 616 938-2838

Greenfield, OH
Classic Car Show
558 Mirabeau Street
Greenfield, OH 45123
PH: 513 982 2748

Lake Forest, IL
Annual Car Meet
Barat College
103 Wildwood Drive
Ingleside, IL 60041
PH: 312 587-0344

Urbana, IL
Annual Show
811 W Green Street
Champaign, IL 61820
PH: 217 356-5722

Wausau, WI
Annual Car Show
Employer's Insurance
Parking
P.O. Box 104
Wausau, WI 54401
PH: 715 845-1507

299

Perfect! *Old acquaintances, a little cheese, salami and a bottle of chablis.*

Utica, MI
Annual Car Show
Ford Test Track
2330 W Clarkston Road
Lake Arion, MI 48035
PH: 313 693-1907

Colorado Springs, CO
Annual Meet
2809 W Willamette
Colorado Springs,
Colorado 80904
PH: 303 475-8367

Minneapolis, MN
Invitational Car Show
Minnehaha State Park
Minneapolis, MN
PH: 612 421-4106

Bloomfield Hills
Indianapolis, IN
Hershey, PA
Oaklahoma
San Antonio, TX
Santa Barbara, CA
Grand Classic
Events (6)
Grand Classics
P.O. Box 443
Madison, NJ 07940

Danbury, CT
Classic Auto Show
Osborne Street Stadium
19 Fleetwood Avenue
Bethel, CT 06801
PH: 203 792-1149

Reston, VA
Porsche Parade

Saskatchewan
International
Antique Car Show
3637 Queen Street
Regina, Saskatchewan
Canada S4S 2G4
PH:306 545-0810

Columbus, OH
Antique Auto Show
5558 Foster Avenue
Worthington, OH 43085
PH: 614 274-8000

Gadsden, AL
Invitational Meet
113 Buckingham Place
Gadsden, AL 35901
PH: 205 547-7143

Spokane, WA
Car Show

Fairgrounds
P.O. Box 176
Veradale, WA 99037

Hamilton, OH
Annual Car Parade
To Fairfield
1050 Garner Road
Hamilton, OH 45013
PH: 513 756-9657

Clinton, IA
Riverboat Days
416 North 3rd Street
Clinton, IA 52732

Knoxville, TN
Antique Car Show
Cherry Street
P.O. Box 3465
Knoxville, TN 37917
PH: 615 933-7433

South Amherst, OH
Auto Racing Festival
Lorain County Speedway
*Cleveland, OH

Iola, WI
Annual Car Show
700 E State Street
Iola, WI 54945
PH: 715 445-2214

Ottawa, KS
Antique Auto Meet
Fairgrounds
Ottawa, KS

Billings, MT
Roaring 20s Auto Club
13th & Broadwater
Billings, MT 59102
PH:406 252-8756

Haverhill, NH
Annual Car Meet
Village Common
Haverhill, NH 03765
PH:603 989-5562

Grand Rapids, MI
Vintage Car Show
Itasca Co Fairgrounds
P.O. Box 131
Grand Rapids
MI 55744

AUGUST

Prescott, AZ
Car Exhibit
Granite Creek Park
Prescott, AZ
PH: 602 778-4360

Piqua, OH
Summer Car Show
804 W Ash Street
Piqua, OH 45356
PH: 513 773-7711

West Warwick, RI
Antique Auto Show
West Warwick, RI
PH: 401 828-3908

North Stonington, CT
Antique
Automobile Meet
Highland Orchards
115 Winnapaug Road
Westerly, RI
PH: 401 348-8797

Pebble Beach, CA
Concours d'Elegance
P.O. Box 597
Pebble Beach, CA 93953
*Monterey, CA

Cartersville, GA
S. Eastern National
Car Show
P.O. Box 121
Cartersville, GA 30120
PH: 404 382-7668

Midland, MI
Trophy Meet
271 Twin Lake Road
Beaverton, MI 48612
PH: 517 689-4580

Eugene, OR
Car Show
859 Nantucket
Eugene, OR 97404
PH: 503 588-3507

Mechanicsburg, PA
Antique Car Jubilee
Williams Grove Park
1 Park Avenue
Mechanicsburg,

PA 17055
PH: 717 697-8266

Warsaw, NY
Antique Car Show
Village Park
8 Murray Street
Warsaw, NY 14569

Leicester, MA
Annual Meet
Junior College
P.O. Box 1063
Leominster, MA 01453
PH: 617 537-7614

Washington, OH
Antique Car Show
Courthouse Lawn
717 Western Avenue
Washington, OH 43160

Macungie, PA
Antique Classic
Das Awkscht Fescht
Box 127
Macungie, PA 18062

Shrewsbury, MA
Antique Auto Show
SAC Park
P.O. Box 171
Rutland, MA 01543
PH: 617 886-4267

Rochester, NY
Antique Auto Show
104 Brookfield Road
Rochester, NY 14610

Elkhart Lake, WI
Concours
2424 Ducharme
Green Bay, WI 54301
PH: 414 435-7975

Pinckneyville, IL
Antique Car Show
Fairgrounds
102 S Grant Street
Pinckneyville, IL 62274
PH: 618 357-8168

SEPTEMBER
Lemoyne, PA
Carlise Event

(April also)
P.O. Box 1974
Lemoyne, PA 17403

Santa Barbara, CA
Concours d'Elegance
1795 San Leandro Lane
Santa Barbara,
CA 93108

Frankfurt, Germany
Frankfurt Auto Show

**Braine l'Alleud,
Belgium**
Salmson-Amilcar
Rally
Amilcar-Pegase-Belgigue
Eug. de Deurwaerder
Rue du Chateau d'Eau 5
1420 Braine l'Alleud
Belgium

Speedway City, IN
Hoosier Auto show
P.O. Box 212
Brownsburg, IN 46112
PH: 317 852-3922

Spartanburg, SC
Antique Car Show
County Fairgrounds
P.O. Box 54
Roebuck, SC 29376

San Diego, CA
Concours d'Elegance
4109 Sports Arena Blvd
San Diego, CA 92110

Wilmington, NY
Antique Auto Rally
Chamber Of Commerce
Wilmington, NY 12997

Enid, OK
Annual Car Show
606 W Oklahoma
Enid, OK 73701
PH: 405 233-8461

Englishtown, NJ
Antique Auto Show
P.O. Box 239
Englishtown, NY

Middle East
Rothmans
Rally Challenge
Cyprus

OCTOBER

Hershey, PA
Antique Show Cars
Hershey, PA
PH: 717 838-6533

Middle East
Rothmans
Rally Challenge
Qatar

DECEMBER

Middle East
Rothmans
Rally Challenge
United Arab Emirates

OTHER EVENTS

Palo Alto
Concours d'Elegance
Opposite
Stanford Stadium
Palo Alto, CA
PH: 415 321k-2790

New York, NY
The Greater
Auto Show

Huntington Beach, CA
Corvette Show
3132 Malloy
Huntington Beach,
California 92646

Turin, Italy
Turin Auto Show

Indianapolis, IN
Milestone Grand
National
Indy Speedway
Box 50850
Indianapolis, IN 16250

Monterey, CA
Historic Car Races
General Racing Ltd
P.O. Box 30628
Santa Barbara,
CA 93105

Eugene, OR
Concours d'Elegance
P.O. Box 270
Eugene, OR 97401

Dearborn, MI
Old Car Festival
Greenfield Village
Dearborn, MI 48121

London, England
London Motorfair

Mechanic Falls, ME
Tri-State Rally
P.O. Box 169
Mechanic Falls,
Maine, 04256

Tokyo, Japan
Tokyo Auto Show

Medfield, MA
Hillclimb New
England Series
70 Greenwich Street
Medfield, MA 02052

Chicago, IL
Chicago Auto Show

Paris, France
Rallye Cing/Cing
Sportive Automotive
Internationale
5 rue Nicolas Chuguet
75017 Paris, France

Auto Auctions Are Fun

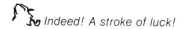
Indeed! A stroke of luck!

Increased Interest In Old Cars

Auctions can be described as having two distinct effects on the public. They are enjoyable to attend and have increased interest in old cars. This is the positive side. There is another. Auctions have helped inflate prices, putting the most desirable cars out of the average person's financial reach. At an auction held in Los Angeles, a 1936 Mercedes 500-K Roadster owned by the late Bud Cohn sold for a cool $400,000—a world record at the time.

Purchase Under Fair Market Value

Don't be too alarmed by those figures. They will cut down the number of people attending auctions. However, the person armed with solid information and a carefully trained eye can still find a good buy. Of automobiles actually sold at auctions, one out of ten is **purchased under fair market value.** Conversely, one out of ten is bought much higher than market value. The remaining eight sell within the range of fair market value.

Think Realistically!

These facts indicate people attending automobile auctions know what antique cars are worth. This can be especially important to consider before paying good money to enter your car for sale at a price it will not bring. Study the market whether buying or selling. Think realistically! As a seller, this will save wasted entry fees. *(Note: See "Outstanding Automotive Publications" in Chapter Three, p. 237 and "Using Value Guides To Estimate Prices" in Chapter Four, p. 289.)*

How Auctions Are Run

Basically this is how most auctions function. There are variations with different companies and locations. The points I'm making will remain valid regardless:

● **Automobiles are consigned by owners to the auction company.** Usually a fee ($50-$100) is charged for each car entered in the auction. This fee must be paid whether the car sells or not. It is paid in advance.

Cars consigned far enough in advance of the auction date are listed in the auction program. This can be a great help in selling your car. It will pay you to inquire!

Upon consignment each car is assigned a number. These numbers determine the order the car will run through the auction. This order is important! I have found the best time for a car to appear on the auction block is about 3:00 p.m. Seems to be more buyers around about this time of day.

● **As a seller, I advise not signing the pink slip (title) releasing your ownership of your car or giving anyone power of attorney to do this, until you see either a cashier's check or cash paid to you for your automobile.**

If you think this release is a part of the consignment form, simply write on the form you are not releasing until paid as above and initial this change. Attend the auction. If the car sells, there's plenty of time to sign the release. Don't give in on this point!

● **There are two different types of auctions, ones with a reserve put on cars and ones without.** A "no reserve" auction is one where there is no minimum bid required to purchase a vehicle. However, almost all auctions operate with cars offered under a reserve clause. This means the owner has registered a minimum bid acceptable for the car. This "reserve" is supposed to be secret from the bidders.

● **Prior to bidding on any automobile you must register with the auction company as a valid bidder.** There usually is a small fee charged for this registration (refundable upon puchase of a vehicle). At this time you will be required to show proof of your ability to pay for any car you might purchase. This is usually done with: (a) letter of credit from your bank, (b) cashier's check or (c) cash. Don't expect the auction company to accept personal checks.

● **At most auctions the company also takes a percentage of the selling price for each automobile sold.** Originally this percentage was paid by the seller not the buyer. This has been modified today in some cases with the seller and the buyer splitting the fee.

General fees run about 10 percent for a car selling at less than $10,000 and 6 percent for those selling over $10,000. Owners often raise their reserve price in order to pay the auction company fees. Now you see the need for studying the market first! Otherwise as a seller all you may get out of the auction is the loss of your entry fee.

● **Plan to arrive at the auction early.** Often there is a preview showing of the automobiles the evening before. Try to select the cars you might be interested in **before the auction starts.** Talk with owners. Ninety percent of the time they are around.

Gather as much information as you can about each vehicle. Take notes. A few carefully worded conversations should enable you to discover the reserve put on each one. Do not bid on automobiles you have not inspected. *(Note: See "The Easy Way To Initially Evaluate Condition" in Chapter Four, p. 285.)*

● **During the auction study the auction area.** Watch for shill bidders. These people work for the auction company by raising the bidding. They can be spotted. Don't bid against them. Look for automobile owners bidding up the price on their own car. This is one of the advantages in arriving early, then later being able to associate owners with their cars.

● **Sometimes good buys can be made after the auction is over from an owner whose car did not sell.** You have nothing to lose by offering less at this time.

Major Auction Companies

Watch local newspapers and automotive magazines for advertisements listing auctions nearest you. Below is a list of major auction companies and their addresses. They will be happy to supply you with a list of their auction dates and locations.

**Classic Car
Auctions Inc**
3212 Wynn Road
Las Vegas, NV 89102

**Hudson And
Marshall Inc**
1 Baconsfield Park
Macon, GA 31211

Kruse Auctioneers Inc
Kruse Building
Auburn, IN 46706

**Vintage Car Auction
Canada Ltd**
127 York Street
Ottawa, Ontario K1N 5T4

Auction Car Rating Code

(Generally accepted)

M . . . . Mint condition, near 100 per cent
E . . . . Excellent condition, 90 points up
R . . . . Repainted and reconditioned interior
U . . . . Unrestored
G . . . . Good, 75 to 89 points
F . . . . Fair, car has been modified or needs reconditioning
P . . . . Poor, needs repairs such as paint, interior, tires

Auto Condition Code

(Additional terms)

- **Concours:** An automobile refurbished to meet the exact requirements for national competition—or outstanding original.

- **Outstanding:** Either the car has been restored or is original. It would require just minor detailing to reach Concours.

- **Sound:** Authentic original or older restoration—may require attention—roadworthy.

- **Serviceable:** Needing appearance and mechanical reconditioning.

- **Recoverable:** A complete car requiring total restoration.

- **Parts Car:** A vehicle beyond salvation, missing major parts, and a poor customization.

Lenders And Loans
For Classic Automobiles

Maryland National Bank
Collector Car Financing Dept
8400 Baltimore Blvd
College Park, MD 20740

**Collector Car
Financing Company**
1703 Spring Street
Smyrna, GA 30080
PH: 404 433-8898

First Pennsylvania Bank
1500 Chestnut Street
Philadelphia, PA 19101
Ph: 215 786-7788

Many additional banks across the United States are interested in financing classic and collector automobiles. I suggest you start with the bank you are doing business with now. Often these loans are made on the basis of past relationship with the customer.

A prosperous adventure for you!

Insurers Of Classic Automobiles

Specialized coverages

At one time, covering a classic automobile with good insurance was difficult if not impossible. Today this has changed. As long as you drive some other car regularly, these companies can insure classic automobiles for about 35 percent of the cost of regular cars. You may also insure, within reasonable limits, for the market value of the car and select the place of repair at time of claim. All the companies write excellent coverage. They'll be happy to send plans and rates to you. Their prices are very competitive.

J. C. TAYLOR, INC
8701 W Chester Pike
Upper Darby, PA 19082
PH: 215 528-6450
Classic car insurance.

CONDON AND SKELLY
P.O. Drawer A
Willingboro, NJ 08046
PH: 609 871-1212
Classic car insurance.

AMERICAN COLLECTORS INSURANCE
P.O. Box 15465
Philadelphia, PA 19149
Classic car insurance.

K & K INSURANCE AGENCY INC
3015 Bowser Avenue
Fort Wayne, IN 46806
PH: 219 744-4101
Race car insurance.

JAMES A. GRUNDY AGENCY
500 Office Center Dr
Fort Washington, PA 19034
PH: 215 628-3100
Classic car insurance.

CHANDLER IBEC INTERNATIONAL LIMITED
Chandler House
5-7 Marshalsea Road
London, SE1 1EF
PH: 01 407-8000
Lloyd's of London racing, rallying and personal accident insurance.

EUROP ASSISTANCE LTD
Europ Assistance House
England
252 Croydon St, Croydon
Surrey, CRO1NF
PH: 01 680-1234
An insurance type policy from England covering accidents, sickness, breakdowns, illnesses, spare parts, return home, etc., while on motoring holidays in Europe. Assistance by multi-lingual phone co-ordinators 24 hours each day.

HYPERFORMANCE INSURANCE
England
Bellevue Ins Brokers Ltd
66 Silver Street
Enfield, Middx.
PH: 01 363-4966
Porsche and Ferrari specialists.

VINTAGE CAR INSURANCE ASSOCIATES
Bywell House
Grange Court
Lagham Road, S Godstone
Surrey, RH9 8HB
PH: 034285 3499
English company catering to drivers of pre-1947 cars.

CLASSIC INSURANCE AGENCY
639 Lindbergh Way
Atlanta, GA 30324
PH: 404 262-2264
Coverage for full stated value. Special interest, high performance and previously uninsurable cars accepted.

Good fortune follows clear thinking!

Pamper Your Antique

Now sir, you have the formula.

Care Is The Name Of The Game

Caring for your collector car is not difficult or expensive. When it comes to care, some do, some don't—you'll be better off if you do. There are few rules, but here are some interesting ones you may recognize.

- In your workshop any tool dropped will roll to the farthest corner—and, before it starts rolling, hit one or both of your feet.
- Sharp metal objects are magnetized by bare feet so they always point up from the floor—especially in the dark.
- All parts falling will come to rest in the exact center of the floor space occupied by the car you're working on.
- If it works, leave it alone! Don't fix it.
- Any object can be broken if the hammer is big enough.

● It is a mistake to ever let any mechanical object realize you're in a hurry.

Here's Your Profit

Despite these rules, **caring for your collector car is enjoyable—profitable too.** There's a delayed reaction to car care. For every dollar you don't spend in upkeep, you'll lose hundreds, maybe thousands in potential earnings when the car is sold. That's your profit being lost!

Formula For Automobile Longevity

Use a figure of about 8-10 percent of your car's original purchase price as a guide to budget for maintanence each year. Start your program right after purchase. Don't delay it. Besides following these basic procedures, there are several general truisms. For example, never make fiberglass body repairs on a metal automobile. They cost less but seldom last long and fool few people. Power steering, oil and transmission fluids should be replaced.

Detergents are harsh to the paint finish. If the car is kept generally clean, you will be surprised how easily it touches up with a soft cloth dampened with a small amount of kerosene mixed in water. A little vinegar added to water provides an excellent solution for cleaning windows. One of the finest all-purpose cleaners, strong yet gentle, is known as GB-60. Not usually found in stores, it can be ordered from G & B Enterprises, Inc., P.O. Box 19236, Portland, OR 97219, PH: 503 641-1040.

Drive the car at least twice a month. A car deteriorates much faster when not used. All automobiles last longer when driven at a slower rate of speed. Dramatically longer! Car owners with over one million miles on their cars cite *driving slowly* as their formula for automobile longevity.

Nine Basic Areas

There are nine basic areas you will need to be concerned with in caring for your collector car:

> **Cooling system**
> **Interior leather**
> **Rubber (molding and tires)**
> **Battery**
> **Brake system**
> **Wood**
> **Paint**
> **Engine protection**
> **Wheels**

● **Cooling system:** Older vehicles present a much greater chance of corrosion in the cooling system, especially when dealing with aluminum cylinder heads, engine blocks, water pumps and passage ways.

Your first procedure is to completely flush the system free of all present water, coolant fluids and sludge. To do this, back flush the system (not nearly as technical or difficult as it sounds). Simple flushing kits with easy instructions can be found at any automotive parts center.

Next, replace all radiator hoses, regardless of age. Check all gaskets and seals for water leaks. Fill your flushed and clean water system with the following mixture. Use a five gallon can and mix three gallons of distilled water with two gallons of quality antifreeze. Then add one-half pint of Malcool 2000. This product can be found at any Detroit Diesel outlet or truck stop. Do this once a year.

● **Interior leather:** Since leather is expensive to replace, great care should be taken to preserve what you have. The first procedure is to thoroughly clean the upholstery with a good saddle soap. Next, apply one of these four products to the leather: Lexol, Clausens Rejuvenator Oil, Neatsfoot Oil or Hide Food, a product found at most Rolls-Royce dealers or saddle shops. Do this at least four times per year.

● **Rubber (molding and tires):** Apply Armor All liberally to all rubber moldings, around door seals, windows, trunk, hood, interior pieces and tires, including the spare. Do this at least as often as you do the interior.

● **Battery:** Poor battery connections are a common problem in older cars (assuming the battery itself is good). A symptom of a poor connection is when attempting to start the car, the starter solenoid makes a clicking noise and the engine will not turn over. Take the battery out and thoroughly clean the outside of it with a solution of baking soda and water.

Use a wire brush to clean the positive and negative battery posts until they shine. Also clean the positive and negative faces where they attach with a wire brush. Before refitting the battery, clean all old acid and dirt from the battery, coat the connections with a heavy grease, Vaseline jelly or similar product.

● **Brake system:** The care you give the car's brake system is of prime importance! Begin by flushing out the entire system, including any hydraulic clutch systems. The most effective way is to completely disassemble all wheel calipers, slave cylinders, master cylinders, etc. Clean all parts both inside and out with lacquer thinner.

Don't use this fluid on rubber "O" rings and seals. Just wipe them clean with a rag. Upon reassembly, use liberal amounts of brake fluid (same type you are going to use in the system) on all rubber seals and inside housings. For this I personally recommend using Dow Silicone Brake Fluid found at most auto parts stores.

A quick, but not as effective way as the above, is to bleed the brake and clutch systems. Afterwards you replace old brake fluid with new. However, all the old fluid and dirt can't be eliminated by this method. This could result in a brake-clutch failure.

● **Paint and wood surfaces:** The first step in preserving either paint or wood is to get the surface clean! Avoid laundry or dishwashing detergents. Use a cleaner, not a combination wax and cleaner. A simple solution of kerosene (small amount) added to a bucket of water is a great cleaning solution. McGuires Cleaner is a very good cleaning agent.

Once the surface is clean use a carnauba-based wax. Wax your car two to three times per year and you will end up with a coating that keeps your car's color finish beautiful.

Preserve the original paint on your car as long as possible. Cars with original paint, all else being equal, will generally bring a higher price. Classic Car Wax Company (Classic Chemical, Arlington, TX 76011) and Visual Ade Products Inc (1571 S. Sunkist, Anaheim, CA 92806) make fine paint restoring products. Try them before repainting!

● **Engine protection:** One of the greatest factors in producing engine longevity is changing your oil and filter regularly. The American Petroleum Institute recommends oil and filter changes every three months, despite manufacturer's extended use claims. I know from my experience with racing engines how important oil changes really are. Do it often. You will not be sorry.

Use a multi-viscosity motor oil such as 10-30 or 20-40 weight. To start any automobile maintenance program, first change the oil and filter. Then run the vehicle 200 to 300 miles and make another change. This plan will not make a poor running engine run well, but oil and filter changes definitely contribute longevity to a fine running engine.

Here is an old and reliable method to clean the inside of

your engine. When the engine is warm, drain all of the oil from it. Replace the oil with a mixture of three parts kerosene to one part of your usual motor oil. Run the engine with this mixture in it for about one minute. Drain every drop of this mixture from the engine. Replace the oil filter if there is one. Refill your engine with quality motor oil.

Most carbon deposits can be removed from the combustion chamber of the engine with this same product—kerosene. While the engine is hot, remove the spark plugs. Put a couple of tablespoons of kerosene into each spark plug hole. Replace the spark plugs. Let the engine set overnight. The kerosene, vaporized by the heat, soaks into and loosens up the carbon. When the engine is started up in the morning the carbon will be blown out.

Carbon can also be removed by water. Run your engine at a fairly high speed. Feed water in through the air intake of the carburetor. Give the engine all the water it will take. A great amount of carbon may be blown out in this way. Run the engine a few extra minutes to make sure everything has been blown out.

● **Wheels:** Care of wheels is important, not only for safety reasons, but for looks as well. Wire wheels should be inspected at least once every 10,000 miles. Replace broken and loose spokes.

Whether your wheels are nickel or chrome plated use a product called Simi-Chrome polish. By using a cheaper brand you risk the chance of etching the surface. Then, to look right, the wheels will have to be replated. This is an expensive operation.

If your car comes with wagon wheels, inspections should be done at least every couple of months. Because of their age, wooden wheels tend to crack easily and this type of wheel is very expensive to replace. Use the same process found in "Paint and wood surfaces" above.

Collector cars require attention. This attention is considered a relaxing occupation to most owners. In addition, the social, educational and financial rewards of collector automobile ownership are many. In the long run, care of your car is the name of the game. It's the easiest way to reap bonus dividends.

Care and profit go together!

Storing Your Classic

On The Safe Side

Last year is always the best time to buy anything. Maybe you did buy last year and now you're wondering how to go about storing your classic automobile. To be on the safe side, there are important pre-storage procedures. When the conversation turns to cars in storage, I inevitably hear, "My car seems to be deteriorating faster now than it did when I used it all the time!" This observation couldn't be more true. Here is the plan for coping with this problem.

Long-Term Storage Planning

Classic and collector automobiles should be driven at least once every two weeks. Special preparations must be made before storing it for longer periods of time. Oil, transmission and **all rubber seals tend to dry up quickly when the car is not in use.** These items are especially critical in long-term storage planning. Unlike a road map with directions for everything except how it can be refolded, here's how to put your car in storage and how to take it out.

Putting Your Car In Storage

To assure successful preservation of your automobile while in storage follow this plan.

Storage Location
Procedure
Remove battery
Jack vehicle up
Drain gasoline
Spark plugs
Engine compartment
Interior preservation
Rubber seals and fittings
Windows

● **Your first consideration should be the location you plan to store the car.** This should be a dry, fully enclosed building. This building must receive as little direct sunlight as possible. Make sure the ceiling has ventilating fans to let the rising heat out during the summer months. Ideally, what you are looking for is a year-around temperature between 60 and 70 degrees.

● **Once you have the location, follow this procedure.** Start the car and bring the water and oil temperatures up to normal operating readings. With the engine still warm, drain the oil. Remove the old filter and replace it with a new one. Next, drain the water from both the engine block and radiator. Don't refill any of these.

● **Remove the battery** and place it on a piece of thick wood. Make sure the water levels in each compartment are at proper levels (above the lead plates). The battery will remain in better contition if recharged once a month.

● **Jack the vehicle up** and place it on four jack stands. The car should remain level with the wheels off the ground.

● **Drain all the gasoline** from the tank. Yes, there is a drain plug. Normal gasoline, standing for a couple of years, changes into a varnish-like substance. This old fuel will destroy your engine! There's no fuel like an old fuel.

Once the tank is empty, add five gallons of 87 octane rated aircraft gasoline. This fuel doesn't turn to varnish and in small amounts won't hurt your engine.

● **Remove the spark plugs.** Using an oil can, squirt a little oil down each plug hole. Preferably use a multi-viscosity engine oil, such as 10-30 weight. **Then, replace the plugs.**

● **Inside the engine compartment,** spray all engine parts not made out of rubber with WD-40 and all rubber pieces and hoses with Armor All.

● **Unless the interior is cloth or mohair, wipe it down with a generous amount of preservative.** I recommend a product called Lexol Leather Preservative for use on leather. Armor All works well on vinyl.

● **Spray Armor All on all rubber around door seals, window moldings, trunk lids, etc., wiping off the excess.** Do the same with both sides and the tread on all five tires.

● **Always leave at least two windows slightly open** to minimize the build up of heat inside the car. Keep the top in the "up" position if the car is a convertible.

Taking The Car Out Of Storage

To bring your classic back to life when you take it out of storage here's what to do—

Charge battery
Check tires
Add gasoline
Refill oil sump
Fill radiator
Remove spark plugs
Prime the engine
Engine warm-up

● **Charge the battery.** Use a low output battery charger (1½ to 4 amp). A charger with more amps might burn out the unit. Fit the battery back in the car, making sure the positive and negative cables are connected properly.

● **Check all tires** for the recommended amount of air pressure and set the car back on the ground.

● **Add five gallons** of the recommended grade of gasoline.

● **Refill the oil sump** with the correct amount of oil, taking into account there is no oil in the new filter.

● **Add one gallon of anti-freeze to the radiator** and continue to fill with water until water comes out the filler neck. Extremely low outside temperatures and/or a larger radiator capacity may require more anti-freeze. Temporarily leave the radiator cap off.

● **Remove the spark plugs.** Once again, apply a couple of squirts of engine oil down each spark plug hole. Leave the plugs out, turn the ignition on and crank the engine over several times. This will lubricate the cylinder walls inside the engine. Replace the spark plugs, making sure you have the ignition wires in the right sequence.

● **Prime the engine** by squirting a small amount of gasoline down the carburetor (s). Then it's time for "Ladies and gentlemen, start your engines." If the engine is a little reluctant to start, prime it again with a small amount of gas to the carburetor.

● **While the engine is warming up,** check the water level in the radiator and fill as necessary. Replace the radiator cap.

Happy motoring!

The Great Collector Car Museums

Remarkable! Their place in history is assured.

Sits Quietly Without Motion

Inside an automotive museum you can sense and smell something called history. What once was considered thundering elegance now sits quietly without motion. Their wagon wheels, cranks and pistons have stopped. Yet, if called upon, these ancient motor cars could and would demonstrate what launched us into the 20th century.

Unique Individuals

If it weren't for the private efforts of a few unique individuals, the fascinating creations of early automotive history would have been

318

lost. The rare old motor cars were easily on the way to extinction! We can thank Bill Harrah, Briggs Cunningham and Bud Cohn, to name but a few, for their preservation. It is appreciated.

Staffed By Experts

Automotive museums strive for a high degree of authenticity. I highly recommend a visit to one before you make an antique automobile purchase or start any restoration project. When debating the type of car to purchase, museums give you good ideas. You'll soon recognize the makes and models most appealing to you. Many museums are staffed by automotive restoration experts. When the subject is approached with discretion, they often will give you valuable assistance with antique motor car problems. Regardless of your own reason for going, prepare for aching feet. Take your sneakers along!

Their Place In History Is Assured

Whether you visit an automobile museum for pleasure or business, take the entire family. It's an experience no one should miss. Antique and classic automobiles. They may no longer be considered thundering elegance, but their place in history is assured.

Automobile Museums

(By State Name & Location)

ARKANSAS
The Museum of Automobiles   (Morrilton)
CALILFORNIA
Briggs Cunningham Automotive Museum   (Costa Mesa)
Jack Passey Jr. Automobile Collection   (San Jose)
Los Angeles County Museum of Natural History   (Los Angeles)
Miller's Horse & Buggy Ranch   (Modesto)
San Sylmar Tour   (Sylmar)

COLORADO
Ray Dougherty Collection   (Longmont)
Forney Transportation Museum   (Fort Collins)
The Veteran Car Museum   (Denver)
CONNECTICUT
Antique Auto Museum   (Manchester)
Bradley Air Museum   (Windsor Locks)
DELAWARE
Magic Age of Steam   (Yorklyn)
DISTRICT OF COLUMBIA
National Museum of History and Technology   (Washington D.C.)

319

FLORIDA
Bellm's Cars and Music of Yesterday   **(Sarasota)**
Early American Museum   **(Silver Springs)**
Horseless Carriage Shop   **(Dunedin)**
Museum of Speed   **(Daytona Beach)**

GEORGIA
Antique Auto and Music Museum   **(Stone Mountain)**
Museum of Automobiles   **(Hamilton)**

HAWAII
Automotive Museum of the Pacific   **(Honolulu)**

ILLINOIS
Excalibur Motorcars Ltd   **(Highland Park)**
Hartung's Automotive Museum   **(Glenview)**
Lazarus Motor Museum   **(Forreston)**
Museum of Science and Industry   **(Chicago)**
Quinsippi Island Antique Auto Museum   **(Quincy)**
Time Was Village Museum   **(Mendota)**

INDIANA
Auburn-Cord-Duesenberg Museum   **(Auburn)**
Cars Of Yesterday   **(Indianapolis)**
Early Wheels Museum   **(Terre Haute)**
Elwood Haynes Museum   **(Kokomo)**
Goodwin Museum   **(Frankfurt)**
Indiana Museum of Transport Communications Inc   **(Noblesville)**
Indianapolis Motor Speedway Hall of Fame   **(Speedway)**

IOWA
Auto Museum   **(Sioux Center)**
Fischer's Colony Museum   **(South Amana)**
Harry E. Burd Collection   **(By appointment—Waterloo)**
Don Jensen Enterprises   **(Humbolt)**

KANSAS
Abilene Auto Museum   **(Abilene)**
Billue's Antique Car Museum   **(Hesston)**
King's Antique Car Museum   **(Hesston)**

KENTUCKY
Calvert Auto Museum   **(Calvert City)**

MAINE
Boothbay Railway Museum   **(Boothbay)**
H. E. Muckler's Highway of Memories Motorama   **(North Woolwich)**
Seal Cove Automobile Museum   **(Seal Harbor)**
Wells Auto Museum   **(Wells)**

MARYLAND
Fire Museum of Maryland Inc   **(Lutherville)**

MASSACHUSETTS
Edaville Railroad Museum   (South Carver)
Heritage Plantation of Sandwich   (Sandwich)
Museum of Transportation   (Brookline)
Sturbridge Auto Museum   (Sturbridge)

MICHIGAN
Detroit Historical Museum   (Detroit)
Gilmore Car Museum   (Hickory Corners)
The Henry Ford Museum   (Dearborn)
Sloan Panorama of Transportation   (Flint)
Poll Museum   (Holland)
Woodland Cars of Yesterday   (Grand Rapids)

MINNESOTA
Hemp Museum   (Rochester)
Woodlands Automotive Museum   (Park Rapids)

MISSOURI
Autos of Yesteryear   (Rolla)
Kelsey's Antique Cars   (Camdenton)
National Museum of Transport   (St. Louis)

MONTANA
Ed Towe Ford Collection   (Helena)

NEBRASKA
Hastings Museum   (Hastings)
Sandhills Museum   (Valentine)
Stuhr Museum of the Prarie Pioneer   (Grand Island)
Harold Warp Pioneer Village   (Minden)

NEVADA
Harrah's Automobile Collection   (Reno)

NEW HAMPSHIRE
Meredith Auto Museum   (Meredith)

NEW JERSEY
Roaring 20 Autos   (Wall)

NEW YORK
Ausable Chasm Antique Auto Museum   (Ausable Chasm)
Automobile Museum of Rome and Restoration Shoppe   (Rome)
Cavalcade of Cars   (Lake George)
Ellenville Motor Museum   (Ellenville)
Golden Age Auto Museum   (Palarine Bridge)
The Long Island Automotive Museum   (Southhampton)
Murchio's Museum of Antique Cars   (Greenwood Lake)
National Motor Racing Museum   (Watkins Glen)
Harry Resnick Motor Museum   (Ellenville)
Upstate Auto Museum   (Bridgewater)
Jim York's Auto Museum   (Howes Cave)

NORTH CAROLINA
Estes-Winn-Blomberg Antique Car Museum   **(Asheville)**
O.A. Corriher Collection   **(Landis)**

OHIO
Allen County Museum   **(Lima)**
Antique Classic Auto Museum   **(Columbus)**
Frederick C. Crawford Auto-Aviation Museum   **(Cleveland)**

OKLAHOMA
Antiques Inc   **(Muskogee)**
William Stewart Collection   **(Shawnee)**

PENNSYLVANIA
Automobilarama   **(Harrisburg)**
Boyertown Museum of Historical Vehicles   **(Boyertown)**
Alan Dent Antique Auto Museum   **(Lighstreet)**
Magee Transportation   **(Bloosburg)**
Paul H. Stern's Antique Cars   **(Manheim)**
Pollock Auto Showcase   **(Pottstown)**
Swigart Museum   **(Huntingdon)**

SOUTH CAROLINA
Joe Weatherly Stock Car Museum   **(Darlington)**
Wings and Wheels   **(Santee)**

SOUTH DAKOTA
Horseless Carriage Museum   **(Rapid City)**
Mitchell Car Museum   **(Mitchell)**
Pioneer Auto Museum and Antique Town   **(Murdo)**

TENNESSEE
Cox's Car Museum   **(Gatlinburg)**
Smoky Mountain Car Museum   **(Pigeon Forge)**

TEXAS
Chapman Auto Museum   **(Rickwell)**
Classic Showcase   **(Kerrville)**
Museum of Time and Travel   **(Odessa)**
Pate Museum of Transportation   **(Fort Worth)**

VERMONT
Cars of Yesterday   **(Castleton Corners)**

VIRGINIA
American Road Museum   **(Williamsburg)**
Car and Carriage Caravan Inc   **(Luray)**
Pettit's Museum of Motoring Memorie   **(Louisa)**
Roaring Twenties Antique Car Museum   **(Hood)**

WISCONSIN
Berman's Auto & Antique Museum   **(Oregon)**
Four Wheel Drive Museum & Historical Building   **(Clintonville)**
Brooks Stevens Automotive Museum   **(Milwaukee)**

Midway Auto Museum	**(Birnamwood)**
Sunflower Museum of Antique Cars	**(Between Tomahawk Lakes)**
Warvel Vintage Car Museum	**(Gillett)**

CANADA

Antique Auto Museum	**(Niagara Falls, Ontario)**
Armstrong's Antique Auto Museum	**(New Brunswick)**
Canadian Automotive Museum	**(South Oshawa, Ontario)**
Car Life Museum	**(Prince Edward Island)**
Elkhorn Manitoba Automobile Museum	**(Elkhorn, Manitoba)**
Musee De L'Auto Ltee	**(Montreal, Qubec)**
Museum of Science and Technology	**(Ottawa)**
Reynolds Museum	**(Wetaskiwin, Alberta)**
Western Development Museum	**(Saskatoon, Saskatchewan)**

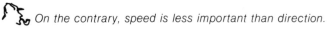 *On the contrary, speed is less important than direction.*

Classifications Of Collectable Cars

(General)

- **Vintage:**   Cars built before 1912
- **Brass Era:**   Cars built 1913-19—brasswork
- **Antique:**   Cars up to 1935 including Brass and Vintage
- **Classic:**   Cars built from 1925-48
- **Milestone Cars:**   Cars built from 1945-67
- **Special Interest Cars:**   Cars built after 1935, valued by special features, performance, styling, etc.
- **Contemporary Classics:**   Cars built after 1945, sought by collectors

Note: See lists of the above for specific accepted cars

(Other Terms)

- **Pre-War Car:**   Car built after World War I
- **Post-War Car:**   Car built after World War II

They're identified by codes.

Car Clubs
Essential And Enjoyable

Separated by a bygone time.

Provide A Foundation

There are literally thousands of car clubs spread around the world. Hundreds more seem to spring up each year. We have selected a number of strong clubs for your reference among the most active. There is no question that these clubs provide a foundation to really have fun with your automobile as a hobby. In all clubs and organizations, you will get the most out of your membership by becoming an active participant in club activities. This was never truer than with a car club.

A Centralized Source Of Information

Most of the clubs listed here are national in scope. Each has many regional chapters. The usual procedure is to join the national club first; then participate in club activities by becoming a member of a regional chapter close to your home. Pick the club of your choice. For the collector, restorer or enthusiast it is a must. Automobile clubs are centralized sources of information. Many publish excellent club magazines for distribution to members. Interesting articles, location of rare parts, automobiles wanted, cars for sale as well as descriptions of club activities make these magazines invaluable.

In this chapter we also list many outstanding automobile events held in various locations around the world. Purposely, these include few specific car club activities. Club calendars are filled with a variety of events designed to please every member at least some of the time. Car clubs should never be overlooked. Regardless of your interests, there is a club to fit. They are a source of enjoyment for individuals and families alike.

Antique Automobile
Club of America

Alas, she was almost too good to be true.

Distinguished Club

The Antique Automobile Club Of America is the country's oldest and largest automotive historical society. It is dedicated to the preservation, restoration and maintenance of automobiles and automotive history. This distinguished club holds countrywide competitive and non-competitive meets and events.

Regions and Chapters

Through its national office this club aids individuals, museums, libraries, historians and collectors dedicated to the preservation of automotive history. The club's official publication is *Antique Automobile*. Amply illustrated, it is distributed bi-monthly to all members. Annual subscriptions are also available to non-members. There are several hundred regions and chapters. Before joining one, you must first become a member of the National Automobile Club of America. Ownership of an automobile is not a prerequisite of membership; however, applicants must be sponsored by a member in good standing.

**Antique Automobile
Club of America**
501 West Governor Road
Hershey, PA 17033
PH: 717 534-1910

Vehicle Classification
Antique Automobile Club Of America

Motor vehicles of all types up to and including models twenty-five years old are grouped, for competitive purposes, into many classes according to age and mechanical features. There are three main groups of vehicles:

Antique
These vehicles are the pre-1930 models.

Classic
Exceptionally fine cars of specific makes, such as Duesenberg, Rolls-Royce, Cord, etc., dating from 1930 through 1942.

Production
These are later models.

The Veteran Motor Car
Club of America

This has long been conceded to be one of America's premiere motor car clubs. It was founded on December 2, 1938, in Boston. The first meet was held in 1939. The purpose of this club is to encourage members in buying, preserving, restoring and exhibiting antique and historically significant automobiles. The club's members are very interested in all printed matter regarding these automobiles. The ownership of an antique car is not a requirement for active membership in this fine club.

The Veteran Motor Car Club of America
105 Elm Street
Andover, MA 01810

Indeed! You know where she is hidden?

Classification Of Cars
The Veteran Motor Car Club Of America

CLASS	TYPE	GROUP
1	Buckboards, 3-Wheelers & Cycle Cars	Through 35 years of age
2	High Wheel Buggy Type cars	Through 35 years
3	Electic Cars	Through 35 years
4	Steam Cars	Through 35 years
5	1,2,3 cylinder cars	Through 35 years
6	Model ''T'' Fords - Brass Radiator	1909-1912
7	Model ''T'' Fords - Brass Radiator	1913-1916
8	Model ''T'' Fords - Black Radiator	1916-1927
9	Gasoline Cars - 4 cyl.	Through 1912
10	Gasoline Cars - More than 4 cyl.	Through 1912
11	Gasoline Cars - 4 cyl.	1913 through 2-wheel brake era
12	Gasoline Cars - More than 4 cyl.	1913 through 2-wheel brake era
13	Gasoline cars - 4 cyl.	4-wheel brake through 1942
14	Gasoline cars - more than 4 cyl.	4-wheel brake through 1942
15	Ford Model ''A''	1928 through 1931
16	Classic Cars - per CCCA Classification	1925 through 1942
17	Commercial Vehicles & Fire Engines	Through 35 years of age
18	Motorcycles	Through 35 years of age
19	Special Interest Cars	Per Milestone Car Society List
20A	Race Cars - non highway equipped	Through 35 years of age
20B	Race Cars - sports type with highway equipment	Through 35 years of age
21	Unclassified Cars other than Milestone, built in 1946 or later, but 25 years of age.	

Classic Car Club Of America

Spirited! She moved with unexpected swiftness.

Twenty-Three Regions Across The United States

The Classic Car Club of America defines a "Classic" as a "fine distinctive automobile, American or foreign, built between 1925 and 1948." You can participate in various national events with or without the ownership of a classic car. At events known as Grand Classics you can enter your automobile in competition where it will be judged for prizes. After becoming a national member, you then join and participate in one of the twenty-three regions across the United States.

Vacation Tour

Like the other large clubs that classify cars, the Classic Car Club recognizes classifications of The Milestone Car Society. When it comes to inclusion of certain automobiles on the list of "Classic" cars, the decisions of the classification committee are final and not subject to membership review. Members and families tour many interesting parts of the United States each year together in their "Classics" on a vacation trip called the CARavan.

**Classic Car Club
of America**
P.O. Box 443
Madison, NJ 07940
PH: 201 377-1925

Recognized Classics
Classic Car Club Of America

A.C.	Lagonda*
Alfa Romeo	La Salle*
Alvis*	Lincoln*
Amilcar*	Lincoln Continental
Aston-Martin*	Locomobile*
Auburn*	Marmon
Austro-Daimler	Maybach
Bentley	McFarlan
Blackhawk	Mercedes-Benz*
B.M.W.*	Mercer
Brewster*	M.G.*
Bucciali	Minerva*
Bugatti	Packard*
Cadillac*	Peerless*
Chrysler*	Pierce-Arrow
Cord	Renault*
Cunningham	Reo*
Dagmar*	Revere
Darracq*	Roamer*
Delaunay Belleville*	Rhor
Doble	Rolls-Royce
Dorris	Ruxton
Duesenberg	Squire
du Pont	S.S. Jaguar*
Franklin*	Stearns Knight
Graham Paige*	Stevens Duryea
Hispano-Suiza	Stutz
Horch	Sunbeam*
Invicta	Talbot*
Isotta-Fraschini	Triumph*
Itala	Vauxhall*
Jordan*	Voisin
Kissel*	Wills St. Claire*

(*Only certain models considered "Classic")

The Milestone Cars

Things desired become things possessed!

Class Endures Forever

These are 1945-67 automobiles judged outstanding, relative to their contemporaries, by The Milestone Car Society. The list today includes over 125 models. The Milestone Car society was founded in 1971. This excellent club publishes a quality quarterly magazine edited by Rich Taylor. One need not own a Milestone Car to become a member.

Car Must Excel

The Milestone Car Society does much the same thing with cars of the 1945-67 era as the Classic Car Club of America has done for 1925-48 car collectors. Their list of cars is also accepted by the Veteran Motor Car Club of America. Any member may nominate a car for consideration of becoming a certified Milestone Car. This ballot is reviewed by a committee, and if deemed worthy, the membership determines if the car is to become a certified milestone. Each car must excel in at least two of the following five categories: styling, engineering, performance, innovation and craftsmanship.

The Milestone Car Society
P.O. Box 50850
Indianapolis, IN 46250

Certified Milestone Cars

AC Ace 1954-61
AC Aceca 1955-61
AC Buckland Open Tourer 1949
AC (Shelby) Cobra 1962-67
Alfa Romeo Giulietta Spyder.................................. 1956-64
Alfa Romeo Giuilietta/Giulia Sprint Speciale 1959-61
Alfa Romeo 6C 2500 super sport 1949
Allard Series J2, K2, K3 1946-56
Apollo 1963-66
Arnolt Bristol 1954-62
Aston Martin DB1 to DB4...................................... 1948-63
Aston Martin DB4, DB5, DB6 (All) 1964-67
Austin Healey 100/100M 1953-56
Austin Healey 100-6 1956-59
Austin Healey 3000 1959-67
Bentley (All)... 1946-64
Bentley S 111, S 3, PV 1965
Bentley SS & T 1966-67
BMW 507 1957-59
Bugatti Type 101 1951
Buick Riviera... 1949, 1963-65
Buick Skylark 1953-54
Cadillac Eldorado 1953
Cadillac Eldorado Brougham 1957-58
Cadillac Eldorado 1955
Cadillac Eldorado 1967
Cadillac Sixty Special 1948-49
Cadillac Sixty-One Coupe (Fastback)........................... 1948-49
Cadillac Sixty-Two Sedanet, Convertible, DeVille 1948-49
Cherolet Bel Air V8 Hardtop Convertible 1955
Chevrolet Corvette... 1953-57
Chevrolet Corvette Convertible 1960
Chevrolet Corvette Convertible 1962
Chevrolet Corvette, Coupe Only 1963
Chevrolet Corvette (All).................................... 1964
Chevrolet Nomad 1955-57
Chrysler 300 (Through "G" Series) 1955-61
Chrysler Town & Country 1946-50
Cisitalia GT (Pininfarina) 1946-49
Citroen DS19 & ID19.. 1955-64
Continental Mark II.. 1956-57
Corvair Monza Spyder 1962-64
Crosley Hotshot/SS 1950-52

Maserati 3500/3700 GT......................................1957-64
M.G. Series TC 1946-49
M.G. Series TD 1950-53
Mercedes-Benz 220A, Coupe & Convertible 1951-54
Mercedes-Benz 190SL.......................................1955-62
Mercedes-Benz 230SL.......................................1963-64
Mercedes-Benz 300 S, SL, SE, 300 Coupe & Convertible 1952-64
Mercedes-Benz 220 S/220SE (Coupe & Convertible) 1956-64
Mercedes-Benz 600...1964
Mercury Sportsman 1946
Morgan Plus Four..1950-64
Muntz Jet 1950-54
Nash-Healey...1951-54
NSU Wankel Spyder 1964
OSCA MT 4 1948-56
Oldsmobile 88 (Coupe, Convertible, Holiday)................1949-50
Oldsmobile Toronado 1966-67
Packard Caribbean...1953-56
Packard Custom (Clipper & Custom Eight)...................1946-50
Packard Pacific/Convertible...............................1954
Packard Panther Daytona...................................1954
Packard Patrician/Four Hundred 1951-56
Pegaso (All) 1951-58
Pontiac Safari..1955-57
Porsche Series 356 1949-64
Porsche 356C 1965
Riley 2.5 (RMA-RME) 1945-55
Rolls-Royce (All) 1947-64
Rolls-Royce S 111, S 3, PV 1965
Rolls-Royce SS & T..1966-67
Shelby 350 GT & 500 GT....................................1965-67
Studebaker Avanti 1963-64
Studebaker Gran Turismo Hawk..............................1962-64
Studebaker Starlight Coupe (All Models)...................1947-49
Studebaker Convertible (All Models) 1947-49
Studebaker Starlight Coupe (Six & V-8)...................1953-54
Studebaker Starliner Hardtop (Six & V-8) 1953-54
Sunbeam Tiger Convertible.................................1965-67
Talbot Lago 4.5 (All) 1946-54
Triumph TR2/TR3 1953-63
Tucker 1948
Volvo P 1800S 2-Door Coupe 1961-67
Willys-Overland Jeepster 1948-51
Woodill Wildfire 1952-58

Note: Provision now exists to add post-1967 cars to the above list provided they are identical to cars already certified as Milestones and at least ten years of age.

Clubs Not Restricted
To One Make Of Automobile

ANTIQUE

★ **Antique Automobile Club
Of America**
501 West Governor Rd
Hershey, PA 17033
350 regions & chapters.

★ **The Antique & Classic
Car Club Of Canada**
P.O. Box 1304
Postal Stattion A
Toronto, Ontario/
Canada M5W 1G7
Purpose to further interest.

AIRFLOW

★ **Airflow Club
Of America**
8554 Boyson Street
Downey, CA 90242
Chryslers and DeSotos.

AUTO HOBBY INDUSTRY

★ **Autorama Guild**
428 Clark Lane
Orange, CT 06477
**Sponsors the Autorama
Show.**

CLASSIC

★ **Classic Car Club
Of America**
P.O Box 443
Madison, NJ 07940
Automobiles 1925-48.

★ **Desert Classic
Car Association**
P.O. Box 1331
Palm Desert, CA 92260

COLLECTIBLES

★ **Historical Automobile
Society of Canada**
RD 2, P.O. Box 6
Rockwood,
Ontario/Canada
Any collectible vehicle.

CONVERTIBLES

★ **Convertible Lovers
Of America**
Box 187
Center Rutland, VT 05736

★ **USA
Convertible Club**
P.O. Box 423
Annnapolis, MD 21401

HORSELESS CARRIAGE

★ **Horseless Carriage
Club Of America**
9031 E Florence Av
Downey, CA 90249
**77 regional groups in
United States.**

LITERATURE

★ **Auto Enthusiasts
International**
P.O. Box 31A
Royal Oak, MI 48068
**Those interested in
automobile literature.**

MILESTONE

★ **The Milestone
Car Society**
P.O. Box 50850
Indianapolis, IN 46250
**Selects certified milestone
cars.**

OLD
CAR COUNCIL

★ **Old Car Council
Of Colorado**
P.O. Box 317
Mead, CO 80542
**31 clubs preserve collectible
autos.**

POSTCARDS

★ **Automotive Postcard
Collectors**

155 Tamarack Drive
Rochester, NY 14622
**Those interested in auto
postcards.**

SHOW CARS

★ **International Show
Car Association**
15075 E Eleven Mile Rd
Roseville, MI 48066
**Sanctions custom vehicle
shows.**

STREET ROD

★ **National Street
Rod Association**
3041 Getwell, 301
Memphis, TN 38118
**Provides leadership for
enthusiasts.**

STREET VAN

★ **National Street
Van Association**
P.O. Box 381
Algonquin, IL 60102
**Organization for van
movement.**

VETERAN

★ **Veteran Motor Car
Club Of America**

105 Elm Street
Andover, MA 01810
**17 regions & 44 intern.
chapters.**

VINTAGE

★ **Vintage Sports Car
Club Of America**
170 Wetherhill Road
Garden City, NY 11530

VOITURES ANCIENNES

★ **Voitures Anciennes
Du Quebec Inc**
C.P. 367 Succursale ''C''
Montreal, Quebec/
Canada H2L 4K3
French language auto club.

WOODIES

★ **National Woodie Club**
5522 W 140th Street
Hawthorne, CA 90250
**Sponsor national & regional
events.**

ENGLISH

★ **Royal Automobile Club**
89-91 Pall Mall
London S.W.1, England

Car Clubs For Enthusiasts

(Each club restricted to one make)

Alas! It can never be quite the same.

ANGLIA

★ **American Anglia Association**
17537 Blythe Street
Northridge, CA 91324

ALFA

★ **Alfa Romeo Association**
2115 El Camino Real
Redwood City CA 94063

★ **Northwest Alfa Romeo Club**
P.O. Box 30581
Seattle, WA 98103

ALLARD

★ **Allard Owners Club USA**
33 Underwood Road
Montville, NJ 07045

ASTON MARTIN

★ **Aston Martin Owners Club**
195 Mt Paran Rd N W
Atlanta, GA 30327

★ **Aston-Martin Owners Club, Ltd**
7440 Armillo Rd
Dublin, CA 94566

AUBURN

★ **Auburn—Cord Duesenberg Club**
Rt 2 Hathaway Rd
Harbor Springs
MI 49740

AUSTIN-HEALEY

★ **Austin-Healey Club**
Pacific Centre
Box 6267
San Jose CA 95150

★ **Austin-Healey Club Of America**
705 Dimmeydale
Deerfield, IL 60015

AVANTI

★ **Avanti Owners Association**
6857 Mulberry Lane
Garden Grove, CA 92645

★ **Avanti Owners
Association International**
3900 Church Road
Mitchellville, MD 20716

BMW

★ **BMW Automobile Club
Of America**
P.O. Box 401
Hollywood, CA

★ **BMW Car Club Of America**
345 Harvard Street
Cambridge MA 02138

BRICKLIN

★ **Bricklin International**
5809 Sable Drive
Alexandria, VA 22303

BUICK

★ **The Buick Club Of America**
P.O. Box 898
Garden Grove, CA 92642

CADILLAC

★ **The Caddilac-LaSalle Club**
3340 Poplar Drive
Warren, MI 48091

CAMARO

★ **The Camaro
Club Of America**
P.O. Box 490344
Atlanta, GA 30349

CHEVROLET

★ **Vintage Chevrolet
Club Of America**
P.O. Box 5387
Orange, CA 92667

★ **Early Four Cylinder
Chevrolet Club Intern.**
11948 Highdale Street
Norwalk, CA 90650

★ **National Nomad Club**
P.O. Box 606
Arvada, CO 80002

CHRYSLER

★ **Chrysler Restorers Club**
426 Orchard Lane
Manheim, PA 17545

★ **Chrysler 300 Club
International Inc**
19 Donegal Court
Ann Arbor, MI 48104

★ **National Chrysler
Products Club, Inc**
P.O. Box 326
Vincentown, NJ 08088

★ **Airflow Club
Of America**
8554 Boyson Street
Downey, CA 90242

CITROEN

★ **Citroen Car Club, Inc**
Box 743
Hollywood, CA 90028

COBRA

★ **Cobra Owners
Club Of America, Inc**
4737 Buffalo Avenue
Sherman Oaks, CA 91403

CORVAIR

★ **Corvair Society Of America**
P.O. Box 2488
Pensacola, FL 32503

CORVETTE

★ **The Classic Corvette Club**
94177 N Rich Road
Alma, MI 48801

★ **National Corvette
Owners' Association**
404 S Maple Avenue
Falls Church, VT 22046

★ **National Corvette
Restorers Society**
P.O. Box 34377
Omaha, NE 68134

★ **Vintage Corvette Club
Of America**
Box T
Atascadero, CA 93422

DATSUN

★ **Z Club Of America**
1065 Market Street
Paterson, NJ 07513

★ **Datsun Owners Club**
363 Woodland Avenue
Brea, CA 92621

DESOTO

★ **W.P.C.Club**
DeSoto, Dodge, Plymouth,
Chrysler, Imperial And
Related
P.O. Box 4705
North Hollywood,
CA 91607

DURANT-STAR

★ **Durant-Star**
Owners' Club
3106 Plymouth Rock Rd
Norristown, PA 19403

DUESENBERG

★ **Auburn-Cord-**
Duesenberg Club Inc
P.O. Box 217
Skippack, PA 19474

EDSEL

★ **International**
Edsel Club
P.O. Box 304
Bellevue, OH 44811

EXCALIBUR

★ **Excalibur**
Owners' Club
1864 W Washington Blvd
Los Angeles, CA 90007

★ **Excalibur Association**
International
P.O. Box 216
N Judson, IN 46366

FERRARI

★ **Ferrari Owners Club**
3460 Wilshire Blvd
Suite 1010
Los Angeles, CA 90012

★ **The Ferrari Club**
Of America
2000 Weber Hills Road
Wyzata, MN 55391

★ **The Ferrari Club**
Of America, Inc

931 Arquilla Drive-432
Glenwood, IL 60425

FIAT

★ **The Fiat Club**
Of America, Inc
Box 192
Somerville, MA 02143

FORD

★ **Model A**
Restorer's Club
P.O. Box 1930 A
Dearborn, MI 48121

★ **Long Beach**
Model T Club
Box 7112
Long Beach, CA 90807

★ **The Early Ford V-8**
Club Of America
P.O. Box 2122
San Leandro, CA 94577

HONDA

★ **Hondacar International**
Box 242
Deptford, NJ 08096

HUDSON

★ **Hudson-Essex**
Terraplane Club
100 E Cross St
Ypsilanti, MI 48197

HUPMOBILE

★ **Hupmobile Club**
P.O. Box AA
Rosemead, Ca 91770

JAGUAR

★ **EJAG North America**
Box 220
Carlisle, MA 01741

★ **The Classic**
Jaguar Association
P.O. Box 61
Costa Mesa, CA 92627

JENSEN

★ **Association Of**
Jensen Owners
1223 Westwood Avenue
High Point, NC 27262

KAISER-FRAZER

★ **Kaiser-Frazer Owners Club**
4015 South Forest
Independence, MO 64052

KISSEL

★ **Kissel Kar Klub**
Frost Pond Road
Locust Valley, NY 11560

LAGONDA

★ **The Lagonda Club**
10 Crestwood Trail
Sparta, NJ 07871

LINCOLN

★ **Lincoln's Of The Sixties Club**
P.O. Box 3067
Longwood, FL 32750

LINCOLN CONTINENTAL

★ **Lincoln Continental Owners Club**
P.O. Box 549
Nogales, AZ 85621

LANCIA

★ **American Lancia Club**
RFD 103 Rancho Real
Del Mar, CA 92014

MASERATI

★ **Maserati Information Exchange**
Box 772
Mercer Island, WA 98040

MAZDA

★ **RX-7 Club Of America**
138 Ardmore Avenue
Hermosa Beach, CA 90254

★ **Mazda RX-7 Club**
1774 S. Alvira Street
Los Angeles, CA 90035

MERCEDES-BENZ

★ **Gull Wing Group Inc**
2229 Via Cerritos
Palos Verdes,
CA 90274

★ **Mercedes-Benz Club Of America**
619 N. Cascade
Colorado Springs,
CO 80903

MERCER

★ **Mercer Associates**
MGT Dept. Texas Tech
Lubbock, TX 79406

MG

★ **North American MGA Register**
4660 Gardenia Av
Cleveland,
TN 37311

★ **American MGB Association**
611 Roger Avenue
Inwood, NY 11696

★ **California MG "T" Register**
4911 Winnetka Av
Woodland Hills,
CA 91364

★ **The Classic MG Club**
1307 Ridgecrest Rd
Orlando, FL 32806

NASH

★ **The Nash Car Club Of America**
635 Loyd Street
Hubbard, OH 44425

OPEL

★ **Opel Club Of America**
Box 4545
Hollywood, FL

OLDSMOBILE

★ **Oldsmobile Club Of America**
145 Latona Road
Rochester, NY 14626

341

★ **Curved Dash Olds Club**
3455 Florida Avenue
N Minneapolis, MN 55427

PACKARD

★ **Packard Automobile Classics**
P.O. Box 2808
Oakland, CA 94618

★ **Packards International**
302 French Street
Santa Ana, CA 92701

PANTERA

★ **Pantera International**
18704 Chase Street
Northridge,
CA 91324

PIERCE-ARROW

★ **PIERCE-Arrow Society, Inc**
135 Edgerton Street
Rochester, NY 14607

★ **Pierce-Arrow Society**
1833 E High Street
Pottstown, PA 19464

PONTIAC

★ **PONTIAC Owners Club**
Box 612
Escondido, CA 92025

★ **Pontiac-Oakland Club International**
P.O. Box 5108
Salem, OR 97304

★ **Pontiac-Oakland Enthusiast's Organization**
2330 W Clarkston Rd
Lake Orion, WI 48035

PORSCHE

★ **Porsche Club Of America**
5616 Clermont Dr
Alexandria, VA 22310

★ **Porsche Owners Club**
Box 54910
Los Angeles, CA 90054

RENAULT

★ **Renault Club Of America**
2709 Pleasantdale Rd
Vienna, VA 22180

SHELBY

★ **Shelby American Automobile Club**
24-C April Lane
Norwalk, CT 06850

SINGER

★ **Singer Owners Club Of America**
1578 Terilyn
San Jose, CA 95122

STEVENS-DURYEA

★ **Stevens-Duryea Associates**
3565 Newhaven Road
Pasadena, CA 91107

STUDEBAKER

★ **Antique Studebaker Club, Incorporated**
P.O. Box 142
Monrovia, CA 91061

SUNBEAM

★ **CAT, California Association Of Tiger Owners**
4508 El Reposo Drive
Los Angeles, CA

★ **Sunbeam Alpine Club**
607 Excalibur Drive
San Jose, CA 95116

★ **Sunbeam Car Club**
592 Baron Street
Toms River, NJ 08753

THUNDERBIRD

★ **Vintage Thunderbird Club Of America**
P.O. Box 2250
Dearborn, MI 48123

TRIUMPH

★ **Triumph Register Of America**
1602 Ramblewood Av
Columbus, OH 43220

★ **Triumph Register**
Box 36477
Grosse Pointe, MI 48236

VOLVO

★ **Volvo America Register**
1203 W Cheltenham Av
Melrose Park, PA 19126

WILLYS

★ **Willys-Overland-**

Knight Registry
241 Orchard Drive
Dayton, OH 45419

WILLS

★ **The Wills Club**
705 S Clyde Avenue
Kissmmee, FL 32741

 *Yes, beauty is ageless.*

Automobile Photography Made Easy

Ah. Automobiles are lovely things.

Satisfying Results

Rewarding automobile photography doesn't have to be expensive. Pictures of your car or other automobiles can be interesting additions to any home or office. Take them yourself! When the photography and framing are done with care, you'll have a satisfying result. One your friends will admire. It's amazing how many people enjoy a good picture of a beautiful automobile. At least half the fun is the search for the right car, location, event or perhaps accessory you may be interested in. It's a rewarding hobby!

It's A Snap!

Fortunately, the end result of automotive photography is not in direct proportion to the amount of money you may have invested in equipment. Nor is it directly related to the gear you are willing to carry. However, always take along lots of film. Use it! Follow the example of professional photographers—take lots of different shots of your subjects. Fine pictures can be produced by anyone willing to take time to arrange and stage the correct surroundings. These steps lead to quality automobile pictures. Photography is not difficult. It's a snap! This basic outline will be a big help. Good luck.

PHOTOGRAPHY OUTLINE

A. BASIC TYPES OF CAMERAS

1. 110 Cameras
   a. Less bulky to carry.
   b. General price range $35-$200.
   c. Ideal basic equipment.
   d. Negatives, if sharp, produce up to 8 x 10.
   e. Normal lens is 24 mm.
2. Medium format cameras
   a. 120 roll film.
   b. Larger camera gives larger negative or transparency.
   c. This usually means better quality in photography.
   d. Normal lens 75 to 105 mm depending on camera.
3. 35 mm S.L.R. cameras
   a. Potential is present for larger enlargements.
   b. Color reproductions can be made from transparencies.
   c. Normal lens 50 mm.
   d. Probably the most flexible camera.
   e. What you see in viewfinder you get on negative.
4. Rangefinder 35 mm cameras.
   a. Excellent cameras.
   b. Inexpensive $59-$175.

B. LENSES

1. Normal lens usually comes with camera. Produces a reasonably undistorted picture in low-light.
2. Telephoto lens suggested for auto racing.
   a. Telephoto allows you to separate the focus of the car from the back or foreground scenery.
   b. Usually impossible to get close enough for good pictures without telephoto lens.
3. Four power (4X) strongest telephoto lens recommended to be handheld.
4. Wide-angle is a luxury lens used for interior shots of cars.
5. Telephoto and wide-angle zoom lenses are good but difficult to use in low-light conditions.
6. Close-up lenses (called macro) and close-up lens sets are used for photographing car ensignias, engine parts and small details.
7. Protect your lens by covering it with a filter (can be clear). Do not use more than one filter except for special effects.

C. SHUTTERS

1. The shutters on cameras can be mechanical or electronically controlled.
   a. Electronic shutter produces consistent exposure.
   b. Electronic shutter needs battery to operate.
   c. Electronic shutter is resistant to dust, moisture and shock.

D. EXPOSURE

1. One type can be set manually.
2. Another can be fully automatic. It is usually either "aperture preferred" or "shutter preferred" *(Note: See following list of terms).*
3. Some camera models have all three: manual, aperture and shutter.
4. Also available in a match the needle inside the viewfinder.
5. Regardless of type, there is a need for you to compensate for the light behind the subject being photographed.

E. SIZE AND WEIGHT

1. The less weight and bulk you have to carry the happier you'll be.

Indeed! This extraordinary bird was no ordinary automobile.

F. LIGHT METERS AND ELECTRONIC FLASH
1. Somewhat unnecessary extra equipment.
2. Electronic flash rarely used in automobile photography.

G. FILM
1. Two basic types of color film.
2. Negative—produces prints.
   a. Prints are more expensive.
   b. The results are less accurate.
3. Reversal film produces transparencies (slides).
   a. Less expensive than prints.
   b. Produces the best and most accurate pictures.

H. ADDITIONAL EQUIPMENT FOR ENTHUSIASTS
1. Unipod or tripod, shutter release cable and a polorized filter (to tone down reflections).

I. LOCATION FOR SHOOTING PICTURES
1. Keep the background simple.
   a. Avoid driveways, poles, wires, ugly trees, parking lots and trash.
   b. Don't have objects in the foreground or background competing with the car for attention.
2. Wet down the surface the car is parked on.
3. Take your photos early in the morning or late afternoon. You may have to filter for color shift.
4. Photograph the car either in all sunlight or all shadows. Don't mix the two in the same photo.
   a. Try different exposure settings on your camera for each angle you photograph.
   b. Try lots of angles. Don't be afraid to use film. Film is not expensive.
5. Use the least possible depth of field. Try adding depth to the photo by placing an object (out of focus) in front.
6. For close ups, put some other part of the car in the photo for reference. An example would be showing part of a fender when photographing a wire wheel, etc.

J. PHOTOGRAPHING THE MOVING AUTOMOBILE
1. Usually done with a 35 mm camera with telephoto lens.
   a. The 200 mm telephoto lens is recommended for 35 mm cameras.
   b. Also could use a 250 mm telephoto lens with a 120 camera (this is expensive equipment).

2. Wide angle lenses can be used if you can get close to the car. Watch for distortion.

3. Panning (moving the camera) to follow the movement of the car gives interesting results.

4. Select a road relatively free of traffic.
   a. Two-lane roads with curves, grass and trees are excellent.
   b. Straightaway shots of cars are usually uninteresting.

5. To hold or stop the action of a moving car you will need a shutter speed of at least 1/500 sec. (maybe faster).

A Few Terms Used In Photography

In purchasing or using any camera it helps to know the meaning of the basic vocabulary. These terms are common to all photography.

Aperture
A circular hole in a thin metal plate located between the lens and film used to regulate the amount of light reaching the film.

Aperture-Preferred
You choose the aperture and camera automatically chooses shutter speed.

ASA
A given value which denotes the speed or sensitivity of a film to light.

Automatic Exposure (AE)
Photocells used to measure the scene brightness as seen through the lens. This photocell automatically sets either the aperture or shutter speed by means of an electronic control circuit.

Cable Release
A long cable that screws into the shutter release on a camera. Used to eliminate camera shake.

Coated Lenses
A thin layer of chemical is deposited on the glass surfaces. Coating reduces flare and gives the lens a color cast.

Depth Of Field
The distance between the nearest point and the farthest point in the picture subject which will come out acceptably sharp on the film.

Diaphragm
Used to reduce the lens opening (aperture) of a camera.

DIN
A system rating the speed of film. Generally found on the film speed setting dial of your camera. European version of ASA.

Lens Speed
Refers to maximum diaphragm opening the lens (light reaching film) of a camera.

Film Speed
Pertains to the rated sensitivity of any film. 25 ASA is slow, 200 ASA is medium and 400 ASA is a fast film speed

Macro Lenses
Lenses used in close-up photography.

Reversal Film
Slide film. The image is reversed during processing to give you a slide.

Shutter-Preferred
You select the shutter speed and the camera selects the aperture (Light reaching the film).

Single Lens Reflex (SLR)
In this camera the user views and focuses through the picture taking lens on the camera.

Telephoto Lens
A camera lens having an enormous focal length. Generally used to bring the picture subject closer.

Wide-Angle Lens
A camera lens used to increase the angle of view. Can also cause distortion.

Zoom Lens
One lens offering many different focal lengths. Also used for special effects.

Identify Your Pictures In Detail

The photographer has a wonderful opportunity to use imagination. Here's an idea. By creating your own special collection portraying state-of-the-art automobile components you can build your own "classic" photo album. You might select photographs of wheels for your collection. The history and color of wheels is a fascinating story. Today the designs are even more exotic and varied than in the past. This means you never have to search far to find new wheels to photograph. A word of caution—(speaking from experience) never take a picture that you can not later identify in detail. As time goes by, captions under the pictures really add the finishing touch to your collection. Without them, you have just another group of pictures.

Phantom

The color photographs in *Automobile Success* were taken from a collection that had its beginning years ago in the manner we have described. You can be sure the collection is a prized possession. The mystique of the automobile is found on each page.

> *She was a phantom of delight*
> *When first she gleamed upon my sight,*
> *A lovely apparition, sent*
> *To be a moment's ornament*
>
> *Wordsworth*

Hard-To-Find
Parts, Repairs And Services

Trust me. Do not believe in miracles—rely on them!

Persistence—The Key To Success

Today's parts hunter is not unlike Dr. Livingston's African search for Stanley. Difficulties encountered trying to locate antique automobile parts, repairs and services may seem almost unsurmountable at times. They aren't! The following list provides excellent sources. Persistence is the key to success! After all, Livingston found Stanley.

This System Protects You

Caution must be excercised when ordering automobile parts by mail or phone. I advise you not to prepay the order. Ask to have the part shipped to you freight collect. Be prepared. You can expect the freight company to ask you for full **cash** payment upon delivery. Most do not accept checks. You may find a seller now and then who will not ship via this method. Go on to the next one. Though inconvenient at times, this system absolutely assures you of receiving your merchandise and the seller getting paid!

When you mail parts for repair, don't send full payment in advance. A better way is to pay no more than half the estimated total or a deposit and the remainder upon delivery.

Suppliers Provide The Answers

You would have little chance of finding needed parts for collectable automobiles without suppliers. The business of locating, purchasing, repairing, storing, selling and shipping these out-of-date items requires skill and patience.

Suppliers Of Rare Auto Parts, Repairs and Services

(Listed by car make)

**Automobile Appraisal
Service For Owners
Buyers & Sellers
Investment Automobiles**
Hunter Harris
The Automobile Consultant
3400 Sausalito Drive
Corona del Mar, CA 92625
PH: 714 760-8834

Antique Auto Parts
Rick's
Box 662
Shawnee Mission,
KS 66201
PH:1-800 255-4100

Appraisal Service
Brian Nelson Jones
P.O. Box 1399
Bloomington, IN 47401

**Austin-Healey
Sprite Parts**
FASPEC
606 SE Madison
Portland, OR 97214
PH: 503 232-7732

**Automobile
(Finding Exotics)
Specialists In Search**
Auto Serach

5047 West 87th Lane
Crown Point, IN 46307
PH: 219 769-4481

Auto Hauling, Enclosed
Passport Transport Ltd
9479 Aerospace Drive
St. Louis, MO 63134
PH: 324 426-6777

Auto Hauling, Enclosed
Horseless Carriage
Carriers, Inc.
61 Iowa Avenue
Paterson, NJ 07503
PH: 800 631-7796

**Auto Hauling
(Cost sharing)**
Peoples Trans-Share
258 S W Alder Street
Portland, OR 97240
PH: 800 547-0933
Or 503 227-2419

Avanti (All)
Avanti Motor Corporation
765 S Lafayette Blvd
South Bend, IN 46623

Avanti/Studebaker (Rare)
Studebaker Auto Parts
Route 8 Box 191
Durham, NC 27704

**Ball & Roller
Bearings & Seals**
Penn Ball Bearing Co
3511 N American Street
Philadelphia, PA 19140

**Bearings, Main
Rod & Cam (Obsolete)**
Terrill Machine Company
RT 2
DeLeon, TX 76444
PH: 817 893-2610

Body Trim (Obsolete)
Obsolete Parts Co
202 N Taylor Street
Nashville, GA 31639
PH: 912 686-5812

**Brake Cylinders
Repair (Early)**
White Post Restorations
White Post, VA 22663
PH: 703 837 1140

British Autos, Parts (All)
British Auto
1635 Creek Street
Rochester, NY 14625
PH: 716 377-1160

British Restoration Parts
BRP
1808 Oak
Kansas City, MO 64108
PH: 816 471-2776

Buick (Classic Parts)
Burchill Antique
Auto Parts
4150 24th Avenue
Port Huron, MI 48060

Buick, Parts (Rare)
Fred & Dan Kanter
76 Monroe Street
Boonton, NJ 07005
PH: 201 334-2400

Cadillac, Antique Parts
Grimaldi Buick-Opel
2225 Dixie Highway
Pontiac, MI 48055
PH: 313 338-6121

**Cadillac, DeSoto,
Dodge & LaSalle Parts**

Jed Efrus
528 Mountain Avenue
Springfield, NJ 07081
PH: 201 376-7590

Calipers (Stainless Steel)
Brakes Corporation
5120 Brookhaven Drive
Clarence, NY 14031
PH: 716 759-6634

**Camaro (Early)
Classic Camaro Parts**
P.O. Box 4277
Palm Springs, CA 92662
PH: 714 849-2303

**Carburetors, Classics
(Rebuild)**
Jim Alexander
Box 144
Maspeth, NY 11378

**Carburetors
Special Service**
Nichols Automotive
734 W Gardena Blvd
Gardena, CA 90247
PH: 213 515-0330

**Carpets & Leather
(Special)**
Bill Hirsch
396 Littleton Avenue
Newark, NJ 07103
PH: 201 243-2858

**Chevrolet, Parts
(Antique)**
Sharon & Sharon
Antique Auto Parts Co
RT 1, Box 33
Alapaha, GA 31622

Chevrolet, Parts (Rare)
Pro Antique Auto Parts
7 Thompson Rd
Warehouse Point,
CT 06088

**Cheverolet, Restoration
(Supplies)**
Harold Drake
20035 Bellemare Avenue
Torrance, CA 90503
PH: 213 370-0080

Chrysler, Parts (All)
Solomon's
Box 115, E Main
East Orwell, OH 44034
PH: 216 437-8622

**Clocks Auto, Amer.
(Repair)**
Auto Clock Shop
1801 Bladensburg Rd, NE
Washington, DC 20002
PH: 202 399-0699

Clock, Repair
Steve's Auto Clock Service
7364 Alba Avenue
Yucca Valley, CA 92284
PH: 714 365-1100

Clocks, Repair (Borg)
Burnell D. Harty
Box 43
Sandy Point, ME 04972

Cobra & Shelby, Parts
Branda Performance
703 Grant Avenue
Altoona, PA 16602
PH: 814 942-1869

Continental, Parts
Reliable Auto
1751 Spruce Street
Riverside, CA 92517
PH: 800 854-4770

Continental, Parts
M. H. Diels
12005 Tulip Grove Drive
Bowie, MD 20715

**Convertible Top
Cylinders
Hydraulic Motor/Pumps**
Hydro-E-Lectric
48-B Appleton Rd
Auburn, MA 01501
PH: 617 832-3081

**Corvair, Parts
Accessories**
American Corvair
Parts, Inc
PO Box 7466
Louisville, KY 40207
PH: 502 267-6835

Corvair, Parts (Rare)
Bill Coyle
1575 Smithtown Avenue
Bohemia, NY 11716
PH: 516 589-3433

**Corvette, Hatchback
(Convertible kit)**
Cars & Concepts, Inc.
Brighton, MI
PH: 800 521-9753

**Corvette
Restoration Parts**
Northland Corvette Supply
19 Airport Drive North
Dodge Center, MN 55927
PH: 507 374-2653

Corvette Parts (Restor.)
Northland Corvette Supply
19 Airport Drive North
Dodge Center, MN 55927
PH: 507 373-2653

Corvette, Special Parts
Corvette Specialists
1835 E Walnut Street
Pasadena, CA 91107
PH: 213 577-2620

Corvette, Special Parts
Corvette Parts
Jim Olson
P.O. Box 1074
Calmet City, IL 60409

Corvette Parts
Butler Corvette
Rt 202
Jaffrey, NH
PH: 603 532-6192

Corvette Parts
The Vette Shop
12115 Self Plaza
Dallas, TX 75218
Ph: 214 328-3124

Corvette Parts
Lincoln's Corvettes
12220 Aurora Av North
Seattle, WA 98133
PH: 1-800 426-7780

Corvette Parts
Corvette America
P.O. Box 427
Boalsburg, PA 16827
PH: 1-800 458-3475

Corvette Parts
Corvette Specialties
8810 Stonehaven Rd
Randallstown, MD 2133
Orders: 1-800 638-3128

Covers (Collector Cars)
Beverly Hills Accessories
202-X S Robertson Blvd
Beverly Hills, CA 90211

**Crosley, Parts
Sourcebook**
Service Motors
1986 NE 148 Street
N Miami, FL 33161
PH: 305 944-7431

Dodge Brothers, Parts
L Watari
511 Molino Street
Los Angeles, CA 90013
PH: 213 622-0970

Dodge & Desoto, Parts
James Ragsdale
134 James Street
Morristown, NJ 07960
PH: 201 539-5307

Dodge, Parts (Rare)
Parts Of The Past
Box 602
Waukesha, WI 53187

**DeSoto, Plymouth
Dodge, Chrysler
Parts (New-Old)**
Murray Motor Company
Box 546
Colby, KS 67701

Duesenberg (All)
Hoe Sportcar
446 Newton Turnpike
Weston, CT 06880

Edsel, Parts (Some)
Robert Midland
Box B
Hawley, PA 18428

**Exhaust Systems
Special**
Burton Waldron
Box C
Nottawa, MI 49075
PH: 616 467-7185

Facel Vega, Parts (Rare)
Kanter
Packard Industries
76 Monroe
Boonton, NJ 07005
PH: 201 334-2400

**Fenders & Bodies
(English)**
Scituate Coachworks, Inc.
PO Drawer 3258
New Bern, NC 28560
PH: 919 637-3686

**Fender Washers
Fasteners**
H C Fastener Co
PO Box P817
Alvarado, TX 76009
PH: 817 783-8150

**Fender Welt, Hood Lace
Overhaul Kits, New
(Classics)**
Stan Coleman
320 South Street, 12A
Morristown, NJ 07960
PH: 201 539-8317

**Ferrari
Parts & Restoration**
Bill Rudd Motors
14326 Oxnard Street
Van Nuys, CA 91401
PH: 213 988-7833

Ferrari
Motor-Sports
International
Box 151 Northern Blvd
Chinchilla, PA 18410
PH: 717 586-9222

Ford, Blocks
Good Old Days Garage
2340 Farley Place
Birmingham, AL 35226
PH: 205 822-4569

**Ford, Literature
(Manuals etc.)**
Vintage Auto Literature
PO Box 1281
Moultrie, CA 31768
PH: 912 985-6860

Ford Parts, Mustang
Glazier's Mustang Barn
531 Wambold Rd
Souderton, PA 18964
PH: 215 723-9674

Ford, Parts (Early)
A & L Parts Specialties
Canton, CT 06019

Ford, Parts (Guaranteed)
The Ford Parts Warehouse
Courthouse Square
Liberty, KY 42539
PH: 606 787-5031

Ford, Parts (Large Stock)
Dean McDonald
R.R. 3, Box 61
Rockport, IN 47635
PH: 812 359-4965

Ford, Parts (Rare)
McDaniel Old Ford Parts
3034 Lakewood
Freeway SW
Atlanta, GA 30310
PH: 404 766-2375

Ford, Parts (Vintage)
Bob's Model A
Cars & Parts
Box 13
Whately, MA 01093
PH: 413 655-2094

Ford, Parts (Vintage)
Sacramento Vintage Ford
1504 El Camino Avenue
Sacramento, CA 95815
PH: 916 922-3444

**Fords, Top Wood Kits
(A s & T s)**
Newood Products Co
4223 N 81st Lane
Phoenix, AZ 85033
PH: 602 269-3755

Gaskets
Gerald Lettieri
132 Old Main Street
Rocky Hill, CT 06067
PH: 203 529-7177

Grills (Reproductions)
C & R Metal Products
P.O. Box 285
Streamwood, IL 60103

**Harnesses & Wiring
(Reproduced)**
J.M.S. Antique
Auto Parts Co.
3915 Kirkwood Highway
Wilmington, DE 19808
PH: 302 995-1131

Headliners
Stan Coleman
320 South St Bldg 12A
Morristown, NJ 07960

Hudson
Clifford 6 = 8 Research
774 Newton Way
Costa Mesa, CA 92627

Hudson, Parts (All)
Solomons
Box 115, 544 E Main
East Orwell, OH 44034
PH: 216 437-8622

Hupmobile
Hupp Factory Service
Auburn, IN 46706

**Interiors
Match Color Kits
Owner & Shop Manuals**
Big T Parts Co
19337 Greenview
Detroit, MI 48219
PH: 800 521-4152

**Interiors
(Spec. Chevrolet)**
Hampton Coach
70 High Street
Hampton, NH 03842
PH: 603 926-6341

Jaguar, Parts (Rare)
Valley Of The Jaguars
Welsh's Enterprises
1108 Oak Grove Avenue
Steubenville, OH

Kaiser-Frazer, Parts
KF Parts
5807 Aldrich Avenue N
Minneapolis, MN 55430
PH: 612 561-6736

Kaiser-Frazer
Henry J, Parts
J E Parker
828E East Walnut
Fullerton, CA 92631

Keys & Locks
Vintage Cars
Bill's Lock Shop
3605 Robin Rd
Toledo, OH 43623

Keys
Protect Against
Loss Of
International Key
Return System
3187 A Airway-1
Costa Mesa, CA 92626
PH: 714 557-7752

Leather, Replica
Cloth & Carpets
Western Hide-Tex
Box 2133 Encinal Station
Sunnyvale, CA 94087
PH: 408 733-7790

Leather (Whole hides)
Raymond A. Wolff
P.O. Box 18,651-B
Milwaukee, WI 53218
PH: 414 464-0220

Lenses, Reproduced
Designs of the Times
1202 Le Gray Avenue
Los Angeles, CA 90042
PH: 213 255-1375

Lexol (Leather Preserve)
Corona Products Co

P.O. Box 1214
Altanta, GA 30301

License Plates, Restored
A. V. Polio
746 N Greenbrier
Orange, CT 06477
PH: 203 795-6434

Magnetos, Rare
George Punden
1520 High School Rd
Sebastopol, CA 95472
PH: 707 823-3824

Manifolds, Porcelainized
West Coast Porcelain
9868 Kale Street
South El Monte, CA 91733
PH: 213 575-1578

Manuals, Owner & Shop
Nat Adelstein
102 Farnsworth Avenue
Bordentown, NJ 08505
PH: 609 888-1000

Manuals (Original)
Howard Hoelscher
4 Pleasant Terrace
Boonton, NJ 07005
PH: 201 334-8510

Maserati
Rob de la rive
Box Reben 22
5612 Vilmergen AG
Switzerland

Mercedes, Parts
Vintage Mercedes Cars
Box 917
Bristol, CT 06010

Mercedes, Parts
Paul's Autohaus, Inc
PO Box 752
Northampton, MA 01060

Mercedes-Benz
Parts & Kits
Don Watkins
RT 1, Box 89
Midway, GA 31320
PH: 912 884-2862

**Metal
Parts Reproduced**
Graphic Enterprises
PO Box 216
West Haven, CT 06516

**Metropolitan
Parts (Rare)**
Metropolitan Pit Stop
5330 Laurel Canyon
North Hollywood, CA 91607
PH: 213 769-1515

MGA, Parts (All)
Scarborough Faire
943 Main street
Pawtucket, RI 02860
PH: 401 724-1357

MG TF, Parts:
Write: Carlos Avallone
Ave. Dr. Luiz Arrolos
Martens 61
Interlogos CEP 04781
Sao Paulo, Brazil

Mirrors, Resilvered
Dan Tilstone
29 N Delaware Rim Drive
Yardley, PA 19067
PH: 215 493-5483

Morgan
Isis Imports Ltd
469 Eddy Street
San Francisco, CA 94109

Morgan
Morgan Motor Co
Pickersleigh Road
Malvern Link
Worcestershire, England

Mufflers, Rare
King & Queen Mufflers
Box 423
Plumsteadville, PA 18949
PH: 215 536-3806

**Mustang
Accessories (Rare)**
Mustang Corral
5891 Westminster
Westminster, CA 92683
PH: 714 531-8850

**Mustang
Carpets (Molded)**
Mustang Mart
655 McGlincy Lane
Campbell, CA 95008
PH: 408 371-5771

**Mustang, Parts
Upholstery**
California Mustang
1249 East Holt
Pomona, Ca 91767
PH: 800 854-1737

Oldsmobile, Parts (Rare)
Mike Fusick
443 North Street
Windsor Locks, CT 06096
PH: 203 623-1589

Packard, Parts (Original)
Special Interest Autos
4320 W Papin
St. Louis, MO 63110
PH: 314 535-7050

**Parts (Rare)
Will Manufacture**
EGGE Machine Co
8403 Allport
Santa Fe Springs,
CA 90670
PH:213 945-3419

**Parts, Machining
Specialists**
Bloomfield Foundry &
Machine
25-A Broadway
Clark, NJ 07066
PH: 201 862-2278

Porsche, Parts (Rare)
PB Tweeks Ltd
4410 N Keystone Avenue
Indianapolis, IN 46205
PH: 317 545-6223

Pierce Arrow
Phil Hill
266 Twentieth Street
Santa Monica, CA 90402

Pierce Arrow
Lynn Steele
21144 Robinwood
Farmington, MI 48024

Pontiac (Vintage)
Buchill Antique Auto Parts
4150 24th Avenue
Port Huron, MI 48060

**Radiators, Duplicate
Original**
Feicht's Restoration
Columbiana, OH 44408
PH: 216 482-9221

Radiators, Early
Harold Coker
5100 Brainerd Rd
Chattanooga, TN 37411

Radio, Speaker Reconing
Speaker Reconing Of Denver
1040 South Gaylord
Denver, CO 80209
PH: 303 778-1617

Radios, Rare Repaired
W. D. Huneycutt
Box 411, Liberty Hill
Hartsville, SC 29550
PH: 803 332-9830

**Research of Rare Parts
(Fee)**
Harrah's Automobile
Collection
P.O Box 10 Reno, NV 89504
PH: 702 786-3232

Rolls-Bentley, Parts
Bob's Auto Parts
Route 9W
Kingston, NY 12401
PH: 914 336-6330

**Rolls Royce & Bentley
Parts (Rare)**
R/sR Parts & Pieces
6 Hidden Hill Rd
Westport, CT 06880
PH: 203 226-0675

**Rolls Royce & Bentley,
Parts**
Rudy's Motor Car Service
Brookside Park
Monmouth Juction, NJ 08852
PH: 201 297-4582

**Rolls-Royce (Engines)
Exchanges**

Antiques Inc
2215 West Shawnee
Muskogee, OK 74401

**Rolls/Bentley
(Rare Parts)
Will Manufacture**
CAR
22456 Orchard Rd
Farmington, MI 48024
PH: 1-800 521-6084
Resid. PH: 313 477-4767

Rubber Fittings (Vintage)
Metro Moulded Parts
3031 2nd Street North
Minneapolis, MN 55411

**Rubber Parts
Reproduction**
Lynn H. Steele
RT 1, Box 71W
Denver, NC 28037
PH: 704 483-5932

Runningboards, Material
Richard Williamson
Box 117
Ocata, FL 32670

**Spark Plug Wire Sets
Reproduced**
Coles's Ign & Mfg
52 Legionaire Dr
Rochester, NY 14617

**Special Parts
Fabrication (Brass)**
The Valley Forge
Restoration
PO Box 1133
Appache Junction, AZ 85220

Spotlights (Original)
Dean McDonald
R.R. 3
Rockport, IN 47635
PH: 812 359-4965

**Studebaker, Avanti,
NSU Wankel Parts**
Performance Unlimited Inc
11192 Prouty Rd
Painesville, OH 44077
PH: 216 354-4403

Studebaker, Parts & Engines
Antique Auto Ranch
N 2225 Dollar Rd
Spokane, WA 99206
PH: 509 535-7789

Studebaker, Parts (Post War)
Newman & Altman
405 W. Sample Street
South Bend, IN 46621
PH: 219 287-3381

Sunvisors, Restoration
Hampton Coach
70 High St, Box 665
Hammpton, NH 03842
PH: 603 926-6341

Thunderbird Parts (Rare)
Clasic Thunderbird Trader
1213 Sam Houston
Garland, TX 75042

Thunderbird, Parts (All)
Big T Parts
19337 Grenview
Detroit, MI 48219
PH: 800 521-4152

Thunderbird, Parts
Larry's Thunderbird Parts
511 S Raymond Avenue
Fullerton, CA 92631
PH: 800 854-0497

Thunderbird, Parts
National Parts Depot
2908 SW 4th Ct
Gainesville, FL 32601

Tires, Rare
Coker Tire Company
1600 E. 25th Street
Chattanooga, TN 37404
PH: 800 251-6336

Tires, Rare
The Lester Tire Company
26881 Cannon Road
Cleveland, OH 44146
PH: 216 439-7200

Tires, Chevrolet Ford (Classic)

Thunderbird Restoration
27 Industrial Park Drive
Hendersonville, TN 37075
PH: 615 824-7959

Tires
Goodyear Tire & Rubber Co
Akron, OH 44316
PH: 216 794-2121

Tires
Michelin Tire Corporation
2500 Marcus Avenue
Lake Success, NY 11040
PH: 516 488-3500

Tires
Pirelli Tire Corporation
600 Third Avenue
New York, NY 10016
PH: 212 490-1300

Tires
Uniroyal
1230 Av of the Americas
New York, NY 10020
PH: 212 756-5840

Tires (Firestone Antique)
Lucas Automotive
2850 Temple Av
Long Beach, CA 90805
PH: 213 595-6721
Also:
2141 W Main
Springfiled, OH 45504
PH: 513 324-1773

Titles (Will Title Any Car)
Titles
2501 4th Avenue South
Birmingham, AL 35233

Top Bows, Classic
Oak Bows
122 Ramsey Avenue
Chambersburg, PA 17201
PH: 717 264-2602

Tops & Carpets (Classics)
The Tufter
1229 S Mission Rd
Fallbrook, CA 92028
PH: 714 723-1121

Trailers (Custom Cars)
Don Jensen Enterprises
Humboldt, IA 50548
PH: 515 332-3343

Trailers (Enclosed, Auto)
Feldman Trailers
P.O. Box 1687
Bowling Green, KY 42101
PH: 502 843-4587

**Transporting, Autos
(Enclosed)**
AMR Co
Box 824
Kearney, NE 68847
PH: 308 236-5344

Triumph, Parts
Nichols Automotive
734 West Gardena Blvd
Gardena, CA 90247
PH: 213 515-0330

Upholstery (Early)
AFTCO Specialty Co
P.O. Box 278
Isanti, MN 55040
PH: 612 742-4025

**Upholstery, Auto
(Antique & Classic)**
LeBaron Bonney Co
14 Washington Street

Amesbury, MA 01913
PH: 617 388-3811

Wheel Covers
Wheel Cover World
4112 E 11th
Tulsa, OK 74112
PH: 918 932-5856

Wire Wheels
Everett Wheel Service
3702 Rucker Avenue
Everett, WA 98201
PH: 206 252-8538

Wire Wheels
Wheel Repair Service
317 Southbridge Street
Auburn, MA 01501
PH: 617 799-6551

Woodgraining, Autos
Elmo's Grainmobile
Rt 4, Box 262
Rusk, TX 75785
PH: 214 683-5930

**Woodgraining
Fords & Packards**
Ron Monte
20 Condit Court
Roseland, NJ 07068
PH: 201 226-3607

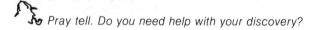

Pray tell. Do you need help with your discovery?

Famous Restoration Shops

Oh yes. When quality counts, here's the solution.

Achieve Reliable Authenticity

A lot of people think restoring an automobile is as simple as connecting tab A to tab B. Believe me, it isn't—not by a long shot! Today most, but not all, authentic restorations are completed, to some extent, by restoration shops. It's one of the best ways to achieve reliable authenticity. Without it you merely have a collection of old and new parts. The end result may be an interesting old automobile—but of lesser value.

Do A Quality Job The First Time

When questions come up, restoration shops can be helpful to you. Most supply hard-to-find parts or know where to obtain them. Any good shop possesses the ability, equipment, facilities and knowledge to do a quality job the first time. Even though you may need only technical advice, this too can be supplied. I suggest establishing a good working arrangement with a reputable restoration shop from the beginning. It can be the best protection of your investment dollars you'll ever make!

When Quality Counts

This story tells the aftereffects of a quality restoration job. At an auction a professionally restored early Mustang brought a world's record price of $9,100. Mustangs of the same vintage but limited to just cosmetic restorations sold for about $4,500. An amazing difference between two selling prices. Quality is obvious!

Restoration Shops

Horseless Carriage Shop . . . . *Dunedin, FL*
Roaring 20's Auto Museum . . . . *Wall, NJ*
Classic Car Investments . . . . *Atlanta, GA*
Vintage Cars . . . . *Nyack, NY*
Hibernia Auto Restorations . . . . *Hibernia, NJ*
Automobile Classics . . . . *Santa Monica, CA*
Egge Machine Company . . . . *Gardena, CA*
Veteran Car Sales . . . . *Denver, CO*
Antiques Inc. . . . . *Muskogee, OK*
The Restoration Engine Shop . . . . *Jamesburg, NJ*
Gaslight Automotive . . . . *Addison, IL*
Classic Auto Restoration . . . . *Farmington, MI*
White Post Restorations . . . . *White Post, VA*
Automotive Restorations, Inc . . . . *Hatfiled, PA*
Stilwell Auto Body . . . . *Zanesville, OH*
Automotive Restorations Inc . . . . *Stratford, CT*

Quality endures!

Old Motoring Terms

Only a few of these early day motoring terms remain in use. Most simply faded away. Today they seem mysterious and out of touch with reality. However, any search for vintage cars can also unearth long unused terms. It's kind'a nice to refer to their meaning.

Atmospheric engine
An early form of steam engine.

Avant train
Before 1900 a power unit attached in front of a horse-drawn vehicle to convert it to an automobile.

Berlina
A closed luxury car with small windows allowing the occupants to see out but not to be easily seen by others.

Bialbero
Italian—twin-camshaft.

Binnacle
The gauge area of a dash. British term.

Bonnet
Term for hood of a car.

Boot
Term for trunk of a car.

British antique auto classifications
Veteran . . . . built before 1905
Edwardian . . . . between 1905-1918
Vintage 1919-1930

Cabriolet
Term for convertible

Coachwork
The automobile body

Convertible
Any car with a folding roof.

Cyclecar
Term for very light production autos prior to 1922.

Cylinder types
''F'' Head . . . . Side exhaust valve and overhead inlet valve.
''L'' Head . . . . Both valves on one side of the cylinder.
''T'' Head . . . . . Exhaust valve on one side; inlet valve on the other side of cylinder.
''I'' Head . . . . Both valves directly over the piston (overhead-valve engine).

Dos-A-Dos
Early 1900s four-seater auto in which four passengers face each other or sit back-to-back.

Drophead coupe
Term for convertible.
G.T.
Grand Touring. An automobile combining sedan and sports car features.
King Of The Belgians
A luxurious open touring car.
Landau
A convertible-styled, chauffeur-driven limousine. Only the roof behind the front side windows was collapsible. Today a term used for a special styling treatment given to the roof line of an automobile.
Landaulet
A small landau with only two seats in the fixed roof portion.
Locomotive
Old term for a heavy, steam-propelled automobile.
Petrol
British term for gasoline.
Roi des Belges
A luxurious open touring car.

Rumble seat
A folding passenger seat recessed in the luggage area of a coupe or roadster. The hinged lid opens to form the backrest of the seat when in use. In England the term is "Dickey."
Runabout
A lightweight sporting-type automobile. Two seats and simple body. Term used especially in United States in early 1900's.
Saloon
British term for sedan. Closed car for four or more passengers with either two or four doors.
Spyder
Originated as a term for a light two-seater sport car. Now used as a description for an open two-seater sports car.
Tonneau
Term first used until about 1915. Describes an open automobile with a bench seat in front and semi-circular seat behind. A part of the back seat was built into the rear door. Now used to describe a cover placed over the rear compartment of a type of automobile.
Torpedo
A long open sports vehicle with an unbroken line from hood to windshield and from the windshield to the back of the car. 1910-20 United States. Until 1930 in France and Italy.
Tourer
Made until about 1930. Originally an open car seating four or more passengers. Later tourers were fitted with detachable screens and curtains.
Tricycle
Early-type open auto using three wheels and a steel-tube frame.

*Tulip Phaeton
A luxurious open touring car.
*Two-Stroke Cycle
Engine requiring only one revolution per cylinder or two piston strokes (up and down) to achieve a power stroke. Not used in cars in United States today, but can still be found in old motorcycles and outboard motors.
*Victoria
A term rarely used after 1900. Two-seater open automobile with a large folding hood.
*Vis-A-Vis
Term used around the turn of the century to describe an automobile with four seats in which two passengers faced the driver.
*Voiture Legere
Not often used for production cars. Usually light racing cars before 1914.
*Voiturette
Early two-seater touring car without a hood.

Thundering Elegance!

Custom-Built Cars Of America

It's elementary. Money made the escape possible.

An Outstanding Performer

The movie "Goldfinger" with James Bond's Aston Martin did much to bring custom cars into the public limelight. Its automatic weapons, ejector seat, radar unit and revolving license plates razzle-dazzed the public in 1964. Although custom cars of today have changed a great deal since 007's DB-4 Aston Martin, they still have the ingredient known as **appeal**! Gone is the spy-fighting artillery. Weaponry has been replaced by sheepskin rugs, 24-carat gold plated dashboards, etched glass and diamond-studded emblems.

Superior Attention Given To Detail And Finish

Technically, custom car manufacturers are known as "coach builders." Most of these companies begin construction of the car by using an existing chassis and drive train, produced by Ford, General Motors or Chrysler. Once this chassis has been stripped and modified the new coachwork (usually manufactured in fiberglass) is placed on it. Interiors are custom designed and refitted. Basically the entire automobile is hand assembled. **Minute attention is given to finish and detail.** Depending on the chassis used, most new car dealers will service the mechanical components of the vehicle.

Beware Of Resale Value Claims

Exercise great care when selecting a custom automobile. Self-deception can be the root of all evil. Although many owners claim their cars have great resale value, this is not always true. Example: I recently watched the owner of a custom car asking $60,000 accept $27,000 as a selling price. The length of time a coach builder has been in business is important. Ask. A good gambler trusts everybody—but always cuts the cards!

Escape From The Ordinary

With price tags of $20,000 and often over $50,000, custom cars appeal to many but can be afforded by few. They are an escape from the main stream of every day life. A blend of uniqueness and individuality separates them from a common world filled with Mercedes and Porsches!

Builders Of Custom Automobiles

(Random order)

Excalibur
Excalibur Automotive Corp
1735 S 106th Street
Milwakee, WI 53214
PH: 414 771-7171

Auburn (Replica)
California Custom Coach
1285 E Colorado Blvd
Pasadena, CA 91106
PH: 213 796-4395

Clenet
Clenet Coachworks, Inc
495 S Fairview Avenue
Santa Barbara, CA 93017
PH: 805 967-1405

Guanci SJJ1
Guanci Automobile Inc
220 North Madison Street
Woodstock, IL 60098
PH: 815 338-1817

Elegante
Elegante Motors, Inc
P.O. Box 20188
Indianapolis, IN 46220
PH: 317 634-5200

DiNapoli Coupe
Pacific Coachworks

57 Depot Road
Goleta, CA 93017

Diamante
Mathews Motor
Coach Corporation
4545 Calle Alto
Camarillo, CA 93010
PH: 805 482-8976

Stutz
Stutz Motor Car Of America, Inc
Time & Life Building
Rockefeller Center
New York, NY 10020
PH: 212 581-0322

Red Stallion (Cobra Repcar)
Red Stallion Ltd
657 H Street
Lincoln, CA 95648
PH: 916 645-8121

Model A Roadster (Repcar)
Model A & T Reproduction Corp
Tower 100, Renaissance Center
Detroit, MI 48243
PH: 313 259-0830

1979 Speedster (Repcar)
Automobili Intermeccanica
2421 South Susan Street
Santa Ana, CA 92704
PH: 714 556-1011

1932 Ford (4-Door Repcar)
Early Times Automotive
1893 South Newcomb
Porterville, CA 93257
PH: 209 781-2206

Daytona Migi (Repcar)
Daytona Automotive
819 Carswell Avenue
Holly Hill, FL 32017
PH: 904 253-2575

Avanti II (Repcar)
Avanti Motor Corporation
765 South Lafayette Blvd
P.O. Box 46634
South Bend, IN 46634
PH: 219 287-1836

Daytona Bird (Repcar)
Old Car Reproductions
5031 South U S 1
Oak Hill, FL 32014
PH: 904 345-3650

1930 Ford (Repcar)
Total Performance Inc
406 South Orchard Street, Rt 5
Wallingford, CT 06492
PH: 203 265-5668

Lincoln Mark V St. Tropez
American Custom Coachworks
P.O. Box 1220
Beverly Hills, CA 90213
PH: 213 278-0643

Cadillac Seville (Custom)
International Automotive Design
20th & Biscayne Blvd
Miami, FL 33137
PH: 800 327-7874

**Seville Tomaso Coupe
(Custom)**
Tomaso Of America Inc
P.O. Box 5692
Little Rock, AR 72215
PH: 501 227-0284

San Remo Dorado (Custom)
Coach Design
Group & Ogner Motors
31344 Via Colinas

Westlake Village, CA 91316
PH: 213 822-9902

Lincoln Cont. Mark V Coloma
Caribou Motor Corporation
1124 San Mateo Avenue
South San Francisco, CA 94080
PH: 415 952-3255

Milan Roadster (Custom)
Milan Coach Builders
4545 Industrial Street, Suite 5A
Simi Valley, CA 93063
PH: 805 527-8174

Del Caballero (Custom)
R.S. Harper, Inc
32639 Groesbeck Highway
Fraser, MI 48026
PH: 313 294-2080

Grandeur Opera Coupe
Grandeur Motor Corp
1405 S W 8th Street
Pompano Beach, FL 33060
PH: 305 947-7990

**Le Cabriolet Cad Convertible
Also Armored Touring Cars**
The Hess & Eisenhardt Company
Blue Ask Road
Cincinnati, OH 45242
PH: 513 791-8888

Cadillac Convertible (Custom)
Ltd Open Motoring
1421 S Ocean Blvd
Pompanmo Beach, FL 33062
PH: 305 735-8801

Eldorado De Cardin (Custom)
Standard Motors, Inc
3050 Biscayne Blvd
Miami, FL 33152
PH: 800 327-5131

LaCrosse (Custom)
Automobili Intermeccanica
2421 Susan Street
Santa Ana, CA
PH: 714 556-1011

Appeal is the trump card!

Kit Cars

Alas! The first rule of intelligent tinkering—save all the parts

Something Out Of The Ordinary

Are you tired of seeing the same Mercedes, Porsches and Ferraris over and over and you think you're a budding Enzo Ferrari, Henry Ford or Carol Shelby? You crave for something different, out of the ordinary, something unique! It has to be so unusual even your neighbors, the Joneses will never have one. You'll even put up with dirty finger nails, smell like Castrol motor oil, and itch for days from working with fiberglass. Then you're ready to build a kit car.

Choose One To Fit Your Lifestyle

Hundreds of different kit cars are available today! Take care to choose one to fit your personal lifestyle. Take stock of your mechanical abilities along with local climatic conditions and cost factors before making the big decision!

The Difference Should Be Obvious

Quality construction showing attention was given to detail at the time the car was built will be the greatest factor leading to a high resale value. In other words the difference between homemade and handmade should be obvious! If it isn't, the day will come you'll wish it was. Probably the same day you decide to sell it.

That Ferrari Look

Low initial cost along with great styling are the biggest advantages of kit cars. In reality you're buying that Ferrari look on a VW budget! Educate yourself. Education is the process of moving from cocksure ignorance to thoughtful uncertainty. Before you go hog wild buying drills, socket sets, impact wrenches, etc., keep these important points in mind:

- **Before purchase** see the kit in the raw! Visit the factory if possible. If you can't do this, locate an owner/builder and discuss problems he might have encountered.

- **Try to acquire the assembly manual.** If it contains thorough instructions, chances of a quality kit are good!

- **Be sure of the time you can devote to this project.** Remember, in order for this new automobile to have any real value, it must show craftsmanship along with quality when completed. There are no shortcuts. Craftsmanship and quality are equal to time spent in construction.

Consider Regulations

You could have to meet federal vehicle safety standards if you build the kit car from the chassis up. It would not make any difference whether you built the car for your own use or to resale to someone else. As a practical matter, **most kit cars are built on the chassis from used vehicles**. This means the kit car keeps the title of the used chassis. This chassis has already qualified as having met federal safety standards.

Get An Insurance Quote

Before you buy any kit car, make sure to ask for a verbal quote on the insurance rates.

Send For Pre-Licensing Requirements

You are not home free yet! Write or call your state Highway Patrol Headquarters. Request a copy of their inspection requirements for these vehicles. The major obstacle in licensing your kit car for street use will be the pre-licensing inspection performed by your local department of motor vehicles or highway patrol.

What Kit Cars Are Available

There are a staggering number of kit cars available today. The list fills a complete book. If you are interested in learning more about kit cars, I suggest you write to Auto Logic Publications, Inc., P.O. Box 2073, Wilmington, Delaware 19899. Ask for *The Complete Guide To Kit Cars, Auto Parts & Accessories* or check for a copy at your local bookstore.

Good luck and happy tinkering!

Convertible Conversions

The Open Air Ride

A new breed from an old idea. Exclusive and expensive. "You are looking at the first and only. . ." Well not quite. But for those who believe the convertible is the ultimate in styling and design, there's no need to settle for anything less. The real thing can be built. Those who seek individuality know the reward is worth the cost.

Companies Building Convertibles

AHA, Inc
EASTERN DISTRIBUTOR
AHA, Inc
510 Savage Road
Belleville, MI 48111
PH: 313 697-7129

WESTERN DISTRIBUTOR
Classic Motor Car Co
Bedford House
1423 Howe Street
Vancouver, British Columbia
V6Z1R9, Canada
PH: 604 683-7021
Mercury Capri.

**American
Custom Coachworks**
P.O. Box 1220
Beverly Hills, CA 90213
PH: 213 272-7908
**Luxury and sport models.
Cadillac, El Dorado, Lincoln,
Thunderbird and Cougar.**

Capital Coachworks
Classic Marketing Group, Inc
#4 Bel Air Village
1640 Peace Portal Drive
Blaine, WA 98230
PH: 206 332-5656
**Oldsmobile, Chevrolet, Buick,
and Pontiac.**

Coach Design Group
31344 Via Colinas

Westlake Village, CA 91361
PH: 213 991-3420
1 800 423-5475
San Remo El Dorado

Flint Corvette
5111 Maywood Avenue
Los Angeles, CA 90041
PH: 213 449-8987
Corvettes.

Global Coach And Armor
Global Marketing, Inc
2000 Century Plaza, 308
Columbia, MO 21044
Cadillac.

Grandeur Motor Co
1405 SW 8th Street
Pompano Beach, FL 33060
PH: 305 946-7990
Lincoln, Cadillac and Toyota.

Hess & Eisenhardt Co
Blue Ash Road
Cincinnati, OH 45242
PH: 513 791-8888
**Cadillac Le Cabriolet, Buick,
Oldsmobile.**

Llynn Motor Car Co
Automobili Intermeccanica
2421 South Susan Street
Santa Ana, CA 92704
Mustang
PH: 714 556-1011

Milan Coachbuilders
Classic Marketing Group, Inc
#4 Bel Air Village
1640 Peace Portal Drive
Blaine, WA 98230
PH: 206 332-5656
Mustang and Cadillac.

National Coach Engineering
American Clout
446 South Winchester Blvd
San Jose, CA 95128

PH: 408 296-3411
Mustang, Trans-Am, Camaro Z28, Berlinetaa, Firebird Formula, Maserati, Datsun 280 ZX, Honda Prelude and American Motors Eagle.

Silcco
8600 NW 53rd Terrace, Suite 124
Miami, FL 33161
PH: 904 629-5834
Lincoln and Mustang.

New looks in an old favorite!

Racing And Rallying

🐿 *Ah. Yes, it's poetry in motion.*

A Joy To Be A Part Of

A special mystique and charisma surrounds automobile racing. Magical. From the lush wooded hills, crystal clear lakes and drifting knackwurst odors of Road America at Elkhart Lake, Wisconsin to stately white casinos, the brilliant Mediterranean and caviar of Monaco at Monte Carlo. From state fair drag races to National Dragster Championships at Indy. From companions around a fire outside the motorhome on the eve of the big race to a table for twelve at Sir Winston's aboard the Queen Mary on the eve of the United States Grand Prix at Long Beach. From having a cold one, maybe two, at the Saturday night Super Modifieds with fellow roundi-pounders to having a cold one, maybe two, at the World 600 at Charlotte with a couple of good ol' boys. No matter where you find it, that's racing. Elusive. Appealing.

You Have A Treat In Store

Racing fans are lucky. They can become personally involved. From the preparations and trials of qualifying to the thrill and excitement of the race itself. Then, everyone experiences the almost haunting time when it's all over. Yes, all this is racing. A magic quality. Entertaining! If you haven't tried it, you have a treat in store.

World Renown Automobile Race Tracks

(Note: Race tracks are not often located inside major cities. To make locating easier the symbol (*) is used to indicate a large city close to the track or in some cases a track close to a city.)

USAC—United States Auto Club
(Oval racing)

*Atlanta, GA
Atlanta Int. Raceway
Hampton, GA

Brands Hatch
England

Brooklyn, MI
Michigan Int. Speedway

College Station, TX
Texas World Speedway

Longpond, PA
Pocono International Raceway

Milwaukee, WI
Wisconsin State Fair Park

Mosport
Ontario, Canada

Ontario CA
Ontario Raceway

Phoenix, AZ
Phoenix International Raceway

Speedway, IN
*(Indianapolis)
Indianapolis Motor Speedway

Trenton NJ
Trenton International Speedway

NASCAR—National Association Stock Car Auto Racing

Bristol, TN
Southeastern 500
Volunteer 400

Brooklyn, MI
Gabriel 400
Cam2 400

Cambridge Junction, MI
Champion Spark Plug 400

Charlotte, NC
World 600
Napa National 500

Darlington, SC
Rebel 500
Southern 500

Daytona Beach, FL
Daytona 500
Firecracker 400

Dover, DE
Mason-Dixon 500
Delaware 500

Martinsville, VA
Virginia 500
Old Dominion 500

Nashville, TN
Music City USA 420
Nashville 420

Pocono, PA
Coca-Cola 500

Richmond, VA
Richmond 400
Capital City 400

Riverside, CA
Winston Western 500
Napa Riverside 400

Rockingham, NC
Carolina 500

Talladega, AL
Winston 500
Talladega 500

Wilkesboro, NC
Gwyn Staley 400
Wilkes 400

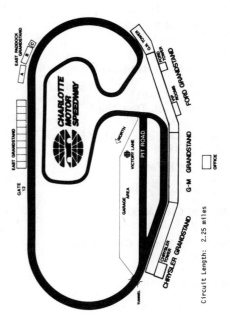

Road Racing—North America

**Brainerd
International Raceway**
*(Minneapolis, MN)
Brainerd, MN 56401
PH: 281 829-9836

Golden State Raceway
*(San Francisco)
Sonoma, CA 95476
PH: 707 938-8448

Grand Prix Trois Rivieres
*Trois-Rivieres, Quebec
PH: 819 378-8335

Hallett Motor Racing Circuit
*Tulsa Ok 74145
PH: 918 664-4131

Laguna Seca Raceway
*Monterey, CA 93940
PH: 408 373-1811

Le Circuit Mt. Tremblant
*(N W of Montreal)
Laval Quest, Que. H7R 3X4
PH: 627-4778

Lime Rock Park
Lakeville, CT
PH: 203 435-2572

Mexico City, Mexico
Ricardo Rodriguez Autodrome

Mid-Ohio Sports Car Course
P.O. Box 3108
*Lexington, OH 44904

Mosport
*(Bowmanville, Ont.)
Toronto, Ont. MtM 3Z9
PH: 416 781-6626

Nelson Ledges Road Course
*(Pittsburgh)
Warren, OH 44484
PH: 216 548-8551

Portland Intern. Raceway
Portland, OR 97258
PH: 503 227-2681

Riverside Intern. Raceway
*Riverside, CA 92508
PH: 714 653-1161

Road America
*(Milwaukee)
Elkhart Lake, WI 53020
PH: 414 876-2900

Road Atlanta
*(Gainesville, GA)
Atlanta, GA 30318
PH: 404 881-8234

Seattle Int. Raceway
*(Kent)
Federal Way, WA
PH: 206 839-7730

Watkins Glen Racing Circuit
Watkins Glen, NY 14891
PH: 607 535-2600

Westwood
*(Port Coquitlam)
Vancouver, B.C. V6B 3T5
PH: 604 687-7711 X 3766

**Mid-Ohio Sports Car Course
Lexington, Ohio**

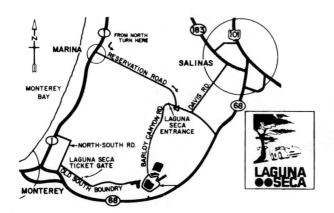

Laguna Seca Raceway
Monterey, California

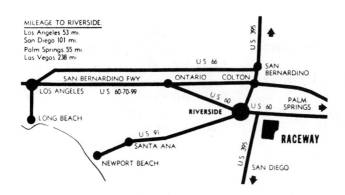

Riverside International Raceway
Riverside, California

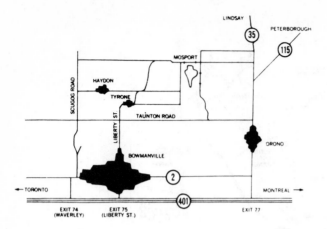

Mosport
Toronto, Canada

Pro Rally Courses

Alpine, TX
Big Bend Bash

Bakersfield, CA
Mikuni La Jornada Trabajosa

California City, CA
Borax Bill Memorial
20 Mule Team Stages

Chillicothe, OH
Sunriser 400

Houghton, MI
Press On Regardless

Issaquah, WA
Nor'Wester

Las Vegas, NV
Nevada Rally

Rolla, MO
100 Acre Wood

Wellsboro, PA
Susquehannock Trail

GRAND PRIX—Formula One

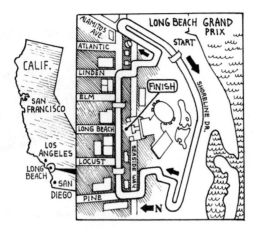

Long Beach, California

Anderstorp, Sweden

Brands Hatch, England

Buenos Aires, Argentina

Hockenheim, Germany

Johannesburg, South Africa

Le Castellet, France

Long Beach, (CA) U.S.

Madrid, Spain

Monte Carlo, Monaco

Montreal, Canada

Monza, Italy

Rio de Janeiro, Brazil

Watkins Glen, (NY) U.S.

Zandevoort, Netherlands

Zeltweg, Austria

Zolder, Belgium

Locations Of The Most Famous Racing Events

Adelaide
Australia
Adelaide International Raceway
*Melbourne

Albi
France
Cicuit d'Albi
*Toulouse

Anderstorp
Sweden
Scandinavian Raceway
*Goteborg

Brands Hatch
England
Brands Hatch Circuit Ltd
*London

Brno
Czechoslovakia
Automotoklub Brno
*Praha

Buenos Aires
Argentina
Autodromo Municipal de la
*Buenos Aires

Clermont-Ferrand
France
Circuit de Montagne
*Clermont-Ferrand

Dijon-Prenois
France
Circuit de Dijon-Prenois
*Dijon

Donington
England
Donington Park
*East Midlands

Enna
Italy
Ente Autodromo di Pergusa
*Palermo

Ensenada
Mexico
Baja International

Estoril, Portugal
Autodromo do Estoril
*Liboa

Francorchamps
Belgium
Circuit National de Francorchamps
*Bruxelles

Fuji
Japan
Fuji International Speedway
*Tokyo

Halifax
Nova Scotia

Hameenlinna
Finnland
Hameenlinnan Moottorirata
*Helsinki

Hockenheim
West Germany
Hockenheim-Ring
*Frankfurt/Main

Imola
Italy
Autodromo 'Dino Ferrari
*Bologna

Interlagos
Brazil
Interlagos
*Viracupos, Congonhas

Jarama
Spain
Circuito Permanente del Jarama
*Madrid

Jyllands-Ringen
Denmark
Jyllands, Ringen, Resenbro
*Tirstrup/Arhus

Kassel-Calden
Germany

Kinnekulle Ring
Sweden
Kinnekulle Ring
*Goteborg

Knutstorp
Sweden
Ring Knutstorp
*Sturup

Kyalami
South Africa
Kyalami Grand Prix Circuit
*Johannesburg

Lakeside
Australia
Lakeside International Raceway
*Brisbane

Le Mans
France
Circuit de la Sarthe
24 Hours of Le Mans
*Paris

Magny-Cours
France
Circuit de Vitesse
*Paris

Mallory Park
Great Britain
Mallory Park Circuit
*Luton, Leicester East

Manfeild
New Zealand
Manfeild Autocourse
*Palmerston North

Mantorp Park
Sweden
Pro/Sport AB
*Kungsangen, Norrkoping

Mexicali
Mexico
Score Mexicali

Misano
Italy

Mondello Park
Ireland
Motor Racing Circuits Ltd
*Dublin

Monthery
France
UTAC Autodrome
*Paris

Mugello
Italy
Autodromo Internazionale
*Milano

Nogaro
France
Circuit Automobile Paul
*Toulouse

Norisring
West Germany
Norisring
*Nurnberg

Nurburgring
Germany

Oulton Park
England
Cheshire Car Circuit
*Manchester

Pau
France
Circuit de Pau
*Toulouse

Paul Ricard
France
ASA Paul Ricard
*Marseille

Pergusa
Italy

Phoenix Park
Ireland
Phoenix Park
*Dublin

Pukekohe
New Zealand
Pukekohe Grand Prix
*Auckland

Ring Knutstorp
Sweden

Riverside
California
Los Angeles Times 6 Hours

Rouen
France
Circuit Rouen les Essarts
*Paris

Salzburgring
Austria
Salzburgring GmbH & Co KG
*Salzburg

Sandown
Australia
Sandown International Motor Racing
*Melbourne

San Juan
Puerto Rico
24 Horas of Puerto Rico

Santamonica
Italy
Autodromo Santamonica
*Rimini

Sebring
Florida
12 Hours of Sebring

Silverstone
England
Silverstone Circuit
*Birmingham

Snetterton
England
Snetterton Circuit
*Luton

Surfers Paradise
Australia
Surfers Paradise International Raceway
*Brisbane

Suzuka
Japan
Suzuka International Racing Course
*Osaka

Teretonga
New Zealand
Teretonga Park
*Wellington

Thruxton
Great Britain
Thruxton Circuit
*Southampton

Vallelunga
Italy
Autodromo Vallelunga
*Rome

Wigram
New Zealand
Wigram Circuit
*Christchurch

F.I.A. Classification Of Racing Groups

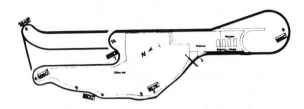

F.I.A.—Federation Internationale de l'Automobile

This is the worldwide governing body of automobile racing. It is also the only international organization grouping together automobile clubs from all over the world. Without reservation, it is the international power governing motor sport.

For the purpose of classification, all automobiles are placed in one of eight different groups. Each group has basic specifications the cars must meet to be eligible to compete in races. Normally all "Group One" cars compete against each other, etc.

"Group Seven" is designated for formula single-seater racing cars. This group consists of three different types of cars known as formula 1, 2, or 3. All are open-wheel racers. Cars in this group are built from the chassis up according to plans (formula) as specified by F.I.A.

The Eight F.I.A. Race Car Groups

GROUP 1
Series-Production Touring Cars
Basic passenger car (with not less than four seats, unless engine is less than 1,000 cc), of which at least 5,000 identical units must have been built in 12 consecutive months. Very little modification from the road car version. Group 1 cars modified beyond this group compete in Group 2.

GROUP 2
Touring Cars
Basic Passenger car (with not less than four seats unless the engine is below 1,000 cc), of which at least 1,000 identical units must have been built in 12 consecutive months. May be highly modified from road version into ultra-fast competition touring cars for racing.

GROUP 3
GTs—Series-Production Grand Touring Cars
Basic luxury road car with not less than two seats, of which at least 1,000 identical units must have been built in 12 consecutive months. Very slightly modified (as in group 1) from road car version. Group 3 cars modified beyond this group compete in Group 4.

GROUP 4
GTs—Grand Touring Cars
Basic luxury road car with not less than two seats, of which at least 400 identical units must have been built in 24 consecutive months. May be highly modified (as in Group 2) from road version into ultra-fast competition GTs for racing.

GROUP 5
Special Competition Cars Derived From Groups 1-4
Basically cars derived from Goups 1-4, but converted into racing cars retaining the silhouette of the original version. Original engine block must be retained, but otherwise may be extensively modified.

GROUP 6
Two-Seater Racing Cars
Specially built cars for closed circuit racing, with open or closed bodywork, no minimum production required.

GROUP 7
International FIA—Formula Single-Seater Racing Cars
Specially built single-seater cars for closed circuit racing, with open bodywork, open wheels and no minimum production required.

★ **Formula One** Grand Prix cars with maximum engine capacity of 3,000 cc (1,500 cc supercharged), with maximum of 12 cylinders.

★ **Formula Two** Maximum engine capacity 2,000 cc with a maximum of six cylinders. No supercharged engines.

★ **Formula Three** Maximum engine capacity 2,000 cc with a maximum of four cylinders. The induction system is fitted with a throttling flange to restrict engine power. Engine must derive from a series production block of which at least 5,000 units have been built in 12 consecutive months.

GROUP 8
Formule Libre Racing Cars
Specially built cars for closed circuit racing not complying with Formula 1-3 regulations. Usually a national (or car manufacturers) formulae.

The Flags System Used Internationally In Auto Racing

GREEN . . . . Course clear. Start of the race
BLUE . . . . Waved—a competitor attempting to pass
YELLOW . . . . Waved—great danger ahead—no passing
YELLOW & RED . . . . Waved—slippery track, great danger ahead
BLACK . . . . Displayed to a car required to stop at pits next lap
RED . . . . All cars stop immediately
WHITE . . . . Service or ambulance vehicles on the course
CHECKERED . . . . Waved at winning car. Held steady for the rest

385

Worldwide Addresses Of Competition Organizations

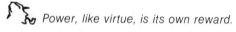

Power, like virtue, is its own reward.

(ACCUS/FIA) Automobile Competition Committee For The United States
1701 K St N W, Suite 1204
Washington, DC 20006
PH: 202 833-9133

(ARRC) American Road Race of Champions
Road Atlanta
Gainsville, GA
Club national racing championships held by SCCA.

(CASC) Formula Atlantic Canadian Automobile Sport Clubs
P.O. Box 97
Willowdale, Ontario
Canada M2N 5S7
PH: 222-5411

(IMSA) International Motor Sports Assoc., Inc.
P.O. Box 3465
Bridgeport, CT 06605
PH: 203 259-5233

(IROC) International Race Of Champions
835 Hopkins Way, Suite 504
Redondo Beach, CA 90277

(SCCA) Sports Car Club Of America
6750 S Emporia
Englewood, CO 80112
PH: 303 770-1044

(USAC) United States Auto Club
4910 W 16th Street
P.O. Box 24001
Indianapolis, IN 46224

(CART) Championship Auto Racing Teams
12626 U.S. 12
Brooklyn, MI 49230

SCORE International
31332 Via Colinas, Suite 103
Westlake Village, CA 91361

NARRA
P.O. Box 814
Nyack, NY 10960

Race Communications Association
P.O. Box 112
North Chili, NY 14514

(NASCAR) National Association Stock Car Auto Racing
P.O. Box K
Daytona Beach, FL 32015

Confederation Of Australian Motor Sport Australia (FIA)
382 Burke Road
Camberwell, Victoria 3124
PH: 03 29-2327

Federation Francaise du Sport Automobile France (FIA)
136, rue de Longchamp
Paris, France 75016
PH: 727 97 39

The Royal Automobile Club England (FIA)
31 Belgrave Square
London SW1X 8QH
PH: 01 235-8601

Royal Irish Automobile Club Ireland (FIA)
34 Dawson Street
Dublin, Ireland C2
PH: 775141/3

ACI/Commissione Sportiva Automobilistica Italiana Italy (FIA)
Via Solferino, 32,
Rome, Italy 00185
PH: 478897

Japan Automobile Federation Japan (FIA)
3-5-8 Shibakoen, Minatoku
Tokyo, Japan
PH: (436) 2811

Asociacion Mexicana Automovilistica Mexico (FIA)
Orizaba No 7
Apartado Postal 244866
Mexico, 7 DF
PH: 514 93 57

Automobile Club de Monaco Monaco (FIA)
23 Boulevard Albert-1er,
BP 314 Monaco
PH: 30 30 72

(NHRA) National Hot Rod Association
4910 W 16th Street
N Hollywood, CA 91602

Club Automovilistico Frances Race organizer—Mexico
Francia No 75 Col Flurida
Mexico 20, D.F.
PH: 564-7877

Rally Automovil Club
Condor No 289-1 Col
Las Aguilas
Mexico-DF
PH: 593-1416

Common Terms
Used In Racing

Racing has a language of its own. Some of it is technical, but much is not. It may surprise you how quickly the knowledge of word meanings will enable you to feel at ease in discussing the sport. We selected just a few of the most commonly used racing terms and gave them a simple explanation.

A-arm
A suspension part connected to the chassis or gearbox. Used to hold the up-right in place on all four wheels.

Aerodynamics
The behavior of air-flow as it passes around a moving car and the forces air exerts on an automobile.

Aerofoils
Devices placed on the car to produce downforce. Usually a wing designed to keep the car on the ground providing better traction.

Alcohol
Fuel used in forms of competition racing. Has advantage of greater internal cooling and slower burning which permits turbocharging.

Anti-roll bar
A bar added to the front or rear of a car and connected to the suspension. This limits body roll while going around a corner.

Apex
The inside tip or point of a curve on a race track.

Autocross
Timed competition runs by drivers who manueuver their cars through a marked course. Originally the event took place on a permanent or temporary circuit having an unsealed surface.

Best races rule
Method for figuring championship points in racing. Points are not based on all races in a season, but on a driver or manufacturer's best placing in a stipulated number of accredited races. This method has recently returned to use in different forms of racing.

Blower
Term for supercharger.

Blown engine:
An engine that is supercharged. In racing, an engine unable to function.

Bumping
Time trials giving drivers with non-qualifying times a chance to gain faster marks—thereby ''bumping'' another driver from the starting grid.

CART
A governing body relative to racing ''Indy'' cars. Located in Brooklyn, MI.

Catch-tank
A residue or overflow tank for fluids.

Chicane
A planned deviation in the layout of a race track. Originally conceived to equalize unequal cars, these are now used mostly as safety features and crowd pleasers.

Cornering
The ability to turn a corner at speed.

Cubic capacity
The volume of the cylinder.

DNF
Race car did not finish.

Drafting
A car closely following the car ahead in order to gain speed. This can be done due to less aerodynamic drag on the following car.

Drift
A planned, controlled four-wheel slide of a racing car in turning certain types of corners.

Dry sump
An engine in which the lubricating oil (by pumps) is stored in a separate tank or cooling radiator instead of the crankcase pan.

Elapsed Time (ET)
In drag racing this is the factor that determines which dragster first reached the finish-line light beam.

Equipe
French term for race team.

Esses
A particular section of track in a road racing course. Track layout consists of a series of slight left and right turns.

F.I.A.
Federation Internationale de l'Automobile—world governing body of automobile racing. The only international organization grouping together automobile clubs from all over the world. The international power governing motor sport.

Flat engines
(Horizontally opposed) Opposing banks of cylinders lying at 180° to each other.

Flying start
Race cars moving together in formation at the start of a race.

Formula
Single-seat, open-wheeled, open-cockpit race cars built to the detailed specifications established by the official governing board.

Fuel weight
A gallon of gasoline weighs 6 pounds.

Funny cars
Used in reference to competition cars with dragster chassis and stock body.

Gasoline alley
(Paddock) Locations of shops for tuning and assembling race car at race track.

Gear ratios
Used in racing to coordinate engine speeds to fit the layout of the race track.

Grand Prix
A Formula 1 race that counts for World Championship points.

Grande Epreuve
French for major test.

Gymkhana
Word that is sometimes substituted for slalom or autocross.

Hairpin
A sharp 180-degree turn (Switchback).

Half shaft
The rotating shaft that sends power from the differential (drive unit) to the wheels. Used in independent rear suspension and front wheel drive.

Header
Pipes or tubes of the exhaust system attached to each cylinder head. Used to carry exhaust gases away from the engine. On highly-tuned engines, header pipes of identical length can produce more power.

Heel and toe
A race driver's technique. The toes of the right foot are used on the brake pedal and the heel on the accelerator. This allows the driver to brake and at the same time blip (quick rev of engine) the throttle for a downshift of gears. This lessens the strain on the gearbox and drive train. The position of the foot makes for quicker reactions. Many fine drivers place toes on accelerator and heel on the brake pedal.

Hemi
Term for an engine with hemispherical shaped combustion chambers. Provides improved efficiency. Used in many sports and racing cars.

Hill-climb
Speed competition up a hill one car at a time, racing against a clock.

Hot rod
A production car that has a number of changes to increase its acceleration and speed.

In-line engine
Engines having the cylinders in a single line.

Kamm tail
Sharply cut-off tail found on many racing and some production cars. Reduces drag.

Lap
One complete tour of a race course.

Lap, to
To establish a lead in excess of the length of the track over a competitor.

Line
Path a racing car follows through a corner. The classic racing line effectively makes the corner as gentle as possible entering wide, clipping the inside apex (tip or point) and exiting wide; the line of least resistance. Once committed at racing speeds it is very difficult to alter the line safely.

Liter (litre)
Used to measure capacity (displacement) of engine (1,000cc equals one liter).

Live Axle
An axle transmitting its power by separate half shafts or side chains.

Methanol (methyl alcohol)
A fuel; distillate. Engines run well on it. Not a petroleum product. It is a coloess, volatile, watersoluble, poisonous liquid. Can be produced synthetically from carbon monoxide and hydrogen. Germany used this source as its primary engine fuel during the Second World War.

Monocoque
A method of race car construction (called chassisless or stressed skin). The skin (body covering) carries a major portion of the stresses on the central structure of the car.

Nitromethane (Nitro)
Blended with gasoline for use in some types of racing engines.

Nomex
Flame-resistant fabric used in clothing for race drivers.

Normally aspirated
Engine that intakes air without assistance of supercharger or turbocharger.

Over-rev
To exceed the maximum engine revolutions an engine is designed for.

Oversteer
The reaction of a car to a turn. If the tendency is for the **rear** of the car to slide out while the front wheels hold stable, the car is said to oversteer

Paddock
The area of race track where cars are stored and prepared.

Pits
Assigned areas for each race car where service by crew members can be performed on that car during the race itself.

Pole position
At the start of a race the place up front taken by the fastest qualifier.

Radius rods
Suspension parts normally control the location of rear wheels

Rallycross
A speed event, on a permanent circuit, with a partly-sealed surface.

Revolutions (revs)
The number of times a crank shaft rotates in one minute. Expressed as revolutions per minute.

Road race
A race over a road or simulated road course with curves and straight aways. The opposite type of racing is thought of as a race run on an oval track.

SCCA
The Sports Car Club of America. Located in Denver, CO. Organized club that sponsors, sanctions and administers many of the amateur and professional road races in America.

Scuderia
Italian term for race team.

Set-up
Term used to describe the various settings or changes that can be used to modify the suspension of a race car.

Shunt
Term for accident in racing.

Slalom
A speed event taking place on a hard surface with changes of direction effected by artificial obstacles, decreasing speed.

Spoiler
A fin or tab attached to the nose or tail of a competition car. The purpose is better aerodynamics.

Stock car
Term for a production car used in racing.

Supercharging
The use of a compressor to raise induction pressure above that normally provided by atmospheric conditions. This allows more fuel to be burned in each cycle producing more power.

Superspeedway
High-banked fast tracks used for stock car racing.

Switchback
That part of a track or road that has hairpin curves.

T-bone
In racing, to strike another car broadside.

Time trials
Pre-race runs to determine starting positions based on best times.

T-Race
Rally-style speed event in Sweden.

Track (tread)
The measurement from one wheel center to the other on the same axle.

Traps
Speed measuring installations on a section of track.
Tuning
Art of getting the maximum amount of power and reliability from an engine.
Turbocharger
An exhaust-driven supercharger (raises the induction pressure).
Understeer
The reaction of a car to a turn. If the tendency is for the **front** of the car to proceed relatively straight ahead instead of following the direction the wheels are turned, the car is said to be understeering.
USAC
The United States Automobile Club. A governing body relative to racing ''Indy'' cars. Located in Indianapolis, Indiana.
Weight
Dry weight—in racing or rallying this is a car without fuel, oil, or water. Curb weight—car with full tank of fuel, oil, and water.
Works car
Car sponsored and maintained in a race by its manufacturer.
Yump
A Scandinavian term used in rallying to descibe a bump big enough to throw a fast car into the air.

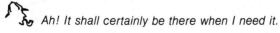 *Ah! It shall certainly be there when I need it.*

Index